FREE $TUFF

for
SENIORS

By Matthew Lesko
with Mary Ann Martello

Publisher's Note

This book is intended for general information only. It does not constitute medical, legal or financial advice or practice. We cannot guarantee the safety or effectiveness of any treatment or advice mentioned. Readers are urged to consult with their personal financial advisors, lawyers, and health-care professionals.

"Consider it pure joy, my brothers, whenever you face trials of many kinds, because you know that the testing of your faith develops perseverance."

— *James 1:2-3 (NIV)*

FC&A Publishing
103 Clover Green
Peachtree City, GA 30269

Produced by the staff of FC&A
Cover images ©1996 PhotoDisc, Inc.

Second Printing, December 1998
ISBN 1-890957-08-9

Table Of Contents

Introduction

I recently turned 50 and I wanted to celebrate. So, as an author of dozens of reference books on government information, I decided to write this book that shows people my age and older that Uncle Sam has over 2,500 places you can turn to for free money, services, discounts, videos, help, publications, and more freebies.

All this stuff is one of the best kept secrets. Why? Because the government doesn't advertise. You'll never see signs in Washington, or anywhere else for that matter, saying **"Seniors can get $5,000 to fix up their home,"** or **"Seniors can get free videos on financial planning,"** or **"Take free college courses,"** or **"Travel free overseas."**

The government has hundreds of millions of dollars of goodies like these that it's giving away to seniors, but Uncle Sam doesn't spend a nickel telling people where to get them. With this book, you'll now know where to go to tap into all these goodies.

There's lots of free stuff in this book that seniors can use to solve serious problems like, how to **get free prescription drugs**, or how to get **free dentures**, or where to go to find the **latest treatment for Alzheimer's**. But the book also has a whole lot of fun, neat stuff such as where to get **free tickets to the symphony, free sewing classes, free fishing videos, free speakers for your group**, and even a **Smithsonian exhibit for your next fundraiser**.

No matter what subject you may be interested in during your golden years ... travel, gardening, or even sex, Uncle Sam has a free source that can make a difference in your life. So why not use it, you've already paid for it.

Warning: This Book is Out of Date

Everything in our country is out of date the moment it is published. Your phone book is out of date as soon as you get it. Your newspaper is even out of date when it hits the streets.

We live in a fast changing world, and there is no way any of us in publishing can always have only the latest information in print. So please be patient. Although we updated and verified each listing right before printing, you may contact one of the offices in this book and find that the telephone number or program has changed.

For a wrong number you can always call the information operator in the city where the office is located and get a new listing. And, if you happen to contact an agency where the program has changed, be sure to ask that office if they know of any additional programs that may also satisfy your request. New programs are always being added or changed, or transferred to a local level.

☆☆☆

Dealing with Bureaucrats: Ten Basic Telephone Tips

An important part of your success in using this book is the careful handling of bureaucrats. Whether you are dealing with your local power company or with the government, you will be speaking to another human being. If you deal with them pleasantly and patiently, you will get quicker service and more of the publications and information that you are interested in.

Here are a few important tips to follow when you attempt to get information of any kind from a government agency over the telephone. Above all, remember that patience is often rewarded — even by weary government bureaucrats!

•Introduce Yourself Cheerfully

Starting the conversation with a cordial and upbeat attitude will set the tone for the entire interview. Let the official know that this is not going to be just another mundane telephone call, but a pleasant interlude in an otherwise hectic day.

•Be Open and Candid

Be as candid as possible with your source. If you are evasive or deceitful in explaining your needs or motives, your source will be reluctant to provide you with anything but the most basic information.

•Be Optimistic

Relay a sense of confidence throughout the conversation. If you call and say "You probably aren't the right person" or "You don't have any information, do you?" it's easy for the person to respond, "You're right, I can't help you." A positive attitude encourages your source to dig deeper for an answer to your question.

2

•Be Courteous

You can be optimistic and still be courteous. Remember the old adage that you can catch more flies with honey than you can with vinegar? Government officials love to tell others what they know, as long as their position of authority is not questioned or threatened.

•Be Concise

State your problem simply. Be direct. A long-winded explanation may bore your contact and reduce your chances for getting a thorough response.

•Don't Be A "Gimme"

A "gimme" is someone who expects instant answers and displays a "give me that" attitude. Be considerate and sensitive to your contact's time, feelings, and eccentricities. Although, as a taxpayer, you may feel you have the right to put this government worker through the mill, that kind of attitude will only cause the contact to give you minimal assistance.

•Be Complimentary

This goes hand in hand with being courteous. A well-placed compliment ("Everyone I spoke to said you are the person I need to ask.") about your source's expertise or insight will serve you well. We all like to feel like an "expert" when it comes to doing our job.

•Be Conversational

Briefly mention a few irrelevant topics such as the weather or the latest political campaign. The more conversational you are without being too chatty, the more likely your source will be to open up and want to help you.

•Return the Favor

You might share with your source information or even gossip you have picked up elsewhere. However, be certain not to betray the trust of either your client or another source. If you do not have any relevant information to share at that moment, call back when you are farther along in your research.

•Send Thank You Notes

A short note, typed or handwritten, will help ensure that a government official source will be just as cooperative in answering future questions.

Free Help To Get A Job

America's population is aging. In fact, by the year 2000 the number of Americans over the age of 65 will exceed the entire population of Canada. The problem is — when they retire, many will discover that their Social Security and pension income just isn't enough to make ends meet. That could very well mean a short retirement for many.

If you find that you do need a job but don't have the skills, there's plenty of free help. All across the country there are free job training programs set up just for seniors who need help getting the job skills they need even if you:

- haven't worked in a long time
- never worked outside the home
- have limitations on your ability to work
- live in a small town or in the country
- receive Social Security income
- do not have a high school education

Free Job Training and Part-Time Jobs

The Senior Community Service Employment program offers part-time training and employment opportunities for eligible low-income persons 55 years of age and older in a variety of public or private nonprofit community service settings, such as senior centers, nutrition programs, social service agencies, libraries, environmental projects, and many others.

The program provides seniors with income and the opportunity to learn new skills or improve the ones they already have. The program also helps you make the transition to the private job market through training, job search support and counseling.

Typical program participants work at such jobs as:

- activities coordinator
- bookkeeper
- cashier
- clerk typist
- custodian
- data entry clerk
- day care worker
- driver
- food service worker
- grounds keeper
- mechanic
- receptionist
- salesperson
- security guard
- teacher's aide

The Job Training Partnership Act program (JTPA) trains and places older workers in full- and part-time jobs with private businesses. Program participants not only receive on-the-job experience, but also have an opportunity to develop job skills and good work habits.

Other services available to seniors in this program include job counseling, help writing your resume, job searches and classroom training. Participating businesses who hire JTPA graduates receive financial and tax incentives for doing so.

The offices listed below will help direct you to job training programs for older workers in your area. They are also great sources for information about general assistance programs for the elderly.

State Job Programs

ALABAMA
Commission on Aging
770 Washington Ave.
RSA Plaza, Suite 470
Montgomery, AL 36130
334-242-5743

This office can refer you to Senior Community Service Employment Program (Title V) sites in your area and general programs and benefits available to older Americans. They can also provide referrals for regional help with Title V through the Senior Aides Program. The National Caucus on Black Aging (334-265-1451) can give you regional assistance with Title V in nine counties, including Montgomery.

Department of Economic and Community Affairs
401 Adams Ave.
P.O. Box 5690
Montgomery, AL 36103-5690
334-242-5300

This office will refer you to Job Training Partnership Act (JTPA) sites in your area.

ALASKA
Older Alaskans Commissions
P.O. Box 110209
333 Willoughby Ave.
Juneau, AK 99801
907-465-3250

These offices can refer you to Senior Community Service Employment

Program (Title V) sites in your area, and give you information on other programs and benefits available to older Americans. They can also send you the *1997 Directory for Older Alaskans.*

Department of Community and Regional Affairs
150 Third St.
P.O. Box 112100
Juneau, AK 99811-2100
907-465-4814, 907-465-5545

This office will refer you to Job Training Partnership Act (JTPA) sites in your area.

ARIZONA
Department of Economic Security
Aging and Adult Administration, 950A
1789 W. Jefferson
Phoenix, AZ 85007
602-542-4446

This office will refer you to Senior Community Service Employment Program (Title V) and Job Training Partnership Act (JTPA) sites in your area. They can also send you the free resource guide, *Senior Pages*, and information about other programs and benefits available to older Americans.

ARKANSAS
Arkansas Division of Aging and Adult Services
P.O. Box 1437, Slot 1412
Little Rock, AR 72201
501-682-2441

This office can refer you to Senior Community Service Employment Program (Title V) sites in your area. By calling the Arkansas Able program (501-660-4110), you can also get more information on senior employment opportunities.

JTPA
Department of Labor
500 West Markham
Suite 220, West Wing
Little Rock, AR 72201
501-371-4487

This office will refer you to Job Training Partnership Act (JTPA) sites in your area.

CALIFORNIA

California Department of Aging
Administrative Services Branch
Senior Employment (Title V) Section
1600 K St.
Sacramento, CA 95814
916-323-0217, 916-323-7515

This office will refer you to Senior Community Service Employment Program (Title V) sites in your area and to regional Private Industry Council offices (phone 800-FOR-A-JOB) for employment information. They will also send you fact sheets on Title V, JTPA, and Older Workers.

JTPA
State of California
Employment Development Department
P.O. Box 826880, MIC 69
Sacramento, CA 94280-0001
916-654-7110

This office will refer you to Senior Community Service Employment Program (Title V) sites in your area, and provide you with information on programs and benefits available to older Americans.

COLORADO

Colorado Department of Labor and Employment
1515 Arapahoa St., T2-400
Denver, CO 80202
303-620-4200

This office will refer you to Job Training Partnership Act (JTPA) sites in your area.

CONNECTICUT

Department of Social Services
Elderly Services Division
25 Sigourney St.
Hartford, CT 06106
860-424-5274

This office will refer you to Senior Community Service Employment Program (Title V) and Job Training Partnership Act (JTPA) sites in your area. They can also give you information on the Older Worker Support Network for employment and training programs for low-income persons age 55 and older (state funded program).

8

DELAWARE
Services for Aging and Adults With Physical Disabilities
Health and Social Services Department
1901 North DuPont Hwy.
Main Building, 2nd Floor Annex
New Castle, DE 19720
302-577-4660

This office will refer you to Job Training Partnership Act (JTPA) sites in your area. They also have information on the Career Exploration Program, Prime Time, a program for workers who are 55 and older to provide workshops, training and job placement (phone 302-573-2474)

DISTRICT OF COLUMBIA
DC Office on Aging
441 4th St. NW, Suite 900 South
Washington, DC 20001
202-724-5622, 202-724-3662

This office will refer you to Senior Community Service Employment Program (Title V) and Job Training Partnership Act (JTPA) sites in your area. They also have information on the Over 60 Employment program information.

Department of Employment Service
500 C St. NW, Room 327
Washington, DC 20001
202-724-7073

This office will refer you to the Senior Aid Program which can in turn refer you to Senior Community Service Employment Program (Title V) and Job Training Partnership Act (JTPA) sites in your area.

FLORIDA
Department of Elder Affairs
4040 Esplanade Way
Tallahassee, FL 32399-7000
850-414-2108, Elder Helpline: 800-96-ELDER (in FL only)
Internet: http://www.state.fl.us/doea/doea.html

For information about Senior Community Service Employment Programs (Title V) and Job Training Partnership Act (JTPA) sites in your area, contact the Elder Helpline listed above.

GEORGIA
Department of Human Services
Division of Aging Services
2 Peachtree St., NW, 36th Floor
Atlanta, GA 30303
404-657-5258, 404-657-5330

This office will refer you to Senior Community Service Employment Program (Title V) and Job Training Partnership Act (JTPA) sites in your area.

HAWAII
Executive Office on Aging
Office of the Governor
250 S. Hotel St., Suite 109
Honolulu, HI 96813-2831
808-586-0100

This office will refer you to Job Training Partnership Act (JTPA) sites in your area.

Honolulu Community Action Program
Department of Labor
830 Punchbowl St., Room 316
Honolulu, HI 96813
808-586-8813/8828

This office will refer you to Senior Community Service Employment Program (Title V) sites in your area.

IDAHO
Commission on Aging
P.O. Box 83720
Boise, ID 83720-0007
208-334-3833

This office will refer you to Senior Community Service Employment Program (Title V) and Job Training Partnership Act (JTPA) sites in your area (free brochures are available). Call the ElderCare Locator to provide community services, including local employment contacts (800-677-1116). Also, an Older Worker Employment Program staff listing is available.

ILLINOIS
Department on Aging
421 East Capitol Ave.
Springfield, IL 62701
217-785-0117, 800-252-8966 (IL only)

This office will refer you to Area Agencies on Aging that can in turn provide you with Senior Community Service Employment Program (Title V) sites in your area.

Department of Commerce and Community Affairs
620 East Adams St.
Springfield, IL 62701
217-782-7500, 217-785-6006

This office will refer you to Job Training Partnership Act (JTPA) sites in your area.

INDIANA
Disability, Rehabilitation and Aging Services
Family and Social Services Administration
402 West Washington St.
Indianapolis, IN 46207
317-232-7000, 317-232-7459

This office will refer you to Job Training Partnership Act (JTPA) sites in your area.

IOWA
Department of Elder Affairs
200 10th St., 3rd Floor
Des Moines, IA 50309
512-281-5187

This office will refer you to Job Training Partnership Act (JTPA) sites in your area.

KANSAS
Department of Aging
Docking State Office Building
1st Floor, Room 150 South
915 SW Harrison
Topeka, KS 66612
913-296-4986

This office will refer you to Senior Community Service Employment Program (Title V) and Job Training Partnership Act (JTPA) sites in your area. They can also refer you to Older Kansans Employment Program (same services as JTPA, but is state funded) sites in your area. Three other programs receive local or private funds for job referral and training: New Directions Program, Services for Seniors, Inc., and Project EARN. Ask for the free booklet, *Employment Services for Workers 55 and Over.*

KENTUCKY
Aging Services Division, Department for Social Services
275 East Main St., 5th Floor W.
Frankfort, KY 40621
502-564-6930

This office will refer you to Senior Community Service Employment Program (Title V) sites in your area. The free booklet, *Senior Community Service Employment Program*, will explain the benefits under this program.

JTPA Coordinator, Office of Training and Reemployment
209 St. Clair St., 4th Floor
Frankfort, KY 40601
502-564-5360

This office will refer you to Job Training Partnership Act (JTPA) sites in your area.

LOUISIANA
Office of Elderly Affairs
Office of the Governor
P.O. Box 80374
Baton Rouge, LA 70898-0374
504-342-7100

This office will refer you to Senior Community Service Employment Program (Title V) and Job Training Partnership Act (JTPA) sites in your area. Ask for the free fact sheet on employment programs.

MAINE
Bureau of Elder and Adult Services, Department of Human Services
State House Station #11
35 Anthony Ave.
Augusta, ME 04333-0011
207-624-5335

This office will refer you to Senior Community Service Employment Program (Title V) sites in your area.

Bureau of Employment Services, Department of Labor
55 State House Station
Augusta, ME 04333-0055
207-624-6390

This office will refer you to Job Training Partnership Act (JTPA) sites in your area.

MARYLAND
Maryland Office on Aging
301 Preston St.
Room 1004
Baltimore, MD 21201
410-767-1102, 800-AGE-DIAL

This office will refer you to Senior Information and Assistance Office in each county that can in turn refer you to Senior Community Service Employment Program (Title V) and Job Training Partnership Act (JTPA) sites in your area. Be sure to ask for the free booklet, *Senior Information and Assistance on Benefits and Services for Older Persons.*

MASSACHUSETTS
Executive Office of Elder Affairs
One Ashburton Place
Boston, MA 02108
617-727-7750, 800-882-2003

This office will refer you to special employment services in your area.

MICHIGAN
Office of Services to the Aging
P.O. Box 30676
Lansing, MI 48909-8176
517-373-8230

This office will refer you to Senior Community Service Employment Program (Title V) sites in your area.

Michigan Job Commission
201 N. Washington Square
Victor Office Center, 4th Floor
Lansing, MI 48913
517-373-9808

This office will refer you to Job Training Partnership Act (JTPA) sites in your area.

MINNESOTA
Minnesota Board on Aging
Human Service Building, 4th Floor
444 Lafayette Rd.
St. Paul, MN 55155
612-296-2770, 800-882-6262 (MN only)

This office will refer you to general programs and services for older

Americans in your area.

Program Specialist, Community Based Services
Department of Jobs and Training
390 N. Robert St., Room 125
St. Paul, MN 55101
612-297-1054

This office will refer you to Senior Community Service Employment Program (Title and Job Training Partnership Act (JTPA) sites in your area.

MISSOURI
Division of Aging
Department of Social Services
P.O. Box 1337
Jefferson City, MO 65102
573-751-3082

This office will refer you to Senior Community Service Employment Program (Title V) sites in your area.

Division of Job Development and Training
P.O. Box 1087
Jefferson City, MO 65102
573-751-7896, 800-877-8698

This office will refer you to Experienced Worker Program (JTPA) sites in your area.

MONTANA
Green Thumb
Box 2587
Great Falls, MT 59403
406-761-4821

This office will refer you to Senior Community Service Employment Program (Title V) sites in your area.

Montana JTP, Inc.
302 N. Last Chance Gulch
Suite 409
Helena, MT 59601
406-444-1309

This office will refer you to Job Training Partnership Act (JTPA) sites in your area.

NEBRASKA
Department on Aging
301 Centennial Mall S.
P.O. Box 95044
Lincoln, NE 68509-5044
402-471-2307

This office will refer you to Senior Community Service Employment Program (Title V) and Job Training Partnership Act (JTPA) sites in your area. They'll also refer you to Older Worker Initiatives in Nebraska.

NEVADA
AARP
P.O. Box 4395, Bonanza Station
Las Vegas, NV 89127
702-648-3356

This office will refer you to Senior Community Service Employment Program (Title V) sites in your area.

Nevada Business Services
930 W. Owens
Las Vegas, NV 89106
702-647-4929

This office will refer you to Job Training Partnership Act (JTPA) sites in your area.

Division for Aging Services
340 N. 11th St., Suite 203
Las Vegas, NV 89101
702-486-3545

This office will refer you to general programs and benefits available to older Americans.

NEW HAMPSHIRE
AARP
P.O. Box 398
Main and Grove Sts.
North Conway, NH 03860
603-356-3117, 800-652-8808 (NH only)

This office will refer you to Senior Community Service Employment Program (Title V) sites in your area. They will also send you free copies of the *New Hampshire Older Worker Employment Network Directory* and the *Senior Employment Program* brochure.

Job Training Council
64 Old Suncook Rd.
Concord, NH 03301-5134
800-772-7001 (NH only), 603-228-9500

This office will refer you to Job Training Partnership Act (JTPA) sites in
your area.

Division of Elderly and Adult Services
Department of Health and Human Services
115 Pleasant St., Annex Bldg., #1
State Office Park South
Concord, NH 03301-3843
603-271-4680

This office will refer you to general programs and benefits available to
older Americans.

NEW JERSEY
Department of Health and Senior Services, Division of Senior Affairs
P.O. Box 807
101 South Broad St., CN 807
Trenton, NJ 08625-807
609-292-4833

This office will refer you to Senior Citizens Information and Referral
Service (phone 800-792-8820) and your Area Agency on Aging that in turn
can refer you to Senior Community Service Employment Program (Title
V) sites in your area. This office also has information on ACTION programs that offer volunteer opportunities through the Foster Grandparent
Program (FGP) and the Senior Companion Program (SCP). Ask for the
free guide, *Federal Programs for Older Persons.*

Department of Environmental Protection and Energy
Division of Personnel, Recruitment Unit
440 East State St., CN 408
Trenton, NJ 08625-0408
609-984-3701

This office will refer you to Senior Environmental Employment Program
(SEEP) sites in your area.

New Jersey Department of Labor
Division of Employment and Training
John Fitz Plaza, Room 407
P.O. Box 055

16

Trenton, NJ 08625-0055
609-292-5005

This office will refer you to Job Training Partnership Act (JTPA) sites in your area.

NEW MEXICO
State Agency on Aging
228 East Palace Ave.
Santa Fe, NM 87501
505-827-7640, 800-432-2080 (only in New Mexico)

This office will refer you to Senior Community Service Employment Program (Title V) sites in your area (free brochure available).

State Department of Labor
Job Training Division
1596 Pacheco St.
Santa Fe, NM 87502
505-827-6827

This office will refer you to Job Training Partnership Act (JTPA) sites in your area.

NEW YORK
State Office For the Aging
2 Empire State Plaza
Albany, NY 12223-1251
518-474-4425, 518-474-1946, 800-342-9871

This office will refer you to local offices for the aging that in turn can refer you to Senior Community Service Employment Program (Title V) and Job Training Partnership Act (JTPA) sites in your area (free briefing books available).

NORTH CAROLINA
Department of Human Resources
Division of Aging
693 Palmer Dr.
Raleigh, NC 27626-0531
919-733-3983

This office will refer you to Senior Community Service Employment Program (Title V) sites in your area. A free program description and history is available.

Department of Commerce, Division of Employment and Training
441 N. Harrington St.
Raleigh, NC 27603

17

919-733-6383

This office will refer you to Job Training Partnership Act (JTPA) sites in your area.

NORTH DAKOTA
Department of Human Services, Aging Services Division
600 S. 2nd St., Suite 1C
Bismarck, ND 58504-5729
701-328-8910, 701-328-2825

This office will refer you to Job Training Partnership Act (JTPA) sites in your area.

Green Thumb
2206 E. Broadway
Bismarck, ND 58501-4930
701-258-8879

This office will refer you to Senior Community Service Employment Program (Title V) sites in your area.

OHIO
Department of Aging
50 West Broad St., 9th Floor
Columbus, OH 43215-5928
614-466-5500, 614-466-1242

This office will refer you to Senior Community Service Employment Program (Title V) sites in your area.

JTPA Division, Ohio Employment Service Division
145 S. Front St.
P.O. Box 1618
Columbus, OH 43215
614-466-3817

This office will refer you to local contact for Job Training Partnership Act (JTPA) sites in your area.

OKLAHOMA
O.E.S.C. - JTPA
2401 N. Lincoln
Oklahoma City, OK 73532
405-557-5323

This office will refer you to Senior Community Service Employment Program (Title V) and Job Training Partnership Act (JTPA) sites in your area.

18

Department of Human Services
Aging Services
312 NE 28th St.
Oklahoma City, OK 73105
405-521-2327

This office will refer you to programs and benefits available to older Americans, and information on the Older Americans Act.

OREGON
Department of Human Resources
Senior and Disabled Services Division
500 Summer St., NE
Salem, OR 97310-1015
503-945-6413

This office will refer you to Senior Community Service Employment Program (Title V) sites in your area.

JTPA
State Economic Development
775 Summer St., NE
Salem, OR 97310
503-373-1995

This office will refer you to Job Training Partnership Act (JTPA) sites in vour area.

PENNSYLVANIA
Department of Aging
555 Walnut St., 5th Floor
Forum Place
Harrisburg, PA 17101-1919
717-783-1550, 717-783-6007

This office will refer you to Senior Community Service Employment Program (Title V) sites in your area.

Department of Labor and Industry
Bureau of Employment Services and Training
7th and Forster Sts., 12th Floor
Harrisburg, PA 17120
717-783-0142

This office will refer you to local contact who in turn can refer you to Job Training Partnership Act (JTPA) sites in your area.

RHODE ISLAND
Department of Elderly Affairs
160 Pine St.
Providence, RI 02903
401-222-2858

This office will refer you to Senior Community Service Employment Program (Title V) and Job Training Partnership Act (JTPA) sites in your area.

SOUTH CAROLINA
Department of Health and Human Services, Office on Aging
P.O. Box 8206
Columbia, SC 29202-8206
803-253-6177

This office will refer you to Senior Community Service Employment Program (Title V) sites in your area. They also have information on Operation Able, a worker/job match service.

JTPA SAU
Employment Security Commission
1550 Gadsden St.
P.O. Box 1406
Columbia, SC 29202
803-737-2660

This office will refer you to local contacts that in turn can refer you to Job Training Partnership Act (JTPA) sites in your area.

SOUTH DAKOTA
Adult Services and Aging Division
120 S. Indiana Ave.
Sioux Falls, SD 57103
605-332-7991

This office will refer you to Senior Community Service Employment Program (Title V) sites in your area.

JTPA
Department of Labor
700 Governors Dr.
Pierre, SD 57501
605-773-5017

This office will refer you to Job Training Partnership Act (JTPA) sites in your area.

TENNESSEE
Commission on Aging
500 Deaderick St.
Andrew Jackson Bldg., 9th Floor
Nashville, TN 37243-0860
615-741-2056

This office will refer you to Senior Community Service Employment Program (Title V) sites in your area.

JTPA
Department of Labor
4th Floor, Andrew Johnson Bldg.
710 James Robertson Pkwy.
Nashville, TN 37243-0658
615-741-1031

This office will refer you to Job Training Partnership Act (JTPA) sites in your area.

TEXAS
Senior Texans Employment Program
5400 Bosque Blvd.
Waco, TX 76710
254-776-7002

This office will refer you to Senior Community Service Employment Program (Title V) sites in your area. Texas also has a state funded program identical to Title V that provides the elderly with job training.

Texas Workforce Commission
101 E. 15th St., Room 112T
Austin, TX 78778-0001
512-936-0345

This office will refer you to Job Training Partnership Act (JTPA) sites in your area.

UTAH
Department of Human Services
Division of Aging and Adult Services
120 North 200 West, Room 325
Salt Lake City, UT 84103
801-538-3910

This office will refer you to Senior Community Service Employment

Program (Title V) sites in your area. Call the Senior Employment office (phone 801-468-2785) for additional Title V program assistance.

Ask for a free copy of the *Senior Resource Directory*, which includes referral numbers for numerous older worker programs.

JTPA
Economic Development and Training Division
2001 South State, S2600
Salt Lake City, UT 84115
801-468-3246

This office will refer you to Job Training Partnership Act (JTPA) sites in your area.

VERMONT
Department of Aging and Disabilities
103 S. Main St.
Waterbury, VT 05671-2301
802-241-2400

This office will refer you to employment resources.

Vermont Associates for Training and Development
Senior Community Service Employment Program
132 N. Main St.
St. Aldans, VT 05478
802-524-3200

This office will refer you to Senior Community Service Employment Program (Title V) sites in your area.

VIRGINIA
Department For the Aging
1600 Forest Ave., Suite 102
Richmond, VA 23229
804-662-9333

This office will refer you to Senior Community Service Employment Program (Title V) sites and Job Training Partnership Act (JTPA) sites in your area. Ask for a Title V and JTPA directory with complete list of local contacts.

WASHINGTON
Job Development and Training
701 Sleater-Kinney Rd., SE, Suite 99A
Lacey, WA 98503
360-786-5586

This office will refer you to Job Training Partnership Act (JTPA) sites in your area.

WEST VIRGINIA
Bureau of Senior Services
1900 Kanawha Blvd. E.
Capitol Complex/Holly Grove, Bldg. 10
Charleston, WV 25305
304-558-3317

This office will refer you to Senior Community Service Employment Program (Title V) sites in your area.

JTPA
Employment Services
States College University System
1018 Kanawha Blvd. E., Suite 700
Charleston, WV 25301
304-558-2664

This office will refer you to Senior Community Service Employment Program (Title V) sites in your area.

WISCONSIN
Division of Workforce Excellence
Department of Workforce Development
Labor and Human Relations
P.O. Box 7972
Madison, WI 53707
608-266-6886

This office will refer you to Job Training Partnership Act (JTPA) sites in your area.

WYOMING
Wyoming Senior Citizens, Inc.
413 West 18th St.
Cheyenne, WY 82001
307-635-1245

This office will refer you to Senior Community Service Employment Program (Title V) and Job Training Partnership Act (JTPA) sites in your area.

Department of Health, Division on Aging
139 Hathaway Building
Cheyenne, WY 82002

307-777-7986

This office will refer you to programs and benefits available to older Americans.

★★★

Get A Job Through The Forest Service

If you are over 55 years of age and meet some income eligibility guidelines, you may be a candidate for the Senior Community Service Employment Program (SCSEP).

This program provides education, retraining and employment opportunities to persons 55 and above. SCSEP's goal is to place seniors in productive unsubsidized employment in the regular working community.

To learn about the program, contact your local Forest Service office or U.S. Forest Service, U.S. Department of Agriculture, SCSEP, Senior, Youth, Volunteer Programs, P.O. Box 96090, Washington, DC 20090; 703-235-8860.

★★★

Make $15 An Hour With The EPA

The Environmental Protection Agency (EPA) has a special program for hiring senior citizens 55 years and over. When an EPA regional office has a shortage of workers, they notify one of the organizations listed below and on page 25, which in turn recruit workers.

Senior citizens get involved in all kinds of activities from conducting national surveys to fulfilling general administrative tasks. The jobs carry unemployment, workmen's compensation, Social Security, and health benefits.

There are 4 levels of pay:
Level 1 — Xerox operators, messengers, telephone assistants; $6-$8
Level 2 — secretaries, administrative assistants; $7.25-$10
Level 3 — writers and editors; $8.50-$11.50
Level 4 — professionals with relevant degrees; $10.50-$15

Senior Environmental Employment Program (SEE)
U.S. Environmental Protection Agency, National Center for
Environmental Research and Quality Assurance
401 M St. SW, Mail Stop 3641

Washington, DC 20460
202-260-2574

For recruitment information contact:

National Association for Hispanic Elderly, 1452 W. Temple St., Suite 100, Los Angeles, CA 90026; 213-487-1922.

National Caucus and Center on Black Aged, Suite 500, 1424 K St., NW, Washington, DC 20005; 202-637-8400.

National Council on the Aging, 409 Third St., SW, Suite 200, Washington, DC 20024; 202-479-1200.

National Older Worker Career Center, 1615 L St., NW, Suite 750, Washington, DC 20036; 202-331-5017.

National Pacific/Asian Resource Center on Aging, Suite 410, 2033 6th Ave., Seattle, WA 98101; 206-624-1221.

☆☆☆

You Are Not The Only One

Feel like you are in the minority at work because you are over 60? You won't feel that way for long.

A report from the General Accounting Office (GAO) shows that the 55 and older age group will be the fastest growing group in the labor force. The report also outlines some options employers are considering in order to deal with the changing demographics, and looks at some different types of retirement. You can also learn from GAO reports that 28% of all the cases filed with the Equal Employment Opportunity Commission (EEOC) deal with age discrimination. You can find out how the EEOC handles complaints, their procedures, and more.

The GAO is the investigative arm of the Congress and conducts audits and evaluations of government programs and activities. The following are reports dealing with employment issues:

* *Multiple Employment Training Programs: Overlap Among Programs Raises Questions About Efficiency* (HEHS 94-193)

* *Federal Personnel: Employment Policy Challenges Created by an Aging Workforce* (GAO/GGD 93-138)

* *The Changing Workforce: Demographic Issues Facing Employers* (GAO/T-GGD 92-61)

- *Age Employment Discrimination: EEOC's Investigation of Charges Under 1967 Law* (HRD 92-82)

- *EEOC: An Overview* (GAO/T-HRD 93-30)

All reports are free and can be requested by contacting U.S. General Accounting Office, P.O. Box 6015, Gaithersburg, MD 20884; 202-512-6000.

☆☆☆

Work Or Retire? It's Up To You

For many people over 60, their job is something they love and enjoy. For others work is what helps pay the bills.

Many seniors look forward to retirement. You can find out how the work force is changing, and that if you keep working your age group will soon control the watercooler.

If you retire, the retirement plans are becoming more complex and varied in order to meet the needs of both the companies and their employees. You can learn about various retirement options on how to make the transition from work to retirement.

The Congressional Research Service (CRS) writes reports which provide an understandable overview of the topic and provide relevant newspaper articles and bibliographies. These reports are free but must be requested through your Congressman. CRS reports dealing with employment include:

- *Jobs: Job Training and Labor Market Issues* (IP246J)

- *Age Discrimination in Employment Act: Recent Enforcement Actions by the EEOC* (87-783A)

- *Early Retirement Incentive Plans under the Age Discrimination in Employment Act of 1967* (88-608A)

- *A Demographic Portrait of Older Workers* (88-636E)

- *Lists of Federal Job Openings* (CRS-1)

- *Older Workers: The Transition to Retirement* (89-28E)

- *Age Discrimination in Employee Benefit Plans* (89-478A)

You can get these and other CRS reports by contacting Your Senator or Representative, The Capitol, Washington, DC 20510; 202-224-3121.

Working and Caring

As the population ages, many workers are finding that they need to take care of their parents or spouse. Caregiving for elderly dependents can involve things such as transporting to doctors appointments, paying bills, or even helping with bathing, dressing, and meal preparation.

Eldercare is a concern to both employers and employees because the time and stress involved in caregiving can be enormous.

The Family and Medical Leave Act allows employees to take up to 12 weeks of unpaid leave in any 12 month period for the birth or adoption of a child; the serious illness of a child, spouse, or parent; and the serious illness of the employee.

Employees must have been working for one year, at least 1,250 hours to qualify, and employers must have at least 50 workers.

The Work and Family Clearinghouse has a free *Work and Family Resource Kit* which provides an overview and options for eldercare. The Clearinghouse can show you how companies similar to yours have established resources and programs to help out this population.

AT&T, Stride-Rite, and Travelers have begun to design innovative programs to decrease employee caregiver problems; your company can too. The Clearinghouse can also answer your Family and Medical Leave questions.

For more information, contact Work and Family Clearinghouse, U.S. Department of Labor, Women's Bureau, 200 Constitution Ave., NW, Washington, DC 20210; 800-827-5335; or contact them online for information and publications available at <http://www.dol. gov/dol/wb>.

Free And Low-Cost Dental Care

Don't let your teeth fall out just because you can't afford to go to a dentist. There are hundreds of programs across the country that offer free and low-cost dental care for seniors and practically anyone else who needs it, **often regardless of your income level.** If you know where and when to look, you may be able to get:

- free or low-cost dentures and repairs,
- automatic senior discounts of 15% to 80%,
- free at-home dental care if you can't get out,
- free dental implants by the best doctors in the world.

Most health insurance plans don't include dental coverage, and this means people often go without regular dental care simply because they think they can't afford it. But you may not be aware of the hundreds of programs that are designed for people like you — programs that actually require that you *don't* have dental insurance so that you can qualify to receive free or largely discounted dental care.

Here are some general examples of the kinds of programs funded all across the country:

Dental Care for the Elderly

You'll find that most states have special programs just for the elderly, especially those who have trouble finding money to pay for dental care on a limited income. Often dentists donate their time and services to make sure the elderly are taken care of. See the state-by-state listing on page 32.

Dental Schools for Everyone

The best-kept secrets about low-cost dental care are the 53 dental schools across the country. They offer quality dental care at a fraction of the cost of private dentists. Many will even set up a repayment plan for you if you can't afford to pay the bill.

Also, researchers at many dental schools receive big money from the federal government to do cutting edge dental research, and these researchers often need patients to work on for free. Be sure to ask about any clinical research underway at the dental school nearest you. See state-by-state listing on page 32.

Free and Low Cost Dental Clinics

Many state and local health departments support dental clinics that offer their services for free or on a sliding fee scale basis. Services are usually limited to those with limited income or those with special needs. See state-by-state listing on page 32.

Free Dental Care For Children

Almost every state runs some kind of dental care program to make sure that kids keep their teeth in good shape. Many of these programs offer their services for free or at huge discounts based upon your ability to pay. Your grandkids should know about this. See state-by-state listing on page 32.

Dental Care for Disabled and Handicapped

There are special programs just for those with mental or physical disabilities, including those with mental retardation, cerebral palsy, multiple sclerosis, and much more.

Many states also have special programs that offer free care for children born with cleft palates. See the state-by-state listing on page 32.

Dental Societies - Dentists Who Volunteer

Each state's Dental Society keeps track of free and low-cost dental programs in their state, so it's a good idea to call them if you have any questions or if you're interested in learning about any new dental programs that start up.

Some Dental Societies also act as a clearinghouse for identifying dentists who volunteer their services to those facing emergencies or those who have other special problems. See the state-by-state listing on page 32.

Free Dentures for Seniors

Don't sit around with false teeth that keep falling out when you eat or hurt so badly that you can't keep them in your mouth.

Many states have discount denture programs where you can receive big savings on false teeth, no matter what your age. See the state-by-state listing on page 32

☆☆☆

Free Tooth Implants and Impacted Molar Removal

These are just two of the many subjects that top dental researchers are studying at the National Institute of Dental Research which is part of the National Institutes of Health in Bethesda, Maryland. Also underway are studies on facial pain, taste disorders, herpes simplex, and dry mouth conditions.

Patients who participate in these clinical trials receive their dental care free of charge. For information about the clinical studies program at the National Institutes of Health, you or your doctor can contact: Clinical Center, National Institutes of Health, Bldg. 10, 10 Center Dr., Bethesda, MD 20892, 301-496-2563.

☆☆☆

Dentists Who Get Government Grants to do Work for Free

Washington is not the only place where doctors receive government grants to conduct dental research and treat patients for free. Each year hundreds of dental schools and other dental research facilities around the country receive money to work on everything from gum disease to denture satisfaction.

You can contact the following office to receive information about ongoing or up-coming dental research in your area.

National Institute of Dental Research
Research Data and Management, Information Section
31 Center Dr., Bldg. 31 2C35, MSC 2290
Bethesda, MD 20892-2290
301-496-4261

Another method of finding these doctors is by contacting the "Dental Schools" in the state-by-state listing on page 32. Dental schools normally receive a good portion of available research.

Dentists on Wheels

If you have trouble getting around because of a handicap or other infirmity, some states, like Illinois, Arizona, and Missouri, have mobile dental vans that will actually come to your home or nursing home and provide you with dental care right there on the spot. See the state-by-state listing.

State-by-State Listing

ALABAMA
Dental Programs
Department of Public Health, Dental Health Division
P.O. Box 303017
Montgomery, AL 36130
334-206-5661

Call your nearest Community Health Center or Clinic for information on reduced fees for dental care. Usually clinics offer a sliding fee scale — qualifications vary. For example, some clinics will treat only children and senior citizens.

Dental School
School of Dentistry
University of Alabama
1919 Seventh Ave., South
Birmingham, AL 35394
205-934-3000, 205-934-4546 (children)
Annual patient visits: 49,617.

Dental Society
Alabama Dental Association
836 Washington Ave.
Montgomery, AL 36104-3893
334-265-1684

Poarch Creek Indian
Health Dept.
5811 Jack Springs Rd.
Atmore, AL 36502
334-368-8630/Indians only

Mostellar Dental Center
525 North Wintzell Ave.
Bayou La Batre, AL 36509
334-824-2347

Jefferson County Health Dept.
1400 6th Ave. South
Birmingham, AL 35202
205-933-9110

University of Alabama, School of Dentistry
1919 7th Ave., South
Birmingham, AL 35233-1785
205-934-3000/Emer. pts. at hosp.

UAB School of Dentistry
Dental Cl.
University Station
Birmingham, AL 35294
205-934-4011

Houston County Health Dept., Childrens Dental Program
Suite 7, 301 West Lafayette
Dothan, AL 36301
334-712-0328

West AL Health Service
E.A. Maddos Center
607 Wilson Ave.
P.O. Box 599
Eutaw, AL 35462
205-372-9225

Stewart (J.W.) Health Center
1409 Springfield Ave.
Gadsden, AL 35902
205-492-0131

Gilbertown Medical Center
Highway 17
P.O. Box 237
Gilbertown, AL 36908
334-843-5354

West AL Health Care Center
2209 W. Main St.
P.O. Box 47
Greensboro, AL 36744
334-624-3014

Lowndes County Health Service
Oak St., P.O. Box 735
Hayneville, AL 36040
334-548-2516

Central No. AL Health Svcs.
751 Pleasant Rd., Box 11187
Huntsville, AL 35814
205-533-6311

Franklin Memorial Primary
Care Center
1303 Dr. Martin Luther
King Ave.
Mobile, AL 36603
334-432-4117

Mobile County Health Dept.
251 N. Bayou
P.O. Box 2867
Mobile, AL 36652
334-690-8158

Lister Hill Health Center
1000 Adams Ave.
Montgomery, AL 36104
334-263-2301

Montgomery Primary
Health Care
3060 Mobile Hwy.

Montgomery, AL 36108
334-293-6670

Henderson (Charles) Child
Health Center
1300 US 231 South, P.O. Box
928
Troy, AL 36081
800-222-9362
334-566-7600/Pts. 13 & under

West AL Dist. Health Dept.
1101 Jackson Ave.
P.O. Box 2789
Tuscaloosa, AL 35403
205-391-5415

Whatley (Maud) Health Center
2731 M.L. King, Jr. Blvd.
P.O. Box 2400
Tuscaloosa, AL 35401
205-758-6647

Central AL/Complete
Health/Midway Clinic
P.O. Box 1331
Tuskegee Inst., AL 36087
334-727-7488

Uniontown Health Services
330 Old Hamburg Rd.
P.O. Box 327
Uniontown, AL 36786
334-628-2661

ALASKA
Dental Programs
Social Services
Department of Public Health
P.O. Box 110610
Juneau, AL 99811-0610
907-465-3090

Limited dental care is available. Call your Community Health Center to get information about whether they offer dental.

Anchorage Neighborhood
Health Center
1217 East 10th Ave.
Anchorage, AK 99501
907-257-4600

Call or write Anchorage Neighborhood Health Center to get information on reduced-fee dental services for adults and children. A sliding fee scale based on income is available.

Senior Citizen Discounts
Anchorage Dental Society
3400 Spenard Rd., Suite 10
Anchorage, AK 99503
907-279-9144

There are no special programs through the Dental Society; however, they do keep a list of referrals of dentists who will give discounts to senior citizens. They are open from 8 AM to noon only.

Dental Society
Alaska Dental Society
3305 Arctic Blvd. #102
Anchorage, AK 99503
907-563-3003

ARIZONA

Dental Programs
Department of Health Services
Office of Oral Health
1740 West Adams St.
Phoenix, AZ 85007
602-542-1866

Low cost dental services are available through various Dental Clinics. They also offer a Homebound program for people who can no longer leave their homes (they will go to nursing homes). Individuals must contact the Office of Dental Health to get eligibility requirements.

Fluoride and Sealant Programs are also available through the public schools. Some Indian Health Centers offer dental for tribal members.

McDowell Dental Clinic
1314 E. McDowell St.
Phoenix, AZ 85006
602-252-1909

The McDowell Clinic provides basic dental work for individuals with HIV. The Area on Aging has contracted with the Office of Dental Health to provide dental services using portable equipment set up at local Senior Centers. Eligibility to access these services is determined by AAA.

Dental Society
Arizona State Dental
Association
131 N. 36th St.
Phoenix, AZ 85018-4761
602-957-4777

ARKANSAS

Dental Programs
Department of Health
Dental Division
5800 West 10th St.
Little Rock, AR 72204
501-661-2279

Limited dental care is available. Three clinics offer dental care at a reduced fee. Low-income is a major factor in determining eligibility. They will also see anyone who is in severe pain due to an emergency. All hospitals keep a listing of dentists who volunteer to treat emergencies. No special programs are available for handicapped or elderly.

Dental Society
Arkansas State Dental Association
920 W. 2nd St., #103
Little Rock, AR 72201-2125
501-771-7650

CALIFORNIA

Dental Programs
Health Services Department
Oral Health
714 P St., Room 550
Sacramento, CA 95814
916-654-0348

Very limited dental care is available through some local Health Centers or Clinics on a sliding fee scale. You'll have to call each individually to see if dental is available.

Senior-Dent
California Dental Association
1201 K Street Mall
P.O. Box 13749
Sacramento, CA 95853
916-443-0505, 800-736-7071
(CA only)

The *Senior-Dent Program* offers dental care at reduced fees to all qualified senior citizens. To qualify you must meet three eligibility requirements: 1) be 60 or older; 2) have an annual income of $16,000 or less; 3) not be receiving dental benefits from Denti-Cal or a dental insurance plan. Participating dentists offer at least a 15% discount. Call for additional information and a participating dentist.

Dental Schools
School of Dentistry, University of California, San Francisco
707 Parnassus Ave.
San Francisco, CA 94143
415-476-1891
Annual patient visits: 52,017.

School of Dentistry
University of California, Los Angeles, School of Dentistry
Box 951668
10833 LeConte Ave.
Los Angeles, CA 90095-1668
310-206-3904
Annual patient visits: 71,627.

School of Dentistry
University of Southern California
925 W. 34th St.
Los Angeles, CA 90007
213-740-2800
Annual patient visits: 31,000.

School of Dentistry
Loma Linda University
11092 Anderson St.
Loma Linda, CA 92350
909-824-4675
Annual patient visits: 105,500.

Dental Society
California Dental Association
P.O. Box 13749
Sacramento, CA 95853-4749
916-443-0505

COLORADO

Dental Programs
Department of Health
Family and Community Health Services, Dentistry
4300 Cherry Creek Dr., South, A4
Denver, CO 80222

303-692-2360

Call your local Health Department or Clinic to get information about reduced fee dental care. When dental care is offered, it is usually on a sliding fee scale based on income. Some will treat both children and adults.

Dental Care for the Handicapped, Donated Dental Services
1800 Glenarm Pl., Suite 500
Denver, CO 80202
303-298-9650

Certain handicapped individuals who meet the following guidelines may be eligible to receive free or low-cost dental care. Patients must meet the following guidelines: 1) mentally or physically disabled including mental retardation, cerebral palsy, MS, or other disabilities; 2) advanced age; 3) Colorado resident; 4) each patient is screened to find those in most need; limited income due to handicap is a major factor. Call for additional information.

Old Age Pension Dental Program
Family and Community Health Services
Dentistry, Ptarmigan Building
4300 Cherry Creek Dr. North
Denver, CO 80222
303-692-2360

The *Old Age Pension Dental Program* is a cooperative effort to provide dental services to a segment of elderly that have an urgent need. Most services offered are denture-related. Individuals must be low income and at least 60 years old. Call to get additional information.

Community Health Center, Dental Program
722 Wahsatch
Colorado Springs, CO 80903
719-475-0783

The Community Health Center, Dental Program provides dental care on a sliding fee scale. Call for more information.

Kids In Need of Dentistry
4155 E. Jewell, Suite 907
Denver, CO 80222
303-691-9130

Call KIND at this number for a referral to one of their five locations nearest you. This program is for children from the ages of 3 to 18 years of age only. They do not take Medicaid.

Salud Clinic
6075 Parkway Dr., Suite 160
Commerce City, CO 80022
303-286-8900

The Salud Clinic accepts both children and adult patients, and fees are based on a sliding scale.

Dental Society
Colorado Dental Association
3690 S. Yosemite Ave., Suite 100
Denver, CO 80237-1808
303-740-6900

CONNECTICUT

Dental Programs
Department of Public Health, Bureau of Community Health
MS 11 DNT

P.O. Box 340308
410 Capitol Ave.
Hartford, CT 06134-0308
860-509-7807

Call your nearest Local Health Department or Clinic to find out information about reduced fees for dental care. Most clinics offer a sliding fee schedule and will accept Medicaid and insurance, though low-income is usually a requirement. Handicap access is also available. Preventive programs are run through the various public school systems and nursing homes. Area dentists volunteer their services to provide low-income elderly with reduced-fee dental care.

Dental Schools
Connecticut Childrens Medical Center
282 Washington St.
Hartford, CT 06106
860-545-9030 (children)

U. Conn Dental Clinic
131 Coventry St.
Hartford, CT 06112
860-714-2140 (children)

U. Conn Dental Clinic
263 Farmington Ave.
Hartford, CT 06112
860-679-2325 (adults)

Dental Society
Connecticut Dental Association
62 Russ St.
Hartford, CT 06106-1589
860-278-5550

DELAWARE

Dental Programs
Division of Public Health

William Center Dental Clinic
805 River Rd.
Dover, DE 19901
302-739-4755

Children in pain, as well as children on Medicaid, are treated. There is very limited reduced fee dental care available in Delaware; however, there are two clinics that treat children and adults on a sliding fee scale. Call 302-428-2269 to get additional information and qualifications.

Nemours Health Clinic
1801 Rockland Rd.
Wilmington, DE 19803
800-292-9538, 302-651-4400

The Nemours Health Clinic offers a Dental Program for senior citizens over 65. There are income requirements, so be sure to call for additional information.

Dental Society
Delaware Dental Society
1925 Lovering Ave.
Wilmington, DE 19806
302-654-4335

DISTRICT OF COLUMBIA

Dental Programs
Department of Public Health, Dental Health Division
4130 Hunt Place
Washington, DC 20019
202-727-0530

Low income is a major factor in determining eligibility for free and low-cost dental care through the DC government. For information on this very limited dental care, you'll need to call your local clinic.

You must be under 21 for most dental clinic programs, and a sliding fee scale is used, based on your ability to pay.

Dental School
College of Dentistry
Howard University
600 W St., NW
Washington, DC 20059
202-806-0007 (adults), 202-806-0008 (adults), 202-806-0307 (children)
Annual patient visits: 128,886.

Dental Society
District of Columbia Dental Society
502 C St., NE
Washington, DC 20002-5810
202-547-7613

The Society will give referrals to clinics that offer low-cost dental care. There are no programs for the elderly.

FLORIDA

Dental Programs
Department of Health and Rehabilitative Services
Public Health Dental Program
1317 Winewood Blvd., Building 5, Suite 121
Tallahassee, FL 32399-0700
904-487-1845

Call your local County Health Department or Clinic for information on low cost dental care. Clinics usually offer a sliding fee scale. Qualifications vary and emphasis is on children. Guidelines are 200% of poverty standards but offer sliding fee scale based on ability to pay.

Dental School
College of Dentistry
University of Florida
1600 Archer Rd.
Gainesville, FL 32610
352-392-4261, Geriatric Clinic: 352-392-9820
Annual patient visits: 47,441.

Dental Society
Florida Dental Association
1111 E. Tennessee St., Suite 102
Tallahassee, FL 32308
800-877-9922, 352-681-3629

GEORGIA

Dental Programs
Department of Human Resources, Oral Health Section
Two Peachtree St., 6th floor
Atlanta, GA 30303
404-657-2574

Call your local Health Department or Clinic to get information on low-cost dental care. Most will treat children and adults, but low-income is a major factor in determining your eligibility. Fluoride and Sealant Programs are available through various public school systems.

Dental School
School of Dentistry
Medical College of Georgia
1459 Laney Walker Blvd.
Augusta, GA 30912
706-721-2696
Annual patient visits: 16,676.

Dental Society
Georgia Dental Association
2801 Buford Hwy., Suite T60
Atlanta, GA 30329
404-636-7553

HAWAII

Dental Programs
Department of Health
Dental Health Division
1700 Lanakila Ave., Room 203
Honolulu, HI 96817
808-832-5710

Dental care is available for very low income individuals who are in the GAP Group, which includes children and adults. A sliding fee scale is used to determine what you pay based on your income. Dental care is also available for the mentally or physically handicapped, as well as homeless individuals. To be treated, you must meet certain criteria, which you can get by calling your local clinic.

Dental Society
Hawaii Dental Association
1000 Bishop St., Suite 805
Honolulu, HI 96813-4281
808-536-2135

IDAHO

Dental Programs
Department of Health and
Welfare, Dental Program
P.O. Box 83720
450 West State St., 1st Floor
Boise, ID 83720-0036
208-334-5966, 800-926-2588

Idaho has a limited dental care program for low-income individuals, but it is very limited for adults. Some restorative dental work is performed. Emergency service for women or children under the age of 21 is available. Call for eligibility requirements. Also, contact your nearest Community Health Center

or Clinic to see if they offer dental assistance. Their fee scales are usually a sliding fee schedule, based on your ability to pay. *Preventive Programs* are offered through the public school system and some nursing homes, which are designed to help educate these groups on the importance of preventing dental problems before they occur.

Senior Care Program
Boise City/Ada County
3010 W. State St., Suite 120
Boise, ID 83703-5949
208-345-7783

The *Dental Access Program* helps low-income people receive assistance with the cost of dentures, denture repair, and extractions. Those eligible include: 1) Age 60 or older; 2) Residents of southwest Idaho; 3) Have limited or fixed income and no available resources to pay for dental work; 4) Must have a dental need that is denture related, 5) No Medicaid.

Dental Society
Idaho Dental Association
1220 W. Hays St.
Boise, ID 83702-5315
208-343-7543

ILLINOIS

Dental Programs
Total Dent Program
Illinois Dental Society
P.O. Box 376
Springfield, IL 62705
800-252-2930 (IL only),
217-525-1406

The *Total Dent Program* is designed to help low- or fixed-income individuals receive needed dental care at a discount rate. To qualify, you must meet ALL of the following requirements: 1) You cannot be eligible for the Public Aide Dental Program or other dental insurance coverage; 2) You must meet Title 20 income requirements; 3) You must be willing to sign a form certifying the above. Dentists who participate in this program offer a fee reduction of at least 20% to participating Illinois residents. Call for additional information.

Denture Referral Service
Illinois Dental Society
P.O. Box 376
Springfield, IL 62705
217-523-8495, 800-323-1743

The Illinois Retired Teachers Foundation sponsors the Denture Referral Service program, which provides dentures to eligible participants. Although you do NOT have to be a retired teacher to participate, you do need to fulfill the following requirements: 1) Resident of Illinois; 2) 65 years or older; 3) Have no public assistance or private dental insurance; 4) You must qualify for the Illinois *Circuit Breaker Program* which requires earnings of less than $14,000 per year.

Portable Dental Equipment
Illinois Dental Society
P.O. Box 376
Springfield, IL 62705-0376
217-525-1406, 800-252-2930

In order to provide needed dental care for the homebound, elderly and physically and mentally handicapped, the Illinois State Dental Society maintains ten portable dental equipment units located throughout the state. Any licensed dentist in the state of Illinois may use the equipment to provide on-site dental care to these special individuals who meet the specified income and physical requirements.

Dental Schools
Dental School
Northwestern University
240 E. Huron, 1st Floor
Chicago, IL 60611
312-503-6837
Annual patient visits: 96,044

This school has a geriatric clinic.

School of Dental Medicine
Southern Illinois University
2800 College Ave.
Building 263
Alton, IL 62002
618-474-7000
Annual patient visits: 33,258

College of Dentistry
University of Illinois
801 S. Paulina St.
Chicago, IL 60612
312-996-7558
Annual patient visits: 70,510

This school also has a program for geriatrics. A doctor with an assistant will visit nursing homes and retirement homes.

Dental Society
Illinois Dental Society
P.O. Box 376
Springfield, IL 62705-0376
217-525-1406

INDIANA

Dental Programs
Department of Public Health
Dental Health Division
2 N. Meridan St.
Indianapolis, IN 46204-3003
317-233-7417

The Dental Program offers reduced-fee dental care. Anyone with low income is eligible. Comprehensive care is available for children, and some limited care for adults. Call your local health center for more information.

Senior Smile Program
Dental Care for Senior
Citizens, Indiana Dental
Association
401 West Michigan St.
P.O. Box 2467
Indianapolis, IN 46206
317-634-2610

Dental care at reduced fees is available at participating dentists to those who meet the following guidelines: 1) 65 or older; 2) have no private dental insurance nor federal, state or other dental health insurance; 3) income no more than $10,000/single or $14,000 for married couples. Call the Indiana Counsel on Aging at 317-254-5465 for more information.

Donated Dental Services,
Dental Care for Handicapped
P.O. Box 872
Indianapolis, IN 46206
317-631-6022

Participating dentists provide free and low-cost dental care to handicapped individuals who meet the following guidelines: 1) mentally or physically disabled including mental retardation, cerebral palsy, MS, or other disabilities; 2) live in Indiana; 3) each patient screened to find those in most need. Limited income due to handicap is a major factor in determining eligibility. Hours are Monday, Tuesday, and Thursday, 9 a.m. to 4 p.m.

Dental School
School of Dentistry
Indiana University
1121 West Michigan St.
Indianapolis, IN 46202
317-274-7957, Clinic: 317-274-8111 (children), 317-274-3547 (adults)
Annual patient visits: 58,495.

Dental Society
Indiana Dental Association
401 West Michigan St., Suite 1000
P.O. Box 2467
Indianapolis, IN 46206-2467
317-634-2610

IOWA

Dental Programs
Department of Public Health, Dental Division
321 East 12th St.
Lucas State Office Building
Des Moines, IA 50319-0075
515-281-5787

Call local Clinics or Health Centers to get information about reduced-fee dental services. A sliding fee schedule is most often used, and most services are for children. Very limited adult care is available with low-income levels used to determine eligibility.

Iowa Dental Elderly Access
Program (IDEA)
Iowa Dental Association
505 Fifth Ave., Suite 333
Des Moines, IA 50309-2379
515-282-7250

This program makes dental services available to Iowa Senior Citizens with limited financial means. Those eligible: 1) 65 or older; 2) Residents of Iowa; 3) Income is 225% or less of the Federal income poverty level; 4) Have no medical or dental insurance coverage for the dental procedures being requested. Discounts off the dentists regular fee will be made available and are determined on an individual basis in consultation with a participating dentist. Call to get more information and an application.

Dental School
College of Dentistry
University of Iowa
322 Dental Science Bldg.
Elliot Ave.
Iowa City, IA 52242-1001
319-335-7499
Annual patient visits: 56,817.

Special care clinic for Geriatrics and Handicapped: (319) 335-7373

Dental Society
Iowa Dental Association
505 Fifth Ave., Suite 333
Des Moines, IA 50309-2379
515-282-7250

KANSAS

Dental Programs
Department of Health and
Environment

Dental Program
Attn: Dr. Corinne Miller
Landon State Office Bldg.
900 SW Jackson, Room 1051
South
Topeka, KS 66612-1290
913-296-6215

A Health Clinic in Wichita offers reduced-fee dental services for individuals with low income. A sliding fee scale is used. There is also a Fluoride Rinse Program available in the public school systems where needed. Dental care for children on Medicaid is available.

Senior Care Program, Kansas
Dental Association
5200 SW Huntoon St.
Topeka, KS 66604-2398
800-432-3583, 913-272-7360

Dental care at reduced fees is available by participating dentists to those who meet the following guidelines: 1) 60 years or older; 2) have no private, federal or state dental insurance; 3) income no more than $10,000/single or $15,000 for married couples. Fees vary but are reduced. Call for additional information.

Dental Society
Kansas Dental Association
5200 SW Huntoon St.
Topeka, KS 66604-2398
913-272-7360

KENTUCKY

Dental Programs
Department of Health, Dental
Health Division
275 East Main St.

Frankfort, KY 40621
502-564-3246

Call your nearest Health Clinic for information on who offers free and low-cost dental care. Income is a major factor used in determining eligibility. There are three such programs now running in Kentucky. All ages are treated using a sliding fee scale to determine ability to pay.

Jefferson County Dental
Park Duval Health Facility
1817 South 34th St.
Louisville, KY 40211
502-774-4401

Those eligible to participate in the dental care program at this facility must meet the following guidelines: 1) Must be a resident of Jefferson County; 2) Must meet low-income guidelines; 3) Must pay on a sliding fee scale based on income level.

Kentucky Physicians Program,
Kentucky Health Care Access
Foundation
275 East Main St.
Frankfort, KY 40621
800-633-8100

Under the Kentucky Physicians Program, all dental work is done by volunteer dentists. Those eligible to receive treatment include: 1) Individuals with no insurance, no Medicaid and be within the Federal Poverty Guidelines; 2) Must be registered as a program participant. The first visit is free. Pharmacies donate medication based on need. Call to get additional information.

Denture Access Program
Kentucky Dental Association
1940 Princeton Dr.
Louisville, KY 40205-1873
502-459-5373

The Denture Access Program offers full dentures at a reduced rate. There are no age requirements to participate. Call for additional information and a referral to a participating dentist.

Dental Schools
College of Dentistry
University of Kentucky
800 Rose St.
Lexington, KY 40536
For appointments to the college clinic: 606-323-6525
Annual patient visits: 38,723.

The university has some programs for the elderly, and a few satellite programs where they go to nursing homes.

University of Louisville, School of Dentistry
Louisville, KY 40292
502-852-5096 (adult)
502-852-5642 (children)
Annual patient visits: 65,914.

Dental Society
Kentucky Dental Association
1940 Princeton Dr.
Louisville, KY 40205-1873
502-459-5373

LOUISIANA

Dental Programs
Department of Public Health,
Dental Health Division
200 Henry Clay Ave.
New Orleans, LA 70118
504-896-1337

The Dental Program offers reduced-rate dental care through your nearest clinic. Louisiana State University offers dentures for those in need, and also restorative work for those under 18 years of age. Anyone with low income under the age of 21 is eligible for these programs. This office also provides referrals for patients with AIDS. For the 24-hour Emergency Dental Service, call 504-897-8250 for more information.

Donated Dental Services
Dental Care for Handicapped
NFDH-Louisiana
LSDU Dept. Pediatric
Dentistry
1100 Florida Ave., Box 139
New Orleans, LA 70119-2799
504-948-6141

Certain handicapped individuals who meet the following guidelines can receive reduced-rate and free dental care through this program: 1) mentally or physically disabled including mental retardation, cerebral palsy, MS, or other disabilities; 2) live in Louisiana; 3) each patient must be screened to find those in most need — limited income due to handicap is a major factor in determining eligibility.

Dental School
School of Dentistry
Louisiana State University
1100 Florida Ave.
New Orleans, LA 70119
504-619-8700
Annual patient visits: 47,247.

Dental Society
Louisiana Dental Association

7833 Office Park Blvd.
Baton Rouge, LA 70809
504-926-1986

MAINE

Dental Programs
Department of Human Services
Division of Dental Health
Bureau of Health
11 State House Station
151 Capitol St.
Augusta, Maine 04333
207-287-3121

Call your nearest Community Health Center or Clinic for information on reduced fees for dental care. Usually fees are based on a sliding scale. Insurance is accepted. Both children and adults are eligible. *American Indian/Alaska Native Tribal Programs* offer direct and/or referral medical/dental services for registered members of federally recognized American Indian/Alaska Native Tribes. These are tribally-directed programs and may differ significantly in eligibility requirements and services.

Senior Dent Program
Maine Dental Association
P.O. Box 215
Association Dr.
Manchester, ME 04351
207-622-7900

The Senior Dent program offers comprehensive dental care to low-income elderly at reduced fees. Those eligible must: 1) be residents of Maine; 2) be 62 or older; 3) Have no dental benefits under a private insurance plan or the Medicaid program; 4) Have an annual income that qualifies them for *Maine's Low Cost Drug Program*. Those eligible will receive at least a 15% discount from the usual and customary fees.

Dental Society
Maine Dental Association
P.O. Box 215
Association Dr.
Manchester, ME 04351-0215
207-622-7900

MARYLAND

Dental Programs
Maryland State Health Department
Dental Health Division - Baltimore
201 West Preston St.
Baltimore, MD 21201-3046
800-492-5231

Under the Maryland Access to Care program, low-income individuals under 21 or over 65 years of age. The program offers reduced fee dental care. Fee schedule for care is based on ability to pay.

Senior Dent Program, Dental Care for Senior Citizens
Maryland State Dental Association
6450 Dobbin Rd.
Columbia, MD 21045-5824
410-964-2880

Senior citizens over 65 years of age living in MD and who meet certain income eligibility requirements may qualify for low-cost dental care. Call for qualifications and more information.

Dental Care for Handicapped
Donated Dental Services
6450 Dobbin Rd.
Columbia, MD 21045-4744
410-964-1944

Certain handicapped individuals who meet the following guidelines may be eligible to receive free or low-cost dental care: 1) mentally or physically disabled including mental retardation, cerebral palsy, MS, or other disabilities; 2) Maryland resident; 3) each patient is screened to find those in most need: limited income due to handicap is a major factor. Call Lois Bidel for more information.

Dental School
Baltimore College of Dental Surgery
University of Maryland
666 W. Baltimore St.
Baltimore, MD 21201
410-706-5603
Annual patient visits: 57,865.

Dental Society
Maryland Dental Association
6450 Dobbin Rd.
Columbia, MD 21045-5824
410-964-2880

MASSACHUSETTS

Dental Programs
Department of Health and Hospitals
Community Dental Programs
1010 Massachusetts Ave.
Boston, MA 02118
617-534-4717

Eighteen Health Center Programs throughout Boston offer low-cost dental care usually on a sliding fee scale based on your income. Requirements vary, so be sure to call to get additional information. Some hospitals offer limited dental. They also operate an HIV referral and treatment program.

Children's Oral Health
250 Washington St., 5th Floor
Boston, MA 02108-4619
617-624-6060

This program offers dental care for individuals who are mentally retarded, have cerebral palsy, and those who are physically disabled. Call for additional information.

Dentistry for All
Massachusetts Dental Society
83 Speen St.
Natick, MA 07160-4144
508-651-7511

The *Dentistry for All Program* is a reduced-fee dental program for low-income individuals who have no dental coverage of any kind. Call to get additional information.

Dental Schools
Harvard School of Dental Medicine
188 Longwood Ave.
Boston, MA 02115
617-432-1423
Annual patient visits: 26,270.

School of Graduate Dentistry
Boston University
100 E. Newton St.
Boston, MA 02118
617-638-4671
Annual patient visits: 34,324.

School of Dental Medicine

Tufts University
One Kneeland St.
Boston, MA 02111
617-636-6547
Annual patient visits: 87,522.

Dental Society
Massachusetts Dental Society
83 Speen St.
Natick, MA 01760-4144
508-651-7511

MICHIGAN

Dental Programs
Department of Public Health,
Dental Health Division
3423 N. Martin Luther King Jr.,
Blvd.
P.O. Box 30195
Lansing, MI 48909
517-335-8898

There are no direct dental services through the State Health Department. You must call your local or county health department for participating clinics and qualifications.

Senior Dent Program
Michigan Dental Association
230 North Washington Square,
Suite 208
Lansing, MI 48933
517-372-9070, 800-589-2632 (MI only)

Dental care at reduced fees are available to senior citizens who meet the following guidelines: 1) 65 or older; 2) have no private dental insurance nor federal, state or other dental health insurance; 3) meet certain low-income requirements. Fees vary, and procedures covered include all types of dental care except full dentures. Over 800 dentists in Michigan participate.

Discount Dentures
Michigan Dental Association
230 North Washington Square,
Suite 208
Lansing, MI 48933
517-372-9070
800-589-2632 (MI only)

Under the *Professionally Acceptable Economy Denture Service (PAEDS)*, qualified patients can receive reduced-fees on full dentures (upper, lower or both) provided by licensed dentists. It also includes examination and x-rays. Those: 1) no age or income eligibility requirements. 2) must call the above number for additional information. Fees vary but are always at a reduced rate. Payment is handled through patient and dentist.

Dental Schools
School of Dentistry
University of Detroit-Mercy
2985 E. Jefferson Ave.
Detroit, MI 48207
313-494-6600
Annual patient visits: 47,152.

School of Dentistry
University of Michigan
1011 North University
Ann Arbor, MI 48109-1078
313-763-6933
Annual patient visits: 88,035.

Dental Society
Michigan Dental Association
230 Washington Square North,
Suite 208
Lansing, MI 48933-1392
517-372-9070

MINNESOTA

Dental Programs
State Health Department
Dental Division
717 Delaware Street SE
Minneapolis, MN 55440
612-623-5529

Call your Local Health Clinic to find out who offers dental care on a reduced-fee scale. Also contact "First Call for Help," 612-224-1133, for additional information on clinics. Low-income is a major factor in determining eligibility.

Senior Partners Care Dental
Program
Minnesota Senior Federation
Iris Park Place
1885 University Ave. W.
Suite 190
St. Paul, MN 55104
800-365-8765, 612-642-1398

The *Senior Partners Care Dental Program* is designed to bridge the Medicare gap, with participating dentists agreeing to provide a 20% discount for all professional dental services. Those eligible must: 1) join the Minnesota Senior Foundation; 2) be 55 or older and retired; 3) meet the annual income criteria of less than 200% of poverty ($1290/single or $1726/ couple per month in 1995); 4) have less than $21,000 in liquid assets (cash savings, stocks, CDs, etc.); 5) NOT be a part of any dental plan.

Wilder Senior Dental Program
516 Humboldt Ave.
St. Paul, MN 55107
612-220-1807

This program is for those 65 years old and older. It is not income-based and they will set up payment plans.

Dental School
School of Dentistry
University of Minnesota
515 SE Delaware St.
Minneapolis, MN 55455
612-625-2495
Call main number to make all appointments
Annual patient visits: 34,078

Dental Society
Minnesota Dental Association
2236 Marshall Ave.
St. Paul, MN 55104-5792
612-646-7454

MISSISSIPPI

Dental Programs
Low-Cost Denture Referral Program
Mississippi Dental Association
2630 Ridgewood Rd.
Jackson, MS 39216-4920
601-982-0442

Under this denture program, patients and dentists negotiate the reduced cost for services based on the patients' ability to pay. Call for additional information.

Dental School
School of Dentistry
University of Mississippi
2500 North State St.
Jackson, MS 39216
601-984-6155
Annual patient visits: 15,097.

Dental Society
Mississippi Dental Association

2630 Ridgewood Rd.
Jackson, MS 39216-4920
601-982-0442

MISSOURI

Dental Programs
Department of Public Health
Dental Health Division
930 Wildwood
P.O. Box 570
Jefferson City, MO 65109
573-751-6247

Call your nearest health center or clinic for information on reduced fees for dental care. Usually clinics offer a sliding fee scale, and qualifications vary, though low income is a major factor considered. Fluoride Rinse Programs are available through the public school system.

Missouri Elks Program for the Handicapped
Truman Medical Center East
7900 Lee's Summit Rd.
Kansas City, MO 64139
816-373-1486

This program offers dental care for physically challenged adults and children through three mobile units, which provide in-home care for those unable to get out on their own. Call for information on eligibility guidelines.

Dental Care for Senior Citizens
Senior Care Program
Missouri Dental Association
230 W. McCarty
P.O. Box 1707
Jefferson City, MO 65102-1707
800-688-1907
573-634-3436 (in Jefferson City)

314-965-5960 (in St. Louis)
816-333-5454 (in KC)

This program provides low-cost dental care to seniors who meet the following eligibility requirements: 1) 60 years or older; 2) income no more than $15,000 (single) or $20,000 (for married couples); 3) you cannot be currently receiving dental care through any public aid program or insurance plan. Participating dentists have agreed to provide a minimum of a 25% discount on services; however, the dentist may charge the usual fee for the initial office visit and examination.

Dental School
School of Dentistry
University of Missouri
650 E. 25th St.
Kansas City, MO 64108-2795
816-235-2100
Annual patient visits: 7,500.

Dental Society
Missouri Dental Association
230 W. McCarty
P.O. Box 1707
Jefferson City, MO 65102-1707
573-634-3436

MONTANA

Dental Programs
Health Services Division,
Dental Department
Health and Environment
Sciences
Cogswell Building
1400 Broadway
Helena, Montana 59620
406-444-0276

Through the Maternal and Child Health department, counties can choose how they wish to use funds for dental care, so call your county health department to find out about treatments. Also Fluoride and Mouthrinse Programs are available for those who are in need.

Dental Society
Montana Dental Association
P.O. Box 1154
Helena, MT 59624-1154
406-443-2061

NEBRASKA

Dental Programs
Health Department, Dental
Health Division
3140 N. St.
Lincoln, NE 68510
402-441-8015

Call your local Clinic to find out if they offer dental care. Low-income is a major factor in determining eligibility, and fees are usually based on a sliding scale. Children are a first priority.

Senior Dent Program
Nebraska Dental Association
3120 O Street
Lincoln, NE 68510-1599
402-476-1704

The *Senior Dent Program* offers dental care at a reduced fee for senior citizens. There are eligibility requirements that include being at least 65 years of age. Call to find out additional information.

Dental Schools
School of Dentistry
Creighton University
2802 Webster St.
Omaha, NE 68178
402-280-2865

49

Annual patient visits: 61,218.

College of Dentistry
University of Nebraska
Medical Center
40th and Holdrege Sts.
Lincoln, NE 68583
402-472-1333 (adult), 402-472-1305 (children)
Annual patient visits: 17,599.

Dental Society
Nebraska Dental Association
3120 O St.
Lincoln, NE 68510-1599
402-476-1704

NEVADA

Dental Programs
Nevada Health Department,
Family Services
505 East King St., Room 201
Carson City, NV 89710-4797
702-687-4740

Call your County Health Department to see if they offer dental. Only very limited, low-cost dental care is available to adults other than possibly extractions due to pain. Most often, programs are only for children. Clark County Dental Society keeps a list of dentists who offer discounts to senior citizens. Call 702-255-7873 to get a referral.

Senior Center Bldg.
1155 East 9th St.
Reno, NV 89502
702-328-2575
This center does referrals only.

Dental Society
Nevada Dental Association
6889 W. Charleston #B
Las Vegas, NV 89117
702-255-4211

NEW HAMPSHIRE

Dental Programs
Department of Health and
Human Services
Dental Division
6 Hazen Dr.
Concord, NH 03301
603-271-4685

New Hampshire has a very limited dental care program for those of low-income. Children are a first priority. Call the toll-free Helpline at 800-852-3345, ext. 4238 to find out about other possible dental assistance. Some state technical colleges offer dental Hygiene Programs.

Denture Program, New
Hampshire Dental Society
23 South State St.
P.O. Box 2229
Concord, NH 03302-2229
603-225-5961

The *Denture Program* offers dentures to anyone who needs them at a reduced rate. There are financial guidelines that need to be met, but the program is for all ages. Call the above number for additional information.

Dental Society
New Hampshire Dental Society
23 South State St.
P.O. Box 2229
Concord, NH 03302-2229
603-225-5961

NEW JERSEY

Dental Programs
Department of Health, Dental
Health Division
P.O. Box 364

50 E. State St., 5th Floor
Trenton, NJ 08625-0364
609-292-1723

Some area hospitals offer dental care on a sliding fee scale based on income, but most services offered are for children. Only limited care is available for adults. Also a limited number of clinics in some towns offer dental care, also using a sliding fee scale.

Senior Dent
New Jersey Dental Association
One Dental Plaza
P.O. Box 6020
North Brunswick, NJ 08902-6020
732-821-9400

The *Senior Dent* program offers increase access to Dental Care for senior citizens by offering at least a 15% discount on services. Those eligible: 1) you must have a PAA (Pharmacy) card; 2) be age 65 or older; 3) have annual income of less than $15,700 (single) or $19,250 (married couple; 4) have no dental insurance or Medicaid benefits. Call the State Division on Aging for additional information at 800-792-8820.

Donated Dental Services
One Dental Plaza
North Brunswick, NJ 08902-4313
732-821-2977

Donated Dental Services offers comprehensive dental care for handicapped individuals. Those eligible: 1) the mentally or physically disabled including mental retardation,

cerebral palsy, MS or other disabilities; 2) New Jersey residents; 3) each patient is screened to find those in most need. Limited income due to disability is a major factor in determining eligibility.

Dental School
New Jersey Dental School
University of Medicine and Dentistry
150 Bergen St.
Newark, NJ 07103
973-972-4300
Annual patient visits: 58,615.

Dental Society
New Jersey Dental Association
One Dental Plaza
P.O. Box 6020
North Brunswick, NJ 08902-6020
732-821-9400

NEW MEXICO

Dental Programs
Department of Health
Dental Division
1190 Saint Francis Dr.
Santa Fe, NM 87502-6110
505-827-2389

Call your nearest Community Health Center or Clinic for information on reduced fees for dental care. Most clinics will charge according to ability to pay, and children are usually a priority. Carrie Tingley Hospital treats mentally disadvantaged and disabled; call 505-843-7493 for additional information. There are also some Indian Health Centers that offer dental care to tribal members.

Community Dental Services, Inc.
2116 Hinkle SE
Albuquerque, NM 87102
505-765-5683

Community Dental Services takes only Medicaid.

Dental Society
New Mexico Dental Association
3736 Eubank Blvd., NE, #1A
Albuquerque, NM 87111-3556
505-294-1368

NEW YORK

Dental Programs
Oral Health Programs and Policies
Health and Hospital Corp.
299 Broadway, Suite 500
New York, NY 10013
212-978-5540

Clinics throughout the city boroughs offer free or reduced cost dental care to children, ages 2 years to 21 years. Call the above number to get additional information about services offered.

Dental Schools
School of Dental and Oral Surgery
Columbia University
630 W. 168th St.
New York, NY 10032
212-305-6726
Annual patient visits: 53,255.

College of Dentistry
New York University
345 E. 24th St.
New York, NY 10010
212-998-9800, Geriatric Clinic: 212-998-9767

Annual patient visits: 269,095.

School of Dental Medicine
State University of New York at Stony Brook
Rockland Hall
Health Science Center
Stony Brook, NY 11794
516-632-8989, 516-632-8967 (children)
516-632-8974 (adults), 516-632-9245 (geriatric clinic)
Annual patient visits: 15,321.

School of Dental Medicine
State University of New York at Buffalo
325 Squire
3435 Main St.
Buffalo, NY 14212-3008
716-829-2821, 716-829-2723 (children)
716-829-2720 (adults)
Annual patient visits: 78,000.

Dental Society
Dental Society of New York
7 Elk St.
Albany, NY 12207
518-465-0044

NORTH CAROLINA

Dental Programs
Health and Natural Resources Environment
Dental Health Department
P.O. Box 29598
Raleigh, NC 27626-0598
919-733-3853

Call your nearest County Health Clinic to see if they offer dental care at a reduced cost. When offered, it is usually on a sliding fee scale and most often for children. Prevention and education are the main focus with *Fluoride and Sealant Programs* throughout the various public school systems.

Senior Smile Program
North Carolina Dental
Association
P.O. Box 12047
Raleigh, NC 27605-2047
919-832-1357

The *Senior Smile Program* offers reduced-fee dental care for senior citizens. This program works under the American Dental Association (ADA). The ADA toll-free number for this program is 800-621-8099. Call for more information.

Dental School
School of Dentistry
University of North Carolina
211 H Brauer Hall
Chapel Hill, NC 27514
919-966-1161
Annual patient visits: 30,395.

Dental Society
North Carolina Dental Society
P.O. Box 12047
Raleigh, NC 27605-2047
919-832-1222

NORTH DAKOTA

Dental Programs
Health Department
Maternal and Child Health
Department
600 E. Blvd. Ave.
Bismarck, ND 58505-0200
701-328-2493

Crippled Children Services offers dental and health care for those in need. Some Indian Health Centers offer dental for tribal members. The Fargo Homeless Project offers emergency dental work for the homeless. No programs other than Medicaid offer dental care, and no clinics offer dental care.

Senior Dent
North Dakota Dental
Association
Box 1332
Bismarck, ND 58502
701-223-8870

The *Senior Dent* program makes a full range of Dental Services available to financially eligible North Dakotans age 55 or older at a reduced fee. Those eligible must: 1) be 55 or older; 2) Not be covered by medical assistance or enrolled in a dental insurance plan; 3) have income that is 125% or less of federal poverty guidelines. Fees vary, but dentists have agreed to offer at least a 33% discount off their regular fees. Contact your local Senior Citizen Center for more information.

Dental Society
North Dakota Dental
Association
P.O. Box 1332
Bismarck, ND 58502-1332
701-223-8870

OHIO

Dental Programs
State Health Department,
Dental Health Division
246 North High
Columbus, OH 43266-0588
614-466-4180

Ohio offers a *Sealant and Fluoride Mouthrinse Program* through the public school system.

Access to Dental Care
Programs, Ohio Dental
Association
1370 Dublin Rd.
Columbus, OH 43215-1098
800-MY-SMILE

The Ohio Dental Association coordinates numerous Access to Dental Care Programs. Free or low-cost dental care is available through the *Access to Dental Care for Children with Special Health Care Needs (CSHCN)* program. This program assists local agencies to increase access to needed oral health services for this special needs group. Funds are also used to provide comprehensive services for high risk children and/or women of child-bearing age, otherwise known as *Child and Family Health Projects (CFSHP)*. Primary Care is also available through some County Health Departments and Clinics. Call for additional information and qualifications.

Dental Services for the
Handicapped
Donated Dental Services
635 W. 7th St.
Cincinnati, OH 45203
513-621-2517

Free and low-cost dental care is available to the handicapped and elderly if they meet the following guidelines: 1) Mentally or physically disabled including mental retardation, cerebral palsy, MS or other disabilities; 2) individuals may also be elderly living on a fixed income; 3) each patient is screened to find those in most need. Limited income due to handicap is a major factor in determining eligibility.

Greater Cincinnati Oral Health
Council
635 W. Seventh St.
Cincinnati, OH 45203
513-621-0248

A charter agency of the United Way, the Public Dental Service Society's dental care programs help special groups such as children from low-income families, the homeless, the aging and those with disabling conditions. 1) Dental Sealant Program: sealants are applied to low-income and handicapped children of Cincinnati. 2) Head Start: provides dental education, consultation and preventive treatment for children of disadvantaged families. 3) Homeless Program: provides dental care for homeless adults and children. 4) Dental Registry for the Elderly and Handicapped: a computerized referral service matches patients with special needs with a dentist who can accommodate these needs.

Dental Schools
College of Dentistry
Ohio State University
305 W. 12th Ave.
Columbus, OH 43210
614-292-2751
Annual patient visits: 51,476.

School of Dentistry
Case Western Reserve
University
2123 Abington Rd.

Cleveland, OH 44106
216-368-3200
Annual patient visits: 86,630.

Dental Society
Ohio Dental Association
1370 Dublin Rd.
Columbus, OH 43215-1098
614-486-2700

OKLAHOMA

Dental Programs
State Department of Health
Dental Health Services
1000 Northeast Tenth St.
Oklahoma City, OK 73117-1299
405-271-5502

Call your local Health Center or hospital to see if dental is offered. When offered, it is usually on a sliding fee scale, and in some instances only for children.

Care-Dent Program
Oklahoma Dental Society
629 West I-44 Service Rd.
Oklahoma City, OK 73118
800-876-8890

Care-Dent offers savings to those who need denture service. Dentists also provide a thorough examination. Call for a participating dentist and more information.

Senior Dent Program
Oklahoma Dental Society
629 West I-44 Service Rd.
Oklahoma City, OK 73118
800-876-8890
405-848-8873

The *Senior Dent Program* offers complete, professional dental care at a reduced fee to those seniors who meet the following guidelines:

1) 65 or older; 2) have no dental insurance; 3) income no more than $10,000/single or $12,000 for a married couple. Dentists offer a 20% discount to qualifying senior citizens. Call for more information.

Disabled Program
D-Dent
4300 North Lincoln Blvd., Suite 205
Oklahoma City, OK 73105
800-522-9510, 405-424-8092

The *D-Dent Program* offers free dental care for the physically disabled. You must apply, and applicants are carefully screened.

Dental School
College of Dentistry
University of Oklahoma
Health Sciences Center
1001 Stanton L. Young Blvd.
P.O. Box 26901
Oklahoma City, OK 73190-3044
405-271-6056
Annual patient visits: 45,615.

Dental Society
Oklahoma Dental Association
629 W. Interstate 44 Service Rd.
Oklahoma City, OK 73118-6032
405-848-8873

OREGON

Dental Programs
Department of Health
Dental Health Division
800 NE Oregon St.
Portland, OR 97232
503-731-4098

Community Access Programs offer reduced-fee dental care to low-income individuals using a sliding fee schedule. Call your nearest Health Clinic for more information. The program requires enrollment at most clinics before treatment can begin. Under the *King Fluoride Program*, children are provided school-based fluoride mouthrinses and tablets.

Low-Cost Denture Program
107 Oakway Center, Suite C
Eugene, OR 97401
541-686-1175

Under this program, residents of Lake County, 55 years or older, and who meet the following guidelines may be eligible to receive low-cost denture care, including full upper and lower dentures, partials, reclines and repairs: 1) receive no public assistance; 2) income no more than $7,500 (single) or $10,500 (married couples). Call for additional qualifications and information.

Dental Care for Senior Citizens
Senior Smile Dental Service
Multnomah Dental Society
1618 W. First, Suite 317
Portland, OR 97201
503-223-4738

Under this program, low income seniors over 60 years old, who live in Multnomah County may be eligible to receive both general and specialized dental care at a 50% reduced fee. Call for more information and to register.

Dental School
School of Dentistry
Sam Jackson Park
Oregon Health Sciences

University
611 SW Campus Dr.
Portland, OR 97201
503-494-8867
Annual patient visits: 44,900.

Dental Society
Oregon Dental Association
17898 SW McEwan Rd.
Portland, OR 97224-7798
503-620-3230

PENNSYLVANIA

Dental Programs
Department of Public Health
Dental Health Division
500 South Broad Street
Philadelphia, PA 19146
215-875-5666

The Dental Program offers reduced-rate dental care through your nearest clinic. Insurance is accepted and fee set according to financial situation. Anyone with low income is eligible, but children are first priority.

Dental Care for Senior Citizens
Access to Care Program
3501 North Front St.
Harrisburg, PA 17110
717-234-5941

Under this program, individuals 65 or over can receive at least a minimum of 15% discount on dental care through 1,700 participating dentists across PA. To be eligible, you must: 1) have no private dental insurance nor federal, state or other dental health assistance; 2) have income no more than $13,000 (single) or $16,200 (married couples). Call the PA Counsel on Aging at 800-692-7256 for more program information.

Dental Care for Handicapped
(Philadelphia only)
Donated Dental Services
Fidelity Bank Bldg.
123 S. Broad St., 22nd Floor
Philadelphia, PA 19109-1022
215-546-0300

Certain low-income mentally or
physically handicapped residents of
Philadelphia may qualify to receive
free or low-cost dental care. Each
patient is screened to find those
most in need: limited income due to
handicap is a major factor.

Dental Schools
School of Dentistry
Temple University
3223 N. Broad St.
Philadelphia, PA 19140
215-707-2900
Annual patient visits: 77,665.

School of Dental Medicine
University of Pennsylvania
4001 Spruce St.
Philadelphia, PA 19104
215-898-8961
Annual patient visits: 85,000.

School of Dental Medicine
University of Pittsburgh
3501 Terrace St.
Salk Hall
Pittsburgh, PA 15261
412-648-8760
Annual patient visits: 59,570.

Dental Society
Pennsylvania Dental
Association
3501 N. Front St.
P.O. Box 3341
Harrisburg, PA 17110
717-234-5941

RHODE ISLAND
Dental Programs
Department of Public Health
Oral Health Division
3 Capital Hill
Providence, RI 02908-5097
401-222-2588

The dental program offers reduced-
fee basic dental care (not crowns or
bridges, for example). Call your
nearest clinic for more information.
Most insurance are accepted and
the pay schedule is according to situation. Anyone with low-income
can qualify.

Travelers Aide Society for the
Homeless
177 Union St.
Providence, RI 02903
401-521-2255

The Travelers Aide Society offers
dental care for the homeless. Call
Linda Dziobeck for more information.

Dental Care for Handicapped
Independence Square
500 Prospect St.
Pawtucket, RI 02860
401-728-9448

Through the *Donated Dental
Services Program,* free and low-cost
dental care is available to the handicapped that meet the following
guidelines: 1) mentally or physically disabled including mental retardation, cerebral palsy, MS, or other
disabilities; 2) live in Rhode Island;
3) each patient must be screened to
find those in most need. Limited
income due to handicap is a major
factor in determining eligibility.

South County
Health Center of South County
One River St.
Wakefield, RI 02879
401-783-0853

Basic dental treatments for all ages
are available. Call Herb Manfield
for more information.

Dental Society
Rhode Island Dental
Association
200 Centerville Rd.
Warwick, RI 02886-4339
401-732-6833

SOUTH CAROLINA

Dental Programs
Department of Health and
Environmental Control
2600 Bull St.
Columbia, SC 29201
803-734-4972

A program through the public
school system offers dental care for
children. Applications are picked up
at participating schools, but not
during the summer. Call your local
Health Center or Clinic to find out if
they offer dental care. Dental usually is for children.

Primary Care Center
P.O. Box 6923
Columbia, SC 29260
803-738-9881

Some Primary Care Clinics or
Centers offer dental on a sliding fee
scale based on income. Call to get
additional information.

Senior Care Dental Program
South Carolina Dental
Association

120 Stonemark Ln.
Columbia, SC 29210-3841
803-750-2277

The *Senior Care Program* offers
dental care to senior citizens at a
reduced fee. The minimum discount is 20%, and there are specific
eligibility guidelines, which you can
get from your local Council on
Aging or Commission on Aging
(Buford: 803-524-1787) or the
Dental Society at 803-750-2277.

Dental School
College of Dental Medicine
Medical University of South
Carolina
171 Ashley Ave.
Charleston, SC 29425
803-792-2611
Annual patient visits: 25,315.

Dental Society
South Carolina Dental
Association
120 Stonemark Ln.
Columbia, SC 29210-3841
803-750-2277

SOUTH DAKOTA

Dental Programs
Department of Health, Dental
Division
Anderson Building
445 E. Capitol Ave.
Pierre, SD 57501
605-773-3361

Although comprehensive dental
care is not offered through local
Health Centers, the *Emergency
Care Referral Program* can put you
in touch with dental care in emergency situations.

Indian Health Program, Indian Health Services
Federal Building
115 4th Ave. SE
Aberdeen, SD 57401
605-226-7501

Dental care is available at no charge for Indians enrolled in a tribe. Call the office above for additional information and find out locations for treatment.

Dental Society
South Dakota Dental Association
P.O. Box 1194
Pierre, SD 57501-1194
605-224-9133

TENNESSEE

Dental Programs
Department of Health, Oral Health Services
Cordell Hull Bldg. 5th Floor
426 5th Ave. North
Nashville, TN 37247
615-741-7213

Contact your Local Health Center or Clinic to find out if they offer reduced-fee dental services. Low income is a major factor in determining eligibility, and a sliding fee scale is most often used. Qualifications vary, and care is primarily for children. Emergency care is offered to adults to alleviate pain. Although there are no special programs for the elderly or disabled, they will be treated based on the above income criteria.

Dental Schools
School of Dentistry

Meharry Medical College
1005 D.B. Todd Blvd.
Nashville, TN 37208
615-327-6669
Annual patient visits: 7,972.

College of Dentistry
University of Tennessee
875 Union Ave.
Memphis, TN 38163
901-448-6257
Annual patient visits: 52,551.

Dental Society
Tennessee Dental Association
P.O. Box 120188
Nashville, TN 37212-0188
615-383-8962

TEXAS

Dental Programs

In Texas, several regional offices of the Texas Public Health Office have additional information on reduced-fee dental care in their regions. Call or write the appropriate region to get additional information.

Region 1
Texas Public Health
1109 Kemper St.
Lubbock, TX 79403
806-744-3577

Region 3
Texas Public Health
2561 Matlock Road
Arlington, TX 76015-1621
817-792-7224

Region 4 & 5 North
Texas Public Health
1517 West Front St.
Tyler, TX 75702
903-595-3585

Region 6
Texas Public Health
10500 Forum Place Drive,
Suite 123
Houston, TX 77036-8599
713-995-1112

Region 7
Texas Public Health
2408 South 37th St.
Temple, TX 76504
817-778-6744

Region 8
Texas Public Health
1021 Garnerfield Rd.
Uvalde, TX 78801
210-278-7173

Region 11
Texas Public Health
601 West Sesame Drive
Harlingen, TX 78550
210-423-0130

Dental Schools
Baylor College of Dentistry
3302 Gaston Ave.
Dallas, TX 75246
214-828-8100
Annual patient visits: 75,411.

Health Science Center
Dental Branch
University of Texas
6516 John Freeman Ave.
Houston, TX 77030
713-792-4056
Annual patient visits: 113,153.

Health Science Center
Dental School
University of Texas
7703 Floyd Curl Dr.
San Antonio, TX 78284
210-567-3222
Annual patient visits: 124,783.

Dental Society
Texas Dental Association
P.O. Box 3358
Austin, TX 78764-3358
512-443-3675

UTAH
Dental Society
Utah Dental Association
1151 E. 3900 South, #B160
Salt Lake City, UT 84124-1216
801-261-5315

VERMONT
Dental Programs
Island Pond Health Center
P.O. Box 425
Island Pond, VT 05846
802-723-4300

This nonprofit Health Center in northeastern Vermont offers eligible residents of specific towns dental care for a reduced fee based on a sliding scale based on their income from the previous year. Fees range from 100% coverage for preventive dental services and 50% coverage for all other services that they provide. No specialty services, such as orthodontics, are available. Call to get additional information and to find out if Health Care Inc. has reduced fee dental care available in your town.

Dental Society
Vermont Dental Society
132 Church St.
Burlington, VT 05401-8401
802-864-0115

VIRGINIA

Dental Programs

Health Department, Dental Division
1500 E. Main, Room 239
Richmond, VA 23219
804-786-3556

Community Health Centers offer dental care at a reduced-fee based on income. Although children are a first priority, adults are treated on an emergency basis. There are approximately 90 such Centers across VA that offer dental care.

Dental School

School of Dentistry
Virginia Commonwealth University
Box 980566
Richmond, VA 23298
804-828-9095
Annual patient visits: 61,722

Dental Society

Virginia Dental Association
P.O. Box 6906
Richmond, VA 23230-0906
804-358-4927

WASHINGTON

Dental Programs

Health Care Authority, Dental Services
P.O. Box 42710
Olympia, WA 98504-2710
360-923-2753

Call your nearest Health Department or Clinic to find out if they offer free or discount dental care. When dental care is offered, it is usually for children and senior citizens, with only limited care for adults. A sliding fee scale is used, and low income is a factor in determining what you're charged. Ask to speak with Connie Mix or Bob Blacksmith to get additional information on these programs.

Seattle-King County Dental Society
2201 Sixth Ave., Suite 1306
Seattle, WA 98121-1832
206-443-7607

The Seattle-King County Dental Society has a listing of clinics and programs that offer free or minimal cost dental care. Contact them for a free copy.

Elderly and Disabled
Washington State Dental Association
2033 Sixth Avenue #333
Seattle, WA 98121
206-448-1914

Under the *Access Program for the Elderly and Disabled,* dental care at a reduced cost is available from participating dentists who meet the following guidelines: 1) 65 or older; 2) have no dental insurance; 3) income no more than $15,670/single or $19,765 for a family; 4) for the disabled, the same criteria for eligibility applies, but there is no age restriction. Eligibility must be recertified every 12 months. Fees are reduced by at least 25% for patients meeting the criteria. Call or write for an application.

Dental School

School of Dentistry
University of Washington
Health Science Building

Northeast Pacific St.
Seattle, WA 98195
206-543-5830
Annual patient visits: 45,500.

Dental Society
Washington Dental Association
2033 6th Ave., Suite 333
Seattle, WA 98121-2514
206-448-1914

WEST VIRGINIA

Dental Programs
Department of Health and
Human Resources
Dental Information
State Capital Complex, Bldg. 6
Charleston, WV 25305
304-926-1700

Very limited dental care is available through the Health Department other than Medicaid: however, below you'll find other contacts that do offer reduced-fee services.

Low-Income Adults, Linkline
One United Way Square
Charleston, WV 25301
800-540-8659, 304-340-3517

Linkline offers reduced-fee dental services for adults 19 to 59, but you must first apply to the program and be accepted. Low income is a major factor in determining your eligibility.

Tiskewah Dental Clinic
600 Florida St.
Charleston, WV 25302
304-348-6613

This dental clinic treats children year-round, and senior citizens during the summer free of charge. Call to find out if you might qualify.

Dental School
School of Dentistry
West Virginia University
The Medical Center
Morgantown, WV 26505
304-598-4810
Annual patient visits: 27,522.

Dental Society
West Virginia Dental
Association
1002 Kanawha Valley Building
300 Capitol St.
Charleston, WV 25301-1794
304-344-5246

WISCONSIN

Dental Programs
Bureau of Public Health
1414 E. Washington Ave.
Madison, WI 53703
608-266-5152

Very limited reduced-fee dental care is available in Wisconsin. Call your local Health Center or Clinic to find out if dental is available.

Wisconsin Dental Society
111 East Wisconsin Ave.
Suite 1300
Milwaukee, WI 53202
414-276-4520

The Wisconsin Dental Society has been working with County Dental Society's to come up with programs to assist the underserved with reduced fee dental services. Keep in contact with them to find out about any new programs that you might qualify for.

Dental School
School of Dentistry
Marquette University

604 N. 16th St.
Milwaukee, WI 53233
414-288-6500
Annual patient visits: 48,235.

Dental Society
Wisconsin Dental Association
111 E. Wisconsin Ave.
Suite 1300
Milwaukee, WI 53202-4811
414-276-4520

WYOMING

Dental Programs
State Health Department
Dental Division
Hathaway Building, 4th Floor
Cheyenne, WY 82002
307-777-7945

The *Marginal Program* for low-income children provides dental care up to 19 years of age. You must apply and be accepted to be eligible. The *Cleft Palate Clinic* offers free diagnostic treatment and referrals. The *Sealant Program* provides sealant treatment for children of low-income families. The *Elderly Program* offers reduced fees for those low-income adults 65 or older. There is no reduced-fee dental care for those individuals 20 to 64 except through *Title 19 Emergency Care program.*

Dental Society
Wyoming Dental Association
330 S. Center St., Suite 322
Casper, WY 82601-2875
307-234-077

Help With Diet And Exercise

S top the insanity of throwing your money away on diet programs, books, and infomercial products. Why pay big money to some diet guru, who maybe spent a few years of his or her life and a few thousand bucks coming up with the latest health fad? Instead, you can contact a government office who spent millions of dollars and hundreds of man years developing the latest scientific information on weight, diet, nutrition, and exercise. And it'll only cost you the price of a stamp or phone call.

From Food Pyramids To Nutritious Snacks

Did you know it takes five servings of fruit and vegetables a day to stay healthy? Or that low fat on a label of a can really means 3g or less of fat per serving?

The Food and Drug Administration (FDA) is the agency that spends all the money coming up with the latest scientific evidence to support findings like these. So if you want the latest answer to your food question, call the FDA and not your mother-in-law. They have a whole lot of information, publications, and brochures waiting to send to you, including:

- *Nutrition and the Elderly*
- *An FDA Guide to Dieting*
- *Fiber: Something Healthy To Chew On*
- *Food and Drug Interactions*
- *Keep Your Food Safe*
- *Facts About Weight Loss: Products & Programs*

All these and more are free by contacting Office of Consumer Affairs, Food and Drug Administration, 5600 Fishers Lane, HFE88, Rockville, MD 20857; 301-827-4420, 800-532-4440; or online at <http://www.fda. gov>.

A Cookbook For Diabetics

If you are sick of those tasteless meals that you're forced to eat because you are a diabetic, the National Diabetes Information Clearinghouse can turn you on to wonderful recipes that don't have to taste like your laundry. Also, if you are wondering how some diabetics are able to keep their condition in check without taking insulin, they can provide you with information on that, as well.

This Clearinghouse is probably the world's best source for anything you need to know about the causes, cures, and treatment for diabetics.

For more information or a complete list of publications, contact National Diabetes Information Clearinghouse, 1 Information Way, Bethesda, MD 20892-3560; 301-654-3327; or online at <http://www.niddk. nih.gov>.

☆☆☆

Free Food At Uncle Sam's House

Now that's a great meal we can all relate to. But it's only for groups that are helping others, like meals for seniors, church groups, school programs, childcare centers, etc.

If you are a nonprofit and trying to improve the nutrition of others, you may be able to get free food from the government. Surplus commodities are distributed to the needy through food banks, charitable institutions, and local government agencies.

Contact your local social services agency (look in the blue pages of your phone book) to find out more about these programs. Or contact U.S. Department of Agriculture, Public Information Office, Food and Consumer Service, 3101 Park Ctr. Dr., Room 819, Park Office Center Bldg., Alexandria, VA 22302; 703-305-2276; or online at <http://www.usda. gov/fcs>.

☆☆☆

Slimming Down Without Health Riders, Thigh Masters, or Screaming Fitness Instructors

You can quit making the boat payment of your personal trainer and grab a free book instead. There are titles that will tell you how to exercise in water and save your joints from developing arthritis, how to develop walking as the only exercise you will need, or how seniors can pep up their life with an easy to do fitness program. They are all from the office that Arnold Schwarzenegger used to run during the Bush Administration.

Some of their free publications include:

- *Pep Up Your Life* (a fitness book for older people)
- *Fitness Fundamentals* (guideline for personal exercise)
- *Exercise and Weight Control*

For these publications and more information, contact President's Council on Physical Fitness and Sports, 200 Independence Ave., SW, HHH Bldg., Room 738H, Washington, DC 20201; 202-690-9000; or online at <http://www.os. dhhs.gov>.

☆☆☆

Weight Watchers Get Competition From Uncle Sam

AND IT'S FREE. Weight Watchers may have prepared meals in the supermarket for dieters living a harried lifestyle, but the government and nonprofit organizations will provide meals to those on low-incomes who find shopping, meal preparation, and cleanup a problem.

There is the Meals-On-Wheels program that delivers to your door, or the congregate meal program run by many churches or senior centers.

To learn what meal options you may have, contact your local senior citizens organization, or the ElderCare Locator, National Association of Area Agencies on Aging, 1112 16th St., NW, Suite 100, Washington, DC 20036; 800-677-1116, which can refer you to a local resource; or online at <http://ageinfo.org/elderloc/ elderloc.html/>.

☆☆☆

Hey! Liver Can Be BAD For You

Kids can call the Food and Nutrition Information Clearinghouse and get the facts so that Mom won't serve something like liver for dinner. And if you want to try and talk Mom into having pizza every night, they can also send you information on how a pizza has more nutritional value than an apple. There is even a free listing of diet videos and free publications on almost any nutrition related topic you can think of. Some of the subjects include:

- *Nutrition and Cancer*
- *Nutrition and Cardiovascular Disease*
- *Nutrition and Diabetes*
- *Nutrition and the Elderly*
- *Nutrition and the Handicapped*
- *Sensible Nutrition*

For more information or for your copies, send a self-addressed, stamped envelope to Food and Nutrition Information Center, U.S. Department of Agriculture, National Agricultural Library, 10301 Baltimore Ave., Room 304, Beltsville, MD 20705; 301-504-5719; or online at <http://www.nalusda. gov/fnic/index.html>.

☆☆☆

Who Says Seniors Are Full Of It?

Constipation can be a serious problem for seniors or it can just be a matter of finding the right diet or exercise program. Curing constipation with the right diet and exercise is a lot easier and cheaper than doctor visits and medication. You can make a simple call to the Aging Information Center and find information on both.

This Center has dozens of free fact sheets and publications that will help seniors with their food and nutrition concerns. Some of the titles include:

- *Be Sensible About Salt*
- *Constipation*
- *Digestive Do's and Don'ts*
- *Hints For Shopping, Cooking, and Enjoying Meals*
- *Nutrition: A Lifelong Concern*

They are available by contacting National Institute on Aging Information Center, P.O. Box 8057, Gaithersburg, MD 20898-8057; 800-222-2225; or online at <http://www. nih.gov/nia>.

☆☆☆

Jog The Dog

Is your family always telling you to slow down? Is mall walking part of your life (or would you like it to be)? What about those $100 jogging shoes the kids got you for Christmas that are sitting in your closet?

The National Institute on Aging has an Exercise Packet containing articles and other helpful information on how exercise can help you live a longer, healthier life. So put on your walking shoes and get moving. Contact the National Institute on Aging Information Center, P.O. Box 8057, Gaithersburg, MD 20898-8057; 800-222-2225; or online at <http://www. nih.gov/nia>.

☆☆☆

How To Pump Up Your Heart

You mean there really is good cholesterol? Yes. It's called high density lipo-proteins. To get more of the good stuff, you may need to change your diet, exercise, and control your weight. A serving of eggs has more cholesterol than a serving of rice. With just a bit of new information, you can easily plan a meal that has less cholesterol and probably tastes twice as good as what you've been eating.

This is the kind of information you can get by contacting the National Heart, Lung, and Blood Institute. They offer free publications on just about anything to do with heart disease, even information on the latest treatments and cures. Publications dealing with food and nutrition include:

- *Eating Right to Lower Your High Blood Cholesterol*
- *Eat Right To Help Lower Your High Blood Pressure*
- *Step by Step: Eating to Lower Your High Blood Cholesterol*
- *Recipes. A Low-Fat Diet*

For your free copies, contact National Heart, Lung, and Blood Information Center, P.O. Box 30105, Bethesda, MD 20824; 301-251-1222; or online at <http://www. nhlbi.nih.gov/nhlbi/nhlbi.htm>.

☆☆☆

Two Carts For The Price Of One

Let Uncle Sam help you with your grocery shopping with some tips on how to get the most out of your nickels and dimes. Your grocery cart can cost you less and be better for your health with just a little planning.

If you are worried about the foods you are eating, and want to make sure your diet is a healthy one, then request some of the consumer information publications available from the Center for Nutrition Policy and Promotion. They conduct research on the nutritive value of foods and the nutritional adequacy of diets and food supplies.

To order the following publications, contact the Government Printing Office Call 202-512-1800, Superintendent of Documents, Washington, DC 20402.

- *Check It Out! The Food Label, the Pyramid and You* $1.25 (001-000-04615-2)
- *Making Healthy Food Choices* $1.50 (001-000-04592-0)
- *Dietary Guidelines and Your Diet* $6.50 (001-000-04598-9)
- *Preparing Foods and Planning Menus Using the Dietary Guidelines* $2.50 (001-000-04527-0)
- *Shopping for Food and Making Meals in Minutes Using the Dietary Guidelines* $3.00 (001-000-04528-6)
- *Eating Better When Eating Out Using the Dietary Guidelines* $1.50 (001-000-04530-0)

For more information contact, Center for Nutrition Policy and Promotion, USDA, 1120 20th St. NW, Suite 200N, Washington, DC 20036; 202-418-2312; or online at <http://www.usda.gov/fcs/cnpp. htm>.

Up To $800 For Food

In Food Stamps, that is. Call your local social service agency listed in the blue pages of your local telephone book and ask about the Food Stamp Program. Senior citizens are given special consideration.

For example, seniors unable to go to the food stamp office to be interviewed may request a phone or home interview instead. Seniors can even be living with others and still qualify as a separate household in order to receive this assistance. They can even go to school and still receive food stamps.

Seniors are required to meet eligibility requirements such as limits on monthly income and available resources, and benefit levels are based on household size and household income. Contact your local social services agency to find out more about special food stamp rules for the elderly.

Contact U.S. Department of Agriculture, Food and Consumer Service, Public Information Office, 3101 Park Ctr. Dr., Room 819, Park Office Center Bldg., Alexandria, VA 22302; 703-305-2276; or online at <http://www.usda.gov/fcs>

Take A Free Cooking Class
With Julia Child's Sister

You can spend $200 for a cooking class at a local school; a cooking video at the bookstore goes for $19.95; or you can take a free cooking class at your local County Cooperative Extension office. This is your local hotline on food where the person won't try to sell you a Butterball turkey.

Your local County Cooperative Extension office frequently has pamphlets, classes, and helpful advice on cooking, good nutrition, and weight loss. Some even offer videos on the subject.

To learn more about what your local office has to offer, look in the blue pages of your phone book for the office nearest you, or you can find the main state office in the state-by-state directory at the end of the book.

For help in locating your county office contact Co-operative State Research, Education and Extension Service, U.S. Department of Agriculture, 14th and Independence Ave. SW, Room 3328 South Bldg., Washington, DC 20250; 202-720-3029; or online at <http://www.recusda. gov>.

Free Legal Help And Consumer Advice

Fire your lawyer! Instead, you can use government resources to answer most of your legal questions for free. You can learn how to write a "Living Will," take on big companies for age discrimination, and even resolve disputes with local stores, just by putting your tax dollars to work for you. If you do need an attorney, you can even use the government to help you find one that you really can afford.

The Pension Tax Guys

No need to pay money to an attorney to interpret the tax issues surrounding retirement and pension plans. You can talk to the guys who wrote the law! The Internal Revenue Service operates a hotline service that allows you to speak to tax attorneys specializing in retirement and pension plan issues.

They are available Monday through Thursday, from 1:30 p.m. to 3:30 p.m. They can be reached at Employee Plans Technical and Actuarial Division, Internal Revenue Service, U.S. Department of the Treasury, Room 6550, CP:E:EP, 1111 Constitution Ave., NW, Washington, DC 20224; 202-622-6074 or 6076.

How To Handle the Power-of-Attorney

Sometimes you need to focus on the big picture of living and let someone else manage the details. There may come a time when you no longer feel able to handle all the responsibilities of managing your own finances.

In many cases, you can sign over a Power-of-Attorney form to a trusted relative or friend that will allow them to make financial decisions in your behalf. When it involves handling your Social Security check, you need to designate the person as a Representative Payee.

This will allow the person to receive your Social Security check, so that they can in turn pay your bills for you. A person can petition the courts to be designated a Representative Payee if their loved one cannot do so themselves due to a physical or mental condition.

To learn more about becoming a Representative Payee, contact your local Social Security office or you may call the Social Security Hotline at 800-772-1213; or online at <http://www.ssa.gov>.

☆☆☆

Free Legal Services

You don't have to go to your neighbor's brother's cousin's kid who is an attorney, unless you want to pay for his legal advice. Uncle Sam has set up law offices all across the country to help those who cannot afford standard legal fees.

It is the Legal Services Corporation's job to give legal help to low-income individuals in civil matters. They are staffed by over 6,400 attorneys and paralegals, and have handled over 1.5 million cases. Each program follows certain guidelines as to what cases it accepts and specific financial eligibility that possible clients must meet.

To learn about the program nearest you, look in the blue pages of your phone book, or contact Legal Services Corporation, 750 First St., NE, 11th Fl., Washington, DC 20002; 202-336-8800; or online at <http://www.lsc.gov>.

☆☆☆

Free Help In Writing Your Will

Fill in the blanks, sign on the line. You've seen those How To Write A Will books in the bookstore. Why not save your money for your grandkids, instead? Many County Cooperative Extension Offices offer classes, pamphlets, and even general forms to help you along the way.

To learn what your local office has to offer, look in the blue pages of your phone book for the office nearest you, or you can find the main state office in the state-by-state directory at the end of the book.

For help in locating your county office contact: Co-operative State Research, Education and Extension Service, U.S. Dept. of Agriculture, 14th & Independence Ave. SW, Room 3328, South Bldg., Washington, DC 20250; or online at <http://reeusda.gov>.

☆☆☆

Lots More Free Legal Help

Don't waste time trying to learn the confusing ins and outs of Social Security or Medicare. Talk directly to an attorney who is on a first name basis with the people who run these programs, and can help you deal with your problem or concern without spending time getting up to speed on the complicated statutes surrounding these programs.

The following is a list of hotlines designed specifically to serve the needs of senior citizens. Services may vary from organization to organization. Some will refer you to lawyers who will offer legal assistance on a sliding fee scale; some will handle your case for you. If your state is not listed below, contact your state Department of Aging listed in the Directory of State Information at the end of this book.

Don't overlook law schools that may be nearby. Many offer legal clinics staffed by law students, although they are supervised closely by top level lawyer professors.

CALIFORNIA
Senior Legal Hotline
Legal Services of Northern
California
1004 18th St.
Sacramento, CA 95814
800-222-1753, 916-442-1212

They will give legal advice and referrals. Some lawyers offer services on a reduced scale based on income. For seniors in northern California only.

DISTRICT OF COLUMBIA
Legal Council for the Elderly
601 E St., NW
Building A, Fourth Floor
Washington, DC 20049
202-434-2120

They give advice and referrals. Services are offered on a reduced fee scale based on age and income.

FLORIDA
Legal Hotline for Older
Floridians
3000 Biscayne Blvd., 4th Floor
P.O. Box 370705
Miami, FL 33137
800-252-5997, 305-576-5997

Lawyer Referral Service
Florida Bar Association
650 Apalachee Parkway
Tallahassee, FL 32399-2300
800-342-8011

This is strictly a referral service for attorneys willing to work for reduced fees.

MAINE
Legal Service for the Elderly
Maine Legal Services
P.O. Box 2723
Augusta, ME 04338-2723
800-750-5353, 207-623-1797

They will give advice and referrals.

75

Services offered to anyone 65 or older, regardless of income.

MICHIGAN
Senior Alliance Inc.
3850 Second St., Suite 160
Wayne, MI 48184
800-347-LAWS (MI only)
313-722-2830

They give advice and referrals over the telephone. They have a list of attorneys that will work pro bono for people 60 or older.

NEW MEXICO
Lawyer Referral Services for the Elderly
P.O. Box 25883
Albuquerque, NM 87125
800-876-6657, 505-797-6005

They give advice and referrals. Some attorneys offer sliding fee scales based on income.

OHIO
ProSeniors Inc.
105 E. Fourth St., Suite 1715
Cincinnati, OH 45202-4008
800-488-6070, 513-621-8721

They give advice and referrals over the telephone. Actual legal services can be done on a sliding scale based on income. ProSeniors also offers an ombudsman service if you are having any long-term health care problems. For example, if you are having trouble with the care given in a nursing home, this agency can investigate the problem.

PENNSYLVANIA
Legal Hotline for Older Americans
Legal Council for the Elderly
P.O. Box 23180
Pittsburgh, PA 15222
800-262-5297, 412-261-5297

They will give legal advice and referrals. Some lawyers offer services on a reduced scale based on income.

TEXAS
Legal Hotline for Older Texans
State Bar of Texas
P.O. Box 12487
Austin, TX 78711-2487
800-622-2520, 512-463-1463

They will give legal advice and referrals. Some lawyers offer services on a reduced scale based on income.

Free Legal Help With Age Discrimination

If the unemployment line is beginning to look like a gathering of the Gray Panthers, then maybe it's time to step back and re-evaluate. For some reason, those layoffs at work seem to affect mostly workers over 40. Do you feel as if your age was a factor in not getting a job for which you were qualified? Age-based discrimination is a serious and growing problem for older adults who depend on their income from working.

Persons 40 years of age or older are protected by the Age Discrimination in Employment Act of 1967. The law prohibits age discrimination in hiring, discharge, pay, promotions, and other terms and conditions of employment. Retaliation against a person who files a charge of age discrimination, participates in an investigation, or opposes an unlawful practice also is illegal.

Last year, the Equal Employment Opportunity Commission received 17,425 complaints of age discrimination. Contact Equal Employment Opportunity Commission, 1801 L St., NW, Washington, DC 20507; 800-669-4000, 800-669-3362 (publications only); or online at <http://www.eeoc.gov>.

☆☆☆

You Have Rights

There's no need to take harassment or bullying on the job sitting down. Here is your chance to fight back. Remember, if your boss or another employee is discriminating against you, they are probably doing it to others and will continue to do it until someone forces them to stop.

If you believe you have been discriminated against by an employer, labor union, or employment agency when applying for a job or while on the job because of race, color, sex, religion, national origin, age, or disability, you may file a charge with the Equal Employment Opportunity Commission (EEOC). The toll-free number will direct you to the appropriate EEOC number for more information and to file a complaint.

The EEOC also distributes a variety of publications including:

- *The American Disability Act: Questions and Answers*
- *Fact Sheet: National Origin Discrimination*
- *Fact Sheet: Religious Discrimination*
- *Sexual Harassment Resource Kit*
- *Information For The Private Sector*

For more information, contact Equal Employment Opportunity Commission, 1801 L St., NW, Washington, DC 20507; 800-669-4000, 800-669-3362 (publications only); or online at <http://www.eeoc.gov>.

☆☆☆

Legal Help Locator

There's one phone number that can hook you up with more services for seniors than there are flavors of ice cream: the Eldercare Locator. This hotline provides access to an extensive network of organizations serving older people at state and local community levels.

The service can connect you to a variety of services, including legal assistance and other advocates and ombudsmen. In some cases, the legal assistance services may actually come to your home or nursing home to help you complete paperwork.

To find out what's available near you, contact the Eldercare Locator, National Association of Area Agencies on Aging, 1112 16th St., NW, Suite 100, Washington, DC 20036; 800-677-1116; or online at <http://www.age-info.org/elderloc/elderloc. html>. The phone lines are open between 9 a.m. and 11 p.m. EST.

Be Your Own Consumer Expert

You'd never guess by watching all those slick ads on TV that one of the most frequent things people complain about is the sale and repair of new cars.

Or what about the health club that gets you to sign up for a life-time membership only to close down the next day? Or even the store that advertises a great deal on a new T.V. only to claim to be "out of stock?"

If you feel you have been deceived or taken advantage of in some way, contact your state Consumer Protection Offices. Depending on the circumstances, the office may contact the offending company and try to resolve the complaint on your behalf. If there are several complaints against a particular company, the Consumer Protection Office may even take legal action.

Look in the Directory of State Information at the back of this book to find the Consumer Protection Office nearest you.

When You Get Caught In The Legal Runaround

Because of a slip-up by your lawyer, you went to jail for a parking ticket. What about the lawyer to whom you paid an expensive retainer only to learn that she seems to have moved to Tahiti permanently? Don't think you're stuck just because they know more about the law than you do.

Often affiliated with the State Bar Associations, Attorney Grievances offices can help you resolve ethical, billing, and theft complaints against lawyers in your state. They can also tell you if an attorney has been sanctioned in any way before you even start to do business with them.

The Attorney Grievance programs deal with ethical complaints; the Fee Arbitration programs will help resolve billing complaints; and the Client Security Trust Funds provides money to clients who have had money stolen from them by their lawyers.

Look in the Directory of State Information at the back of this book to find the program nearest you.

When All Else Fails

You have done your best, written letters, documented phone calls, yet you still feel as if you haven't been helped.

Use the power of the voting booth, and call your Senator or Representative. Each one has support staff set up to solve the problems of the people who voted them into office and keep them happy so that they'll keep voting for them. Offices are located in both Washington, D.C. and in their home districts.

Remember, these are the people who vote to renew an agency's budget, so they can usually have their way with government agencies. Businesses also know laws and regulations can help them or hurt them, so they are not going to want to bite the hand that feeds them.

To locate your U.S. Senator or Representative, look in the blue pages of your phone book, or contact The Capitol, Washington, DC 20510; 202-224-3121; or online at <http://www.house.gov> or <http://www.senate.gov>.

Mug the Muggers

Victims of Crimes have united in an effort to get criminals to repay their victims.

Millions of people and their families are victimized by crime every year. Congress enacted a law to establish a Crime Victims Fund to compensate innocent victims of violent crime. Part of the money is given to help compensate victims or their families for costs relating to such crimes as muggings, and even murder.

One of the nice things about this money is that it does not come out of the pockets of taxpayers; rather it is collected from the criminals themselves through criminal fines, forfeited bail bonds, penalty fees, and forfeited literary profits.

To learn who you need to talk to in your state, contact Office of Congressional and Public Affairs, Office of Justice Programs, U.S. Department of Justice, 633 Indiana Ave., NW, Room 1244, Washington, DC 20531; 202-307-0781; or online at <http://www.ojp.usdoj.gov>.

Money And Help For Your Home Or Apartment

For many people over 65, their homes are their only asset. What if you can't afford the taxes, will you be kicked out on the street? The house didn't seem so big when you had four kids, but now that you are all alone, you have to struggle just to keep it up.

What about if you are trying to find an affordable apartment? If you know where to look, there are all kinds of information about different housing opportunities for the older crowd, along with help to fix up your house or get a home equity loan, and much more.

Did you know:

- Almost 21 million households in the U.S. are headed by people 65 years or older.
- 8.9 million are headed by persons over 75.
- Two-thirds of renters are single.
- 4 million households spend more than 35 percent of their incomes on housing.
- 45% of public housing units are occupied by older adults.

Your Home Cash Machine

Just because the house you bought 30 years ago for $30,000 is now worth $500,000, doesn't mean that you are living on easy street. In fact, chances are that if you are over 65, you are struggling to make ends meet.

But it just doesn't have to be this way. To make your life easier, you can convert the value of your home into ready cash without having to sell your house and move. You can use this cash to get in-home care, someone to cut your lawn, pay for a new furnace or roof, get a new T.V., or even take your grandkids to McDonald's. But you have to be careful in the way that you do it.

To help you out, the Federal Trade Commission has several free publications that explain more about the different types of mortgage options:

- *Home Equity Credit Lines*
- *Home Financing Primer*
- *Mortgage Money Guide*

- *Reverse Mortgages*

For your copies or more information, contact Public Reference, 6th & Pennsylvania Ave. NW, Room 130, Federal Trade Commission, Washington, DC 20580; 202-326-2222; or online at <http://www.ftc.gov>.

☆☆☆

Choosing The Best Way To Live

Maybe your house is too large to manage. Maybe you need someone to come in and clean and cook. Or just maybe a roommate's the answer.

A free copy of *Your Home, Your Choice (Living Choices for Older Americans)* will help you make the right decision and show you where to get more help for any decision you make.

Contact Public Reference, 6th & Pennsylvania Ave. NW, Room 130, Federal Trade Commission, Washington, DC 20580; 202-326-2222; or online at <http://www.ftc.gov>.

☆☆☆

Rent at Big Discounts

Want to find an apartment you can afford in a building filled with people your own age? No need to look any further than your local public housing office. They have a special program called, Supportive Housing for the Elderly (Section 202).

If you meet certain income guidelines, your rent will be no higher than 10-30% of your adjusted income. An added plus is that many of these buildings also offer Service Coordinators, the concierge of special services for seniors. They can hook you up with special transportation, medical programs, food assistance, and more.

If your nonprofit or consumer cooperative sees a need for housing services for elderly persons, you can take advantage of the Section 202 program. Capital advances are made to eligible private, nonprofit sponsors to finance the development of rental housing with supportive services for the elderly.

The advance is interest free and does not have to be repaid as long as the housing remains available for very low-income elderly persons for at least 40 years. You can also take advantage of the fact that the Service Coordinators are an eligible expense under this program.

Contact the HUD field office nearest you to learn how you can apply. The HUD Field Offices for each state are listed in the Directory of State Information in the back of this book.

A Thousand Bucks To Fix Up Your House

Need money to perform rehabilitation or fix up your home? As part of the HOME Investment Partnership Program, the HOME Repair/Modification Programs For Elderly Homeowners program makes low interest loans available to low-income individuals for home repair services.

Money is distributed through over 500 sites, so to locate the closest program and application information, contact the Community Connections, P.O. Box 7189, Gaithersburg, MD 20898; 800-998-9999.

Park It In A Trailer Park

Join the crowd of over 1,227,000 seniors who own or rent trailer homes. No lawn to mow, no big house to clean.

Many senior citizens live in trailer homes for the convenience and camaraderie of trailer park living. The U.S. Department of Housing and Urban Development (HUD) insures loans for people to finance the purchase of manufactured homes and/or lots. The loans, called Title 1, are made by private lending institutions, and are available to any person able to make the cash investment and the loan payments.

To learn more about this insurance program, contact the HUD Field office near you, or Assistant Secretary for Housing, Federal Housing Commissioner, U.S. Department of Housing and Urban Development, 451 7th St. SW, Room 9100, Washington, DC 20410; 202-708-3600; or online at <http://www.hud.gov>

Get Cash From Your Home

Do you have a home, but no money to pay for repair bills or even your own medical bills?

The Home Equity Conversion Mortgage (HECM) allows a homeowner, 62 years of age or older, to borrow against the equity in his or her home and free up cash for home improvements, medical costs, or other living expenses. Loans do not have to be repaid until the homeowner moves from the home, sells the home, or dies.

The HECM program enables older Americans to continue living independently in their own homes. This program is now available in 47 states and is often referred to as a reverse mortgage.

If you would like more information on applying for the program, contact the HUD field office near you (listed in the Directory of State Information in the back of this book), or contact Assistance Secretary for Single Family Housing, U.S. Department of Housing and Urban Development, 451 7th St. SW, Room 9100, Washington, DC 20410; 202-708-3600; or online at <http://www.hud.gov>.

☆☆☆

Apply for Valets and Room Service

No, you are not living in a luxury hotel, but actually in your own apartment. For many seniors, as they get older, they need help with housekeeping, bathing, and more.

The Congregate Housing Services Program (CHSP) is a demonstration program designed to help the elderly remain in rented dwellings as they age. Some public housing agencies and nonprofit Section 202 sponsor meals and other support services such as housekeeping, aid in grooming, dressing, and other activities to maintain personal appearance and hygiene for frail elderly and nonelderly handicapped residents.

Each participant must pay 10 to 20 percent of their income for the meals program, plus they may have to pay a flat fee for other supportive services. Total fees can be no more than 20% of his/her adjusted income.

There is a listing on page 85 of those who participate in the program, as well as the local U.S. Department of Housing and Urban Development or Rural Housing and Community Development Service offices. Keep in mind that many other elderly housing facilities offer similar services to residents.

For more information, contact the program nearest you from the list on page 85, or contact Assistant Secretary for Housing-Federal Housing Commissioner, U.S. Department of Housing and Urban Development, 451 7th St. SW, Room 9100, Washington, DC 20410; 202-708-3600.

Congregate Housing Services Program Grantee List

ARKANSAS
North Arkansas Human Services
P.O. Box 2578
Batesville, AR 72503
501-793-8934

CALIFORNIA
Community Development
Commission
2 Coral Circle
Monterey Park, CA 91755
213-890-7125

Marin County HA
30 N. San Pedro Rd.
P.O. Box 4282
San Rafael, CA 94913
415-491-2348

Spanish Speaking Unity Council
1900 Fruitvale Ave., Suite 2A
Oakland, CA 94601-2468
510-535-6913

COLORADO
Archdiocesan Housing Committee
1580 Logan, #700
Denver, CO 80203
303-830-0215

Francis Heights, Inc.
2626 Osceola St.
Denver, CO 80212-1258
303-433-6268, ext. 224

CONNECTICUT
Mansfield Retirement Community
One Silo Circle
Storrs, CT 06268-2018
860-429-9933

State of Connecticut
Department of Social Services
25 Sigourney St., 10th Floor
Hartford, CT 06106

860-424-5283

DELAWARE
Wilmington Housing Authority
400 N. Walnut St.
Wilmington, DE 19801
302-429-6775

FLORIDA
Ft. Pierce Housing Authority
707 N. 7th St.
Fort Pierce, FL 34950-4501
561-461-7281

Dade County HUD
P.O. Box 350250
Miami, FL 33135-0250
305-644-5290

Dowling Park Home, Inc.
P.O. Box 4307
Dowling Park, FL 32060
904-658-3333

Dowling Park Apartments, Inc.
P.O. Box 4307
Dowling Park, FL 32060
904-658-3333

Kinneret Inc. & Kinneret II
515 S. Delaney Ave.
Orlando, FL 32801-3841
407-425-4537

HAWAII
Hale Mahaolu
200 Hina Ave.
Kahului, Maui, HI 96732-1821
808-871-4792

Opportunities for the Disabled, Inc.
64-1510 Kamehameha Hwy.
Wahiawa, HI 96786
808-622-3929, ext. 123

ILLINOIS

The Lambs, Inc.
P.O. Box 520
Libertyville, IL 60048-0520
847-362-4636

Bloomington Housing Authority
104 E. Wood St.
Bloomington, IL 61701-6768
309-829-3360, ext. 214

INDIANA

Muncie Housing Authority Agency
409 E. First St.
Muncie, IN 47302
317-288-9242

IOWA

Waterloo Housing Authority
620 Mulberry St. Carnegie
Waterloo, IA 50703
319-233-0201

Ecumenical Housing, Inc.
2671 Owen Court
Dubuque, IA 52002
319-556-5125

Alverno Apartments, Inc.
3525 Winsor Ave.
Dubuque, IA 52001-0419
319-582-2364

Charles City Housing Commission
1000 S. Grand Ave.
Charles City, IA 50616
515-228-6661

KANSAS

HA of the City of Atchison
103 S. 7th St.
Atchison, KS 66002
913-367-3323

LOUISIANA

Village de Memoire I/NCSCHMC
1001 N. Reed St.

Ville Platte, LA 70581
318-363-0162

MAINE

Methodist Conference Home
46 Summer St.
Rockland, ME 04841-2939
207-596-6477

Old Town Housing Authority
100 S. Main St.
P.O. Box 404
Old Town, ME 04468-1572
207-827-6151

Brunswick Housing Authority
P.O. Box A
Brunswick, ME 04011-1541
207-725-8711

Summer Street Housing
Preservation, Inc.
46 Summer St.
Rockland, ME 04841-2939
207-596-6477

MARYLAND

HA of Baltimore City
417 E. Fayette St., Room 265
Baltimore, MD 21202-3431
410-396-4271

The Arc of Southern Maryland
P.O. Box 1860
Prince Frederick, MD 20678
410-535-2413

MASSACHUSETTS

Bethany Homes
10-12 Phoenix Row
Haverhill, MA 01832
508-374-2160

MI Residential
189 Maple St.
Lawrence, MA 01841-3761
508-682-7575

86

Jewish Community Housing
30 Wallingford Rd.
Brighton, MA 02135-4753
617-254-1861

MICHIGAN
Jewish Federation Apts., Inc.
6700 W. Maple Rd.
West Bloomfield, MI 48322
810-661-5220

Plymouth Opportunity
Non-Profit Housing
593 Deer St.
Plymouth, MI 48170-1701
313-422-1020

Jewish Federation Apts., Inc.
15100 W. Ten Mile Rd.
Oak Park, MI 48237
810-967-4240

Moore Non-Profit Housing Corp.
401 W. Jolly Rd.
Lansing, MI 48910-6607
517-393-4442

Detroit Int. Stake Adult Housing
16651 Labser Rd.
Detroit, MI 48219
313-538-0360

Potential Development
Homes, I
P.O. Box 1978
Jackson, MI 49204
517-784-4426

MINNESOTA
St. Paul Housing Authority
480 Cedar St., Suite 600
St. Paul, MN 55101-2240
612-298-5664, ext. 3083

Duluth Housing Redevelopment
Authority
222 E. Second St.

Duluth, MN 55816-0900
218-726-2857

HRA City of South St. Paul
125 Third Ave. North
South St. Paul, MN 55075-2097
612-455-1560

St. Paul Public Housing Agency
480 Cedar St., Suite 600
St. Paul, MN 55101-2240
512-298-5665, ext. 3083

MISSISSIPPI
Mississippi Regional HA
No. 5
P.O. Box 419
Newton, MS 39345-0419
601-683-3371

MISSOURI
Crown Center for Senior Living
8350 Delcrest Dr.
St. Louis, MO 63124-2166
314-991-2055, ext. 222

St. Louis Housing Authority
5655 Kingsbury
St. Louis, MO 63112
314-367-1686

Murphy-Blair Senior Commons
2600 Hadley St.
St. Louis, MO 63106
314-539-9625

MONTANA
Northern Cheyenne Tribe
P.O. Box 128
Lame Deer, MT 59043
406-477-6284

NEBRASKA
Falls City Housing Authority
800 E. 21st St.
Falls City, NE 68355-2349
402-245-4204

Lincoln Area Agency on Aging
129 N. 10th St., Room 222
Lincoln, NE 68508
402-441-6175

NEW HAMPSHIRE
Manchester Housing Authority
198 Hanover St.
Manchester, NH 03104-6125
603-624-2146

Laconia HRA
25 Union Ave.
Laconia, NH 03246-3558
603-524-2112

Keene Housing Authority
105 Castle St.
Keene, NH 03431
603-352-6161

Somersworth Housing Authority
9 Bartlett Ave.
P.O. Box 31
Somersworth, NH 03878
603-692-2357

Nashua Housing Authority
101 Major Dr.
Nashua, NH 03060-4783
603-883-5661

NEW JERSEY
Plainfield Housing Authority
510 E. Front St.
Plainfield, NJ 07060-1424
908-769-6335

Trent Center
511 Greenwood Ave.
Trenton, NJ 08609-2108
609-394-0093

NEW YORK
New York City Housing Authority
250 Broadway, Room 1503
New York, NY 10007
212-306-3330

Schenectady Municipal HA
375 Broadway
Schenectady, NY 12305-2519
518-382-8651

NORTH CAROLINA
Bell House, Inc.
2400 Summit Ave.
Greensboro, NC 27405-5014
910-621-0938

High Point Housing Authority
500 E. Russell Ave.
P.O. Box 1779
High Point, NC 27261-1779
910-887-2661, ext. 60/35

East Salem Homes, Inc.
8 W. Third St., Suite 400
Winston Salem, NC 27101
910-725-3564

NORTH DAKOTA
Fargo Housing Authority
2525 N. Broadway
Fargo, ND 58102-1439
701-293-7870

Senior Meals and
Services, Inc.
P.O. Box 713
Devil's Lake, ND 58301
701-662-5061

OHIO
Cincinnati Metrop Housing
Authority
16 W. Central Pkwy.
Zone 10
Cincinnati, OH 45210
513-675-5585

Alpha Phi Alpha Homes
695 Dunbar Dr.
Akron, OH 44311-1315
216-376-8787

Central Ohio Area Agency on Aging
174 E. Long St.
Columbus, OH 43215
614-645-3886

OKLAHOMA

Cherokee Nation Housing Authority
P.O. Box 948
Tahlequah, OK 74465-0948
918-456-0671, ext. 241

Muskogee Fairhaven Manor,
Phase I
500 Dayton
Muskogee, OK 74403
918-682-4300

OREGON

Housing Authority of Portland
135 SW Ash St.
Portland, OR 97204
503-273-4522

PENNSYLVANIA

Philadelphia Housing Authority
801 Arch St., 5th Floor
Philadelphia, PA 19107
215-684-4421

OIC Housing
1717 W. Hunting Park Ave.
Philadelphia, PA 19140
215-229-9000

Riverview Towers, Phase I Inc.
52 Garetta St.
Pittsburgh, PA 15217-3231
412-521-7876

East Brady Heights
106 E. North St.
New Castle, PA 16101
412-654-8659

RHODE ISLAND

United Methodist Retirement
Center

40 Irving Ave.
East Providence, RI 02914
401-438-4456

SOUTH DAKOTA

South Dakota HDA
221 South Central
Pierre, SD 57501
605-773-4532

TENNESSEE

St. Peter Manor
108 N. Auburndale
Memphis, TN 38104-6405
901-278-8200

Orange Grove Center
615 Derby St.
P.O. Box 3249
Chattanooga, TN 37404-0249
423-493-2919

TEXAS

W. Leo Daniels Towers
8826 Harrell St.
Houston, TX 77093
713-692-8541

REAL, Inc.
301 Lucero
Alice, TX 78332
512-668-3158

UTAH

St. Mark's Gardens
514 North 300 West
Kaysville, UT 84037-3103
801-544-4231

WISCONSIN

Residential Care
424 Washington Ave.
Oshkosh, WI 54901
414-236-6560

WYOMING
RENEW
2 North Main, Suite 406
Sheridan, WY 82801
307-674-4200

Money To Pay The Rent

Almost 25% of seniors rent the places they live in. But if you are struggling to pay rent, there is a U.S. Department of Housing and Urban Development (HUD) program that may be able to help you. Under the Section 8 Rental Assistance Program, low-income renters can receive special vouchers to cover part of their rent.

Low-income doesn't have to mean poor. For example, in some parts of Ohio the eligible income for a single person can go up to $24,700. With the vouchers, the most you will have to pay is 30% of your adjusted income for rent.

To apply for this type of assistance, contact your local public housing agency (look in the blue pages of your phone book), or the HUD field office for your state. The HUD Field Offices for each state are listed in the Directory of State Information in the back of this book.

Small Town Rent Money

Senior citizens have enough to worry about without wondering if they have the money to pay the rent.

If you live in a rural area and need some help with rent, contact the Rural Housing and Community Development Services (formerly Farmers Home Administration), which provides payments to make up the difference between the tenants' payments and the Rural Housing-approved rents for the housing.

To be eligible, low-income families must occupy Rural Rental Housing, Rural Cooperative Housing, and Farm Labor Housing projects financed by the Rural Housing and Community Development Services.

To learn more, contact your local office of Rural Housing and Community Development Services (look in the blue pages of your phone book), or Rural Housing Services, U.S. Department of Agriculture, 14th and

Independence Ave. SW, Room 5321, Washington, DC 20250; 202-720-1599; or online at <http://www. rurdev.usda.gov/agency/rhs/rhsprog.html>.

How Safe Is Your Home?

Every day there are stories in the paper about the dangers of lead paint, radon, or carbon dioxide.

The Environmental Protection Agency is responsible for controlling environmental pollution and can answer all your questions. They have brochures and pamphlets describing how to check for radon and what should be done about it; the proper use of pesticides; how to garden chemically free; recycling; how to find and use safe drinking water; and indoor and outdoor air pollution.

For all your environmental questions, contact Public Information Center 3404, U.S. Environmental Protection Agency, 401 M St., SW, Washington, DC 20460; 202-260-5922; or online at <http://www. epa.gov>.

1% Loans To Move To The Country

You can move away from congestion, nosy neighbors, and smog by checking out a program designed to help you get a home in the country. The program is called Section 502, and it's set up just for low-income families to buy new or existing houses in rural areas. Borrowers may reduce the interest rate to as low as 1 percent, and for some borrowers the loan term may be as long as 38 years. There are income requirements you must meet to qualify.

For information on the loans and eligibility requirements, contact your local Rural Housing office (formerly Farmers Home Administration) or Rural Housing Services, U.S. Department of Agriculture, 14th & Independence Ave. SW, Room 5334, Washington, DC 20250; 202-720-1474; or online at <http://www.rurdev.usda.gov/ agency/rhs/rhsprog.html>.

✩✩✩

$15,000 To Spruce Up Your Home

Need a new furnace, roof, water heater, or even plumbing in your house? Don't let your house deteriorate around you.

If you live in a small town and don't make much money, you can apply for a grant to fix up your home from the Rural Housing Preservation Grants (Section 504). The average grant is $7,500, but you can get up to $15,000. The money comes from the government, but is given to local groups who in turn give it out to local homeowners.

To learn more about the program, to identify local groups giving out the money, or to learn eligibility requirements, contact your local Rural Housing and Community Development Services (formerly Farmers Home Administration).

You may also contact Multiple Family Housing Loan Division, Rural Housing Services, U.S. Department of Agriculture, AG Box 7081, Washington, DC 20250; 202-720-1606; or online at <http://www.rurdev.usda.gov/agency/rhs/rhsprog.html>.

☆☆☆

Continuing Care Communities

Many elderly choose to move from their homes and into continuing care retirement communities (CCRCs), also called life-care communities. Typically these provide housing, personal care, nursing home care, and a range of social and recreation services as well as congregate meals.

Residents enter into a contractual agreement with the community to pay an entrance fee and monthly fees in exchange for benefits and services. The contract usually remains in effect for the remainder of a resident's life.

The definition of these communities continues to be confusing and inconsistent due to the wide range of services offered, differing types of housing units, and different contracts. There have been some problems with refunds or of cancelling the contract if someone changes their mind.

The American Association of Homes for the Aging has a consumer guidebook which provides information about the various contracts and services, as well as outlines the benefits and risks.

Continuing Care Retirement Communities Guidebook is available for $6.95 by contacting American Association of Homes and Services for the Aging, Suite 500, 901 E St., NW, Washington, DC 20004; 202-783-2242, or calling the Publication Dept. at 800-508-9442.

No Down Payment Necessary

You don't even have to wear your uniform to qualify. If you are a veteran or an unmarried surviving spouse of a vet, you may be eligible for a loan guarantee for the purchase and refinancing of a home, condo, or manufactured home.

Veterans Affairs (VA) guarantees part of the total loan so a veteran may obtain a mortgage on a home or condominium with a competitive interest rate — and without a down payment, if the lender agrees. VA requires a down payment for the purchase of a manufactured home.

To learn who can qualify, details of financing, and more, contact Veterans Assistance Office, U.S. Department of Veterans Affairs, 810 Vermont Ave., NW, Washington, DC 20420; 800-827-1000; or online at <http://www.va.gov>.

Can't Pay Your Property Taxes?

There is no need to gripe about the local school board voting in another tax increase for the schools when your kids have long since graduated. Many seniors own houses mortgage free, yet cannot afford to pay their property taxes. Property tax deferral programs are popular in many states, and enable older home owners to postpone paying their taxes until they sell their homes or die. Many states even offer property tax relief of varying amounts to seniors.

The state pays taxes to the local government for the homeowner. These payments accrue with interest as a loan from the state to the homeowner, secured by equity in the home. Upon death or prior sale of the home, the loan is repaid to the state from the proceeds of the sale of the estate. To learn more about this program, contact your State Department of Taxation.

☆☆☆

Save Your House Profit From The Tax Man

Say you want to sell your house in Ohio for $150,000 and buy a condo in Florida for $30,000. The new law says that you can keep all the money for yourself.

The Internal Revenue Service has done away with the one-time exclusion rule for those over the age of 55. Now when you sell your home you can exclude from your income any profit up to $500,000. There are several rules you have to meet to enjoy this new benefit, including having to both own and live in the home for two out of the last five years. You can take advantage of this benefit every two years.

Certain use and ownership restrictions apply, so request Publication 523, *Selling Your Home,* from the Internal Revenue Forms Line at 800-829-3676; or online at <http://www.irs.gov>.

Roommate Hotline

Maybe you haven't had a roommate other than your spouse since college, but it may be time to reconsider. An option for many elderly so they can stay in their homes is to get a roommate. Shared housing is a way to help with bill payments, as well as the social benefits of having someone else around. According to statistics, 670,000 people over 65 share housing with nonrelatives; that's a 35 percent increase from over a decade ago.

There are a number of shared housing projects in existence today. One of the largest is called Operation Match, which is a division in the housing offices of many cities. It helps match people looking for an affordable place to live with those who have space in their homes and are looking for someone to aid with their housing expenses.

To learn more about this type of program, contact the housing office in your area (look in the blue pages of your phone book), or contact the ElderCare Hotline for a referral to an appropriate agency at 800-677-1116; or online at <http://www. ageinfo.org/elderloc/elderloc.html>.

$1,600 To Keep You Warm This Winter

Storm windows, insulation, and even weather stripping, can help reduce your fuel bill. The elderly can receive assistance to weatherize their homes and apartments at no charge if they meet certain income guidelines. States allocate dollars to nonprofit agencies for purchasing and installing energy-related repairs, with the average grant being $1600 per year.

Contact your State Energy Office or the Weatherization Assistance Programs Branch, 5E066, U.S. Department of Energy, 1000 Independence

Ave., SW, Washington, DC 20585; 202-586-8295; or online at <http://www.eren.doe.gov>.

☆☆☆

Can't Pay Your Energy Bill?

Get a break, and be part of over 1,500,000 seniors who get a deal on their heating and cooling bill. Even if you own or rent your home or apartment, you may be eligible for Low Income Home Energy Assistance Program (LIHEAP).

Although eligibility requirements vary from state to state, the household's income must not exceed 150% of the poverty level or 60% of the state median income. Payments may be made directly to eligible households or to home energy suppliers, and may take the form of cash, vouchers, or payments to third parties, such as utility companies or fuel dealers.

To learn more about the program, you may contact the State LIHEAP coordinator from the list below, or Administration for Children and Families, 370 L'Enfant Promenade, 5th Floor West, Suite 509, Washington, DC 20444.

LIHEAP Coordinators

ALABAMA
Mr. Willie D. Whitehead
LIHEAP Coordinator
Department of Economic and
Community Affairs
401 Adams Ave.
P.O. Box 5690
Montgomery, AL 36103-5690
334-242-5365

ALASKA
Ms. Mary Riggen-Ver
Energy Assistance Coordinator
Department of Health and Social
Services
Division of Public Assistance
400 W. Willoughby Ave., #301
Juneau, AK 99801-1731
907-465-3058
Fax: 907-465-3319

ARIZONA
Ms. Juanita Garcia, Program
Manager
Arizona Department of Economic
Security
Community Services Administration
086Z-A
P.O. Box 6123-010A
Phoenix, AZ 85005
602-542-6611
Fax: 602-229-6655

ARKANSAS
LIHEAP Unit
OCS/Division of County Operations
Department of Human Services
P.O. Box 1437, Slot 1330
Little Rock, AR 72203-1437
501-682-8726
Fax: 501-682-6736

CALIFORNIA
Ms. Toni Curtis
Deputy Director of Programs
California Department of
Economic Opportunity
700 N. 10th St., Room 272
Sacramento, CA 95814
916-323-8694
Fax: 916-327-3153
800-433-4327 (in CA only)

COLORADO
Ms. Ann Peden
LIHEAP Administrator
Division of Self Sufficiency
Department of Social Services
1575 Sherman St., 3rd Floor
Denver, CO 80203
303-866-5972
Fax: 303-866-5098

CONNECTICUT
Ms. Marion Wojick
Program Supervisor
Energy Services Unit
Department of Social Services
25 Sigourney St., 6th Floor
Hartford, CT 06105
860-424-5891
Fax: 860-424-4952

DELAWARE
Ms. Leslie Lee, Energy Program
Manager
Department of Health and Social
Services
Div. of State Service Centers
Carvel State Office Building
4th Floor, P.O. Box 8911
Wilmington, DE 19801
302-577-3491
Fax: 302-577-2383

DISTRICT OF COLUMBIA
Mr. Richard Kirby, Chief

Citizen Energy Resources Div.
DC Energy Office
2000 14th St. NW, Suite 300
Washington, DC 20001
202-673-6700
Fax: 202-673-6725

FLORIDA
Mr. Robert Lakin
Program Coordinator
Bureau of Community Assistance
Dept. of Community Affairs
2555 Shumard Oak Blvd.
Tallahassee, FL 32399-2100
850-488-7541
Fax: 850-488-2488

GEORGIA
Mr. Preston Weaver, Director
Office of Community Services
Division of Family and Children
Services
Two Peachtree St., NW
Atlanta, GA 30303-3180
404-656-6697
Fax: 404-657-3299

HAWAII
Ms. Patricia Williams
LIHEAP Coordinator
Hawaii Department of Human
Services
810 Richards St., Suite 500
Honolulu, HI 96813
808-586-5734
Fax: 808-586-5744

IDAHO
Ms. Neva Kaufman
LIHEAP Program Specialist
EOO, Division of Welfare
Department of Health and Welfare
450 W. State St.
Statehouse
Boise, ID 83720

208-334-5732
Fax: 208-332-7343

ILLINOIS

Ms. Kathy Hauger
Office of Human Services
Department of Commerce and
Community Affairs
620 E. Adams St., 5th Floor
Bressmer Building
Springfield, IL 62701
217-524-8029

INDIANA

Ms. Maria Larson
LIHEAP Coordinator
Family and Social Services
Administration
Division of Family and Children
402 W. Washington St., Room 481
Indianapolis, IN 46206
317-232-7015
Fax: 317-232-7079

IOWA

Ms. Sue Downey, Chief, Bureau of
Energy Assistance
Division of Community Action
Agencies
Department of Human Rights
Lucas State Office Building
Des Moines, IA 50319
515-281-3838/3943
Fax: 515-242-6119

KANSAS

Ms. Kathy Valentine
Energy Program Administrator
Division of Income Maintenance,
DSRS
Docking State Office Bldg.
915 SW Harrison St., 6th Floor
Topeka, KS 66612-1570
913-296-3349
Fax: 913-296-1158

KENTUCKY

Mr. Patrick Bishop, Manager
Energy Assistance Branch, DMD
Dept. of Social Insurance
Cabinet for Human Resources
275 E. Main St., 3rd Floor W.
Frankfort, KY 40621
502-564-4847
Fax: 502-564-6907

LOUISIANA

Mr. Lonnie Didier, Program Manager
Department of Social Services
Office of Community Services
P.O. Box 3318
Baton Rouge, LA 70821
504-342-2274
Fax: 504-342-2268

MAINE

Ms. Jo-Ann Choate
LIHEAP Coordinator
Maine State Housing Authority
353 Water St.
P.O. Box 2669
Augusta, ME 04330-4633
207-626-4600
Fax: 207-626-4678

MARYLAND

Ms. Sandra Brown, Director
Energy Assistance Program
Community Services Administration
Dept. of Human Resources
311 W. Saratoga St.
Baltimore, MD 21201
410-767-7218
Fax: 410-333-0256

MASSACHUSETTS

Mr. James A. Hays, Director
EOCD/BEP
Saltonstall Bldg., Room 1803
100 Cambridge St.
Boston, MA 02202

617-727-7004, ext. 533
Fax: 617-727-4259

MICHIGAN
Ms. Shirley Nowakowski
Director, Energy Services
Department of Social Services
325 S. Grand Ave.
P.O. Box 30037
Lansing, MI 48909
517-335-3588
Fax: 517-335-4801

MINNESOTA
Mr. Mark D. Kaszynski
Energy Assistance Program
Coordinator
Division of Community Based
Services, EPU
390 N. Robert St., Room 125
St. Paul, MN 55101
612-297-2590
Fax: 612-282-5900

MISSISSIPPI
Mr. Godwin Agulanna
LIHEAP Division Director
Division of Community Services
Mississippi Department of Human
Services
750 N. State St.
Jackson, MS 39202-3524
601-359-4769
Fax: 601-359-4370

MISSOURI
Mr. Charles F. Wright, Administrator
Division of Family Services
Energy Assistance Unit
P.O. Box 88
Jefferson City, MO 65103
314-751-0472
Fax: 314-526-5592

MONTANA
Mr. Jim Nolan, Chief

Division of Family Assistance
Department of Social and
Rehabilitation Services
P.O. Box 4210
Helena, MT 59604-4210
406-447-4260
Fax: 406-447-4287

NEBRASKA
Mr. Bill Davenport
Public Asst. Unit
Program and Planning Specialist
Department of Social Services
310 Centennial Mall South, 5th Floor
P.O. Box 95026
Lincoln, NE 65809-5026
402-471-9172
Fax: 402-471-9455

NEVADA
Ms. Vickie DeKoekkoek
LIHEAP Program Manager
Nevada Department of Human
Services, Welfare Division
2527 N. Carson St.
Carson City, NV 89710
702-687-6919
Fax: 702-687-1272

NEW HAMPSHIRE
Mr. Richard M. Johnson
Fuel Asst. Program Manager
Governor's Office of Energy and
Community Services
57 Regional Dr.
Concord, NH 03301-8506
603-271-2611
Fax: 603-271-2615

NEW JERSEY
Mr. John R. Simzak, Coordinator
Home Energy Assistance Unit
DHS, Division of Family
Development, CN 716
Trenton, NJ 08625

609-588-2488
Fax: 609-588-3369

NEW MEXICO
Ms. Loretta Williams
Community Development and
Commodities Section
NM Human Services Dept.
P.O. Box 26507
Albuquerque, NM 87125
505-841-2693
Fax: 505-841-2691

NEW YORK
Mr. Steven Ptak, Director
Bureau of Energy Programs
NY State Department of Social
Services
40 N. Pearl St.
Albany, NY 12243-0001
518-474-9321
Fax: 518-474-9347

NORTH CAROLINA
Ms. Alice Smith
Program Consultant
Public Assistance Section
Division of Social Services
Dept. of Human Resources
325 N. Salisbury St.
Raleigh, NC 27603
919-733-7831
Fax: 919-715-5457

NORTH DAKOTA
Mr. Ron Knutsen
LIHEAP Coordinator
Energy Assistance and Emergency
Services
Dept. of Human Services
State Capitol Bldg.
Judicial Wing, 3rd Floor
Bismarck, ND 58505
701-328-4882
Fax; 701-328-2359

OHIO
Ms. Vicky Mroczek
Program Administrator
Home Energy Assistance Program
Ohio Dept. of Development
P.O. Box 1001
Columbus, OH 43216-1001
614-644-6858
614-728-6832

OKLAHOMA
Mr. Ron Amos, Program Supervisor
Division of Family Support Services
Dept. of Human Services
P.O. Box 25352
Oklahoma City, OK 73125-0352
405-521-4089
Fax: 405-521-4158

OREGON
Ms. Linda Marquam
LIHEAP Coordinator
Community Services
Oregon Housing and Community
Services
1600 State St.
Salem, OR 97310-0161
503-986-2094
Fax: 503-986-2020

PENNSYLVANIA
Ms. Joan Brenner, LIHEAP Director
Div. of Cash Assistance, DPW
Complex 2, Room 224
Willow Oak Building
P.O. Box 2675
Harrisburg, PA 17105
717-772-7902
Fax: 717-772-6451

PUERTO RICO
Ms. Lucila B. Rivera, Specialist
Division of Policy and Procedures
Department of Social Services
P.O. Box 11398

San Juan, Puerto Rico 00910
809-722-7361
Fax: 809-722-4605

RHODE ISLAND
Mr. Matteo Guglielmetti
Energy Assistance Program
Manager
Department of Administration
Division of Central Services
One Capitol Hill
Providence, RI 02903
401-277-6920
Fax: 401-277-1260

SOUTH CAROLINA
Mr. Michael Hawkins
Director of Division of Economic
Opportunity
1205 Pendleton St.
Columbia, SC 29201
803-734-0662
Fax: 803-734-0356

SOUTH DAKOTA
Ms. Abbie Rathbun
Program Administrator
Office of Energy Assistance
Department of Social Services
206 W. Missouri Ave.
Pierre, SD 57501-4517
605-773-4131
Fax: 605-773-6657

TENNESSEE
Mr. Steve Neece
Dept. of Human Services
Citizens Plaza Bldg.
400 Deaderick St.
Nashville, TN 37219
615-313-4764
Fax: 615-532-9956

TEXAS
Mr. J. Al Almaguer
Program Manager

Energy Assistance
Texas Department of Housing and
Community Affairs
P.O. Box 13941
Austin, TX 78711-3941
512-475-3951
Fax: 512-475-3935

UTAH
Mr. Sherm Roquiero
Home Energy Assistance Target
Program
Office Family Support Administration
120 N. 200 West, 3rd Floor
P.O. Box 45000
Salt Lake City, UT 84145-0500
801-538-8644
Fax: 801-538-8888

VERMONT
Mrs. Judy Rosenstrike
LIHEAP Block Grant Manager
Department of Social Welfare
103 S. Main St.
Waterbury, VT 05676
802-241-2889
Fax: 802-241-2830

VIRGIN ISLANDS
Ms. Kathryn C. Mills, Commissioner
Dept. of Human Services
Knud Hansen Complex, Building A
1003 Hospital Ground
Charlotte Amalie, Virgin Islands
00802
809-774-1166
Fax: 809-774-3466

VIRGINIA
Ms. Charlene Chapman, Energy
and Emergency Assistance Unit
Virginia Department of Social
Services
Theater Row Building
730 E. Broad St., 7th Floor
Richmond, VA 23219-1849

804-692-1750
Fax: 804-692-1704

WASHINGTON
Mr. William Graham
EAP/ECIP Coordinator
Department of Community
Development
Division of Community Services
9th and Columbia Building - N/X
GH51
Olympia, WA 98504
360-753-3403
Fax: 360-586-5880

WEST VIRGINIA
Mr. Robert R. Kent, HHR
Specialist, Sr. Income Maintenance
Bureau
Department of Health and Human
Resources
Building 6, Room B-749
State Capitol Complex
Charleston, WV 25305

304-558-8290
Fax: 304-558-2059

WISCONSIN
Mr. Steve Tryon, Energy
Assistance Program Supervisor
Energy, Poverty and Refugee
Services
Energy Assistance Unit
Department of Health and Social
Services
Madison, WI 53707-7935
608-266-7601
Fax: 608-267-3652

WYOMING
Ms. Evon Williams
Consultant, LIHEAP Program
Department of Family Services
3rd Floor Hathaway Building
Cheyenne, WY 82002-0490
307-777-6095
Fax: 307-777-3693

✩✩✩
There Is More Than Hope

You can stay in your home a little longer with a new program called HOPE for Elderly Independence. You can receive help with dressing, bathing, grooming, eating, and cleaning at little cost to you, as well as help with paying the rent through Section 8 rental certificates. This is a demonstration program designed to combine rent certificates along with support services to help the frail elderly remain in their homes.

To learn if the project is currently being undertaken in your town, contact your local public housing office, or you may contact the Rental Assistance Division, Office of the Assistant Secretary for Public and Indian Housing, U.S. Department of Housing and Urban Development, Operations Division, 451 7th St. SW, Room 4220, Washington, DC 20410.

✩✩✩

Some Housing Reports

Want to know about the different housing options available to seniors? What are the pros and cons of congregate housing for the elderly? Is the government actually doing anything to help this group find affordable housing? Want to know what your congressman knows about housing for the elderly?

Most likely they got most of their information from reading reports done by the Congressional Research Service (CRS). These reports are written by experts in various fields (usually PhDs) at the request of Congress, but are great resources for everyone. They provide an understandable overview of the topic and provide relevant newspaper articles and bibliographies. These reports are free but must be requested through your Congressman.

CRS reports dealing with housing include:

- *Congregate Housing: The Federal Program and Examples of State Programs* (86-918E)
- *Description of Residential Facilities for the Elderly* (84-19 EPW)
- *Elderly and Handicapped Housing: Recent Developments in Section 202* (89-667E)
- *Evolution of Section 202: Housing for the Elderly* (93-645-E)
- *Federal Housing Programs Affecting Elderly People* (88-576E)
- *Housing for the Elderly and Handicapped: Section 202, Issue Brief* (IB84038)
- *Housing for Older Persons Act of 1995: HR 660* (95-443E)

You can get these and other reports by contacting Your Senator or Representative, The Capitol, Washington, DC 20510; 202-224-3121.

Free Health Information And Treatment

Access the Best Research on How to Live Longer

To live longer and healthier lives. From everything you hear on the T.V. and read in the paper you'd think otherwise. But findings show that the heart adapts well to the effects of age; that memory and problem solving remain strong; and that older adults are no more conservative or cranky or prone to complaining about their health than they were when young.

Where does this new information come from? You can learn how to live longer, get a good night's sleep, and even start an exercise program just by contacting the National Institute on Aging (NIA). NIA researches all kinds of subjects on aging, as well as the diseases and special problems of older people. They are also conducting the longest running scientific examination of human aging ever undertaken called the *Baltimore Longitudinal Study of Aging*.

On top of that, NIA can answer your questions and provide you with all kinds of free publications on a wide variety of topics including:

General Information About NIA
- *Aging Research: Practice, Promise, and Priorities*
- *NIA Publications List*
- *Research for a New Age*
- *With the Passage of Time: The Baltimore Longitudinal Study of Aging*

Information for Health Professionals
- *Extramural Training and Career Opportunities in Aging Research*
- *Grants Packet*
- *Hearts and Arteries: What Scientists are Learning About Age and the Cardiovascular System*
- *In Search of the Secrets of Aging*
- *Research Training in Geriatrics and Gerontology*
- *Urinary Incontinence Kit*
- *Working With Your Older Patient: A Clinician's Handbook (with Continuing Medical Education credit)*

Information for the Public

- *Accidental Hypothermia: The Cold Can be Trouble for Older People*
- *Hyperthermia: A Hot Weather Hazard for Older People*
- *Menopause*
- *Resource Directory for Older People*
- *Talking With Your Doctor: A Guide for Older People*
- *What's Your Aging IQ?*
- *Who? What? Where? Resources for Women's Health and Aging*

NIA's Age Pages provide a quick, practical look at some of the health topics that interest older people.

Diseases/Disorders/Conditions

- *Aging and Alcohol Abuse*
- *Arthritis Advice*
- *Cancer Facts for People Over 50*
- *Constipation*
- *Dealing With Diabetes* (S)
- *Depression: A Serious but Treatable Illness*
- *Forgetfulness in Old Age*
- *High Blood Pressure: A Common But Controllable Disorder*
- *HIV, AIDS and Older Adults*
- *Osteoporosis: The Bone Thinner*
- *Prostate Problems*
- *Stroke Prevention and Treatment*
- *Urinary Incontinence*

Health Promotion/Disease Prevention

- *Aging and Your Eyes*
- *A Good Night's Sleep*
- *Be Sensible About Salt*
- *Dietary Supplements: More is Not Always Better*
- *Don't Take It Easy—Exercise!*
- *Foot Care*
- *Hearing and Older People*
- *Heat, Cold, and Getting Old*
- *Hints for Shopping, Cooking, and Enjoying Meals*
- *Life Extension: Science or Science Fiction?*
- *Managing Menopause*
- *Nutrition: A Lifelong Concern*
- *Pneumonia Prevention: It's Worth A Shot*
- *Sexuality in Later Life*
- *Shots for Safety*
- *Skin Care and Aging*

- *Smoking: It's Never Too Late To Stop*
- *Taking Care of Your Teeth and Mouth*
- *What to do About Flu*

Medical Care

- *Considering Surgery?*
- *Finding Good Medical Care for Older Americans*
- *Hospital Hints*
- *Who's Who in Health Care*

Medications

- *Arthritis Medicines*
- *Hormone Replacement Therapy: Should You Take It?*
- *Medicines: Use Them Safely*
- *Safe Use of Tranquilizers*

Planning for Later Years

- *Getting Your Affairs in Order*
- *When You Need a Nursing Home*

Safety

- *Accident Prevention*
- *Crime and Older People*
- *Health Quackery*
- *Preventing Falls and Fractures*

Contact National Institute on Aging, Public Information Office, 9000 Rockville Pike, Building 31, Room 5C27, Bethesda, MD 20892; 800-222-2225; or online at <http://www.nih.gov/nia>.

☆☆☆

Get Your Own Facts On Your Own Heart

Although we're not sure whose mother it was, but someone once said that whoever controls your heart controls your head. Now it is time to take some action on your own.

Don't let high blood pressure or cholesterol rule your life. With some help from the National Heart, Lung, and Blood Institute you can learn about the target numbers you need to shoot for, as well as how to eat better to put you in control.

The National Heart, Lung, and Blood Institute (NHLBI) conducts research on these topics and more, and responds to questions on cholesterol, high blood pressure, blood resources, sleep disorders, obesity, and asthma. They can conduct database searches to locate materials, and they distribute a wide variety of educational publications for both the consumer and professional. Some of the publications available include:

- *Controlling High Blood Pressure*
- *Take Steps — Prevent High Blood Pressure*
- *Facts About Heart Disease and Women*
- *So You Have High Blood Pressure*
- *Step by Step: Eating To Lower Your High Blood Cholesterol*
- *Check Your Healthy Heart IQ*

Many other publications are also available. Request a free catalog. Contact National Heart, Lung, and Blood Institute Information Center, P.O. Box 30105, Bethesda, MD 20824-0105; 301-251-1222; 800-575-WELL (recorded message line); or online at <http://www.nhlbi.nih.gov/nhlbi/ nhlbi.htm>.

☆☆☆

Taking the Scare Out of Cancer

No one likes to think about the "C" word. But think about this: the earlier cancer is found, the better your chances of beating it. There are simple tests you can take that can help find cancer early, long before any symptoms appear. Research is showing that this has helped increase the survival rate dramatically for certain types of cancer.

The toll-free Cancer Information Service (CIS) can provide accurate, up-to-date information about cancer and cancer-related resources near you. Information is also available about treatment studies currently accepting patients and is available to doctors through a database known as PDQ (Physician Data Query).

The National Cancer Institute also distributes free publications on specific types of cancer, treatment methods, coping with cancer, and other cancer-related subjects. Just a few of the publications available include:

- *Cancer Tests You Should Know About: A Guide For People 65 And Over*
- *Anticancer Drug Information Sheets*
- *Advanced Cancer: Living Each Day*
- *Chemotherapy and You: A Guide To Self Help During Treatment*
- *Questions and Answers About Pain Control*
- *What Are Clinical Trials All About?*
- *Radiation Therapy And You*
- *Facing Forward: A Guide for Cancer Survivors*

- *Eating Hints: Recipes and Tips*

Contact National Cancer Institute, Office of Cancer Communications, Building 31, Room 10A16, 31 Center Dr., NSC2580, Bethesda, MD 20892-2580; Cancer Information Service 800-4-CANCER; or online at <http://www.nic.nih.gov>.

Your Very Own Yellow Pages

Ever get tired of not knowing which way to turn or who to call?

Never fear, *The Resource Directory for Older People* is here. This is the yellow pages for associations and organizations that deal with issues faced by people over 50. Everything from the Administration on Aging to Young Women's Christian Association is included in this comprehensive directory. Each listing includes the address and phone number, mission statement, services, and publications.

No need to feel like you are fighting a battle alone. Now there are over 250 places to call. To receive your copy, contact National Institute on Aging, Information Center, P.O. Box 8057, Gaithersburg, MD 20898; 800-222-2225; or online at <http://www.nih.gov/nia>.

☆☆☆

Keep Your Own Choppers

Just because you're over 65 doesn't necessarily mean you should be watching those commercials for denture cleaners more closely. In fact, who would ever have guessed that a majority of seniors still have their own set of pearly whites, and with each passing year fewer and fewer are losing them.

This is due in large part to water fluoridation, brushing and regular visits to the dentist, not to mention the exciting new research on the causes, prevention, diagnosis, and treatment of dental disease.

The National Institute on Dental Research can answer your questions about problems with your teeth and send you all kinds of free publications to keep them healthy and happy. Contact National Institute of Dental Research, Information Office, Building 31, Room 2C35, 31 Center Dr., MSC2290, Bethesda, MD 20892-2290; 301-496-4261; or online at <http://www.nidr.nih.gov>.

☆☆☆

When Aspirin Isn't Enough

If you suffer from chronic headaches, sometimes even several doses of aspirin may not do the trick. Believe it or not, in the Ninth Century the recommended treatment involved drinking a concoction of elderseed, cow's brain, and goat's dung dissolved in vinegar.

Although that may sound appealing to some of you out there, for the rest of us, new treatment options have greatly improved our lives. Drug therapy, biofeedback training, stress reduction, and elimination of certain foods from the diet are just a few of the most common methods of preventing and controlling migraines and other types of headaches.

The National Institute of Neurological Disorders and Stroke has put together a publication entitled, *Headache: Hope Through Research*, that provides journal articles, research reports, and other resources for headache sufferers. For your free copy, contact the National Institute of Neurological Disorders and Stroke, Information Office, Building 31, Room 8A06, 31 Center Dr., MSC 2540, Bethesda, MD 20892-2540; 800-352-9424; or online at <http://www.ninds.nih.gov>.

Sugar Alert

Sugar doesn't need to be a four letter word to those 11 million Americans who have diabetes. In fact, it doesn't even have to be a five letter word to those who can spell.

With the proper diet and exercise program, in many cases you can actually reverse or reduce insulin resistance, which is one of the underlying causes of diabetes. And how about this: some formerly overweight diabetics no longer have the disease after shedding pounds.

The National Diabetes Information Clearinghouse can answer any of your questions regarding diabetes and will send you the Diabetes Dateline newsletter and a calendar of meetings and educational programs. They also have a wonderful collection of free publications on diabetes and how it can be controlled:

- *Diabetes Dictionary*
- *Insulin Dependent Diabetes*
- *Questions to Ask Your Doctor About Blood Sugar Control*
- *Non-insulin Dependent Diabetes*
- *Do Your Level Best: Start Controlling Your Blood Sugar*

A complete list of publications is available by contacting the Clearinghouse at National Diabetes Information Clearinghouse, 1 Information Way, Bethesda, MD 20892-3560; 301-654-3327; or online at <http://www.niddk.nih.gov>.

Aches and Pains

If your joints ache, join the crowd. Over 50% of people over 65 suffer from some form of arthritis, whether it is a mild stiffness in your joints when it rains to full-blown osteoarthritis. But for many, a simple change in diet and exercise could result in an improvement in their condition.

The National Institute of Arthritis and Musculoskeletal and Skin Diseases (NIAMS) conducts research on a number of chronic, disabling diseases, including osteoarthritis, rheumatoid arthritis, muscle diseases, osteoporosis, Paget's disease, back disorders, gout, and more.

The Clearinghouse can answer questions, provide you with publications, and search the Combined Health Information Database (CHID) for other references on specific topics. Some of the free publications include:

- *Lupus* (AR-96) 6/95
- *Osteoarthritis* (AR-73) 9/94
- *Behcet's Syndrome* (AR69) 12/89
- *Back Pain* (AR-78)
- *Arthritis* (AR-27)

For more information, contact National Arthritis and Musculoskeletal and Skin Diseases Information Clearinghouse, 1 AMS Circle, Bethesda, MD 20892-3675; 301-495-4484; or online at <http://www. nih.gov/niams>

☆☆☆

Prostate Solutions

Research shows that if a man lives long enough, he's almost certain to have some kind of non-cancerous problem with his prostate. Fortunately, there are also many effective treatments.

To learn more about prostate problems and treatment options other than prostate cancer, contact the National Kidney and Urologic Diseases Information Clearinghouse. They can answer questions, provide publications, and can conduct a search on the Combined Health Information Database (CHID) for more information.

Some of the free publications include:

- *Prostate Enlargement: Benign Prostatic Hyperplasia*
- *Age Page: Prostate Problems*

For more information, contact National Kidney and Urologic Diseases Information Clearinghouse, 3 Information Way, Bethesda, MD 20892-3580; 301-654-4415; or online at <http://www.niddk.nih.gov>.

☆☆☆

Should You Get Your Flu Shot?

Each winter, millions of people suffer from the unpleasant effects of the "flu." For most people, a few days in bed, a few more days of rest, aspirin, and plenty to drink will be the best treatment. For older people though, the flu can be life-threatening.

A flu shot can give your body time to build the proper immunity. To better understand infectious diseases and the immune system, the National Institute of Allergy and Infectious Diseases conducts research and clinical trials. They have a free publication titled, Flu, that can give you some great tips for the Flu season.

For more information, contact National Institute of Allergy and Infectious Diseases, Office of Communications Building 31, Room 7A50, 31 Center Dr. MSC2520, Bethesda, MD 20892-2520; 301-496-5717; or online at <http://www.niaid.nih.gov>.

☆☆☆

Drink Your Broccoli?

Well you don't have to drink it, but broccoli is a good source of calcium, in addition to cheese and milk. Getting enough calcium and maintaining a good exercise program are two steps you can take to help prevent or delay the onset of osteoporosis.

To learn more about the causes, risk factors, and treatment of osteoporosis, contact National Resource Center on Osteoporosis and Related Disease, National Osteoporosis Foundation, 1150 17th St., NW, Suite 500, Washington, DC 20036-4603; 202-223-0344; or online at <http://www.osteo.org>.

☆☆☆

Stroke Clearinghouse

Here's some great news: strokes can be prevented today. In fact, the death rate from strokes has fallen as much as 50% since 1970.

This decline has come about, in part, because of new tests and treatments. There is even some evidence that common aspirin can reduce your chances of stroke. In addition, many people are adopting sensible health habits such as controlling their high blood pressure.

The free publication, *Stroke: Hope Through Research*, outlines some of the causes, tests and treatments for strokes.

The National Institute of Neurological Disorders and Stroke (NINDS) supports and conducts research and research training on the cause, prevention, diagnosis and treatment of hundreds of neurological disorders. Some of their studies involve Alzheimer's disease, Parkinson's disease, Huntington's disease, multiple sclerosis, and amyotrophic lateral sclerosis. Some of the other free publications they have available include:

- *Dizziness: Hope Through Research*
- *Multiple Sclerosis: Hope Through Research*
- *Parkinson's Disease: Hope Through Research*
- *Shingles: Hope Through Research*

Contact the National Institute of Neurological Disorders and Stroke, Information Office, Building 31, Room 8A06, 31 Center Dr. MSC 2540, Bethesda, MD 20892-2540; 800-352-9424; or online at <http://www.ninds.nih.gov>.

Osteoporosis and Related Bone Diseases

Information ranging from slip and fall prevention to fibrous dysplasia is available from the Osteoporosis and Related Bone Diseases National Resource Center (ORBD-NRC). ORBD-NRC's resource database provides current information on subjects such as:

- *Osteoporosis*
- *Paget's disease of bone*
- *Osteogenesis imperfecta*
- *Primary hyperparathyroidism*

Contact the ORBD-NRC to receive free publications or facts sheets from: Osteoporosis and Related Bone Diseases National Resource Center, 1150 17th St. NW, Suite 500, Washington, DC 20036-4603, 800-624-BONE;

or online at <http:/www.osteo.org>.

★★★

Incontinence Is Not Inevitable

You would think from the humiliating diaper commercials that incontinence is the Number 1 problem faced by seniors today. But in reality only 1 in 10 suffer from it, and in most cases it can be treated and controlled, if not cured.

Believe it or not, incontinence often results from the use of medications or certain common medical conditions. Once your doctor finds out the cause, there may be simple steps you can take to help correct this problem.

The National Kidney and Urologic Diseases Information Clearinghouse can answer questions and provide information about all kidney and urologic diseases. They have free publications and can conduct a search on the Combined Health Information Database (CHID) for more information on a specific subject. Some of the free publications include:

- *Urinary Tract Infections In Adults*
- *Kidney Stones in Adults*
- *End-Stage Renal Disease*
- *Age Page: Urinary Incontinence*

For more information, contact National Kidney and Urologic Diseases Information Clearinghouse, 3 Information Way, Bethesda, MD 20892-3580; 301-654-4415; or online at <http://www.niddk.nih.gov>.

Help For Heartburn

No need to spend the rest of your life chugging antacids for that upset stomach. Besides tasting lousy, some recent research has shown a possible link between aluminum-based antacids and Alzheimer's.

But there are simple home remedies for heartburn. Just by avoiding some everyday foods such as peppermint, orange juice (naturally high in acid), and chocolate among other things, you can help control your heartburn. You can even try elevating the head of your bed six inches, although ask your spouse first.

Although they can't cure your heartburn or ulcer, the National Digestive Diseases Information Clearinghouse does offer helpful information about digestive diseases. They have free publications, and can conduct a search on the Combined Health Information Database (CHID) to provide you with references for further reading. Some of the fact sheets they have include:

- *Heartburn*
- *Constipation*
- *Hemorrhoids*

- *Pancreatitis*
- *Cirrhosis of the Liver*
- *Gallstones*

They also have information packets on many digestive diseases. For more information, contact National Digestive Diseases Information Clearinghouse, 2 Information Way, Bethesda, MD 20892-3570; 301-654-3810; or online at <http://www.niddk.nih.gov>.

☆☆☆

Turn Down The Volume

Now you have the government backing you up when you tell the kids to turn down the rock-and-roll. Over one-third of people who have hearing impairments can trace the damage to exposure to loud sounds.

If you are currently shopping around for a hearing aid, you know that the choices you have are as varied as their price tags. You can learn more about the causes of hearing loss, hearing aid information, and the latest research on the topic from the National Institute on Deafness and Other Communication Disorders, which conducts research on the diseases and disorders of hearing, balance, smell, taste, voice, speech, and language.

They can answer your questions, and have publications which explain common problems and inform you of the latest research being undertaken. For a publications list or more information contact National Institute on Deafness and other Communication Disorders Clearinghouse, 1 Communication Ave., Bethesda, MD 20892-3456; 800-241-1044; or online at <http://www.nih.gov/nidcd>.

☆☆☆

Sneezing? Blame Your Parents

Most allergies can be blamed on inheriting them from your parents. You wanted their Louis IV chairs but instead ended up with their hay fever. Oh well.

Once you've finished yelling at them, there are some more effective steps you can take to improve your daily life. For example, the 1970's are over, and it's okay to get rid of the shag rug. Give the kid next door five

113

bucks to mow your lawn for you. And if you're a real thrill seeker, give the cat a bath every week.

To learn about the different types of allergies and their treatment options, contact the National Institute of Allergy and Infectious Diseases, and they will send you free publications and information to help you survive the sniffle season.

- *Allergic Disease: Medicine for the Public*
- *Something in the Air: Airborne Allergens*
- *Food Allergy and Intolerances*
- *Allergies: Living With Allergies*
- *How to Create a Dust-Free Bedroom*

For more information, contact National Institute of Allergy and Infectious Diseases, Office of Communications Building 31, Room 7A50, 31 Center Dr. MSC2520, Bethesda, MD 20892-2520; 301-496-5717; or online at <http://www.niaid.nih.gov>.

Vision Blurry?

So you don't have 20/20 vision anymore. Look on the bright side, without your glasses your daughter-in-law is a far more attractive woman now.

Seriously, most people retain good eyesight well into their 80's and beyond. Some tips to help you see clearly include having regular health checkups to detect diseases that cause eye problems such as diabetes; having a complete eye exam every 2 or 3 years; and seeking eye health care more often if you have diabetes or a family history of eye problems.

The National Eye Institute (NEI) conducts research on the prevention, diagnosis, treatment, and pathology of diseases and disorders of the eye, and has free publications including:

- *Cataracts*
- *Don't Lose Sight of Glaucoma*
- *Don't Lose Sight of Diabetic Eye Disease*
- *Don't Lose Sight of Cataracts*
- *Don't Lose Sight of Age-Related Macular Degeneration*
- *Diabetic Retinopathy*

For more information, contact National Eye Institute, Information Office, Building 31, Room 6A32, 31 Center Dr. MSC 2510, Bethesda, MD 20892-2510; 301-496-5248; or online at <http://www.nei.nih.gov>.

✩✩✩

Don't Drink and Medicate

Many seniors are on drugs — serious prescription medications that when mixed with alcohol can cause serious problems, such as falls and broken bones, and even hard core addiction. And it's also not uncommon for some seniors to use alcohol to help them deal with the loneliness accompanied with being old.

The National Clearinghouse for Alcohol and Drug Information is a wonderful resource to learn more about alcohol and drug addiction. They can answer your questions and provide you with free publications on the safe use of prescriptions, drug and alcohol abuse, and treatment information.

To learn more, contact the National Clearinghouse for Alcohol and Drug Information, P.O. Box 2345, Rockville, MD 20847; 800-729-6686; or online at <http://www.health.org>.

☆☆☆

Everyone Gets The Blues Now And Then

It's part of life. Being down in the dumps over a period of time is a common problem among the elderly, but it doesn't have to be a normal part of growing old. For most people, depression can be treated successfully, and while some depression may require drug treatments, many others require simple changes in diet and exercise.

The National Institute of Mental Health conducts research to learn more about the causes, prevention, and treatment of mental and emotional illnesses. They can answer your questions and have publications on a wide variety of topics, including:

- *Alzheimer's Disease*
- *Depressive Illness: Treatments Bring New Hope*
- *Plain Talk About Depression*
- *Plain Talk About Handling Stress*
- *If You're Over 65 and Feeling Depressed ... Treatment Brings New Hope*
- *Panic Disorder*

For more information, contact National Institute of Mental Health, Information Resources and Inquiries Branch, Room 7C02, 5600 Fishers Lane, MSC 8030, Bethesda, MD 20892; 301-443-4513; or online at <http://www.nimh.nih.gov>.

115

Move To Florida and Look Even Older

Forget shoveling snow — you're moving to Arizona or Florida to enjoy the sunshine and feel younger. But you'd better think twice about enjoying the warm sun too much. No matter what age you are, the sun can do all kinds of harmful things to your skin, not the least of which is accelerate aging.

Read up on tanning and suncare products through two free publications from the Federal Trade Commission, titled Indoor Tanning and Sunscreens. These will help you keep your skin beautiful and healthy.

To receive your copies, contact Public Reference, Room 130, Federal Trade Commission, 6th St. & Pennsylvania Ave. NW, Washington, DC 20580; 202-326-2222; or online at <http://www.ftc.gov>.

Quack Alert

Ignore those seductive ads in the supermarket tabloid newspapers. No amount of rubbing, wrapping, massaging, or scrubbing will cure your arthritis. And no over-the-counter cream, lotion, or device can prevent baldness, induce new hair to grow, or cause hair to become thicker.

There are all kinds of miracle cure scams aimed at older people who are vulnerable to their unrealistic claims. The Federal Trade Commission has several pamphlets to help educate you about health fraud. Some of the free titles include *Health Claims: Separating Fact From Fiction, and Healthy Questions (To Ask Health Care Specialists)*.

To receive your copies, contact Public Reference, Room 130, Federal Trade Commission, 6th St. and Pennsylvania Ave. NW, Washington, DC 20580; 202-326-2222; or online at <http://www.ftc. gov>.

Information Clearinghouses on Problems With the Elderly

Would you like to learn more about nutrition and the elderly? What about how to help post-stroke patients rehab? Need videotapes to help your geriatric workers better understand the needs of the elderly?

As the elderly population grows each year, the need for doctors, nurses, and other health professionals trained in geriatrics also increases. The Bureau of Health Professions supports a nationwide network of Geriatric Education Centers whose purpose is to provide education and training opportunities in geriatrics.

Centers maintain resource clearinghouses and develop curriculum and teaching materials. A catalog of selected materials produced by the centers is available at no charge.

For additional information, contact Geriatric Education Centers Coordinator, Bureau of Health Professions, U.S. Department of Health and Human Services, 5600 Fishers Lane, Room 8-103, Rockville, MD 20857; 301-443-6887.

The following is a list of the Geriatric Education Centers which are specifically for health care professionals and students:

ALABAMA
University of Alabama at Birmingham Geriatric Education Center
CH-19, Suite 201
933 19th Street South
Birmingham, AL 35294-2041
205-934-1094
Fax: 205-934-7354

CALIFORNIA
California Geriatric Education Center
Department of Medicine
University of California
Los Angeles, 32-144 CHS
10833 Le Conte Ave.
Los Angeles, CA 90095-1687
310-312-0530
Fax: 310-312-0538

Stanford Geriatric Education Center
703 Welch Road
Suite H-1
Stanford, CA 94305-0151
415-723-7063
Fax: 415-723-9692

COLORADO
Colorado Geriatric Education Center
Health Sciences Center
Office of Academic Affairs
Box A094
4200 E. 9th Ave.
Denver, CO 80262
303-270-8974
Fax: 303-270-7729

DISTRICT OF COLUMBIA
Washington DC Geriatric Education Center Consortium
George Washington University Medical Center
Dept. of Health Care Sciences
2150 Pennsylvania Ave., NW
Room 2B-417
Washington, DC 20037
202-994-4731
Fax: 202-994-7023

FLORIDA
Miami Area Geriatric Education Center
University of Miami
1425 NW 10th Ave.
Sieron Building, 2nd Floor (D303)
Miami, FL 33136
305-243-6270
Fax: 305-243-4804

University of Florida Geriatric
Education Center
P.O. Box 100277
University of Florida
Gainesville, FL 32610-0277
352-395-0274
Fax: 352-338-9884

University of South Florida
Geriatric Education Center
Suncoast Gerontology Center
University of South Florida
Medical Center Box 50
12901 Bruce B. Downs Blvd.
Tampa, FL 33612
813-974-4355
Fax: 813-974-4251

HAWAII

Pacific Islands Geriatric Education
Center
347 N. Kuakini Street, HPM-9
Honolulu, HI 96817
808-523-8461
Fax: 808-528-1897

ILLINOIS

Illinois GEC Network
University of Illinois at Chicago
College of Associated Health
Professions
1640 W. Roosevelt Rd.
MC626, Room 438
Chicago, IL 60608-6904
312-413-1520
Fax: 312-996-6942

IOWA

Iowa Geriatric Education Ctr.
Center on Aging
300 CAMB
University of Iowa Hospitals
Iowa City, IA 52242
319-335-5756
Fax: 319-335-7025

KENTUCKY

Ohio Valley Appalachia Regional
Geriatric Education Center
University of Kentucky
658 S. Limestone St.
Lexington, KY 40506-0442
606-257-8314
Fax: 606-323-4940

LOUISIANA

Louisiana Geriatric Education
Center
Louisiana State University
School of Medicine
1542 Tulane Ave.
New Orleans, LA 70112
504-568-5842
Fax: 504-568-6735

MASSACHUSETTS

Harvard Upper New England
Geriatric Education Center
Division on Aging
Harvard Medical School
643 Huntington Ave.
Boston, MA 02115
617-432-2620
Fax: 617-734-4432

MICHIGAN

Geriatric Education Center of
Michigan
B-544 West Fee Hall
Michigan State University
East Lansing, MI 48824
517-353-7828
Fax: 517-353-6613

MINNESOTA

Minnesota Area Geriatric
Education Center
School of Public Health
Box 197 Mayo
420 Delaware Street, SE
University of Minnesota

118

Minneapolis, MN 55455
612-626-3886
Fax: 612-624-8448

MISSISSIPPI
Mississippi GEC
University of Mississippi Medical
Center
2500 N. State Street
Jackson, MS 39216-4505
601-984-6190
Fax: 601-984-6659

MISSOURI
Missouri Gateway Geriatric
Education Center
St. Louis University
School of Medicine
1402 S. Grand Blvd., Room M238
St. Louis, MO 63104
314-577-8462
Fax: 314-771-8575

NEVADA
Nevada Geriatric Education Center
University of Nevada at Reno
Sanford Center of Aging
Mackay Science Bldg. /146
University of Nevada Reno
Reno, NV 89557-0133
Fax: 702-784-1814

NEW JERSEY
New Jersey Geriatric Education
Center
University of Medicine and
Dentistry of New Jersey
School of Osteopathic Medicine
42 East Laurel Rd., Suite 3200
Stratford, NJ 08084-1504
609-566-7141
Fax: 609-556-6419

NEW MEXICO
New Mexico Geriatric Education
Center

UNM Center for Aging
1836 Lomas Blvd., NE
University of New Mexico
Albuquerque, NM 87131-6086
505-277-0911
Fax: 505-277-6878

NEW YORK
Columbia University-New York
Geriatric Education Center
Columbia University
Division of Nursing
50 W. 4th St., Room 429
Shinkin Hall
New York, NY 10012
212-998-5618
Fax: 212-995-4770

Finger Lakes Geriatric Education
Center
University of Rochester
Monroe Community Hospital
535 E. Henrietta Rd.
Rochester, NY 14620
716-760-6350
Fax: 716-760-6376

Western New York Geriatric
Education Center
Buffalo VA Hospital
Administration Center
Division of Geriatrics
Buffalo, NY 14125
716-829-3097
Fax: 716-862-3414

NORTH CAROLINA
Appalachian Geriatric Education
Center Consortium
Bowman Gray School of Medicine
Medical Center Boulevard
Winston-Salem, NC 27157-1051
910-716-4284
Fax: 910-716-7359

OHIO
Western Reserve Geriatric
Education Center
12200 Fairhill Road
Cleveland, OH 44120
216-368-5433
Fax: 216-368-3118

OREGON
Oregon Geriatric Education Ctr
Oregon Health Sciences University
Portland VAMC Mail Code (14G)
P.O. Box 1034
Portland, OR 97207-1034
503-721-7821
Fax: 503-721-7807

PENNSYLVANIA
Delaware Valley Geriatric
Education Center
University of Pennsylvania
Institute on Aging
3615 Chestnut St.
Philadelphia, PA 19104
215-898-1579
Fax: 215-573-8684

Geriatric Education Center of
Pennsylvania
121 University Place, 6th Floor
School of Medicine
University of Pittsburgh
Pittsburgh, PA 15260
412-624-9190
Fax: 412-624-5529

PUERTO RICO
Geriatric Education Center of
University of Puerto Rico
School of Medicine
Medical Sciences Campus
G.P.O. Box 5067
San Juan, PR 00936
809-751-2478
Fax: 809-765-0514

RHODE ISLAND
Rhode Island Geriatric Education
Center
University of Rhode Island
Program in Gerontology
White Hall, 2 Heathman Rd.
Kingston, RI 02881
401-874-5311
Fax: 401-874-2061

TENNESSEE
Meharry Consortium Geriatric
Education Center
1005 D.B. Todd Boulevard
Nashville, TN 37208
615-327-6947
Fax: 615-327-6880

TEXAS
Texas Consortium of Geriatric
Education Centers
Baylor College of Medicine
One Baylor Plaza, Room M320
Houston, TX 77030-3498
713-798-4611
Fax: 713-798-6688

South Texas Geriatric Education
Center
Department of Dental Diagnostic
Science
7703 Floyd Curl Drive
San Antonio, TX 78284-7921
210-567-3370
Fax: 210-567-3337

UTAH
Geriatric Research
Education & Clinical Center
VA Medical Center (182)
500 Foothill Blvd.
Salt Lake City, UT 84148
801-582-1565, ext. 2522
Fax: 801-583-7338

VIRGINIA

Virginia Geriatric Education
Center
Virginia Commonwealth University
520 N. 12th Street
The Lyons Building
Richmond, VA 23298-0228
804-828-9060
Fax: 804-828-7905

WASHINGTON

Northwest Geriatric Education
Center
University of Washington
Box 358123
Seattle, WA 98195
206-685-7478
Fax: 206-685-3436

WEST VIRGINIA

Mountain State Geriatric
Education Center
West Virginia University
Center on Aging
P.O. Box 9127
Morgantown, WV 26505
304-293-2081
Fax: 304-293-2700

WISCONSIN

Wisconsin Geriatric Education
Center
Marquette University
Academic Support Facility
P.O. Box 1881
Milwaukee, WI 53201-1881
414-288-3712
Fax: 414-288-1973

Get The Inside Scoop on the Health Budget

Seems like all we hear about in the news these days is balancing the budget and lowering the deficit. Maybe at your expense.

Of course, one suggestion to accomplish this is to cap Medicare spending. How would this affect the everyday lives of older people? Will they be forced to join HMOs? Will new changes cover nursing home care or prescription drugs?

Before they vote on any issue, your Congressman usually looks over one of the reports written by the Congressional Research Service (CRS). These CRS reports provide an overview of an issue, and include bibliographies, newspaper articles, and more.

Copies of the CRS reports are free to the public, but you have to request them through your Representative or Senator. Some of the reports dealing with health include:

- *Health: Long-Term Health Care* (IP402H)
- *Medicare: An Overview* (IP467M)
- *Characteristics of Nursing Home Residents and Proposals for Reforming Coverage of Nursing Home Care* (90-471EPW)
- *Elderly Home Care: Tax Incentives and Proposals for Change* (89-662E)
- *Public Opinion on Long-Term Health Care Needs, Costs and*

Financing (90-151GOV)
- *Housing for Older Persons Act of 1995: HR660* (95-443E)

These and other titles dealing with older people are available by contacting Your Representative or Senator, The Capitol, Washington, DC 20510; 202-224-3121.

☆☆☆

What Treatment Is Best For You

Seems like everybody's got an opinion about how you should treat a condition or disease. Even doctors disagree with one another. That's when it gets really confusing. All you want to know is "What's best for me?"

To help both you and your doctor make the best treatment choices, the Agency for Health Care Policy and Research (AHCPR) has developed some practical guidelines that you can use to help you with your health care choices.

In addition, they also look at research on health services, health care, and home health care. Some of the publications they have available include:

- *Pain Control After Surgery: A Patient's Guide* (AHCPR 92-0021)
- *Cataract in Adults: A Patient's Guide* (AHCPR 93-0544)
- *Depression is a Treatable Illness: A Patient's Guide* (ANCPR 93-2553)
- *Preventing Pressure Ulcers: A Patient's Guide* (AHCPR 92-0048)
- *Urinary Incontinence in Adults: A Patient's Guide* (AHCPR 92-0041)
- *Early Alzheimer's Disease*
- *You Can Quit Smoking*
- *Treating Your Enlarged Prostate*
- *Be Informed: Questions to Ask Your Doctor Before You Have Surgery*
- *Choosing and Using a Health Plan*
- *Prescription Medicines and You*
- *What You Should Know About Stroke Prevention*

For your free copies or more information, contact Agency for Health Care Policy and Research, P.O. Box 8547, Silver Spring, MD 20907; 800-358-9295; or online at <http://www.ahcpr.gov>.

☆☆☆

Someone Else Is Also Checking Your Pulse

Many seniors worry that they don't have enough health coverage, so they spend billions on additional, and often unnecessary, insurance. A recent government study looked into this issue, and what they found out might save you thousands of dollars on your insurance premiums. This free report from the General Accounting Office (GAO) looks at typical coverage that older Americans carry and potential problems.

The GAO publishes results of research into issues that face the elderly, including:

- *Health Insurance for the Elderly: Owning Duplicate Policies Is Costly and Unnecessary* (HEHS 94-185)
- *Medicare: Beneficiary Liability for Certain Paramedic Services May Be Substantial* (HEHS 94-122BR)
- *Mammography Services: Impact of Federal Legislation on Quality, Access, and Health Outcomes* (HEHS-98-11)
- *Housing for the Elderly: Information on HUD's Section 202 and Home Partnership Programs* (RCED-98-11)
- *Medicare Home Health: Success of Balanced Budget Act Cost Controls Depends on Effective and Timely Implementation* (T-HEHS-98-41)
- *Health Care Services: How Continuing Care Retirement Communities Manage Services for the Elderly* (HEHS-97-36)
- *Retiree Health Insurance: Erosion in Employer-Based Health Benefits for Early Retirees* (HEHS-97-150)

All reports are free and can be requested by contacting U.S. General Accounting Office, P.O. Box 6015, Gaithersburg, MD 20884-6015; 202-512-6000; or online at <http://www.gao.gov>.

☆☆☆

Medicare Medigap Medimess

One of the most burning questions facing older Americans today is: "Should I buy health insurance from Art Linkletter?" If only life were that simple.

For those who are covered by Medicare, the maze of questions about insurance coverage is confusing and frustrating, but the toll-free Medicare hotline can answer your questions and refer you to local offices if necessary. They also distribute free information booklets including:

- *Guide to Health Insurance for People with Medicare* (518B)
- *Medicare: Coverage for Second Surgical Opinion* (521B)
- *Medicare: Hospice Benefits* (591B)
- *Medicare and Managed Care Plans* (592B)
- *Medicare and Other Health Benefits* (593B)

- *Medicare Coverage of Kidney Dialysis and Kidney Transplant Services* (594B)
- *Manual De Medicare* (595B) Spanish Edition
- *Medicare: Savings for Qualified Beneficiaries* (596B)
- *Medicare and Your Physician's Bill* (520B)
- *Continuous Improvement* (637B)

For more information, contact the Medicare Hotline, Health Care Financing Administration, 6325 Security Blvd., Baltimore, MD 21207; 800-638-6833; or online at <http://www.hcfa.gov>.

☆☆☆

More Health Insurance for the Poor

Being poor doesn't get you much in this country, but one of the things it may get you is free health insurance under the Medicaid program.

Medicaid is funded by the Federal and state governments to provide medical assistance for certain low-income persons. Each state designs and administers its own Medicaid program, setting eligibility and coverage standards.

Although originally intended to provide basic medical services to the poor and disabled, Medicaid has also become the primary source of public funds for nursing home care. Look in the blue pages of your phone book for your local Medicaid office.

☆☆☆

Your Brain: Use It or Lose It

New studies show that people who don't have much education or high levels of job achievement have at least twice the risk for developing Alzheimer's disease as those who do. Clearly this doesn't account for everyone who suffers from Alzheimer's — take Ronald Reagan for example — but there is a suggestion that when it comes to your brain, you need to use it or lose it. Other promising research is underway to find the causes and treatments of this disease.

And as for caring for a person with Alzheimer's, which can be emotionally, physically, and financially stressful, help is nearby. The Alzheimer's Disease Education and Referral (ADEAR) Center is a national resource that provides information on diagnosis, treatment issues, patient care, caregiver needs, long-term care, education and training and research activities. They also maintain a database which includes references to patient and professional materials. The ADEAR

Center distributes a quarterly newsletter and other publications such as:

- *Alzheimer's Disease Fact Sheet*
- *Multi-infarct Dementia Fact Sheet*
- *Forgetfulness in Old Age: It's Not What You Think*
- *Progress Report on Alzheimer's Disease*
- *Alzheimer's Disease Centers Program Directory*
- *Differential Diagnosis of Dementing Diseases*
- *Alzheimer's Disease: A Guide to Federal Programs*
- *Caring and Sharing: A Catalog of Training Materials from Alzheimer's Disease Centers*
- *Talking With Your Doctor: A Guide for Older People*

For more information, contact Alzheimer's Disease Education and Referral Center, P.O. Box 8250, Silver Spring, MD 20907; 301-495-3311, 800-438-4380; or online at <http://www.alzheimers.org>.

Free Treatment ... Taking Part In Finding A Cure

Although there is currently no way to prevent or cure Alzheimer's disease, the research continues. In fact, a recent study has possibly located a genetic marker for Alzheimer's. Other areas of investigation range from the basic mechanisms of Alzheimer's disease to managing the symptoms and helping families cope with the effects of the disease.

The National Institute on Aging currently funds 28 Alzheimer's Disease Centers (ADC's) at major medical institutions across the nation. These centers offer free diagnosis and treatment for those who volunteer for the research. There are also support groups and other special programs for volunteers and their families.

Contact the Center nearest you from the list below and ask for information about services they may provide, as well as satellite clinics they may have at other locations.

Alzheimer's Disease Centers Program Directory

ALABAMA
University of Alabama at
Birmingham
Lindy E. Harrell, M.D., Ph.D.
Professor
Department of Neurology

University of Alabama at
Birmingham
1720 7th Ave.,
South Sparks Center 454
Birmingham, AL 35294-0017
Director: 205-934-3847

Fax: 205-975-7365
Information: 205-934-9775

CALIFORNIA

University of California, Davis
William J. Jagust, M.D., Director
University of California, Davis
Alzheimer's Disease Center
Alta Bates Medical Center
2001 Dwight Way
Berkeley, CA 94704
510-204-4530
Fax: 510-204-4524

University of California, Los Angeles
Jeffrey L. Cummings, M.D.
Professor
Department of Neurology and
Psychiatry
University of California, Los Angeles
710 Westwood Plaza
Los Angeles, CA 90024-1769
Director: 310-206-5238
Fax: 310-206-5287
Information: 310-206-5238

University of California, San Diego
Leon Ihal, M.D., Chairman
Department of Neuroscience
(0624)
University of California
San Diego School of Medicine
9500 Gilman Dr.
La Jolla, CA 92093-0624
Director: 619-534-4606
Fax: 619-534-1437
Information: 619-622-5800

University of Southern California
Caleb E. Finch, Ph.D.
Division of Neurogerontology
Ethel Percy Andrus Gerontology
Center
University Park, MC-0191
3715 McClintock Avenue

University of Southern California
Los Angeles, CA 90089-0191
Director: 213-740-1758
Fax: 213-740-8253
Information: 213-740-7777

GEORGIA

Emory University/VA Medical
Center
Suzanne S. Mirra, M.D., Professor
Department of Pathology and
Laboratory Medicine
Emory University School of
Medicine
VA Medical Center (151)
1670 Clairmont Rd.
Decatur, GA 30033
404-728-7714
Fax: 404-728-7771

ILLINOIS

Rush-Presbyterian-St. Lukes
Medical Center
Denis A. Evans, M.D.
Professor of Medicine
Rush Alzheimer's Disease Center
Rush-Presbyterian-St. Lukes
Medical Center
1653 West Jackson, Suite 675
Chicago, IL 60612
Director: 312-942-3350
Fax: 312-942-2861
Information: 312-942-4463

Northwestern University
Marsel Mesulam, M.D., Director
Cognitive Neurology and
Alzheimer's Disease Center
Northwestern University Medical
School
320 East Superior St.
Searle 11-450
Chicago, IL 60611
Director: 312-908-9339
Fax: 312-908-8789

126

INDIANA
Indiana University
Bernardino Ghetti, M.D.
Professor of Pathology, Psychiatry,
Medical and Molecular Genetics
Department of Pathology, MS A142
Indiana Alzheimer's Disease Center
Indiana University School of
Medicine
635 Barnhill Drive
Indianapolis, IN 46202-5120
Director: 317-274-1590
Fax: 317-274-4882
Information: 317-278-2030

KANSAS
University of Kansas
Charles De Carli, M.D., Director
Department of Neurology
University of Kansas Medical Center
3901 Rainbow Boulevard
Kansas City, KS 66160-7117
913-588-6952
Fax: 913-588-6965

KENTUCKY
University of Kentucky
William R. Markesbery, M.D.
Director
Sanders-Brown Research Center
on Aging
101 Sanders-Brown Building
University of Kentucky
800 S. Lime
Lexington, KY 40536-0230
606-233-6040
Fax: 606-258-2866

MARYLAND
The Johns Hopkins Medical
Institutions
Donald L. Price, M.D.
Professor of Pathology Neurology
and Neuroscience
The Johns Hopkins University
School of Medicine
558 Ross Research Building
720 Rutland Ave.
Baltimore, MD 21205
410-955-5632
Fax: 410-955-9777

MASSACHUSETTS
Boston University
Neil William Kowall, M.D.
Alzheimer's Disease Center
Geriatric Research, Education and
Clinical Center
Bedford VA Medical Center
200 Springs Rd.
Bedford, MA 01730
Director: 617-687-2632
Fax: 617-687-3515
Information: 617-687-2916

Harvard Medical School/
Massachusetts General Hospital
John H. Growdon, M.D.
Department of Neurology
Massachusetts Alzheimer's
Disease Research Center
Massachusetts General Hospital
WAC 830
Boston, MA 02114
617-726-1728
Fax: 617-726-4101

MICHIGAN
University of Michigan
Sid Gilman, M.D.
Professor and Chair
Department of Neurology
Michigan Alzheimer's Disease
Research Center
University of Michigan
1914 Taubman St.
Ann Arbor, MI 48109-0316
Director: 313-936-9070
Fax: 313-936-8763
Information: 313-764-2190

MINNESOTA

Mayo Clinic
Ronald Petersen, M.D.
Associate Professor
Department of Neurology
Mayo Clinic
200 First St., SW
Rochester, MN 55905
Director: 507-284-4006
Fax: 507-284-2203
Information: 507-284-1324

MISSOURI

Washington University
Leonard Berg, M.D.
Alzheimer's Disease Research Center
Washington University Medical
Center
The Health Key Bldg.
4488 Forest Park Blvd.
St. Louis, MO 63108-2293
314-286-2881
Fax: 314-286-2763
Information: 314-286-2881

NEW YORK

Columbia University
Michael L. Shelanski, M.D., Ph.D.,
Director
Alzheimer's Disease Research Center
Columbia University
Department of Pathology
630 W. 168th St.
New York, NY 10032
Director: 212-305-3300
Fax: 212-305-5498
Information: 212-305-8056

Mr. Sinai School of Medicine/
Bronx VA Medical Center
Kenneth L. Davis, M.D.
Professor and Chairman
Department of Psychiatry
Mount Sinai School of Medicine
Mount Sinai Medical Center

1 Gustave L. Levy Place
Box #1230
New York, NY 10029-6574
Director: 212-824-7008
Fax: 212-860-3945
Information: 212-241-8329
Fax: 212-996-0987

New York University
Steven H. Farris, Ph.D.
Aging and Dementia Research
Center
Department of Psychiatry (THN314)
New York University Medical Center
550 First Avenue
New York, NY 10016
212-263-5703
Fax: 212-263-6991
Information: 212-263-5700

University of Rochester
Paul D. Coleman, Ph.D., Professor
Department of Neurobiology and
Anatomy
Box 603
University of Rochester Medical
Center
601 Elmwood Ave.
Rochester, NY 14642
716-275-2581
Fax: 716-273-1132
Information: 716-275-2581

NORTH CAROLINA

Duke University
Allen D. Roses, M.D.
Director and Principal Investigator
Joseph and Kathleen Bryan
Alzheimer's Disease Research Center
2200 Main St., Suite A-230
Durham, NC 27705
Director: 919-286-3228
Fax: 919-286-3406
Information: 919-286-7299

OHIO
Case Western Reserve University
Peter J. Whitehouse, M.D., Ph.D.,
Director
Alzheimer's Disease Center
University Hospitals of Cleveland
11100 Euclid Ave.
Cleveland, OH 44106
216-844-7360
Fax: 216-844-7239

OREGON
Oregon Health Sciences University
Earl A. Zimmerman, M.D., Chairman
Department of Neurology, (L-226)
Oregon Health Sciences University
3181 SW Sam Jackson Park Rd.
Portland, OR 97201-3098
Director: 503-494-7321
Fax: 503-494-7242
Information: 503-494-6976

PENNSYLVANIA
University of Pennsylvania
John Q. Trojanowski, M.D., Ph.D.,
Professor
Pathology and Laboratory Medicine
University of Pennsylvania School
of Medicine, Room A009,
Basement, Maloney/HUP
36th and Spruce Sts.
Philadelphia, PA 19104-4283
Director: 215-662-6921
Fax: 215-349-5909
Information: 215-662-6920

University of Pittsburgh
Steven DeKosky, M.D., Director
Alzheimer's Disease Research Center
University of Pittsburgh Medical
Center
Montefiore University Hospital 4
West, 200 Lothrop St.
Pittsburgh, PA 15213

Director: 412-624-6889
Fax: 412-624-7814
Information: 412-692-2700

TEXAS
Baylor College of Medicine
Stanley H. Appel, M.D., Director
Alzheimer's Disease Research Center
Department of Neurology
Baylor College of Medicine
6501 Fannin, NB302
Houston, TX 77030-3498
Director: 713-798-6660
Fax: 713-798-7434
Information: 713-798-6660

University of Texas
Southwestern Medical Center
Roger N. Rosenberg, M.D., Director
Alzheimer's Disease Research Center
Zale Distinguished Chair and
Professor of Neurology and
Physiology
University of Texas
Southwestern Medical Center at
Dallas
5323 Harry Hines Blvd.
Dallas, TX 75235-9036
Director: 214-688-3239
Fax: 214-688-6824
Information: 214-648-3198

WASHINGTON
University of Washington
George M. Martin, M.D., Professor
Department of Pathology
Box 357470, HSB K-543
University of Washington
1959 NE Pacific Ave.
Seattle, WA 98195-7470
Director: 206-543-5088
Fax: 206-685-8356
Information: 206-543-6761

☆☆☆

Healthy Hotline

People are living longer — a lot longer. In fact, the average life expectancy has almost doubled in the last hundred years in America. But that doesn't necessarily mean that older people are spending their remaining years healthy and happy.

In fact, because people are living longer, they are contracting some diseases in larger numbers than ever before. The report, Healthy Older People, finds that older people are very interested in maintaining and improving their health, but need information about specific habits and how they are connected to chronic disease.

You can learn about what programs public and private organizations have used to spread the word. The National Health Information Center serves as an information and referral service, directing people to organizations that can provide health information, and also distributing resource guides on popular health topics. A catalog of publications is available free, and the prices of the publications range from $1-$4. Some of the publications include:

- *Federal Health Information Centers and Clearinghouses*
- *Toll-Free Numbers for Health Information*
- *Healthy Older People: The Report of a National Health Promotion Program* ($4)
- *Locating Resources for Healthy People 2000 Health Promotion Projects* ($5)

For a catalog and referral information, contact National Health Information Center, Office of Disease Prevention and Health Promotion, P.O. Box 1133, Washington, DC 20013-1133; 800-336-4797; or online at <http://nhic-nt.health.org>.

☆☆☆

Taking Medication Safely

Swallow capsules whole. Don't chew tablets. Drink plenty of fluids. Do this, don't do that. Can't you read the label?

There are so many things to remember when taking medication, it's not surprising that many people end up not taking them properly. Does it really matter if a tablet isn't taken at precisely the right time? What if you miss a dose?

The Food and Drug Administration's (FDA) Office of Consumer Affairs answers all these questions and more. They can refer you to other offices within the FDA for more information and has free publications that deal with drugs, medical devices, and health concerns. Some of the publications include:

- *Buying Medicine? Stop, Look, Look Again!*
- *How To Take Your Medicines: Acetaminophen-Codeine*
- *How To Take Your Medicines: Antihistamines*
- *How To Take Your Medicines: Beta Blocker Drugs*
- *How To Take Your Medicines: Cephalosporins*
- *How To Take Your Medicines: Diuretics*
- *How To Take Your Medicines: Erythromycin*
- *How To Take Your Medicines: Estrogens*
- *How To Take Your Medicines: Nonsteroidal Anti-inflammatory Drugs*
- *How To Take Your Medicines: Penicillins*
- *Testing Drugs In Older People*
- *When Medicines Don't Mix*

For these publications and more information, contact Drug Information Branch, Food And Drug Administration, 5600 Fishers Lane, HFD-210, Rockville, MD 20857; 800-532-4440; or online at <http://www.fda.gov>.

☆☆☆

Check Out The Drugs First

Since you started taking estrogen, you've been getting sudden headaches and gaining some weight. Coincidence or conspiracy? You don't have to wait for Oliver Stone to do a movie about it — the Center for Drug Evaluation and Research does all kinds of research on side effects of prescription drugs, and can answer a whole variety of drug-related questions.

They are also the ones who make sure drug companies follow guidelines for warning labels. They can provide you with information on types of medications, such as estrogen, as well as send you the package insert for specific medications.

For more information, contact Center for Drug Evaluation and Research, Food and Drug Administration, 5600 Fishers Lane, HFD210, Rockville, MD 20857; 800-532-4440; or online at <http://www.fda.gov>.

Free Hospital Care

Those annoying people from the collection agency won't leave you alone, even though you've told them a thousand times you don't have any money to pay for that gallbladder operation you had last year.

You might be able to get them off your back without having to pay a cent, simply by calling the Hill-Burton Hotline. Under this program, certain hospitals and other health care facilities provide free or low-cost medical care to patients who cannot afford to pay. You may qualify even if your income is up to double the Poverty Income Guidelines. You can apply before or after you receive care, and even after the bill has been sent to a collection agency.

Call the Hotline to find out if you meet the eligibility requirements and to request a list of local hospitals who are participating. For more information, contact Hill-Burton Hotline, Health Resources and Services Administration, 5600 Fishers Lane, Room 747, Rockville, MD 20857; 800-638-0742; 800-492-0359 (in MD); or online at <http://www.hrsa.dhhs.gov>.

Health Stats

A majority of older adults rated their health as good, reported no problems in every day living, and are living longer than ever before. And only 1% of people admit cheating on their taxes. Just goes to show you make statistics say anything you want.

But if you are a statistics junkie who needs his fix, call up the National Center for Health Statistics and ask for the report, Access to Health Care: Older Adults. You will be the hit of the next cocktail party. Or you'll be the first one shown to the door.

For a catalog of reports or more information, contact National Center for Health Statistics, 6525 Belcrest Rd., Hyattsville, MD 20782; 301-436-8500; or online at <http://www.cdc.gov/nchswww/nchshome.htm>.

Get Free Medical Care

Each year over 150,000 patients receive free medical care by some of the best doctors in the world. Many are older patients suffering from common conditions, like Alzheimer's, cataracts, and heart disease.

Medical researchers get millions of dollars each year to study the latest causes, cures, and treatments to these diseases. If your condition is being studied somewhere, you might qualify for what is called a "clinical trial" and get treatment for free.

There are several ways to find out about ongoing clinical trials across the nation. Your first call should be to the National Institutes of Health (NIH) Clinical Center. NIH is the federal government's focal point for health research and is the largest biomedical research organization in the world. The 300 acre NIH campus houses research laboratories, offices and the Warren Grant Magnuson Clinical Center.

Approximately 9,000 patients are admitted each year to the Clinical Center. Another 85,000 outpatients visit the ambulatory care 13-story clinic adjacent to the hospital. Your doctor should contact the Patient Referral Line to find out if your disease is being studied, and to be put in contact with the primary investigator who can then tell if you meet the requirements for the study.

An information brochure is available describing the Clinical Center programs. For more information, contact Clinical Center, National Institutes of Health, Building 10, Room 1C255, 10 Center Dr., MSC 1170, Bethesda, MD 20892-1170; 301-496-4891.

☆☆☆

Your Medical Library

Want the latest medical research for your condition? What about doing a literature search? The National Library of Medicine is the world's largest medical research library, containing more than 4.5 million journals, technical reports, books, photographs, audiovisual materials covering hundreds of biomedical areas and related subjects.

References to journal articles can be retrieved quickly through MEDLINE. These computerized databases include hospital and health care literature, toxicology information, medical ethics information, cancer literature, and more.

You can learn about accessing MEDLINE, and receive a listing of regional medical libraries by contacting National Library of Medicine, 8600 Rockville Pike, Bethesda, MD 20894; 800-272-4787; or online at <http://www.nlm.nih.gov>.

☆☆☆

Free Care From Those Getting The Money

If you don't trust your doctor about what he or she says about your arteries, you can conduct your own medical research. You can even learn who's being awarded research grants to study your health condition, simply by requesting a CRISP (Computer Retrieval for Information on Scientific Projects) search to be done by the Division of Research Grants.

The search can provide you with information on grants awarded by the National Institutes of Health, Food and Drug Administration, and other government research institutions, universities, or hospitals that deal with the topic in which you are interested. In some cases, the researchers may be looking for people willing to take part in clinical trials.

To learn how to request a search, contact Office of Extramural Research (NIH), 6701 Rockledge Dr., Rockledge Bldg. #2, MSC 7772, Bethesda, MD 20814-7772; 301-435-0656; or online at <http://www.nih.gov> (go to grants and contracts).

Rehab Assistance

You hope it never gets to that point, but recovering from a stroke is a long struggle, including those who care for stroke victims. The National Rehabilitation Information Center provides information covering all types of physical and mental disabilities.

For example, do you need to find a special kind of wheelchair or communication board? What about handrails for the bathroom? The Center can conduct a search of their database to learn about research, journal articles, and more dealing with your topic of interest.

To learn more about the information and assistance this Center can provide, contact National Rehabilitation Information Center, Suite 935, 8455 Colesville Rd., Silver Spring, MD 20910; 301-588-9284; 800-346-2742.

☆☆☆

New Cancer Cure?

Ever seen a shark with cancer? You probably never wanted to get close enough to find out. Well, it's so rare that researchers have begun looking into what sharks have that we don't, and they think they may have found it — in the sharks' cartilage. In a Cuban study, a number of cancer patients who received shark cartilage treatments showed significant improvement.

But before you spend $115 on a bottle of shark cartilage pills, contact the National Cancer Institute. They'll send you a series of articles on this controversial treatment to help you better decide if it's for you. Contact: National Cancer Institute, Bldg. 31, Room 10A16, 31 Center Dr., NSC 2580, Bethesda, MD 20892; 1-800-4-CANCER; or online at <http://www.nci.nih. gov>.

Prostate Cancer Treatment

The numbers aren't encouraging. Prostate cancer is on the rise, and more than 80% of cases occur in men over the age of 65.

But listen to the promising news: there's a new test to detect prostate cancer earlier, which could mean more lives will be saved. The test is called the Prostate-specific antigen test, or PSA. Right now, the government is sponsoring clinical trials at ten locations across the country to test how effective the PSA screening test is in men between the ages of 60 and 74.

If you're interested in participating in this free research project, call the National Cancer Institute's toll-free hotline at 1-800-4-CANCER; or online at <http://www.nci. nih.gov>.

Quit Lighting Up

You can lower your risk of developing osteoporosis, having a heart attack, getting pneumonia, and setting your bed on fire. And earn $750 in savings to take a trip to the Bahamas. All you have to do is stop smoking for a year.

But you're probably wondering if it's really worth it after smoking for so long. It is, according to the Office on Smoking and Health. They collect and distribute information on the health risks associated with smoking and secondhand smoke, as well as material on smoking cessation methods:

- *Don't Let Another Year Go Up In Smoke: Quit Tips*
- *Good News For Smokers 50 and Older: It's Never too Late to Quit!*
- *Out of the Ashes: Choosing a Method to Quit Smoking*
- *Office on Smoking and Health's Information Resources*
- *Significant Developments Related to Smoking and Health*

The Office also has a fax service where they will fax you these and other articles. For a publications list or more information, contact Office on Smoking and Health, Centers for Disease Control, 4770 Buford Hwy., NE, Mail Stop K-12, Atlanta, GA 30341; 770-488-5705; 800-CDC-1311 (publications and fax service); or online at <http://www.cdc.gov/tobacco>.

☆☆☆

Denied Again?

Did your insurance company claim a medical treatment was experimental or unnecessary, so they denied your claim? Have you been denied coverage, but you feel you qualify?

Contact your state's Insurance Commissioner. They handle complaints involving insurance policies, including premiums, deductibles, claims, or anything else related to your insurance coverage. They will review your complaint, and if they find that your insurance company has acted in an unlawful or unethical way, they have the power to force the insurance dealer to compensate you or correct whatever mistake they have made.

To locate your state Insurance Commissioner, look in the Directory of State Information at the end of this book.

☆☆☆

Can't Pay Your Premium?

For most elderly, Medicare takes care of a majority of their health care bills, but there is still the deductible and the Medicare Part B premium.

Many states have developed programs to provide coverage for low income elderly. Usually called Qualified Medicare Beneficiary Program, these programs provide benefits to individuals who do not qualify for Medicaid, but cannot afford some of the expenses of Medicare.

Most programs cover the premiums and annual deductible for Medicare Part B, plus the payment of co-insurance and deductible amounts for the services of Medicare.

To learn if your state has such a program, contact your state Department on Aging, located in the Directory of State Information at the end of this book.

☆☆☆

Travel Cheap

Now it's time to head out on the highway and look for some adventure. You probably have a few ideas of where you would like to go, but Uncle Sam can offer some valuable advice. Here you might find new ideas for your vacations that you might never hear from your travel agent.

☆☆☆

All Aboard For 15% Discounts

Traveling by train can make getting somewhere a lot more fun. We all know how adventurous AMTRAK can be at times — sit back and view the countryside, and if you are 62 or older you can save 15% on the lowest available fare to wherever you want to go.

By calling their toll-free hotline, AMTRAK will send you a free travel planner which offers travel tips and services, as well as a listing of their special vacation packages. Contact AMTRAK, 60 Massachusetts Ave., NW, Washington, DC 20002; 800-USA-RAIL.

☆☆☆

Hiking and Swimming Resorts

Whoever thought that spending time on property owned and operated by the U.S. Army could be fun? Boot camp for seniors? Far from it. For some strange reason, the Army owns thousands of square miles of some of the best recreational areas in the country, with picnic areas, swimming beaches, hiking trails, boating, canoeing, fishing, ice fishing, hunting, and snowmobiling.

For a list of recreational areas, contact U.S. Army Corps of Engineers, Directorate of Civil Works, Natural Resources Management Branch, CECW-ON, 20 Massachusetts Ave., NW, Washington, DC 20314; 202-761-0247; or online at <http://www.hg.usace.army.mil>.

What Your Travel Agent Won't Tell You About Foreign Travel

Wouldn't it have been nice if someone had told you before you went to Rome that you should not have kept your money and your wallet together in your purse? Who knew that those little kids didn't really want to take your picture in front of St. Peter's but wanted your money instead?

This is just one piece of free advice you can read about in *Travel Tips for Seniors*, a free publication containing basic information on insurance, medication, travel warnings, and passports. And if you are unfortunate enough to run into problems overseas, the pamphlet also includes information on the kinds of assistance you can expect from U.S. embassies and consulates around the world.

For your copy, contact Overseas Citizens Services, U.S. Department of State, 2201 C St., NW, Room 4800, Washington, DC 20520; 202-647-5225; or online at <http://travel.state.gov>.

George Washington Slept Here (Really)

Some people dream of seeing a baseball game in every major league city. For some reason (and we won't ask), you want to sleep in every bed George Washington slept in. To get some help in plotting out your specific itinerary, contact the Advisory Council on Historic Places.

They will send you a free list of State Historic Preservation Officers who will no doubt know where George and all of his friends liked to hang out. They can also tell you about other historic and archeological sites in other states that you might want to check out.

Contact Advisory Council on Historic Preservation, 1100 Pennsylvania Ave., NW, Suite 809, Washington, DC 20004, 202-606-8503; or online at <http://www. achp.gov>.

Hello Mrs. Jones ... You've Just Won A Free Vacation

Many older people are especially vulnerable to the lure of cheap vacation offers. Before you sign up to take a cross-country flight for a free weekend in Las Vegas, you can get some free advice from a lawyer who specializes in dealing with travel schemes. Some of these opportunities really are too good to be true.

The Federal Trade Commission will send you this advice in a free pamphlet, *Telemarketing Travel Fraud*. It will provide you with information and tips to help prevent you from being taken by swindlers who are interested in only one thing — your money. Contact Public Reference, Room 130, Federal Trade Commission, Washington, DC 20580; 202-326-2222; or online at <http://www.ftc.gov>.

☆☆☆

Meaningful Memories For Vets

Commemorating the 50th anniversary of World War II can turn an overseas vacation into a meaningful experience. World War II veterans and their families can honor their friends and family by visiting military burial grounds on foreign soil. The American Battle Monuments Commission maintains cemeteries around the world where 124,921 U.S. war dead are interred.

Each year the Commission publishes attractive, free pamphlets which highlight individual memorials, and include locations, site descriptions and photographs, brief histories of the battles in which the deceased fought, and directions from the nearest major airports. Free issues covering specific memorials are available.

For more information, contact American Battle Monuments Commission, 2300 Clarendon Blvd., Suite 500, Arlington, VA 22201; 703-696-6897.

☆☆☆

Free Passports For Families Of Vets

It's hard to believe that a passport can cost up to $75, but did you know that you can get it free of charge if you are a member of a family visiting an overseas grave site of a veteran? So when you are planning your next trip to Paris, keep dear Uncle Harry in Normandy in mind.

Eligibility for these free passports includes widows, parents, children, sisters, brothers, and guardians of the deceased who are buried or commemorated in permanent American military cemeteries on foreign soil.

For additional information, write to the American Battle Monuments Commission, 2300 Clarendon Blvd., Suite 500, Arlington, VA 22201; 703-696-6897.

Enjoy The Outdoors

$10 will get you Yellowstone, Yosemite, and Mount Ranier. That's not bad considering that the U.S. Government paid $100 and three rabbit pelts for all of them!

Well, actually the $10 will get you the Golden Age Passport, which is a lifetime entrance pass to those national parks, monuments, historic sites, recreation areas, and national wildlife refuges. It entitles you to a 50% discount on fees for facilities and services, such as camping, swimming, parking, boat launching, and cave tours. The Federal Recreation Passport Program booklet describes the various passes to the parks which are available.

The National Parks Service (NPS) preserves historical, natural, and recreational areas of national significance. You can enjoy talks, tours, films, exhibits, publications, and other interpretive media about the parks.

The National Parks Service also operates campgrounds and other visitor facilities at the parks. Reservations can be made through MISTIX 800-365-2267. The NPS provides many publications about the various parks. They also have a map and guide which shows you the locations of the parks throughout the U.S. and the facilities each park offers.

For a complete catalog of free or for sale publications, contact the National Park Service, Office of Information, P.O. Box 37127, Washington, DC 20013; 202-208-4747; or online at <http://www. nps.gov>.

⭐⭐⭐

Buffalo and Cattle Refuges

Maybe you hated watching Buffalo play in the Super Bowl, but you'll love them at the National Wildlife Reserve. And if buffalo don't do it for you, then there are plenty of Texas longhorn cattle, as well as deer and elk who will gladly pose for pictures.

Wichita Mountains in Oklahoma and Fort Niobrara in Nebraska preserve these animals in their natural habitat. For more information, contact Fort Niobrara National Wildlife Refuge, Hidden Timber Route, HC 14,

Box 67, Valentine, NE 69201; or 402-376-3789. Wichita Mountains Wildlife Refuge, Rt. 1, Box 448, Indiahoma, OK 73552; 405-429-3221. Another resource is National Bison Range, Moise, MT 59824; 406-644-2211.

Hotline to 10,000 "Rooms"

Maybe you don't need marble bathrooms or a king-size bed, or even room service for you to call it a vacation. All you need is a place to pull in for the night.

You can call the Forest Service toll-free hotline to make a reservation at one of the 156 National Forests, where you can hike, fish, camp, ski, or just relax on over 100,000 miles of trails and 10,000 recreation sites. Call the toll-free number to make reservations for any of the National Forests at 800-280-CAMP; or online at <http://www.fs.fed.us>.

See Uncle Sam's Buffalo Herds Free

Land Between the Lakes offers recreation for tourists on over 300 miles of undeveloped shoreline. Three primary campgrounds offer over 1,000 sites and numerous informal shoreline campgrounds.

Land Between the Lakes also boasts their own resident buffalo herd — the largest publicly-owned herd east of the Mississippi River.

For more information on recreation opportunities, contact Land Between the Lakes, Resource and Development, Tennessee Valley Authority, 100 Van Morgan Dr., Golden Pond, KY 42211; 502-924-2000; or online at <http://www. lbl.org>.

Have Them Pay Your Ticket

Did you know that the government will pay you $50 a day to teach kids in Tanzania to throw a shot putt, or $100 a day to talk about women's rights in Bangladesh? And that includes round-trip airfare.

If you have had a unique American experience or hold a particular expertise, you can join the likes of Sandra Day O'Connor, Sally Ride, and

John Updike who are just a few of those who have taken part in the U.S Speakers Program. You will get a chance to meet with government officials, journalists, labor leaders, students, entrepreneurs, and anyone who wants to know more about the United States.

Every year about 600 Americans are sent overseas for short-term speaking programs. If selected, you could be eligible to receive $100 a day, plus expenses. A U.S. Speaker's tour generally includes informal lectures or discussions, followed by questions and answers with a small group of experts.

No, you cannot teach golf in Paris. This program is for bonafide experts in a field. For more information, contact U.S. Speakers Program, U.S. Information Agency, 301 4th St., SW, Washington, DC 20547; 202-619-4764.

☆☆☆

Camping On Uncle Sam's Land

The Recreation Guide to Bureau of Land Management (BLM) Public Lands features a map outlining all of the public lands used as recreational areas. Designations on the map include campgrounds, visitors centers, national wild and scenic rivers, national wilderness areas, and national historic and scenic trails.

Contact Office of Public Affairs, Bureau of Land Management, U.S. Department of the Interior, 18th and C Sts., NW, Washington, DC 20240; 202-452-5125; or online at <http://www.blm.gov>.

☆☆☆

Powwow With The Experts

You want to dance with some wolves? Maybe you would just settle for looking at ancient Indian artifacts in a glass case? The Bureau of Indian Affairs runs three museums full of all kinds of Indian folk art. They'll send you free pamphlets and brochures about their respective programs and exhibition activities.

Contact the museums directly at Southern Plains Indian Museum, P.O. Box 749, Anadarko, OK 73005; 405-247-6221; Museum of the Plains Indian, P.O. Box 400, Browning, MT 59417; 406-338-2230; or Sioux Indian Museum, P.O. Box 1504, Rapid City, SD 57709; 605-348-0557.

See A Million Dollars

Do you want to know how to make a million dollars a day? Literally. Take a free self-guided tour at the Bureau of Engraving and Printing, which features actual money being made, cut, and counted.

Although the armed guards discourage sampling the goods, you can still enjoy yourself by buying uncut sheets of currency, engraved prints, small bags of shredded currency, and other neat stuff.

For more information, contact the Bureau of Engraving and Printing, U.S. Department of Treasury, 14th and C Sts., SW, Washington, DC 20228; 202-874-3019; or online at <http://www.dep.treas. gov>.

See Your Congressman Actually Work

You can now go to Washington, DC to see all your favorite T.V. stars — Sonny Bono, Gopher from Love Boat, and even Fred Thompson from the Tom Clancy movies.

The U.S. House of Representatives meets in the House Chamber in the south wing of the Capitol. You can be seated in the side and rear galleries while these well known personalities discuss cutting your benefits and increasing their salaries.

Seats are available to those who secure passes from their Representative on a first come, first serve basis: one helpful hint might be that rotten vegetables will not set off the metal detectors. Contact your member of Congress, U.S. House of Representatives, Washington, DC 20515; 202-224-3121; or online at <http://www. house.gov>.

Get Your Own VIP White House Tour

Don't stand in that long line out back of the White House waiting to see Hillary's china pattern, or Bill's jogging shoes. Do what the insiders do: call your member of Congress and join the special VIP tours that are held every Tuesday through Saturday from 10 a.m. to 12 noon, unless the White House is closed for some official function. Who knows? You might even see Newt Gingrich's mother waiting in line with you.

You can get free passes that allow you to tour the White House earlier in the day to avoid the crowds, but you need to get these special passes from your member of Congress (call well in advance of your scheduled trip to Washington).

To learn about the White House tours contact, White House, 1600 Pennsylvania Ave., NW, Washington, DC 20500; 202-456-1414. Contact your Senator or Representative, The Capitol, Washington, DC 20515; 202-224-3121; or online at <http://www.whitehouse.gov>.

Music At The Capitol

If listening to five hours of debate over Social Security cuts isn't music to your ears, then you might want to check out the American Festival/Concerts at the Capitol performed by the National Symphony during the spring and summer months.

The Armed Service bands and choral groups of the Air Force, Army, Marine Corps, and Navy provide summer nighttime entertainment in public concerts. Concerts are free, seating is on the lawn, and picnics are in order. Contact Architect's Office, Room SB-15, U.S. Capitol Bldg., Washington, DC 20515; 202-228-1793.

A Hotline For Your Cool Boat

Against your children's better advice, you sold the house, and bought a cabin cruiser. Before you go tearing around the harbor terrorizing the locals, you'd better find out if you need a license to drive that thing, or maybe even learn the difference between starboard and starfish.

The Boating Safety Hotline can provide you with information on such topics of interest to boaters as safety recalls, publications, Coast Guard department contacts and addresses, public education courses, and free Coast Guard services. A free consumer information packet is available. The hotline also takes consumer complaints about safety defects and violations.

Contact Boating Safety Hotline, Consumer and Regulatory Affairs Branch (G-NAB-5), Office of National Safety and Waterways Services, U.S. Coast Guard, 2100 2nd St., SW, Room 1109, Washington, DC 20593;

800-368-5647; or online at <http://www.dot. gov/dotinfo/uscg/>.

Is A Cheap Vacation In Haiti Worth Two Years In Jail?

The next time your travel agent calls with a cheap two weeks on some island in the Caribbean, first call the Overseas Citizens Service and make sure that the current political situation on that island won't turn your two weeks on the beach into two years behind bars. Believe it or not, some people in this world actually don't like Americans.

This office can provide financial and medical assistance when necessary, foreign visa and entry requirements, and they even issue travel warnings for countries where travel may be dangerous.

For more information, contact Overseas Citizens Services, Bureau of Consular Affairs, 2201 C St., NW, Room 4800, Washington, DC 20520; 202-647-5225; or online at <http://travel.state.gov>.

Know Before You Go

Before you get any big ideas about bringing back five boxes of cigars from Havana or 10 cases of vodka from Russia to sell to your friends, check it out first with the U.S. Customs Service. They can tell you how much duty you will have to pay, so you will know how much profit you can make from your scheme.

They can also tell you about the items that they will confiscate, quarantine, or even let you bring in free. For more information, contact Public Information Office, U.S. Customs Service, U.S. Department of the Treasury, P.O. Box 7407, Washington, DC 20044; 202-927-6724; or online at <http://www.customs.ustreas.gov>.

Check Out The Plants

You never thought it would come to this, but you actually like watching the grass grow. The government knew this all along and that is why the Botanic Garden is open to the public from 9 a.m. to 9 p.m. daily, June through August, and from 9 a.m. to 5 p.m. the rest of the year.

Of course, if you want to watch other things grow, that's okay too — they grow all kinds of plants that you and your green thumb have probably managed to kill over the years. They may even be able to give you some tips on how to spruce up your own yard.

Contact Public Programs Office, U.S. Botanic Garden, 245 1st St., SW, Washington, DC 20024; 202-226-4082.

Picture Perfect Passports

If you are unclear about whether you need a passport to go to Mexico or if you need a vaccine to go to Nigeria, then contact Passport Services. You will hear a recorded message which explains the documents you need and application process for obtaining a passport, as well as reporting the loss or theft of your passport.

It explains how to get any reports of a birth or death of any U.S. citizen who is in another country. You will also be directed to the proper agencies for information regarding naturalization, travel warnings, customs regulations, and shots required by various countries.

For more information, contact Passport Services, Bureau of Consular Affairs, U.S. Department of State, 2201 C St., NW, Room 5813, Washington, DC 20520; 202-647-0518; or online at <http://travel.state.gov/passport_services.html>.

☆☆☆

Do You Have Your Shots?

Chances are that contracting an infectious disease like malaria, typhoid, or the plague isn't the point of that exotic vacation you're planning. If it is, you can skip this item, but for the rest of you who are going to be traveling outside the U.S., you might be interested in finding out about any disease outbreaks in the countries you will be visiting, along with any vaccine requirements you'll need to follow.

The Centers for Disease Control's Voice Information System allows anyone using a touchtone phone to get pre-recorded information on

International Travelers' Health issues. The system can also transfer you to a public health professional if you need additional information.

The system is available 24 hours a day, although the health professionals are available Monday through Friday, 8 a.m. until 4:30 p.m. Contact Centers for Disease Control at 888-232-3228; or online at <http://www.cdc.gov>.

☆☆☆

Hotlines For Some Hot Places

Before you plan your dream vacation to Arkansas to see Bill Clinton's birthplace, call the hotline listed below to learn about all kinds of special senior discounts for your hotel, restaurant, or theaters.

If you are scouting out destinations, or planning a visit to a particular city, each state's Travel and Tourism Office can be a great help. They can send you all kinds of maps, brochures, and other valuable information. If you want to know where to find hotels, motels, or restaurants, cafes, diners, movie theaters, supermarkets, drug stores or even churches, this is the place to start. They can even tell you if there are special discounts or programs for seniors.

Other information from state tourism offices might include highway conditions, weather advice, local hotel/motel rates, and the best places to eat. In general, each state will provide information packages containing a travel guide, a calendar of events, state maps, and brochures from private, state, and regional tourist attractions.

State Tourism Offices

ALABAMA
334-242-4169
800-ALABAMA
http://www.touralabama.org/

ALASKA
907-465-2012
http://www.commerce.state.ak.us

AMERICAN SAMOA
684-633-1091-2-3

ARIZONA
602-230-7733
800-824-8257

http://www.arizonaguide.com

ARKANSAS
501-682-1088
800-NATURAL
http://www.ono.com/arkansas

CALIFORNIA
916-322-2881
800-TO-CALIF
http://gocalif.ca.gov

COLORADO
303-592-5510
800-COLORADO

CONNECTICUT
800-CT-BOUND
http://www.state.ct.us/tourism. htm

DELAWARE
800-441-8846
302-739-4271
http://www.de.state.us

DISTRICT OF COLUMBIA
202-789-7000
http://www.washington.org

FLORIDA
904-488-5607
888-735-2872
http://www.fla.us.com

GEORGIA
404-656-3553
800-VISIT-GA
http://www.georgiaonmymind. com

GUAM
671-66-5278-79
800-US3-GUAM

HAWAII
808-586-2550
http://www.gohawaii.com

IDAHO
208-334-2470
800-635-7820
http://www.visitid.org

ILLINOIS
312-814-4732
800-226-6632
http://www.enjoyillinois.com

INDIANA
317-232-8860
800-824-8376
http://www.indianatourism.com

IOWA
515-242-4705
800-345-4692

http://www.state.ia.us/tourism

KANSAS
913-296-2009
800-2KANSAS
http://www.kansascommerce.com

KENTUCKY
502-564-4930
800-225-TRIP
http://www.state.ky.us./tour/
tour.htm

LOUISIANA
504-568-6968
800-33-GUMBO
http://www.louisianatravel.com

MAINE
207-289-5710
800-533-9595

MARIANAS
670-234-8327

MARYLAND
410-767-6277
800-543-1036
http://www.mdisfun.org

MASSACHUSETTS
617-727-3201
800-447-MASS
http://www.mass_travel.com

MICHIGAN
517-373-0670
800-543-2937
http://www.michigan.org

MINNESOTA
612-296-2755
800-657-3700
http://www.exploreminnesota. com

MISSISSIPPI
800-WARMEST
601-359-3297
http://www.mississippi.org

MISSOURI
573-751-4133
800-877-1234

MONTANA
406-444-2654
800-VISIT-MT
http://travel.mt.gov/

NEBRASKA
402-471-3794
800-228-4307
http://www.ded.state.ne.us/tourism

NEVADA
702-687-4322
800-NEVADA8

NEW HAMPSHIRE
603-271-2665
800-FUNINNH
http://www.visitnh.gov

NEW JERSEY
609-292-6963
800-JERSEY7
http://www.state.nj.us

NEW MEXICO
800-545-2040
505-827-7400
http://www.newmexico.org/

NEW YORK
518-474-4116
800-CALL-NYS
http://iloveny.state.ny.us

NORTH CAROLINA
919-733-4171
800-VISIT-NC
http://www.visitnc.com

NORTH DAKOTA
800-437-2077
701-328-2525
http://www.ndtourism.com

OHIO
614-466-8844
800-BUCKEYE
http://www.ohiotourism.com

OKLAHOMA
405-521-3981
800-652-6552
http://www.otrd.state.ok.us/

OREGON
800-547-7842
http://www.traveloregon.com

PENNSYLVANIA
717-787-5453
800-VISIT-PA
http://www.state.pa.us

PUERTO RICO
89-721-1576-2402
800-866-STAR
http://www.discoverpr.com

RHODE ISLAND
800-845-2000
401-277-2601
http://www.visitrhodeisland.com

SOUTH CAROLINA
803-734-0122
800-364-3634
http://www.prt.state.sc.us/sc

SOUTH DAKOTA
800-SDAKOTA
605-773-3301
http://www.state.sd.us

TENNESSEE
615-741-2158

TEXAS
512-462-9191
800-8888-TEX
http://www.traveltex.com

UTAH
801-538-1030
800-200-1160
http://www.utah.com

VERMONT
802-828-3236
800-VERMONT
http://www.vermont.com

VIRGINIA
804-786-2051
800-VISITVA
http://www.virginia.org

VIRGIN ISLANDS
809-774-8784
800-372-8784

WASHINGTON
360-753-5600
800-544-1800
http://www.tourism.wa.gov

WEST VIRGINIA
304-558-2286
800-CALL-WVA
http://www.state.wv.us/tourism

WISCONSIN
608-266-2345
800-432-TRIP
http://www.landsend.com

WYOMING
307-777-7777
800-225-5996
http://www.state.wy.us/ commerce/
tourism/index.htm

Help With Your Retirement Fund & Pension Questions

Y ou gave your notice at the office, and now it is time to kick back and relax. Let Uncle Sam offer some assistance for those nagging financial questions that you might have. You can learn how to check on your retirement, pension, taxes, and more. All you need to do is pick up your phone and call.

Little-Known Tax Tidbits

Did you know that the IRS considers you 65 on the day before your 65th birthday? Why? I don't know, but you qualify for some added tax bonuses when you hit that magic number. It could be the only time you are actually happy to turn a year older!

Trying to fill out those simple tax forms each year can sometimes be a frustrating experience. The Internal Revenue Service has several different options to make things go a little smoother for you.

Do you need to file? Can you use the 1040EZ? Want to know how to figure out the donations you gave to your church?

The Information Line provides answers to all your tax questions, and can assist you in completing your income tax return. They can also refer your call to tax specialists for answers to your more detailed tax questions. You can also listen to pre-recorded answers on over 140 frequently asked tax questions on the Tele-Tax Line.

For more information on your taxes, contact Internal Revenue Service, U.S. Department of the Treasury, 1111 Constitution Ave., NW, Washington, DC 20224; 800-829-1040 Information Line; 800-829-3676 Forms Line; 800-829-4477 Tele-Tax Line; or online at <http://www.irs. gov>.

Learn How to Prepare Tax Forms

Are you the kind of person who has to see it before you believe it? The Internal Revenue Service distributes films and videos on a variety of tax topics.

For example, "A Vital Service" aims at enlisting groups and organizations into the Volunteer Income Tax Assistance Program in which IRS trains volunteers to help the low-income, elderly, non-English speaking, and the handicapped complete their tax returns.

This video is available from Audio/Visual Branch, Public Affairs Division, IRS, U.S. Department of the Treasury, 1111 Constitution Ave., NW, Washington, DC 20224; 202-622-7541; or online at <http://www.irs.gov>.

☆☆☆

Get Your Taxes Done For Free

But, don't worry, these guys from the IRS don't charge by the minute. And what's great about this group is that they go where they are needed — to nursing homes, community centers, and even to your home if you can't get out.

The program is called, Tax Counseling for the Elderly, and offers free tax help to people who are 60 years and older. Many of the volunteers are retired and are affiliated with nonprofit groups, so it's basically a nice group of people willing to lend a hand to others in completing those "simple" tax forms that are oftentimes not so simple to fill out.

The IRS Information Line can refer you to the closest program, so call 800-829-1040; or online at <http://www.irs.gov>.

☆☆☆

Special Tax Help For Seniors

The tax guys thought only of you when they wrote *Tax Information For Older Americans* (Pub. 554). It answers all those specific tax questions about your filing status, retirement benefits, life insurance proceeds, and more. It will even help you keep most of what you made (up to a point anyway) on the sale of your house if you meet certain requirements.

The IRS Forms Line distributes all of the IRS tax forms and instruction books. Some of the forms dealing with elderly concerns include:

- *Tax Information on Selling Your Home* (pub. 523)
- *Credit for the Elderly or Disabled* (pub. 524)
- *Comprehensive Tax Guide to U.S. Service Retirement Benefit* (pub. 721)
- *Pension and Annuity Income* (pub. 575)
- *Tax Information for Handicapped and Disabled Individuals* (pub. 907)

- *Social Security Benefits and Equivalent Railroad Retirement Benefits* (pub. 915)
- *Medical and Dental Expenses* (pub. 502).

For your copies, contact the IRS Forms Line at 800-829-3676; or online at <http://www.irs.gov>.

☆☆☆

A List of Little-Known Tax Deductions

We all feel like we pay, and we pay, and we pay. Now here is someone who is looking out for your needs for a change. If you are a senior citizen or know someone who is, it is important to get a copy of a free publication titled, *Protecting Older Americans Against Overpayment of Income Taxes*.

Designed to ensure that older Americans claim every legitimate income tax deduction, exemption, and tax credit, this publication is very easy to understand and provides many examples and checklists. It is updated annually in January and includes a section on income tax items which will change in the following year.

For your free copy, contact Special Committee on Aging, U.S. Senate, SDG 31, Washington DC 20410; 202-224-5364; or online at <http://www. senate.gov/committee/aging.html>.

☆☆☆

Has Your Check Arrived?

Think you're not getting ahead? Think again. You're better off now than those folks who retired 30 years ago. The median income for married couples is now $23,817, and that's a 79% increase, even with an adjustment for inflation.

Today 92% of seniors receive Social Security which was designed to replace a portion of the income a person loses when they retire, die, or become disabled with monthly benefits based upon a worker's earnings. In August of 1992, the average check was for $630.

Social Security has established a hotline to answer all your questions. You can learn how to get a duplicate Social Security card, change your address, and even learn how much you would earn each month if you retired today.

153

It actually is very important to get a copy of your Personal Earnings and Benefits statement each year. The statement is free and records your income for each year from which your future benefits will be determined. Contact Social Security Hotline at 800-772-1213; or online at <http://www. ssa.gov>.

Up to $5000 To Help You Pay Your Bills

If your check is too small to live on, don't be discouraged. If you don't qualify for Social Security, or if your benefits are very low, you may qualify for Supplement Security Income (SSI).

This program was established to help poor seniors over 65 and the blind and disabled meet basic living needs. To qualify you must meet a maximum monthly income test.

Some of the income and services you receive are excluded when they calculate your monthly income in relation to your personal expenses. Those who meet SSI's eligibility usually automatically qualify for Medicaid coverage and Food Stamps benefits.

Studies have found that only between 40 percent and 60 percent of seniors poor enough to qualify for SSI actually receive benefits under the program. To find out if you qualify, contact your local Social Security office or call the Social Security Hotline at 800-772-1213; or online at <http://www.ssa.gov>.

Your Pension Watchdogs

There are a lot of pensions to watch as they grow or even lose value, as over 50 million workers and retirees are covered by employer-sponsored pension plans. In fact, 19% of all income for seniors comes from private and government employee pensions.

Most private plan participants are covered under a defined-benefit plan, which generally bases the benefit paid in retirement either on the employee's length of service or on a combination of his or her pay and length of service.

The Pension Benefit Guaranty Corporation (PBGC) keeps an eye on these different benefit plans and takes over those that are underfunded.

They have several free publications concerning this issue to help you look out for your best interests.

Employer's Pension Guide provides a general overview of the responsibilities under federal law of employers who sponsor single-employer defined benefit pension plans.

Your Guaranteed Pension answers some of the most frequently asked questions.

Your Pension: Things You Should Know About Your Pension Plan serves as an explanation of pension plans: what they are, how they operate, and the rights and options of participants.

For more information, contact Public Affairs, Pension Benefit Guaranty Corporation, 1200 K St., NW, Washington, DC 20005; 202-326-4000; or online at <http://www.pbgc.gov>.

☆☆☆

For Those Who Served Our Country

Military veterans are entitled to retirement pay after 20 years of service. In 1990, 1.6 million retirees and survivors received military retirement benefits. There are actually three types of benefits provided by the military: standard retirement benefits, disability retirement benefits, and survivor benefits.

Service members who retire from active duty receive monthly payments based on a percentage of their final monthly base pay being received at the time of retirement. Base pay comprises 65-70 percent of total pay and allowances. The formula used to compute benefits varies depending upon when you entered the service, length of service, and age at retirement.

Full benefits begin immediately upon retirement; the average retiring enlisted member begins drawing benefits at 43; the average officer at 46. Benefits continue until the death of the participant. The Military Survivor Benefit Plan allows a military retiree to have a portion of his or her retired pay withheld to provide a benefit to his/her survivors.

Veterans may also be eligible for support if they have limited income when they have 90 days or more of active military service. They must be permanently and totally disabled for reasons not due to the military.

To learn more about the retirement plans, contact the U.S. Department of Veterans Affairs, 810 Vermont Ave., NW, Washington, DC

20420; 800-827-1000; or online at <http://www.va.gov>.

✮✮✮

I've Been Working On The Railroad

For all those engineers, conductors, linesmen, and caboose riders, the Railroad Retirement System is the one responsible for managing the retirement system. It covers all railroad firms and distributes retirement and disability benefits to employees, their spouses, and survivors.

Workers must amass 120 months of employment to qualify for a pension. In some cases, military service may be counted as railroad service. The average annuity paid in 1996 was $1,565.

The Board has several fact sheets including a booklet titled *Railroad Retirement and Survivor Benefits*, which explains who qualifies, how to apply, and more. For more information, contact Railroad Retirement Board, 844 North Rush St., Chicago, IL 60611; 312-751-4500; or online at <http://www.rrb.gov>.

✮✮✮

For Those Employees Of The Big Guy

Uncle Sam takes care of those dutiful bureaucrats through the Federal Employees Retirement System (FERS). FERS is comprised of three parts: a defined-benefit plan, Social Security, and a Thrift Savings Plan.

In the defined-benefit plan, workers earn 1% of the average of their highest three consecutive years of wages for each year of service completed. You also contribute to Social Security. The Thrift Savings Plan (TSP) is similar to the 401(k) plans used by private employers. Sound complicated? It's not, once you do your required reading.

To learn more specific details about the plan and retirement information, contact Federal Employees Retirement System, Office of Personnel Management, 1900 E St., NW, Washington, DC 20415; 202-606-0490; or online at <http://www.opm.gov>.

How To Check Up on Your Pension

It's a good idea to check its pulse, blood pressure, and heart rate. You want to make sure your pension is around longer than you are.

The Pension and Welfare Benefits Administration can help you do that. They require administrators of private pension and welfare plans to provide plan participants with easily understandable summaries of plans; to file those summaries with the agency; and to report annually on the financial operation of the plans.

Free publications include: *What You Should Know About The Pension Law*, which gives a summary of what is required of pension plans, and *How To File A Claim For Your Benefit*, which explains what you need to do to receive your benefit.

Contact Public Information, Pension and Welfare Benefits Administration, U.S. Department of Labor, 200 Constitution Ave., NW, Room N5656, Washington, DC 20210; 202-219-8921; or online at <http://www.dol.gov/dol/pwba>.

☆☆☆

Keeping An Eye On Your Pension Money

Sure, the Pension Benefit Guaranty Corporation (PBGC) says they will cover the pension plans that are underfunded, but what if several of the big ones collapse at the same time? Would they all be protected? A General Accounting Office (GAO) report showed that no one would get their check.

What if your company offers you a lump-sum retirement? A GAO report looks at several of these offers and examines the pros and cons.

Some titles of the GAO reports focusing on income security issues include:

- *Financial Audit: Pension Benefit Guaranty Corporation's 1992 and 1991 Financial Statements* (GAO/AIMDD 93-21)
- *Lump-Sum Retirements* (GAO/GGD 93-2R)
- *Pension Plans: Hidden Liabilities Increase Claims Against Government Insurance Program* (GAO/HRD 93-7)
- *Pension Plans: Labor Should Not Ignore Some Small Plans That Report Violations* (GAO/HRD 93-45)
- *Pension Restoration Act* (GAO/HRD 93-7R)
- *Private Pensions: Protections for Retirees' Insurance Annuities*

Can Be Strengthened (GAO/HRD 93-29)
- *Underfunded State and Local Pension Plans* (GAO/HRD 93-9R)

All reports are free and can be requested by contacting U.S. General Accounting Office, P.O. Box 6015, Gaithersburg, MD 20884; 202-512-6000; or online at <http://www.gao.gov>.

Free Prescription Drugs

Millions of older Americans are going without needed medications, even though they could be getting them for free. Why? Many do not have adequate insurance, and they understandably think that is the end of the story.

An American Association of Retired Persons (AARP) report even found that about 8 million Americans over 45 now say that they have to cut back on necessary items such as food or fuel to pay for their medications. Of the top 20 most widely prescribed drugs taken by older Americans, most do not have lower-priced generic substitutes.

The average prescription price is about $20. In fact, if an older person with an average income of $8,700 took just 10 prescriptions a year, and had no insurance coverage, that individual would spend 27% of his/her income ($2,400/$8,781) on prescription drugs.

Discount Drug Program

Help could be just a phone call away. Ten states have special drug programs that give huge discounts to seniors who are ineligible for Medicaid and who don't have private insurance. For example, seniors in New Jersey can get their prescriptions for only $5, and in Maine they can get them for as little as $2.

Often all it takes is a phone call and filling out a simple form. You will have to meet income eligibility, but you can make upwards of $23,000 a year and still be eligible in New York, for example. If your state is not listed below, contact your state Department of Aging listed in the Directory of State Information in the back of this book, but also check out the free drug programs sponsored by the drug manufacturers themselves. You will find a detailed description of this program following the listing of the state-by-state drug programs.

CONNECTICUT
Conn PACE
P.O. Box 5011
Hartford, CT 06102
800-423-5026 (in CT)
860-832-9265

Eligibility Requirements:
- You must be 65 years old or older, or those who receive Social Security disability.
- You must have lived in Connecticut for six months.
- Your income cannot exceed $13,800 if you are single, and $16,600 if you are married.
- You may not have an insurance plan that pays for all or a portion of each prescription, a deductible insurance plan that includes prescriptions, or Medicaid.

Cost:
- You pay a $25 one time registration fee.
- You pay $12 for each prescription.
- You must get generic drugs whenever possible, unless the doctor writes on the prescription, brand drug only.

DELAWARE
Nemours Health Clinic
915 N. Dupont Blvd.
Milford, DE 1963
302-424-5420
800-763-9326

Eligibility Requirements:
- You must be a Delaware resident.
- You must be a U.S. citizen.
- You must be 65 or older.
- Income requirements for single $11,900; for married $16,300.

Cost:
- You must pay 20% of the prescription drug cost.

ILLINOIS
Pharmaceutical Assistance Program
Illinois Department of Revenue
P.O. Box 19021
Springfield, IL 62794
800-624-2459
217-785-7100

Eligibility Requirements:
- You must be 65 years of age or older, or over 16 and totally disabled, or a widow or widower who turned 63 before spouse's death.
- You must be a resident of Illinois.
- Your income must be less than $14,000.
- You must file a Circuit Breaker claim form.

160

Cost:
- Pharmaceutical Assistance card will cost either $40 or $80, depending upon your income.
- Your monthly deductible will be $15 if the cost of your card is $40, and $25 if the cost of your card is $80.
- You must choose the generic brand when available, unless you are willing to pay the difference in price.

MAINE
Elderly Low-Cost Drug Program
Bureau of Taxation
State Office Building
Augusta, ME 04333-0024
207-626-8475

Eligibility requirements:
- You must be a Maine resident.
- You may not be receiving SSI payments.
- You must be at least 62 years old or part of a household where one person is 62 years old.
- Your income may not exceed $10,300 if you live alone; $12,700 if you are married or have dependents.

Cost:
- Each drug will cost $2 or 20% of the price allowed by the Department of Human Services, whichever is greater.

MARYLAND
Maryland Pharmacy Assistance Program
P.O. Box 386
Baltimore, MD 21203-0386
410-767-5397
800-492-1974

Eligibility:
- For anyone in the state who cannot afford their medications. Income requirements vary, so it is best to call.
- Permanent resident of Maryland

NEW JERSEY
Pharmaceutical Assistance to the Aged and Disabled (PAAD)
Special Benefit Programs
CN 715
Trenton, NJ 08625
800-792-9745
609-588-7049

Eligibility:
- You must be a New Jersey resident.
- Your income must be less than $17,500 if you are single, or less than $21,519 if you are married.
- You must be at least 65 years of age.
- Drugs purchased outside the state of New Jersey are not covered, nor any pharmaceutical product whose manufacturer has not agreed to provide rebates to the state of New Jersey.

Cost:
- You pay $5 for each covered prescription. PAAD collects payments made on your behalf from any other assistance program, insurance, or retirement benefits which may cover prescription drugs.

NEW YORK
Elderly Pharmaceutical Insurance Coverage EPIC
P.O. Box 15018
Albany, NY 12212
800-332-3742
518-452-6828

Eligibility Requirements:
- You must be 65 or older.
- You must reside in New York State.
- Your income must not exceed $18,000 if you are single; or $23,700 if you are married.
- You are not eligible if you receive Medicaid benefits.

Cost:
- You pay between $3-$23 per prescription depending upon the prescription cost.
- There are two plans for EPIC. You can pay an annual fee depending upon your income to qualify right away. The annual fee ranges from $20 to over $75, which can be paid in installments. The EPIC Deductible plan is that you pay no fee, but you pay full price for your prescriptions until you spend the deductible amount. The deductible amount also varies by income and starts at $468.

PENNSYLVANIA
PACE Card
(Pennsylvania Pharmaceutical Assistance Contract For The Elderly)
Pennsylvania Department of Aging
P.O. Box 8806
400 Market St., 6th Floor
Harrisburg, PA 17101-2301

717-787-7313
800-225-7223

Eligibility Requirements:
- You must be 65 or older.
- Your income cannot exceed $14,000 if you are single; $17,200 for married couples.
- You must also live in the state for at least 90 days.
- PACE NET program has higher income eligibility requirements and you must also meet the $500 prescription deductible.

Cost:
- You pay an $8.00 co-payment for each prescription. You may not purchase drugs out of state.
- PACE limits drug amounts to no more than a 30-day supply or 100 pills. There are no vacation supplies allowed.

RHODE ISLAND
Rhode Island Pharmaceutical Assistance to the Elderly (RIPAE)
Rhode Island Department of Elderly Affairs
160 Pine St.
Providence, RI 02903
401-277-3330

Eligibility Requirements:
- You must be a Rhode Island resident.
- You must be 65 years old.
- Your income must not exceed $15,042 if you are single; $18,804 if you are married.
- You cannot have any other prescription drug coverage.

Cost:
- Members pay 40% of the cost of prescription drugs used to treat certain illnesses.

VERMONT
VScript program
Department of Social Welfare
Medicaid Division
103 South Main St.
Waterbury, VT 05671
802-241-3971
800-529-4060

Eligibility Requirements:
- You must be a resident of Vermont.
- You must be at least 65.

- You may not have income in excess of 175% of the federal poverty guidelines.
- You may not be in a health insurance plan that pays for all or a portion of the applicant's prescription drugs.

Cost:
- There will be a co-payment requirement. The amount will be a percentage of the charge for a drug, with the percentage amount determined at the beginning of each fiscal year.

☆☆☆

Free Medications Directly From Drug Companies

Valium, Prozac, Dilantin, Insulin — these are just a few of the medications you can get FREE directly from the drug companies themselves.

That's right: drug companies don't want everybody to know this, but they will give certain people who can't afford their medications their drugs free of charge. I guess they don't want to tarnish their greedy bad guys image by publishing these benevolent programs.

So, what's the catch? It sounds too easy. All that many of these companies require for you to participate in these "indigent patient programs" is that your doctor write them a note stating that you cannot afford the drugs that you need. Your doctor is the one that needs to make the call.

Once the forms are filled out, you will be able to pick your drugs up directly from your doctor's office for free. Your doctor can call the toll-free Pharmaceutical Manufacturers Association (PMA) hotline to get more information about individual manufacturer indigent patient programs.

Call 800-PMA-INFO, or you can write Pharmaceutical Manufacturers Association, 1100 15th St., NW, Washington, DC 20005, or the Special Committee on Aging, U.S. Senate, SD-G31, Washington, DC 20510; 202-224-5364; or online at <http://www.senate.gov/~aging>.

Directory of Pharmaceutical
Manufacturers Programs

Allergan Prescription Pharmaceuticals

Contact: Allergan Patient Assistance Program, Physician Services, Mailstop #T1-2G, 2525 Dupont Drive, Irvine, CA 92612, 800-347-4500, ext. 7791. Drugs covered are: Betagan, Epifrin, Pilagan, Propine, OTC, Alphagan. Eligibility is determined at the physician's discretion. If there are one or two people in the house, their income should be under $12,000; three or more, they should make under $19,000. Their glaucoma medicine should not be covered by any other insurance, partially or completely. The time limitation is six months.

Alza Pharmaceuticals

Contact: Indigent Patient Assistance Program, Attn: Sales Service Dept. M6, ALZA Pharmaceuticals, P.O. Box 10950, Palo Alto, CA 94303-0802, 415-962-4297. Drugs covered are: Testoderm, Ocusert, Progestasert. Eligibility is determined by ALZA Pharmaceuticals based on patient household annual income. Patients must be ineligible for any other third-party reimbursement or support program.

Amgen, Inc.

Contact: Amgen Safety Net Programs, Medical Technology Hotlines, 1-800-272-9376 (202-637-6698 in Washington, D.C.). Drugs covered are: Epogen, Neupogen. For patients on dialysis only. Amgen's SAFETY NET Program for Epogen and Neupogen is designed to assist those patients who are medically indigent. Eligibility is based on patient's insurance status and income level. The program is based on a 12 month patient year rather than on a calendar year.

Astra Merck, Inc.

Contact: Patient Assistance Program, Astra Merck Information Center, 800-236-9933. Drugs covered are: Plendil, Prilosec, Tonocard. Health care provider must apply on behalf of a patient who has a medical need and a financial hardship that would prevent the patient from filling their prescription. Astra Merck's Patient Assistance Program is available to patients who do not have insurance reimbursement for prescriptions, are not eligible for governmental assistance programs (e.g., Medicaid), or who do not have other means to pay for their medication. The time limitation is three months.

Astra USA, Inc.

Contact: FOSCAVIR Assistance and Information on Reimbursement Program, State and Federal Associates, 1101 King St., Alexandria, VA 22314; 800-488-3247, 703-683-2239. Drugs covered are: Foscavir. If patient is not covered for outpatient prescription drugs under private insurance or a public program, patient's income must fall below level selected by the company. Patient may or may not be poor, but retail drug purchase would cause hardship. If patient is covered for outpatient prescription drugs, he or she may be eligible for assistance with deductibles or maximum benefit limits. Eligibility is determined by the company based on income information provided by the physician.

Athena Neurosciences

Contact: Indigent Patient Program, Athena Neurosciences, Inc., 800 Gateway Blvd., South San Francisco, CA 94080. Drugs covered are: Permax. The patient must be a resident of the United States, have a net worth of less than $30,000 and no third-party prescription drug coverage. The time limitation is three months.

Bayer Corporation, Inc

Contact: Bayer Indigent Patient Program, 400 Morgan Lane, West Haven, CT 06516, 800-998-9180. Drugs covered are: Adalat, ANA, Biltricide, Chlo-Amine, Cipro, Cort Dome Suppositories, Domepaste, DTIC Dome, Mezlin, Mithracin, MRV, Mycelex, Nimotop, Pollen Extract, Precose, Stilphostrol, Tridesilon, Venomil. Patient must be a U.S. resident. Physician must certify patient is not eligible for, or covered by, government-funded reimbursement or insurance program for medication; patient is not covered by private insurance; and patient's household income is below federal poverty-level guidelines. Physician must indicate condition for which drug is to be prescribed and certify that drug will be used for indicated use only. Physician must agree to follow patient through therapy. All applications are subject to a case-by-case evaluation by Bayer Corporation.

Berlex

Contact: Berlex Laboratories Cardiovascular Assistance Program, Berlex Laboratories, 800-423-7539. Drugs covered are: Betapace, Quinaglute. Patients must have an adjusted annual gross family income below $20,000 and be ineligible for any public or private health insurance; or have an adjusted family income below $15,000 and be uninsured for prescription drugs. Enrollment forms must be completed by the physician.

Contact: Betaseron Indigent Patient and Support Program, Berlex

Laboratories, 800-788-1467. Drugs covered are: Betaseron. Patients must be uninsured and ineligible for Medicare or Medicaid and have an annual income of less than $50,000. For patients with incomes less than $20,000, Betaseron is provided free of charge.

Contact: Patient Assistance for Cancer Treatment, Berlex Laboratories, 800-473-5832. Drugs covered are: Fludara. The program is designed to provide access to Fludara through injection for uninsured cancer patients with an annual income of less than $25,000 with no dependents or less than $45,000 with dependents. The physician should contact the program with information on the patient.

Boehringer Ingleheim Pharmaceuticals, Inc.

Contact: Partners in Health, P.O. Box 368, Ridgefield, CT 06877-0368, 800-556-8317. Drugs covered are: Alupent, Atrovent, Catapres, Mexitil, Serentil. Eligibility is determined solely by BIPI. Patient must be a U.S. citizen ineligible for prescription assistance through Medicaid or private insurance. Patient must meet established financial criteria. The time limitation is three months.

Bristol-Myers Squibb

Contact: Bristol-Myers Squibb, Patient Assistance Program, P.O. Box 9445, McLean, VA 22102-9998; 800-736-0003; 703-760-0049 (fax). Most Bristol-Myers Squibb Pharmaceutical products are covered by the program. This program is designed to provide temporary assistance to patients with a financial hardship who are not eligible for prescription drug coverage through Medicaid or any other public or private health program. Patients who meet the program's eligibility criteria are provided BMS products free of charge.

DuPont Merck Pharmaceutical Company

Contact: DuPont Merck Pharmaceutical Company Patient Assistance Program, P.O. Box 80723, Wilmington, DE 19880-0723, 800-474-2762. Drugs covered are: Coumadin, Lodosyn, Sinemet, Symmetrel, Trexan, Vaseretic. Eligibility is based on the patient's insurance status and income level/assets. Patients should have exhausted all third-party insurance, Medicaid, Medicare, and all other available programs. The patient must be a resident of the U.S. The time limitation is one month.

Eli Lilly and Company

Contact: Lilly Cares Program Administrator, Eli Lilly and Company, P.O. Box 9105, McLean, VA 22102, 800-545-6962. Most Lilly prescription products and insulins are covered. Eligibility is determined on a case-by-case basis in consultation with each prescribing physician. Eligibility is based on the patient's inability to pay and lack of third-party drug payment assistance, including insurance, Medicaid, government subsidized clinics, and other government, community, or private programs. Inpatients and those who can obtain drug reimbursement from any other source are not eligible. Requests for replacement drugs cannot be honored. Medications are provided directly to the physician for dispensing to the patient. Quantity of supply is dependent upon type of product being prescribed. All Lilly medications must be used as recommended in product labeling.

Contact: Gemzar Patient Assistance Program, 888-443-6927. Drugs covered are: Gemzar. Applications for the program are available by calling the toll-free Gemzar Hotline. Applicants who are determined to be eligible based on program income criteria will be approved on the basis of these additional criteria: no medical insurance, and ineligible for any programs with a drug benefit provision, including Medicaid; third-party insurance, Medicare, and all other programs have been denied coverage for Gemzar in writing, and all appeals have been exhausted.

Fujisawa USA, Inc.

Contact: Susan Lindsey, 847-317-8874, or Beth McNamara, 847-317-8617. Drugs covered are: NebuPent. This program is designed to provide NebuPent (pentamidine isethionate) to AIDS patients who could not otherwise afford this treatment. All requests for consideration must be written by a physician and should include the patient's medical, financial, and insurance information.

Contact: Prograf Patient Assistance Program, c/o Medical Technology Hotline, P.O. Box 7710, Washington, DC 20044-7710, 800-4-PROGAF, 800-477-6472, or 202-393-5563 in the Washington, DC area. Drugs covered are: Prograf capsules. The purpose of this program is to help improve access to oral Prograf for patients who have no health insurance for Prograf and limited financial resources. To be eligible for this program, patients must meet income and insurance requirements set by Fujisawa USA.

Gilead Sciences, Inc.

Contact: Gilead Sciences Support Services, 800-GILEAD, or 713-760-0049 (fax). Drugs covered are: VISTIDE. This program is designed to assist both insured and uninsured patients in receiving reimbursement for VISTIDE. To determine eligibility for this program, physicians or patients may request a Patient Assistance Program application for VISTIDE and mail or fax the completed form to Gilead Sciences Support Services.

Glaxo Wellcome Inc.

Contact: Glaxo Wellcome Inc., Patient Assistance Program, P.O. Box 52185, Phoenix, AZ 85072-2185; 800-722-9294 or 800-750-9832 (fax). All marketed Glaxo Wellcome prescription products are covered. The Patient Assistance Program is intended to serve patients who do not have or qualify for private insurance or government-funded programs, and is not intended to supplant or replace government sponsored programs. The program is designed as an interim solution to assist financially disadvantaged individuals until alternative funding can be found. Income eligibility is based on the U.S. poverty level adjusted for household size. The Patient Assistance Program is dedicated to providing patients and their providers with information or guidance in finding alternative reimbursement venues for needed medicines. The provision of free medication is a philanthropic activity of Glaxo Wellcome, and therefore, the Patient Assistance Program is considered the payer of last resort. The time limitation is 90 days.

Hoechst Marion Roussel, Inc.

Contact: Indigent Patient Program, Hoechst Marion Roussel, Inc., P.O. Box 9950, Kansas City, MO 64134-0950, 800-221-4025. Most prescription medications are covered by this program. Eligibility is determined by the physician based on patient's income level and lack of insurance. Physicians are encouraged to participate in the spirit of this partnership by also providing their services free of charge. The intent of the program is to provide access to products for patients who fall below the federal poverty level and have no other means of health care coverage. The program is restricted to indigent patients.

Immunex Corporation

Contact: Professional Services Immunex Corporation, 800-466-8639 or 202-587-0430. Drugs covered are: Leukine. Physician must attest that the patient requires the drug and that all reimbursement options have been tried. The time limitation is three cycles.

Janssen Pharmaceutical

Contact: Janssen Patient Assistance Program. 1800 Robert Fulton Drive, Reston, VA 22091-4346; 800-544-2987. Drugs covered are: Duragesic, Ergamisol, Hismanal, Imodium, Nizoral, Propulsid, Sporanox, Vermox. The products offered in this program are offered free of charge to persons who meet specific medical criteria and lack financial resources and third-party insurance necessary to obtain treatment. Reimbursement specialists determine eligibility for each patient. Janssen requests physicians not charge patients for professional services. The time limitation is one or two months' supply; varies by product.

Contact: Janssen Cares, The Risperdal Patient Assistance Program, 4828 Parkway Plaza Blvd., Suite 120, Charlotte, NC 28217-1969, 800-652-6227, 704-357-0036 (fax). Drugs covered are: Risperdal. The program will ensure that this product is available free of charge to any persons who meet specific medical criteria and lack financial resources and third-party insurance necessary to obtain treatment. Reimbursement specialists determine eligibility for each patient. Janssen requests physicians not charge patients for professional services. The Risperdal Reimbursement Support Program is designed to answer physicians' and patients' questions and solve problems related to Risperdal reimbursement as efficiently and quickly as possible.

Knoll Pharmaceutical Company

Contact: Knoll Indigent Patient Program, Knoll Pharmaceutical Company, Telemarketing, 3000 Continental Drive, North, Mount Olive, NJ 07828-1234. Drugs covered are: Isoptin, Rythmol, Collagenase Santyl, Synthroid. Physician must submit appropriate documentation proving patient indigence to company. The time limitation is three months.

The Liposome Company, Inc.

Contact: Financial Assistance Program for ABELCET, 800-335-5476. Drugs covered are: ABELCET. Patients must be uninsured and not eligible to receive reimbursement through any other third-party drug reimbursement program, such as Medicaid, local or federal agency programs, Blue Cross/Blue Shield, private insurance programs and private foundations, and unable to pay for the product out-of-pocket. Eligibility is determined by The Liposome Company based on medical and financial information provided on behalf of the patient by the hospital or physician.

McNeil Pharmaceutical

Contact: Ortho-McNeil Patient Assistance Program, One Phoenix Drive, Lincoln Park, NJ 07035, 800-281-5192. Drugs covered include most McNeil Pharmaceutical products. Patient should not have insurance coverage for prescription medications. Patient's income must fall below the federal poverty level and retail purchase would cause hardship.

Merck Human Health

Contact: Allergan Patient Assistance Program, 800-994-2111. Most Merck products with the exception of vaccines and injectibles are covered.

Anti-cancer injectibles are available. The program is designed to provide temporary assistance to patients who have no access to insurance coverage for prescription medications and are truly unable to afford prescription medications. The patient must have exhausted all options for prescription benefits and coverage including private insurance, HMOs, Medicaid, Medicare, state pharmacy assistance programs, Veterans Assistance, and any other Social Services agency support. Completed applications are reviewed on a case by case basis. The time limitation is three months.

Contact: Support, 800-850-3430. Drugs covered are: Crixivan. This program assists patients who are uncertain of their insurance coverage in locating payment sources for Crixivan. It is designed for uninsured patients who qualify and for whom no alternative source of coverage can be identified. All patients are reviewed on a case by case basis.

Novartis Pharmaceuticals

Contact: Patient Support Program, Jackie Laguardia, P.O. Box 9764, McLean, VA 22102-9764, 888-455-6655. Drugs covered are: Actigall, Anafranil, Anturane, Apresazide, Apresoline, Aredia, Brethaire, Brethine, Cataflam, Cytadren, Desferal, Esdrix, Estraderm, Habitrol, Ismelin, Lamprene, Lioresal, Lopressor, Lotensin, Lotrel, Ludiomil, Metriprone, Vivelle, PBZ, Rimactane, Ser-Ap-Es, Slow-K, Tegretol, Tofranil, Transderm, Voltaren. The patient should not be covered for outpatient prescription drugs under private insurance or a public program. Patient should be financially unable to afford the cost of the medication. This program will provide temporary assistance while the patient seeks alternative sources of payment.

Ortho Biotech, Inc.

Contact: The Ortho Biotech FAP (Financial Assistance Program) Program, 1800 Robert Fulton Drive, Suite 300, Reston, VA 22091-4345; 800-553-3851. Drugs covered are Procrit, Leustatin. Program will ensure that Procrit and Leustatin are made available free of charge to any persons who meet specific medical criteria and lack financial resources or third-party insurance necessary to obtain treatment. A reimbursement specialist determines eligibility for a patient. Ortho Biotech requests that physicians not charge FAP patients for professional services.

Ortho Pharmaceutical Corporation

Contact: Ortho-McNeil Patient Assistance Program, One Phoenix Drive, Lincoln Park, NJ 07035, 800-281-5192. Most Ortho products are covered. Patient should not have insurance coverage for prescription medications. Patient's income must fall below the federal poverty level and retail purchase would cause hardship.

Parke Davis

Contact: Parke Davis Patient Assistance Program, P.O. Box 1058, Somerville, NJ 08876, 908-725-1247. Drugs covered are: Acupril, Cognex, Loestrin, Neurontin, Zarontin. Patients must not be eligible for other sources of drug coverage and must be deemed financially eligible based on company guidelines and physician certification. The time limitation is three months.

Pasteur Merieux Connaught

Contact: Indigent Patient Program, Customer Account Manager, Pasteur Merieux Connaught, Route 611, P.O. Box 187, Swiftwater, PA 18370, 800-822-2463. Drugs covered are: Imovax, Imogam, TheraCys, BCG. Eligibility is determined on a case by case basis and limited to those individuals who have been identified as indigent, uninsured and ineligible for Medicare and Medicaid. Physician must waive all fees and certify that the product will not be sold, traded, or used for any other purpose but to treat mentioned patient.

Pfizer Inc.

Contact: Pfizer Prescription Assistance, P.O. Box 25457, Alexandria, VA 22313, 800-646-4455. Most Pfizer outpatient products with chronic indications are covered by this program. Difucan and Zithromax are covered by a separate program. Any patient that a physician is treating as indigent is eligible. Patients must have incomes below $12,000 (single) or $15,000 (family). Patients must not be eligible for or be receiving third-party or Medicaid reimbursements for their medications. No copayment or cost-sharing is required by the patient.

Contact: Diflucan and Zithromax Patient Assistance Program; 800-869-9979. Drugs covered are: Diflucan, Zithromax. Patient must not have insurance or other third party coverage, including Medicaid, and must not be eligible for a state AIDS drug assistance program. Patient must have an income of less than $25,000 a year without dependents, or less than $40,000 a year with dependents.

Contact: Sharing the Care, Pfizer Inc., 235 E. 42nd St., New York, NY 10017-5755; 800-984-1500. Certain Pfizer single-source products are covered. The program is a joint effort of Pfizer, the National Governors' Association, and the National Association of Community Health Centers. It works solely through community, migrant, and homeless health centers that are certified by the federal government as meeting criteria for Section 330, 329, or 340 of the Public Health Service Act, and that have an in-house pharmacy. The program includes the participation of approximately 330 health centers throughout the United States. To be eligible to participate, the patient must be registered at a participating health center, must not be covered by any public or private insurance covering pharmaceuticals, must not be Medicaid-enrolled, and must have a family income that is equal to or below the federal poverty level. Pfizer reserves the right to limit enrollment and health centers.

Contact: Arkansas Health Care Access Program, 800-984-1500. All Pfizer products are covered. Must be an Arkansas state resident to qualify. Eligible individuals are certified by the Arkansas Local County Department of Human Services as being Arkansas residents below the federal poverty guidelines, who do not have federal health insurance benefits and do not qualify for any government entitlement programs. No copayment or cost-sharing is required by the patient. Physician must waive his or her fee for the initial visit. This program does not apply to individuals during hospital inpatient stays.

Contact: Kentucky Health Care Access Program, Mr. Keith Knapp, Executive Vice President, Kentucky Health Care Access Foundation, 12700 Shelbyville Rd., Suite 1000, Louisville, KY 40243, 800-633-8100, 502-244-4214. All Pfizer products are covered. Must be a Kentucky resident to qualify. Eligible individuals are certified by the Kentucky Cabinet for Human Resources as Kentuckians below the federal poverty standards, who do not have health insurance benefits and do not qualify for any government entitlement programs. No copayment or cost-sharing is required by the patient. Physician must waive his or her fee. This program does not apply to individuals during hospital inpatient stays.

Contact: Commun-I-Care, Ms. Parker Sparrow, Director, Commun-I-Care, P.O. Box 12054, Columbia, SC 29211, 800-763-0059, 803-254-0320. All Pfizer products are covered. Eligible individuals must be South Carolina residents. Individuals are certified by Commun-I-Care as below the federal poverty line and not covered by any government entitlement programs. No copayment or cost-sharing is required by the patient. Physician must waive his or her fee. This program does not apply to individuals during hospital inpatient stays.

Pharmacia and Upjohn

Contact: Pharmacia and Upjohn Prescription Medication Assistance Program, Pharmacia and Upjohn RXMap, P.O. Box 29043, Phoenix, AZ 85038, 800-242-7014 for self-administered drugs. Contact Pharmacia and Upjohn RXMap, P.O. Box 9525, McLean, VA 22102, 800-366-5570 for non-self-administered drugs. Pharmacia and Upjohn products are covered.

This program was developed to provide Pharmacia and Upjohn prescription drug therapy to eligible patients who have special needs during a short term financial hardship. A patient may be eligible for this program if he or she is a resident of the United States, has special needs due to a short term financial hardship, has no prescription coverage under any other plans, and has sought or is seeking assistance through other funding sources.

Procter & Gamble Pharmaceuticals Inc.

Contact: Procter & Gamble Pharmaceuticals, Inc., P.O. Box 231, Norwich, NY 13815, 800-448-4878. Drugs covered are: Asacol, Dantrium Capsules, Didronel, Macrodantin, Macrobid. To qualify, patients should not have insurance coverage for prescriptions or be eligible for Medicaid reimbursements. The intent of the program is to ensure access to products for patients who fall below the federal poverty level and have no other means of health coverage. Each patient's case is handled strictly on an individual basis. The company relies on the physician's assessment of need to determine eligibility. Application forms are provided by the company for the physician to complete. An original prescription duly signed by the attending physician for one of the company's products is required.

Rhone-Poulenc Rorer Inc.

Contact: Rhone Poulenc Rorer Indigent Access Program, Medical Affairs/Indigent Access Program, Rhone-Poulenc Rorer Inc., P.O. Box 5094, 500 Arcola Rd., Mailstop #4C29, Collegeville, PA 07110, 610-454-8110. All products are included, with some limitations. This program is administered on a case-by-case basis. A patient is eligible to apply to the program if there is a medical and financial need for assistance as identified by a physician, social agent or agency, and if the effort to obtain assistance from all third-party payers, Medicaid, Medicare, and all other local, state or federal government support has been exhausted. The physician is requested to fill out a form provided by RPR and to send the completed form along with a valid prescription to the program.

R&D Laboratories

Contact: Patient Support Program, R&D Laboratories, Inc., 4094 Glencoe Avenue, Marina del Rey, CA 90292; 800-338-9066. Most products are covered. Eligibility is decided by physician or health care provider.

Roche Laboratories

Contact: Roche Medical Needs Program, Daria Lemongello, Senior Program Coordinator, Medical Services, Roche Laboratories, 340 Kingsland St., Nutley, NJ 07110, 800-285-4484. Drugs covered are: Roche and former Syntex product line with some exceptions. Physicians make the determination. Those eligible are private practice outpatients who are considered to be medically eligible and who are not eligible to receive Roche drugs through any other third-party drug reimbursement program, Medicaid, local or federal agency programs, Blue Cross/Blue Shield, private insurance programs, and private foundations. Inpatients and those who can obtain drug reimbursement from other sources are not eligible.

Roxane Laboratories, Inc.

Contact: Patient Assistance Program, 1101 King St., Suite 600, Alexandria, VA 22314, 800-274-8651. Drugs covered are: Marinol, Oramorph, Roxanol, Roxicodone, Viramune. Product will be provided free of charge to patients through their physician or pharmacist, provided the patient is uninsured and meets annual income requirements. Physicians must call on behalf of the patient.

Sandoz Pharmaceuticals

Contact: Sandoz Patient Assistance Program, National Organization for Rare Disorders, P.O. Box 8923, New Fairfield, CT 06812, 800-999-6673. Drugs covered are: Clozaril, Neoral, Sandimmune, Sandogobulin, Sandostatin, Parlodel. Eligibility is determined by financial need based on information provided by applicant. This program will provide temporary assistance while the patient seeks alternative sources of payment.

Sanofi Winthrop Pharmaceuticals

Contact: Sanofi Winthrop Pharmaceuticals, Needy Patient Program, Product Information Department, 90 Park Avenue, New York, NY 10016; 800-446-6267. Drugs covered are: Aralen, Breonesin, Bronkometer, Danocrine, Drisdol, Hytakerol, Isuprel, Mytelase, NegGram, pHisoHex, Plaquenil, Primaquine, Photofrin, Trancopal. Eligibility is determined on a case by case basis. The time limitation is six months to a year.

Schering Laboratories/Key Pharmaceuticals

Contact: For Intron A/Eulexin Products: 800-521-7157. For other products: Schering Laboratories/Key Pharmaceuticals, Patient Assistance Program, P.O. Box 52122, Phoenix, AZ, 85072, 800-656-9485. Drugs covered are: Diprolene, Diprosone, Fulvicin, Lotrimin, Lotrisone, Normodyne, Optimine, Proventil, Trinalin, Vancenase. The program is designed to assist those patients who are truly in need and are not eligible for private or public insurance reimbursement and cannot afford treatment. Patient eligibility is determined on a case-by-case basis based on economic and insurance criteria. Physician must call on behalf of the patient. Social Worker can call and give the company the patient information but the Physician and patient have to fill out the application form.

Searle

Contact: Searle Patients in Need Foundation, 5200 Old Orchard Rd., Skokie, IL 60077; 800-542-2526; 847-470-6633 (fax) or Local Searle Sales Representative. Drugs covered are: Aldactazide, Aldactone, Calan, Kerlone, Calan, Norpace, Cytotec, Quinolone, Maxaquin. The physician determines a patient's eligibility for the program based on medical and economic need. Searle provides guidelines for physicians to consider, but they are not requirements. The guidelines suggest that: patient suffers from conditions for which a Searle product in the Patients in Need program may be appropriate; patient does not qualify for outpatient prescription drugs under private insurance, a public program, or other assistance that pays in whole or in part for prescription drugs; patient's income falls below a level suggested by Searle. Searle does not review documentation for eligibility. Physicians must call to obtain a certificate for patient.

Serono Laboratories, Inc.

Contact: Serono Laboratories' Helping Hand Program, Gina Cella, Director, Corporate Communications, Serono Laboratories, Inc., 100 Longwater Circle, Norwell, MA 02061, 617-982-9000, 617-982-1369 (fax). Drugs covered are: Metrodin, Fertinex. Patients are eligible if they are not covered for outpatient prescription drugs under private insurance or a public program. Eligibility is determined by the physician based on company guidelines.

Contact: Patient Assistance Program, Gina Cella, Director, Corporate Communications, Serono Laboratories, Inc., 100 Longwater Circle, Norwell, MA 02061, 617-982-1369. Drugs covered are Serostim. Physicians must call on behalf of patient.

SmithKline Beecham Pharmaceuticals

Contact: Access to Care Program, SmithKline Beecham, One Franklin Plaza-FP1320, Philadelphia, PA 19101, 800-546-0420. Drugs covered are: Amoxil, Bactroban, Compazine, Dexedrine, Dibenzyline, Dyazide, Dycill, Famvir, Menest, Monocid, Omni, Ornade, Relafen, Ridaura, Stelazine, Tagamet, Timentin. Patient's annual household income must be less than $25,000. Patient must have no medical insurance and be ineligible for government or private programs that cover the cost of prescription pharmaceuticals. Patient must be a resident of the United States. Individual physicians determine which patients are eligible and would benefit most from the Access to Care Program. Physicians must submit forms to enroll

What Do You Think?

1. How satisfied are you with your recent purchase?
01. ☐ Dissatisfied
02. ☐ Somewhat Dissatisfied
03. ☐ No Opinion
04. ☐ Satisfied
05. ☐ Very Satisfied

2. How likely are you to buy from us again?
01. ☐ Definitely Not
02. ☐ Possibly
03. ☐ No Opinion
04. ☐ Likely
05. ☐ Very Likely

3. In the past 12 months, I have ordered products through the mail:
01. ☐ 0-2 times
02. ☐ 3-5 times
03. ☐ 6-8 times
04. ☐ 9 or more times

4. Recently, I bought the following items through the mail. (Multiple boxes may be checked.)
01. ☐ food
02. ☐ magazines / publications
03. ☐ craft supplies
04. ☐ video tapes
05. ☐ music CD's
06. ☐ computer CD's
07. ☐ books
08. ☐ clothing
09. ☐ collectibles
10. ☐ sports equipment
11. ☐ health products
12. ☐ household items
13. ☐ other (please list)

5. Check the hobbies and interests of you and your spouse. (Multiple boxes may be checked.)

You or Spouse
01. ☐ drawing / painting
02. ☐ needlework
03. ☐ sewing
04. ☐ knitting / crochet
05. ☐ quilting
06. ☐ cross stitch
07. ☐ furniture making
08. ☐ woodworking crafts
09. ☐ other (please list favorites):

10. ☐ workshop / do-it-yourself / home repair
11. ☐ antiques / fine art
12. ☐ other collectibles
13. ☐ other collectibles (please list):

14. ☐ car / auto repair
15. ☐ motorcycles
16. ☐ home video games
17. ☐ computer

6. Please indicate any medical reference books you own.
01. ☐ Mayo Clinic's
02. ☐ American Medical Assoc.'s
03. ☐ Merck's Manual
04. ☐ The Wellness Encyclopedia
05. ☐ Other (please specify)

7. _Please check all that apply to you and your family._ **We have or plan to purchase within the next several months:**
01. ☐ a camcorder
02. ☐ a CD player for music
03. ☐ a VCR
04. ☐ pre-recorded videotapes
05. ☐ a computer (No CD ROM)
06. ☐ a computer (with CD ROM)

If you have or plan to buy a computer, the computer is an....
a. ☐ IBM compatible
b. ☐ Apple/Mac format

8. Please check if you access any of these services with your computer.
01. ☐ Compuserve
02. ☐ Prodigy
03. ☐ America Online
04. ☐ Internet via other service providers

9. Check the topics of the books or videotapes that you buy.
01. ☐ cooking
02. ☐ gardening
03. ☐ do-it-yourself
04. ☐ travel
05. ☐ self-improvement
06. ☐ history
07. ☐ personal finance
08. ☐ science
09. ☐ religious / inspirational
10. ☐ children's
11. ☐ art
12. ☐ nature / outdoors
13. ☐ medical references
14. ☐ health (self-help)
15. ☐ novels
16. ☐ mystery / suspense
17. ☐ nonfiction
18. ☐ other (please list)

10. I am
01. ☐ female   02. ☐ male

11. My age is:
01. ☐ 17 – 22 years
02. ☐ 23 – 28 years
03. ☐ 29 – 34 years
04. ☐ 35 – 40 years
05. ☐ 41 – 46 years
06. ☐ 47 – 52 years
07. ☐ 53 – 58 years
08. ☐ 59 – 64 years
09. ☐ 65 – 70 years
10. ☐ 71 – 80 years
11. ☐ over 80 years

12. What region of the country is your primary residence?
01. ☐ Northeast
02. ☐ Southeast
03. ☐ Northwest
04. ☐ Southwest
05. ☐ Midwest

13. What is the SEX and AGE of children and other adults in your household?

	Male	Female	Age in years
01.	☐	☐	
02.	☐	☐	
03.	☐	☐	
04.	☐	☐	
05.	☐	☐	
06.	☐	☐	
07.	☐	☐	
08.	☐	☐	

14. My education level is:
01. ☐ High school
02. ☐ High school graduate
03. ☐ Graduate / vocational / technical / trade school
04. ☐ Some college
05. ☐ College graduate
06. ☐ Graduate degree
07. ☐ Other (please list)

15. What is your, and your spouse's, employment status?

	You	Spouse
01. Professional	☐	☐
02. Managerial / Administrative	☐	☐
03. Technical / Clerical / Sales	☐	☐
04. Precision production / craft / repair	☐	☐
05. Production / construction / mechanical	☐	☐
06. Agricultural / forestry / fishing	☐	☐
07. Self-employed	☐	☐
08. Homemaker - not employed outside the home	☐	☐
09. Unemployed	☐	☐
10. Retired	☐	☐

16. My annual household income is:
01. ☐ up to $15,000
02. ☐ $15,000 – $25,000
03. ☐ $25,001 – $35,000
04. ☐ $35,001 – $50,000
05. ☐ $50,000 – $75,000
06. ☐ $75,000 – $100,000
07. ☐ over $100,000

Comments?

We often like to talk with our customers, first hand, to hear their opinions. If you are willing to receive a phone call from us, please provide your name and phone number.

_____ (name)

(_____) _____
(area code)   (phone number)

Thank you for your help. Your response will make a difference!

Survey item lists (numbered 18–51)

18. ☐ photography
19. ☐ video making
20. ☐ electronics
21. ☐ investments
22. ☐ personal business
23. ☐ science
24. ☐ travel
25. ☐ cooking
26. ☐ gardening / yard
27. ☐ house plants
28. ☐ decorating
29. ☐ fashion
30. ☐ music
31. ☐ nature / wildlife
32. ☐ health / fitness
33. ☐ hiking / camping
34. ☐ motor boating / sailing
35. ☐ bicycling
36. ☐ golfing
37. ☐ running
38. ☐ tennis
39. ☐ fishing
40. ☐ hunting
41. ☐ shooting
42. ☐ other sports, (please list favorites):
43. ☐ coin / stamp collecting
44. ☐ nonfiction reading
45. ☐ fiction reading
46. ☐ religious / inspirational reading
47. ☐ history
48. ☐ cultural events
49. ☐ current affairs
50. ☐ activities related to your career
51. ☐ other (please list)

FC&A, 103 Clover Green, Peachtree City, GA 30269

L-S(CS)DS-199
Printed in USA

patients in the program. A three month's supply is available at one time.

Contact: AmeriCares Paxil Access to Care Program, 800-729-4544. Drugs covered are: Paxil. When the physician determines that a patient may benefit from Paxil, he may provide them with one AmeriCares Paxil Access to Care certificate along with a prescription for 30 Paxil tablets in such as deemed appropriate. Please note: the physician's signature is required on the coupon verifying that the patient meets eligibility requirements.

Contact: Oncology Access to Care Program Hotline, 800-699-3806. Drugs covered are: Kytril, Hycamtin. Physician must call on behalf of the patient.

Solvay Pharmaceuticals, Inc.

Contact: Patient Assistance Program, Solvay Pharmaceuticals, Inc., c/o Phoenix Marketing Group, One Phoenix Drive, Lincoln Park, NJ 07035, 800-788-9277. Drugs covered are: Cortenema, Creon, Curretab, Dermacort, Dexone, Duphalac, Estratab, Estratest, Lithobid, Lithonate, Lithotabs, Luvox, Orasone, Rowasa. The patient's eligibility is determined on a case-by-case basis in consultation with each prescribing physician and is based on a patient's inability to pay, lack of insurance, and ineligibility for Medicaid. The patient must be a resident of the United States. The physician is enocuraged to waive his or her fee. The free product must be provided to the patient for whom it is requested. Up to three months supply is available at one time.

3M Pharmaceuticals

Contact: Indigent Patient Pharmaceutical Program, Medical Services Department, 275-3E-09, 3M Center, P.O. Box 33275, St. Paul, MN 55133-3275; 800-328-0255, 612-733-6068 (fax). Drugs covered are: Alu-Cap, Alu-Tab, Calcium Disodium Versenate, Disalcid, Maxair, Medihaler, Norflex, Norgesic, Tambocor, Theolair, Urex. Patients whose financial and insurance circumstances prevent them from obtaining 3M Pharmaceuticals drug products considered to be necessary by their physician are eligible. Consideration is on a case-by-case basis.

Wyeth-Ayerst Laboratories

Contact: The Norplant Foundation, P.O. Box 25223, Alexandria, VA 22314; 703-706-5933. Drugs covered are Norplant. Eligibility is determined on a case-by-case basis and limited to individuals who cannot afford the product and who are ineligible for coverage under private and public sector programs. The time limitation is a five-year contraceptive system.

Contact: Wyeth-Ayerst Laboratories Indigent Patient Program, John E. James, Professional Services, IPP, 555 E. Lancaster Ave., St. Davids, PA

19087, 800-568-9938. Drugs covered are: Sectral, Cyclospasmol, Premarin, Isordil, Phenergan, Orudis, Wytensin, Cordarone. Eligibility is limited to individuals who have been identified by their physicians as low income and ineligible for any third-party payment. A limited supply of specific products is provided directly to the physician for dispensing to the patient.

Zeneca Pharmaceuticals

Contact: Patient Assistance Program, Zeneca Pharmaceuticals Foundation, P.O. Box 15197, Wilmington, DE 19850-5197. Drugs covered are: Accolate, Arimidex, Casodex, Kadian, Nolvades, Sorbitrate, Sular, Tenoretic, Tenormin, Zestril, Zestoretic, Zoladex. Determination is made by the company based on income level/assets and absence of outpatient private insurance, third party coverage, or participation in a public program. There is an allowance for short-term compassionate supplies in the case of unique financial circumstances. Physician should call on behalf of the patient.

Alphabetical Listing by Drug

This section identifies the name of medications frequently prescribed for older Americans and the manufacturers of the drugs which are covered under an indigent patient program listed in this directory. If a drug that you take is NOT listed here, it still may be provided under a medication assistance program; it is suggested that your physician call the company to determine if it is covered by an assistance program.

If the manufacturer of a particular drug is not listed in this directory, it is suggested that the patient or physician call the company directly to determine if the company has an indigent patient program. Drug Manufacturer telephone numbers can be found in the Physician's Desk Reference.

Drug/Manufacturer

A

A/T/S/Hoechst Marion
Abelcet/Liposome Company
Accolate/Zeneca
Accutane/Roche Laboratories
Aclovate/Glaxo Wellcome
Actigall/Novartis
Acupril/Parke Davis
Adalat/Bayer Corporation
Adriamycin/Pharmacia and Upjohn
Albuterol/Bristol-Myers Squibb

Aldactazide/Searle
Aldomet/Merck
Alkeran/Glaxo Wellcome
Allegra/Hoechst Marion
Almaryl/Hoechst Marion
Alphagan/Allergan
Altace/Hoechst Marion
Alu-Tab/3M
Alu-Cap/3M
Alupent/Boehringer Ingleheim
Amantadine/Bristol-Myers Squibb
Amicar/Immunex

Amin-Aid/R&D Laboratories
Aminohuppurate/Merck
Amoxil/Smithkline Beecham
Amoxicillin/Bristol-Myers Squibb
Ampicillin/Bristol-Myers Squibb
ANA/Bayer Corporation
Anafranil/Novartis
Anaprox/Roche Laboratories
Ancobon/Roche Laboratories
Antivenin/Merck
Antivert/Pfizer Inc
Anturane/Novartis
Apresazide/Novartis
Apresoline/Novartis
AquaMephyton/Merck
Aralen/Sanofi Winthrop
Aramine/Merck
Aredia/Novartis
Arimidex/Zeneca
Asacol/Procter and Gamble
Atarax/Pfizer Inc
Atenolol/Bristol-Myers Squibb
Atrovent/Boehringer Ingleheim
Attenuvax/Merck
AVC/Hoechst Marion
Azactam/Bristol-Myers Squibb
Azmacort/Rhone-Poulenc Inc

B

Bactrim/Roche Laboratories
Bactroban/Smithkline Beecham
Barotras/Rhone-Poulenc Inc
Beclovent/Glaxo Wellcome
Beconase/Glaxo Wellcome
Bentyl/Hoechst Marion
Benztropine/Bristol-Myers Squibb
Berocca/Roche Laboratories
Betagan/Allergan
Betapace/Berlex
Betaseron/Berlex
Biavax/Merck
BiCNU/Bristol-Myers Squibb
Biltricide/Bayer Corporation

Blenoxane/Bristol-Myers Squibb
Breonesin/Sanofi Winthrop
Brethaire/Novartis
Brethine/Novartis
Bricanyl/Hoechst Marion
Bronkometer/Sanofi Winthrop
Bumex/Roche Laboratories
BuSpar/Bristol-Myers Squibb

C

Calan/Searle
Calci-Chew/R&D Laboratories
Calci-Mix/R&D Laboratories
Calcimar/Rhone-Poulenc Inc
Calcium Disodium Versenate/3m
Calel-D/Rhone-Poulenc Inc
Cantil/Hoechst Marion
Capoten/Bristol-Myers Squibb
Capozide/Bristol-Myers Squibb
Captopril/Bristol-Myers
Carafate/Hoechst Marion
Cardene/Roche Laboratories
Cardizem/Hoechst Marion
Cardura/Pfizer Inc
Casodex/Zeneca
Cataflam/Novartis
Catapres/Boehringer Ingleheim
Caverjject/Pharmacia and Upjohn
Ceclor/Eli Lilly
CeeNU/Bristol-Myers Squibb
Cefaclor/Bristol-Myers Squibb
Cefadroxil/Bristol-Myers Squibb
Cefadyl/Bristol-Myers Squibb
Cefazolln/Bristol-Myers Squibb
Ceftin/Glaxo Wellcome
Cefzil/Bristol-Myers Squibb
CellCept/Roche Laboratories
Cephalexin/Bristol-Myers
Cephulac/Hoechst Marion
Chibroxin/Merck
Chlo-Amine/Bayer Corporation
Cholestyramino/Bristol-Myers
    Squibb

Chronulac/Hoechst Marion
Cimetidine/Bristol-Myers Squibb
Cipro I.V/Bayer Corporation
Claforan/Hoechst Marion
Cleocin/Pharmacia and Upjohn
Clinoril/Merck
Clomid/Hoechst Marion
Cloxacillin/Bristol-Myers Squibb
Clozaril/Novartisd
Cogentin/Merck
Cortosporin/Glaxo Wellcome
Cognex/Parke Davis
Colestid/Pharmacia and Upjohn
Collagenase Santyl/Knoll
Compazine/Smithkline Beecham
Cordarone/Wyeth-Ayherst
  Laboratories
Cort dome Suppositories/Bayer
  Corporation
Cortenama/Solvay
Cortone/Merck
Corvert/Pharmacia and Upjohn
Cosmegen/Merck
Coumadin/DuPont Merck
Cozaar/Merck
Creon/Solvay
Crixivan/Merck
Crystodigin Tablets/Eli Lilly
Cuprimine/Merck
Curretab/Solvay
Cutivate/Glaxo Wellcome
Cyyclobenzebprine/Bristol-
  Myers Squibb
Cyclospasmol/Wyeth-Ayherst
  Laboratories
Cyclospotrin/Novatis
Cytadren/Novartis
Cytotec/Searle
Cytoxan/Bristol-Myers Squibb
Cytovene/Roche Laboratories

D

d-Biotin/R&D Laboratories

Dalmane/Roche Laboratories
Danocrine/Sanofi Winthrop
Dantrium Capsules/Procter
  and Gamble
Daranide/Merck
Daraprim/Glaxo Wellcome
Darvocet/Eli Lilly
Darvon/Eli Lilly
DDAVP/Rhone-Poulenc Inc
Decadron/Merck
Demser/Merck
Depo-Provera/Pharmacia and
  Upjohn
Dermacort/Solvay
Dermatop/Hoechst Marion
Desferal/Novartis
Desyrel/Bristol-Myers Squibb
Dexedrine/Smithkline Beecham
Dexone/Solvay
Diabe Vite/R&D Laboratories
Diabinese/Pfizer Inc
Dialume/Rhone-Poulenc Inc
DiBeta/Hoechst Marion
Dibezyline/Smithkline Beecham
Dicioxacillin/Bristol-Myers Squibb
Didronel/Procter and Gamble
Diflucan/Pfizer Inc
Dilacor/Rhone-Poulenc Inc
Dilantin/Parke Davis
Dipentum/Pharmacia and Upjohn
Diprolen/Schering
  Laboratories/Key
Diprosone/Schering
  Laboratories/Key
Disalcid/3M
Ditropan/Hoechst Marion
Dlltiazem/Bristol-Myers Squibb
Dobutrex/Eli Lilly
Domepaste Bandages/Bayer
  Corporation
Doxyeyellne/Bristol-Myers Squibb
Drisdol/Sanofi Winthrop
DTIC Dome/Bayer Corporation
Duricef/Bristol-Myers Squibb

Duiril/Merck
Duphalac/Solvay
DURAGEXIC/Janssen
Duricef/Bristol-Myers Squibb
Dyazide/Smithkline Beecham
Dycill/Smithkline Beecham
Dynapen/Bristol-Myers Squibb

E

EC-Naprosyn/Roche Laboratories
Edecrin Sodium/Merck
Edecrin/Merck
Efudex/Roche Laboratories
Emete-con/Pfizer Inc
Emgel/Glaxo Wellcome
Epifrin/Allergan
Epivir/Glaxo Wellcome
Epogen/Amgen, Inc
Ergamisol/Janssen
Esdrix/Novartis
Esophotrast/Rhone-Poulenc, Inc
Estrace/Bristol-Myers Squibb
Estraderm/Novartis
Estradiol/Bristol-Myers Squibb
Estratab/Solvay
Etopophos/Bristol-Myers Squibb

F

Famvir/Smithkline Beecham
Feldene/Pfizer Inc
Fertinex/Serono Laboratories, Inc
Flexeril/Merck
Flonase/Glaxo Wellcome
Flovin I.V./McNeil
Floxin Tablets/McNeil
Fludara/Berlex
Fluorouracil/Roche Laboratories
Fosamax/Merck
Foscavir Injection/Astra
Fungizone/Bristol-Myers Squibb
Fulvicin/Schering
    Laboratories/Key

G

Gantanol/Roche Laboratories
Gemfibrozil/Bristol-Myers Squibb
Geocillin/Pfizer Inc
Glipizide/Bristol-Myers Squibb
Glucagon/Eli Lilly
Glucophage/Bristol-Myers Squibb
Glucotrol/Pfizer Inc
Grifulvin V/Ortho

H

Habitrol/Novartis
Halcion/Pharmacia and Upjohn
Haldol Decanoate/McNeil
Halotestin/Pharmacia and Upjohn
Heparin Sodium/Eli Lilly
Hiprex/Hoechst Marion
Hismanal/Janssen
Hivid/Roche Laboratories
HP Achta/Rhone-Poulenc Inc
Humalog/Eli Lilly
Humatrope/Eli Lilly
Humorsol/Merck
Humulin/Eli Lilly
Hycamtin/Smithkline Beecham
Hydrea/Bristol-Myers Squibb
Hydrocortone/Merck
Hydroxychlorquine/Bristol-
    Myers Squibb
Hygroton/Rhone-Poulenc Inc
Hytakerol/Sanofi Winthrop
Hyzaar/Merck

I

Idamycin/Pharmacia and Upjohn
Ifex/Bristol-Myers Squibb
Iletin/Eli Lilly
Imitrex/Glaxo Wellcome
Imodium/Janssen
Imogam/Pasteur Merieux Connaught

Imovax/Pasteur Merieux Connaught
Imuran/Glaxo Wellcome
Indapamide/Bristol-Myers Squibb
Indocin/Merck
Inversine/Merck
Invirase/Roche Laboratories
Ismelin/Novartis
Isoptin SR/Knoll
Isordil/Wyeth-Ayherst Laboratories
Isuprel/Sanofi Winthrop

K

K-Lyte/Bristol-Myers Squibb
Kadian/Zeneca
Kefurox/Eli Lilly
Kefzol/Eli Lilly
Kemadrin/Glaxo Wellcome
Kantrex/Bristol-Myers Squibb
Kenalog/Bristol-Myers Squibb
Klatrix/Bristol-Myers Squibb
Klonopin/Roche Laboratories
Kytril/Smithkline Beecham

L

L-Carnitine/R&D Laboratories
Lacrisert/Merck
Lamictal/Glaxo Wellcome
Lamprene/Novartis
Lanoxicaps/Glaxo Wellcome
Lanoxin/Glaxo Wellcome
Larodopa/Roche Laboratories
Lasix/Hoechst Marion
Leucovorin/Immunex
Leukeran/Glaxo Wellcome
Leukine/Immunex
Leustatin/Ortho Biotech Inc
Levo-Dromoran/Roche Laboratories
Levoprome/Immunex
Librax/Roche Laboratories
Limbritol/Roche Laboratories
Lioresal/Novartis
Lithobid/Solvay
Lithonate/Solvay

Lithotabs/Solvay
Lodosy/DuPont
Loestrin/Parke Davis
Lopressor/Novartis
Loprox/Hoechst Marion
Lorabid/Eli Lilly
Lotensin/Novartis
Lotensin HCT/Novartis
Lotrel/Novartis
Lotrimin/Schering
    Laboratories/Key
Lotrisone/Schering
    Laboratories/Key
Lovenox/Rhone-Poulenc Inc
Lozol/Rhone-Poulenc Inc
LPF/Immunex
Ludiomil/Novartis
Luvox/Solvay
Lysodren/Bristol-Myers Squibb

M

M-R-Vax/Merck
M-M-R/Merck
Macrobid/Procter and Gamble
Macrodantin/Procter and Gamble
Mag-Carb/R&D Laboratories
Mandol/Eli Lilly
Marax/Pfizer Inc
Marinol/Roxane
Matulane/Roche
Maxair/3M
Maxaquin/Searle
Maxlplme/Bristol-Myers Squibb
Medihaler/3M
Mefoxin/Merck
Megace/Bristol-Myers Squibb
Menest/Smithkline Beecham
Mephyton/Merck
Mepron/Glaxo Wellcome
Meruvax/Merck
Mesnex/Bristol-Myers Squibb
Methotrexate/Immunex Novatrone
Metipirone/Novartis

Metoclopramide/Bristol-Myers
  Squibb
Metoprolol Tartrate/Bristol-
  Myers Squibb
Metrodin/Serono Laboratories, Inc
Mevacor/Merck
Mexitil/Boehringer Ingleheim
Mezlin/Bayer Corporation
Microbuten/Pharmacia and Upjohn
Micronase/Pharmacia and Upjohn
Midamor/Merck
Minipress/Pfizer Inc
Minizide/Pfizer Inc
Mintezol/Merck
Mithracin/Bayer Corporation
Monistat-Derm/Ortho
  Pharmaceutical
Monocid/Smithkline Beecham
Monopril/Bristol-Myers Squibb
MRV/Bayer Corporation
Mucomyst/Bristol-Myers Squibb
MumpsVax/Merck
Mustargen/Merck
Mutamycin/Bristol-Myers Squibb
Mycelex/Bayer Corporation
Mycostatin/Bristol-Myers Squibb
Myleran/Glaxo Wellcome
Mytelease/Sanofi Winthrop

N

Nadolol/Bristol-Myers Squibb
Nafcillin/Bristol-Myers Squibb
Nalcecon/Bristol-Myers Squibb
Naprosyn/Roche Laboratories
Naproxin/Bristol-Myers Squibb
Nasacort/Rhone-Poulenc Inc
Nasalide/Roche Laboratories
Nasarel/Roche Laboratories
Natalins/Bristol-Myers Squibb
Navane/Pfizer Inc
Navelbine/Glaxo Wellcome
Nebcin/Eli Lilly
NebuPent/Fujisawa

NegGram/Sanofi Winthrop
Neoatigmine/Bristol-Myers
  Squibb
Neodecadron/Merck
Neoral/Novartis
Neosporin Opthalmic/Glaxo
  Wellcome
NephrAmine/R&D Laboratories
Nephro-Fer/R&D Laboratories
Nephro-Calci/R&D Laboratories
Nephro-Vite/R&D Laboratories
Nephro-Derm/R&D Laboratories
Neupogen/Amgen, Inc.
Neurotin/Parke Davis
Niacin/Bristol-Myers Squibb
Nicobid/Rhone-Poulenc Inc
Nicolar/Rhone-Poulenc Inc
Nimotop/Bayer Corporation
Nitrazine/Bristol-Myers Squibb
Nitro-Bid/Hoechst Marion
Nitrolingual/Rhone-Poulenc Inc
Nizoral/Janssen
Nolvades/Zeneca
Norflex/3M
Norgesic/3M
Normodyne/Schering
  Laboratories/Key
Noroxin/Merck
Norpace/Searle
Norplant/Wyeth-Ayherst
  Laboratories
Norpramin/Hoechst Marion
Norvasc/Pfizer Inc
Nydrazid/Bristol-Myers Squibb

O

Ocusert/Alza
Ogen/Pharmacia and Upjohn
Omni/Smithkline Beecham
Oncaspar/Rhone-Poulenc Inc
Oncovin/Eli Lilly
Ophithaine/Bristol-Myers Squibb
Optimine/Schering

Laboratories/Key
Oramorph/Roxane
Orasone/Solvay
Oratrast/Rhone-Poulenc Inc
Ornade/Smithkline Beecham
Orudis/Wyeth-Ayherst
Laboratories
Ovcon/Bristol-Myers Squibb
Oxacillin/Bristol-Myers Squibb
Oxistat/Glaxo Wellcome

P

Pancrease Capsules/McNeil
Parafon Forte DSC/McNeil
Paraplayten/Bristol-Myers Squibb
Parlodel/Novartis
Pavabid/Hoechst Marion
Paxil/Smithkline Beecham
PBZ/Novartis
Pediotic Suspension/Glaxo
Wellcome
PedvaxHib/Merck
Penetrex/Rhone-Poulenc Inc
Penicillin/Bristol-Myers Squibb
Pentasa/Hoechst Marion
Pepcid/Merck
Periactin/Merck
Permax/Athena Neurosciences
Phenergan/Wyeth-Ayherst
Laboratories
pHisoHex/Sanofi Winthrop
Photophrin/Sanofi Winthrop
Pilagan/Allergan
Plaquenil/Sanofi Winthrop
Platinol/Bristol-Myers Squibb
Plendil/Astra Merck
Pneumovax/Merck
Pollen Extract/Bayer Corporation
Polycillin/Bristol-Myers Squibb
Polysporin Opthalmic/Glaxo
Wellcome
Potassium CI/Bristol-Myers Squibb
Pravachol/Bristol-Myers Squibb

Precose/Bayer Corporation
Premarin/Wyeth-Ayherst
Laboratories
Prilosec/Astra Merck
Primaquine/Sanofi Winthrop
Primaxin/Merck
Principen/Bristol-Myers Squibb
Prinivil/Merck
Prinizide/Merck
Procardia/Pfizer Inc
Prochlorperazine/Bristol-Myers
Squibb
Procrit/Ortho Biotech Inc
Progestasert/Alza
Prograf/Fujisawa
Proloprim/Glaxo Wellcome
Prollxin/Bristol-Myers Squibb
Pronestyl/Bristol-Myers Squibb
Propine/Allergan
Propulsid/Janssen
Prolixin/Bristol-Myers Squibb
Pronestyl/Bristol-Myers Squibb
Proscar/Merck
Protamine Sulfate/Eli Lilly
Proventil/Schering
Laboratories/Key
Provera/Pharmacia and Upjohn
Purinethol/Glaxo Wellcome

Q
Questran/Bristol-Myers Squibb

R
Rauzide/Bristol-Myers Squibb
Recombivax/Merck
Regroton/Rhone-Poulenc Inc
Relafen/Smithkline Beecham
Renova/Ortho
ReoPro/Eli Lilly
Retin-A/Ortho
Retrovir/Glaxo Wellcome
Ridaura/Smithkline Beecham
Rifadin/Hoechst Marion

Rifamate/Hoechst Marion
Rifater/Hoechst Marion
Riultek/Rhone-Polenc Inc
Rimactane/Novartis
Risperdal/Janssen
Rocaltrol/Roche Laboratories
Rocephrin/Roche Laboratories
Roferon-A/Roche Laboratories
Romazicon/Roche Laboratories
Rowasa/Solvay
Roxanol/Roxane
Roxicodone/Roxane
Rubex/Bristol-Myers Squibb
Rythmol/Knoll

S

Sandimmune/Novartis
Sandoglubulin/Novartis
Sandostatin/Novartis
Seconal/Eli Lilly
Sectral/Wyeth-Ayherst
    Laboratories
Seldane/Hoechst Marion
Semprex-D/Glaxo Wellcome
Septra/Glaxo Wellcome
Ser-Ap-Es/Novartis
Serentil/Boehringer Ingleheim
Serevent/Glaxo Wellcome
Serostim/Serono Laboratories, Inc
Silvadene/Hoechst Marion
Sinemet CR/DuPont Merck 1
Sinemet/DuPont Merck
Sinequan/Pfizer Inc
Slo-Phylllin/Rhone-Poulenc, Inc
Slo-bid/Rhone-Poulenc Inc
Slow-K/Novartis
SMZ-TMP/Bristol-Myers Squibb
Sorbitrate/Zeneca
Sorzone/Bristol-Myers Squibb
Spectazole/Ortho
Spec-T Sore/Bristol-Myers Squibb
Sporanox/Janssen
Stadol/Bristol-Myers Squibb

Stelazine/Smithkline Beecham
Stilphostrol/Bayer Corporation
Sumycin/Bristol-Myers Squibb
Symmetrel/DuPont Merck
Synalar/Roche Laboratories
Synthroid Tablets/Knoll
Syprine/Merck

T

Tace/Hoechst Marion
Tagamet/Smithkline Beecham
Tambocor/3M
Taxol/Bristol-Myers Squibb
Taxotere/Rhone-Poulenc Inc
Tazidime/Eli Lilly
Tegison/Roche Laboratories
Tegretol/Novartis
Tegretol-XR/Novartis
Temovate/Glaxo Wellcome
Tenuate/Hoechst Marion
Teslac/Bristol-Myers Squibb
Testoderm/Alza
Theolair/3M
TheraCys/Pasteur Merieux
    Connaught
Theragran/Bristol-Myers Squibb
Thioguanne/Glaxo Wellcome
Thioplex/Immunex
Ticlid/Roche Laboratories
Tilade/Rhone-Poulenc Inc
Timentin/Smithkline Beecham
Timolide/Merck
Timoptic/Merck
Tobramycin/Bristol-Myers Squibb
Tofranil/Novartis
Tolectin/McNeil
Tonocard/Astra Merck
Topicort/Hoechst Marion
Trancopal/Sanofi Winthrop
Trandate/Glaxo Wellcome
Transdermal Nitro and
    Voltaren/Novartis
Trental/Hoechst Marion

Trexan and Vaseretic/DuPont
Tridesilon/Bayer Corporation
Trimox/Bristol-Myers Squibb
Trimpex/Roche Laboratories
Trinalin/Schering
  Laboratories/Key
Trusopt/Merck
Tubocurarine/Bristol-Myers
  Squibb
Tussar/Rhone-Poulenc Inc
Tylenol with Codeine/McNeil
Tylox Capsules/McNeil

U

Ultram/McNeil
Urecholine/Merck
Urex/3M

V

Vagistat-1/Bristol-Myers Squibb
Valium/Roche Laboratories
Valtrex/Glaxo Wellcome
Vancenase/Schering
  Laboratories/Key
Vancocin HCI/Eli Lilly
Vantin/Pharmacia and Upjohn
Vaqta/Merck
Varivax/Merck
Vascor/McNeil
Vaseretic/Merck
Vasodilan/Bristol-Myers Squibb
Vasotec/Merck
Velban/Eli Lilly
Veetids/Bristol-Myers Squibb
Velosef/Bristol-Myers Squibb
Venomil Maintenance/Bayer
  Corporation
Venomil Individual/Bayer
  Corporation
Ventolin/Glaxo Wellcome

VePesid/Bristol-Myers Squibb
Vermox/Janssen
Vesanoid/Roche Laboratories
Vesprin/Bristol-Myers Squibb
Vibra-Tabs/Pfizer Inc
Vibramycin/Pfizer Inc
Videx/Bristol-Myers Squibb
Viramune/Roxane
Viroptic/Glaxo Wellcome
Vistaril/Pfizer Inc
Vistide/Gilead
Vivactil/Merck
Vivelle/Novartis
Voltaren-XR/Novartis
Vumon/Bristol-Myers Squibb

W

Wellbutrin/Glaxo Wellcome
Wellcovorin/Glaxo Wellcome
Wytensin/Wyeth Ayherst
  Laboratories

X

Xanax/Pharmacia and Upjohn

Z

Zantac/Glaxo Wellcome
Zarotin/Parke Davis
Zerit/Bristol-Myers Squibb
Zestoretic/Zeneca
Zestril/Zeneca
Zinecard/Pharmacia and Upjohn
Zithromax/Pfizer Inc
Zocor/Merck
Zyrtec/Pfizer Inc
Zofran/Glaxo Wellcome
Zoladex/Zeneca
Zoloft/Pfizer Inc
Zovirax/Glaxo Wellcome
Zyloprim/Glaxo Wellcome

Help With Your Sex Life

Use it or lose it. Research shows that a pattern of regular sexual activity helps to preserve sexual ability in later life. So try to avoid those "Not tonight, I have a headache" days. Most older people want — and are able to lead — an active, satisfying sex life. There are some normal changes that may affect sex, but as long as you're aware of what is happening and why, your sex life can continue to be great! Read on to learn about physical changes and what to expect.

Is Estrogen Really The Fountain Of Youth?

It will make you young, beautiful, and sexy. No, we are not talking about the latest hair care product. Estrogen is getting a lot of hype these days as a cure-all for aging women who wish to remain youthful and sexually active through menopause and beyond.

Estrogen is taken by millions of women and does help relieve symptoms of menopause such as hot flashes, and other vaginal changes that can cause problems during sex. Some vaginal changes can be treated with local applications of creams that contain estrogen, which may lower the risk to the rest of the body from estrogens that are taken orally.

The Food and Drug Administration (FDA) has information on estrogen to help women understand the benefits and risks of this drug when deciding the best course of therapy. Contact the Center for Drug Evaluation and Research, Food and Drug Administration, 5600 Fishers Lane, HFD-8, Rockville, MD 20857; 301-827-4573, 800-532-4440; or online at <http://www.fda.gov/cder>.

Impotence ... When Love Is A Let Down

It is not exactly an easy subject to talk to your doctor about, but many elderly men suffer from impotence.

You don't have to forgo sex in your remaining years because of this problem. Many types of sexual dysfunction can now be treated successfully.

Close to 10 million men suffer from impotence and Uncle Sam can give you the latest on medical therapies, from penile implants to encounter sessions. There are 15 different models of penile implants and they all have a 90% success rate.

The National Kidney and Urologic Diseases Information Clearinghouse can answer questions and provide information about impotence and penile implants. They have free publications and can conduct a search on the Combined Health Information Database (CHID) for more information on a specific subject.

For more information, contact National Kidney and Urologic Diseases Information Clearinghouse, 3 Information Way, Bethesda, MD 20892-3580; 301-654-4415; or online at <http://www.niddk.nih.gov>.

Are Your Hot Flashes Getting Hotter?

Menopause doesn't have to be the hormonal hurricane women have faced in the past. Mood swings, hot flashes, depression ... the list goes on. But many women still rely on outdated information when trying to adjust to "the change."

Taking estrogen and progesterone, known as HRT, can help relieve the problems of menopause, although they are not without problems of their own. Research is currently being undertaken regarding the use of these drugs.

The National Institute on Aging has a free booklet titled *Menopause* which explains the changes women go through as their bodies change. Lower estrogen levels can affect sexual intercourse, but there are steps you can take to make sex a pleasurable experience once again. For your copy, contact National Institute on Aging, Information Center, P.O. Box 8057, Gaithersburg, MD 20898; 800-222-2225; or online at <http://www.nih.gov/nia>.

☆☆☆

Bald Is Sexy

Don't look for some over-the-counter miracle to solve your balding pate. Bad hair days are bad hair days. Our government hair and drug experts say over-the-counter drugs don't work, but some prescription drugs and implant techniques can keep you from indulging in those "Hair Club" offers on late night TV.

Get the facts. Contact Center for Drug Evaluation and Research, Food and Drug Administration, 5600 Fishers Lane, HFD-8, Rockville, MD 20857; 301-827-4573, 800-532-4440; or online at <http://www.fda.gov/ cder>.

Find Your Lover On The Freeway

Looking for your future Mercedes Benz driving boyfriend? You can get a mailing list from your state Department of Motor Vehicles (DMV) which includes information on men in your zip code who own BMWs and Mercedes Benzs. This information is available for a fee in 47 states. Contact your Department of Motor Vehicles in your state capital.

Also for a fee, your full service DMV can provide you with a person's current address if you have their full name, date of birth, and city. Most states have an office through which you can trace auto tags, but the request usually has to be made in writing. Each state operates the service a little differently, and may charge a small fee. You can receive information such as to whom the car is registered, their address, the year and make of car, and the serial number of the car. Contact your state Department of Motor Vehicles located in your state capital for more information.

☆☆☆

Sexy Seniors Do It, Too

A recent poll found that many Americans are enjoying each other's charms well into their seventies. Many of them even swear that sex, like wine, gets better with age.

With age, women do not ordinarily lose their physical capacity for orgasm nor men their capacity for erection and ejaculation. There is, however, a gradual slowing of response, especially in men. This slowing down is currently considered part of normal aging, but may be eventually treatable or even reversible.

A pattern of regular sexual activity (which may include masturbation) helps to preserve sexual ability. When problems occur, they should not be viewed as inevitable, but rather as the result of disease, disability, drug reactions, or emotional upset, and may require medical care.

Illness, disabilities, and even some medicines can affect sex or sexual desire.

The National Institute on Aging has a free publication titled *Age Page: Sexuality in Later Life* which provides information on normal physical changes, effects of illness or disability, and other factors that may affect sex for older adults. For your free copy, contact National Institute on Aging, Information Center, P.O. Box 8057, Gaithersburg, MD 20898; 800-222-2225; or online at <http://www.nih.gov/nia>.

AIDS: Changing Sex In The Nineties

AIDS is not something that affects only the young, but is found in every age group. In fact, over 40,000 people received their AIDS diagnosis when they were 50 years or older.

And it's not just contracted from unprotected sex. Even having your gallbladder removed puts you at risk because of the possibility of being exposed to AIDS tainted blood. There is so much information out there regarding AIDS — how do you know what is true and what's not?

The National AIDS Hotline can answer questions about HIV transmission and prevention, HIV testing, and HIV/AIDS treatments. Callers can receive referrals to national, state, and local HIV/AIDS service organizations. There is a catalogue of brochures, pamphlets, reports, posters, and audiovisuals that are available free or at a very low cost.

For more information, contact National AIDS Hotline, P.O. Box 13827, Research Triangle Park, NC 27709; 800-342-AIDS; 800-458-5231 (publications); or online at <http://www.cdcnac.org>.

Gifts, Bargains And Hobbies

With your retirement, you may finally have some extra time now to enjoy your favorite pastimes. Whether it's gardening, sewing, shopping for bargains, watching videos, or even tracking down your family history, Uncle Sam can help you.

The government has videos on every topic imaginable for your viewing pleasure. Did you know that through government auctions you can get great gifts for the kids and grandkids? You can even improve your fishing technique with some lessons, courtesy of the government. All it takes is a few phone calls and you are on your way to getting much more out of your free time.

Free Sewing Classes

You never know when it will come in handy to know 100 things to do with a yard of fabric. If you are using your retirement time to get back into sewing, or even want to teach sewing classes to kids, a great resource is your County Cooperative Extension Office. They frequently offer courses, workbooks, and even videos about how to sew. Some even focus on certain projects like Christmas gifts or draperies.

To learn more about what is available in your area, look in the blue pages of your phone book for the office nearest you, or you can find the main state office in the Directory of State Information at the end of the book. For more information, contact Extension Service, U.S. Department of Agriculture, Room 3328, Washington, DC 20250; 202-720-3029; or online at <http://www.reeusda.gov>.

Free Photos of Bill, Hill, and Socks

Whether you are a Republican or Democrat, President Clinton is the one in charge these days.

You can get free photos of the President and/or the First Lady, and even get an 8x10 of First Feline Socks. Remember that they won't know if you are throwing darts at the picture or not.

All you need to do is send a letter with your request to Presidential Correspondence, White House, Photo Department, Attention Stephen Nolet, Old Executive Office Building, Room 94, Washington, DC 20502; or online at <http://www.whitehouse.gov>.

☆☆☆

Help for Model Ship Builders

If miniature ship building is a pastime for you, then turn to the National Archives for help in making your replicas accurate. The brochure, Pictures of United States Navy Ships: 1775-1941, lists pictures available covering sailing ships to submarines, in addition to steamships, aircraft carriers, battleships, cruisers, destroyers, and torpedo boats.

For the brochure and ordering information, contact Still Pictures Branch, National Archives and Records Administration, 8601 Adelphi Rd., College Park, MD 20740; 301-713-6625, ext. 221; or online at <http://www.nara.gov>.

☆☆☆

WWII Memorabilia

General Douglas MacArthur storming the shores. Ships burning in Pearl Harbor. Inspirational posters. World War II can come alive again through slides, pictures, and posters from the National Archives.

Thousands of pictures are maintained by the Archives, so to help you with your selection they have developed a brochure, Pictures of World War II, which describes what is available.

For the brochure and ordering information, contact Still Pictures Branch, National Archives and Records Administration, 8601 Adelphi Rd., College Park, MD 20740; 301-713-6625, ext. 221; or online at http://www.nara.gov>.

Borrow Old Faithful

For those armchair travelers who want to learn more before they go, or even for those that never got to see some of this country's natural wonders, the Park Service can bring them directly to you.

The photography library of the U.S. Park Service will lend you pictures and slides of national parks, monuments, battlefields, and other points of interest. This is a great resource for Civil War buffs.

Contact Photo Library, Office of Public Affairs, National Park Service, U.S. Department of Interior, 18th and C Sts., NW, Washington, DC 20240, 202-208-4997.

Photos of the Natural Wonders

Volcanoes, earthquakes, the Grand Canyon, and Niagara Falls are just a few of the thousands of pictures available from the U.S. Geological Survey. Pictures date back to 1869, but unfortunately there is no real catalog to consult, so why not develop a wish list of your very own?

To obtain information on ordering or purchasing prints, negatives or transparencies, contact the library directly. Contact Photographic Library, MS914, U.S. Geological Survey, Box 25046, Federal Center, Denver, CO 80225, 303-236-1010; for the hearing impaired, 303-236-0998 TTY.

☆☆☆

Bones And Fossils Headquarters

For all those fossil hunters out there, the government has an office just for you. The National Park Service provides technical assistance to federal and state agencies on the identification, evaluation, and preservation of archeological properties, and has a series of technical publications and a database of archeology bibliographies.

For more information, contact Archeological and Ethnography Division, National Park Service, Department of the Interior, P.O. Box 37127, Suite 210, Washington, DC 20013-7127, 202-343-4101; or online at <http://www. nps.gov>.

Free Videos of The One That Got Away

Back up your fishing adventures with evidence. The Fish and Wildlife Service lends slides and still photos to lend credibility to even the tallest tale that you can dream up to tell your buddies.

The Audio Visual Department of the Fish and Wildlife Service has a collection of both black and white pictures and color slides of fish and wildlife and there is no charge for their lending service. You can even contact your regional Fish and Wildlife office for free loaner films and videos to get you excited about the upcoming fishing season.

Contact Broadcast and Audio Visuals, Fish and Wildlife Service, 18th and C Sts., NW, Washington, DC 20240, 202-208-5611; or online at <http://www.fws.gov>.

Our African Heritage On Film

An exhaustive collection of photographs of African art and life is available from the Eliot Elisofon Photographic Archives.

The collection is divided into two major categories: art, which includes photographs of art objects in the permanent collection, as well as in public and private collections; and field, which contains images of African life. An overall guide to the collection and a price list are available upon request.

Contact National Museum of African Art, 950 Independence Ave., SW, Washington, DC 20560, 202-357-4654.

A Picture For Those Who Served

If Mom or Dad ever served in the Armed Forces, surprise them on their next birthday with a photo of their base, aircraft, or ship. You can get them an 8x10, so that the next time they say, "When I was in the service we did things this way," you can understand what they're talking about.

The Still Media Records Center of the Defense Department has an archive of over 135,000 photographs. For a general information sheet and current price list, contact Defense Visual Information Center, Attn: Still

Media Operations, 1363 Z St., Bldg. 2730, March Air Force Base, CA 92518; 909-413-2515.

A Fisherman's Dream

Did the movie *A River Runs Through It* excite you about fly fishing? *"Pathway to Fishing"* is a 12-part, hour-long instructional program covering fish biology, aquatic ecology, angler ethics, methods for handling fish, and information about where to go fishing.

Although a bit pricey at $61, it's packed with a User's Guide, 12 support posters and an instructional video. Contact U.S. Fish and Wildlife Service, Pathway To Fishing, 1849 C St., NW, ARLSQ-820, Washington, DC 20240, 202-208-5611.

When The Fish Aren't Biting

Everyone needs a little down time, so when you are taking a break from the fishing boat, you can at least read up on the topic.

A free shopping list of government fishing publications (doc. number SB209) is available which provides information on fisheries and fish research, and another list (doc. number SB57) provides information on charts and marine posters.

For your copies, contact Superintendent of Documents, Government Printing Office, Washington, DC 20402, 202-512-1800.

For Archaeologists Who Won't Get Their Hands Dirty

Here is your own home study course to help you make your own rare find. *Participate in Archeology* is a free brochure which provides some basic information on archeology, and lists magazines, books, videos, and agencies and organizations through which you can receive additional information.

Contact National Park Service, Natural Cultural Resources,

Archeological and Ethnography Division, U.S. Department of the Interior, 1849 C St., NW, Suite 210, Washington, DC 20240, 202-208-4747; or online at <http://www.nps.gov>.

☆☆☆

Join In on a Free Archaeological Dig

Never liked staying on the sidelines? Well then, dig in. "Passport In Time" helps you open a window on the past by allowing you to join activities such as archaeological excavation, site mapping, drafting, laboratory and art work, collecting oral histories, restoration, and much more.

Projects vary in length and there is no registration cost or fee. You may even receive a small stipend to off-set your living expenses.

For information on upcoming opportunities, contact Passport In Time Clearinghouse, P.O. Box 31315, Tucson, AZ 85751-1315; 800-281-9176; or online at <http://www.fs. fed.us/recreation/opp_to_vol.html>.

☆☆☆

Free Information About Sick Pets

For most pet owners, their pets are like their children. You worry about what they are eating, and you worry when they are sick.

The Center for Veterinary Medicine can answer all your pet food and nutrition questions. They have fact sheets and articles about choosing food for your pets, as well as information sheets on common pet illnesses and veterinary terms.

Do what is right for your pet. To receive free copies of these fact sheets, contact Center for Veterinary Medicine, Food and Drug Administration, 7500 Standish Place, Rockville, MD 20855; 301-594-1755; or online at <http://www.cvm.fda.gov>.

☆☆☆

How to Care for Your Cat Or Cow

They are not just for livestock anymore. Many County Cooperative Extension Service Offices have information pamphlets, classes, or even videos on the care and feeding of animals.

Want to learn how to take better care of your pet? What about dog training classes? To learn what your local office has to offer look in the blue pages of your phone book for the office nearest you, or you can find the main state office in the Directory of State Information at the end of the book.

For more information, contact Extension Service, U.S. Department of Agriculture, Room 3328, Washington, DC 20250; 202-720-4111; or online at <http://www. reeusda.gov>.

☆☆☆

Learn About Endangered Species

You actually may not need to go any farther than your own backyard to find rare and wonderful things. If you are a card-carrying birder, the Fish and Wildlife Service has information booklets on attracting birds to your yard, and even information on different homes for birds.

If you are worried about endangered species, they can provide you with information on the Endangered Species Act, a list of endangered and threatened species, as well as information sheets on many species. Contact U.S. Fish and Wildlife Service, 4401 N. Fairfax Dr., Arlington, VA 22203; 703-358-1711; or online at <http://www.fws.gov>.

☆☆☆

Another Elvis Sighting

You may think you've seen Elvis around town, but don't think you're all that special — so have millions of others. What you probably saw was Elvis' face on millions of envelopes. What Elvis did for the Post Office is to make stamp collecting even more the rage.

Join the crowd with some help from the U.S. Postal Service, and request their free brochure, *Introduction to Stamp Collecting*, which will help you learn how to start and maintain a collection. Contact your local post office or write U.S. Postal Service, 475 L'Enfant Plaza West, SW, Washington, DC 20260; or online at <http://www. usps.gov>.

Get the Ship Passenger Logs
of Ellis Island Arrivals

Gathering up all those branches, limbs, and splinters can be an incredible treasure hunt. If you are putting together your family tree, let the National Archives help you along.

They maintain ship passenger arrival records dating back into the 1800's, and they will even do the research for you! If they find your ancestor, they will send you a notice. The logs consist of 2x3 foot sheets listing age, amount of money, language spoken, even their height and weight. There is a cost of $10 if you want to purchase the log.

For more information, contact Reference Services Branch, National Archives and Records Administration, 8th St and Pennsylvania Ave., NW, Washington, DC 20408; 202-501-5400; or online at <http://www.nara.gov>.

Bountiful Botany

Ferns, ivies, poinsettias, orchids, chrysanthemums. Fact sheets to keep you reading and digging are available to answer some of your plant questions. The Horticulture Services Division of the Smithsonian Institution has a series of fact sheets, which includes information on how to help the plant grow, potential problems, fertilization, and cultivation.

For more information, contact Horticulture Services Division, Arts and Industries Building, Room 2282, MRC 420, Smithsonian Institution, Washington, DC 20560; 202-357-1926.

Call The Plant Doctor

Bring me your tired, sick, and decaying plants... Almost all Cooperative Extension Service offices (which are located in every county) have a horticulture hotline, where you can talk to gardening experts, and even bring in samples of your plants for diagnoses. There is usually no fee for this service.

They can even help you deal with squirrels digging up your bulbs, and deer eating your trees. Look in the blue pages of your phone book for the office nearest you, or find the main state office in the Directory of State Information at the end of this book.

For more information, contact Extension Service, U.S. Department of Agriculture, Room 3328, Washington, DC 20250; 202-720-4111; or online at <http://www. reeusda.gov>.

Free Books on Tape

You used to love reading, but since your eyes have started to get bad, you've all but given up enjoying a good book anymore.

Before you give up altogether, listen to this: the National Library Service (NLS) maintains a large collection of books, magazines, journals, and music materials in Braille, large type, and recorded formats for individuals who cannot read or use standard printed materials because of temporary or permanent visual loss or physical limitations. Reading materials and necessary playback equipment for books on record and cassette are distributed through a national network of cooperating libraries.

Books in the collection are selected on the basis of their appeal to a wide range of interests. Bestsellers, biographies, fiction, and how-to books are in great demand.

Contact your local library to find out what they have available to you, or you may contact Handicapped Readers Reference Section, National Library Service for the Blind and Physically Handicapped, Library of Congress, Washington, DC 20542; 202-707-9275; or online at <http://lcweb.loc.gov/nls/nls.html>.

Jewelry Cheaper Than Out of Someone's Trunk

No need to locate the nearest shady dealer to find a great deal. The U.S. Customs agents are on the lookout for you. These are the guys that confiscate items brought into this country illegally.

You can get diamond rings for half price, fancy cars for a fraction of their cost, and anything else you can imagine including airplanes, boats, and fine linens. These items are auctioned off all over the U.S. For information on auctions, contact EG&G Dynatrend, 3702 Pender Dr., Suite 400,

Fairfax, VA 22030; 703-273-7373; or online at <http://www.ustreas.gov/treasury/bureaus/customs/general.html>.

Great Bargains at Uncle Sam's Shopping Mall

At one time or another everything is shipped by mail, including the latest CDs, videos, books, toys, ostrich eggs, and even suits of armor. When the government can't deliver something, it is collected in the back of the post offices and auctioned off around the country. I personally got 100 stuffed animals for $1.00 each.

The postal auctions are held at four Mail Recovery Centers across the U.S. To locate the center nearest you, contact your local postmaster.

Bargains on Bombs, Bases, and Butterfly Catchers

Everyone would love to have their own B-52, but there are just not enough to go around. But if you can't have that, what else does the Department of Defense have that you could use?

With the Defense cutbacks taking place, you can now buy tents, sporting equipment, computers, horses, furniture, telephone systems, photographic equipment, and even entire military bases. The merchandise is sold at over 200 locations worldwide.

Information on local and national sales is available in the free booklet *How To Buy Surplus Personal Property From DOD*. To obtain your booklet, contact Defense Reutilization and Marketing Service, International Sales Office, P.O. Box 5275 DDRC, 2163 Airways Blvd., Memphis, TN 38114; 888-352-9333 (press 2).

A Drug Confiscated Limo For $1.00

No. You can't get one for $1.00, but you can get one at bargain prices. (Just hope they don't want it back when they get out of jail). You can also get boats, planes, antiques, exquisite jewelry, and luxury homes that have been confiscated from drug traffickers or other criminals.

Major sales are advertised the third Wednesday of every month in *USA Today*.

For more information, write U.S. Marshals Service, 600 Army-Navy Dr., Arlington, VA 22202; 202-307-9087. You can also call 703-557-9753 to receive a list of contractors throughout the U.S. who are authorized to sell confiscated property.

Get a Horse and Ride'em Cowboy

You don't have to go to the Wild West to re-enact the movie *City Slickers*. Horses roaming on government land can be adopted for only $125. Or you can get a burro for $75. And if you're lucky, you can get two for the price of one if a mare is with foal.

For details, write the Bureau of Land Management, U.S. Department of the Interior, P.O. Box 12000, Reno, NV 89520; 702-785-6400.

☆☆☆

Fly a Flag in Your Honor

No need to struggle with a gift idea for your "Made In America" relative. As a special gift for a loved one or for yourself, you can purchase an American flag that has been flown over the Capitol. It comes with a certificate verifying the date on which the flag was flown.

You can request a specific date, such as a birthdate, anniversary, or even the day someone was discharged from the Service. These flags cost between $6.50-$17 depending upon the size and material, and can be purchased through your Senator or Representative. To learn more, contact your Senator or Representative, The Capitol, Washington, DC 20510; 202-224-3121.

☆☆☆

Cash In on Another's Banking Problems

Tired of putting money into a bank and not seeing much in return? The Federal Deposit Insurance Corporation (FDIC) sells a wide variety of assets from failed banks including loans, real estate such as undeveloped land, hotels, shopping malls, single-family homes, condominiums, and apartment complexes. They even sell personal property including computers, phone systems, furniture, fixtures, plants, and more.

For information about the sales, contact the FDIC, 550 17th St., NW, Washington, DC 20429-9990; 202-736-0000.

Help Your Garden Grow

Rather not have your tomatoes glow in the dark? You can get your vegetables and flowers to be the talk of the neighborhood without using pesticides that may turn your insides into mush.

You can learn how to fertilize and protect your plants without adding harmful chemicals with some help from the Environmental Protection Agency. They have fact sheets and information booklets on pesticides, organic gardening, and even composting.

To learn more, contact Public Information Center, U.S. Environmental Protection Agency, 401 M St., SW, 3404, Washington, DC 20460; 202-260-5922; or online at <http://www.epa.gov>.

News Of The Day

Remember when you got the news before the movies? Those same newsreels are available for viewing through the National Archives. The Universal Newsreels cover the period between 1929-1967. Like other newsreels, it appeared semi-weekly at theaters, averaging ten minutes per issue.

You can view the newsreels at the Archives, or you can pay a nominal fee to a service to have them make a special copy for you. Find out what exciting things were happening in the world on the day you were born! Contact the Motion Picture, Sound, and Video Branch, National Archives, 8601 Adelphi Rd., College Park, MD 20740; 301-713-7060; or online at <http://www.nara.gov>.

☆☆☆

Sound Bites From History

Want to hear Amelia Earhart talking about the future of flight? Or Thomas Edison talking about the future of electricity? You can also hear famous speeches by past Presidents, Supreme Court oral arguments, NASA recordings of air-to-ground communications, and even National Public Radio broadcasts. There are more than 160,000 sound recordings to choose from! All you need to do is start compiling a list.

You can go to the National Archives and make copies for free or there are service providers who will make copies for you for a fee. For more information contact the Motion Picture, Sound, and Video Branch, National Archives, 8601 Adelphi Rd., College Park, MD 20740; 301-713-7060; or online at <http://www.nara.gov>.

Your Very Own Ansel Adams

Many of us would like to own great works of art, but our budget doesn't quite extend that far. Now here's your chance to purchase your very own copy of an Ansel Adams print. And what is nice about these is that the photographs are not copyrighted. So if you want to put together notecards or calendars, you are well within your rights.

In 1941 Mr. Adams was commissioned to create a photo mural of nature protected by the U.S. National Parks. The National Archives holds the 226 photographs taken for this project. Photos include the Grand Canyon, Grand Tetons, Rocky Mountains, Yellowstone, and more. A complete listing is available and includes how you can order and purchase a print of your own.

For more information contact: Still Picture Branch, National Archives, 8601 Adelphi Rd., College Park, MD 20740; 301-713-6625, ext. 234; or online at <http://www. nara.gov>.

Money, Help And Cheap Tickets For Art Lovers

Grandma Moses didn't start painting until her late seventies, and was still at it when she turned 100. Pablo Picasso was still drawing at 90. Even Tolstoy and George Bernard Shaw were productive writers well into their eighties. To find out where you can turn your talent into money for yourself or your group, as well as help in bringing in artists to inspire you, read on.

Money From The Big Guys

The National Endowment for the Arts (NEA) may be fighting for their very existence these days, but don't fear — they've been on the government hit list for many years, and somehow have always managed to survive in one form or another.

The Endowment Funds Fellowships: Congressional legislation has eliminated all but the following fellowships to individuals — Creative Writing Fellowships, American Jazz Masters Awards, and National Heritage Awards. Call 202-682-5400 for information on these awards, or contact them online at <http://arts.endow.gov>.

Grants to Organizations:

All applications must be for a specific project, not seasonal. Each organization may submit only one application for one of the four themes which are: (1) Heritage and Preservation — for projects which reflect one of the many traditions which form our country or projects which seek to preserve significant works of art; (2) Creation and Presentation — for the creation of new work or the presentation of new or existing work of any culture; (3) Education and Access — for projects which intend to reach audiences which may not have been reached in the past or to provide exposure to art forms which previously have enjoyed little or no exposure; (4) Planning and Stabilization — focusing on planning which seeks to sustain the arts, building partnerships or developing resources.

Your organization must decide which one of the four themes that your project falls under. If your application is rejected under one theme your organization may not reapply under another. Interested organizations may call 202-682-5400 for the free guide *Reinventing the National Endowment for the Arts.*

All the grants listed in this section fall under one of the previously mentioned four themes. Depending on the actual project, the theme will vary. It is up to the organization to decide which theme to apply under. The individual programs no longer exist.

For more information, contact Public Information Office, National Endowment for the Arts, Nancy Hanks Center, 1100 Pennsylvania Ave., NW, Washington, DC 20506; 202-682-5400; or online at <http://arts.endow.gov>.

☆☆☆

Start a Local Theater or Dance Company

If your arts group develops work reflective of your own community, you may be eligible for grants.

These grants are to professionally directed arts organizations that are rooted in culturally diverse, inner-city, rural, or tribal communities. Matching grants are available to help create, exhibit, or present works representative of the culture of a community, and to provide a community with access to all types of quality art.

To learn more about eligibility requirements, contact Public Information Office, National Endowment for the Arts, 1100 Pennsylvania Ave., NW, Washington, DC 20506; 202-682-5400; or online at <http://arts.endow.gov>.

☆☆☆

$20,000 To Write The Great American Novel

For all those writers and poets out there, the Literature Fellowship Program wants to support you. They offer fellowships to creative writers of fiction, non-fiction, and poetry as well as translators of works into English.

The money can be used to cover expenses while you write, conduct research, or travel. It can also be used to sponsor residencies and reading series.

Competition for fellowships is extremely competitive. To learn more, contact Literature Fellowships, National Endowment for the Arts, Room

772, 1100 Pennsylvania Ave., NW, Washington, DC 20506; 202-682-5451, 202-682-5428.

Priceless Art For Your Home

Who needs expensive auction houses selling culture to the highest bidder? The National Gallery of Art can help people like you and me start our own collections. All you need is $5, and you can get a jump start on your collection.

Black and white photographs and 35 mm slides of works from the National Gallery of Art's permanent collections are available for sale (color transparencies for rental). For ordering information, contact National Gallery of Art, Office of Visual Services, Constitution and 6th St., NW, Washington, DC 20565, 202-842-6231, fax 202-842-2356; or online at <http://www.nga.gov>.

☆☆☆

$10,000 For Craftspeople and Storytellers

If you create works in a traditional art form, then look to the Heritage and Preservation Program for assistance. This program supports traditional arts that have grown through time within the many groups that make up our nation — groups that share the same ethnic heritage, language, occupation, religion, or geographic area.

These folk arts include music, dance, poetry, tales, oratory, crafts, and various types of visual art forms. Money can be used for festivals, tours, workshops, residencies, exhibits, and more.

To learn about eligibility, contact the Heritage and Preservation Program, National Endowment For The Arts, Room 710, 1100 Pennsylvania Ave., NW, Washington, DC 20506; 202-682-5449.

☆☆☆

Get a Smithsonian Exhibit For a Fundraiser

The Smithsonian can bring art to you, whether you live in a major metropolitan area or a rural one. The Smithsonian Institute Traveling

Exhibition Services (SITES) sponsors 80 to 100 different exhibits at any given time in museums and other locations around the country.

The participation fee varies from $500 to $20,000. The exhibitions range from popular culture, to fine arts, photography, historical exhibits, or topics of interest to children. The collections are most frequently sent to other museums, libraries, historic homes, or even schools and community centers.

Request a free *SITES* Updates catalog to see what is currently available. Contact Smithsonian Institute Traveling Exhibition Service, Smithsonian Institution, 1100 Jefferson Dr., SW, Room 3146, Washington, DC 20560; 202-357-3168.

☆☆☆

Get Your Local Gallery to Cater More to Seniors

Want to reach people of all ages and disabilities? In conjunction with the National Endowment for the Arts, the National Assembly of State Arts Agencies has compiled a comprehensive arts access book titled, *Design for Accessibility: An Art Administrator's Guide.* The book helps people design spaces and programs that accommodate individuals throughout their lives.

You can also learn about how to open up existing programs and outreach to people who would otherwise not experience your arts programs. For more information, contact the Office for Special Constituencies, National Endowment for the Arts, 1100 Pennsylvania Ave., NE, Washington, DC 20506; 202-682-5532; or online at <http://arts.endow.gov>.

☆☆☆

Music That Will Bring Tears To Your Eyes

And not ringing to your ears. Tired of all that loud music, where you can't understand the words, and aren't sure you want to? The Folkways Records Archive has an incredible collection of music from around the world, and from America's past.

You can hear Jelly Roll Morton, Leadbelly, Pete Seeger, Woody Guthrie, great fiddlers, balladeers, gospel singers, and more. They even have recordings of the spoken word. Cassette tapes are available for under $10.

To receive a free catalog, contact Smithsonian/Folkways Recordings, Office of Folklife Programs, 955 L'Enfant Plaza, Suite 2600, Smithsonian Institution, Washington, DC 20560; 202-287-3262; or online at

<http://www.si.edu/folkways>.

☆☆☆

Free Loan of Famous Masters

You can tell your house guests to sit back and enjoy the show, as you move from masterpiece to masterpiece on your slide projector. They really didn't want to see those pictures of your vacation to Florida anyway.

The National Gallery's lending library of 30,000 images of art will impress your friends and influence your enemies. There is no catalog, so start a wish list and find out what the National Gallery can fulfill on it. Slides consist only of National Gallery's holdings and objects.

The slide images can be borrowed through inter-library loan system. For the Public Lending Guide or more information, contact National Gallery of Art, Slide Library, Constitution and 6th St., NW, Washington, DC 20565, 202-842-6100; or online at <http://www.nga.gov>.

☆☆☆

Free Videos and CDs of Famous Artists

While the Mortons are watching *Top Gun* for the hundredth time next door, you can be watching something with a little class and learning about Leonardo, Matisse, or Impressionism.

The National Gallery of Art has over 150 videos, films, and video-discs covering specific artists or time periods. These programs are loaned free of charge to you in an effort to bring the Gallery to the world.

To receive a complete catalog of programs, contact Department of Education Resources, Education Division, National Gallery of Art, 4th St. and Constitution Ave., NW, Washington, DC 20565; 202-842-6875; or online at <http://www.nga.gov>.

☆☆☆

Artists and Performers Will Give You a Free Show

You won't be able to get Picasso or Warhol, but you will be able to get some incredible artists, musicians, actors, and craftsmen to come to your senior citizens' center, nursing home, or other nonprofit organization gathering.

Most states have Project Grants or Artist in Residence Programs to help cover some of the expenses involved in bringing various art forms to the community. To find out what programs are available and the requirements for each program, contact your State Arts Group from the list on page 215.

☆☆☆

Take Your Own Art Show On The Road

Grandparents Theater In The Round? High-Stepping Seniors? If you are part of an arts group that would like to go on tour, take advantage of the Touring Programs offered in many states.

These programs help share the cost of bringing artists, dancers, musicians, storytellers and others to local community organizations. Contact your State Arts Group from the list on page 215 to learn more about the steps necessary to qualify.

☆☆☆

Money to Have Your Own Art Exhibit

If your work didn't get into the Metropolitan Museum of Art, don't give up. Your group can still have a show of its own. States offer grants to produce exhibits, workshops, and performances. Your senior citizen photography group, painting class, or even the artwork created by nursing home residents may qualify.

Contact your State Arts Group from the list on page 215 to learn more about the steps necessary to qualify.

☆☆☆

Free Art Speakers for Your Group

Want someone to come to your group and talk "Art?" You can get a certified (not certifiable) artist to come share words of wisdom about his or her craft, or you can even learn what special programs your local arts group offers to seniors.

Many State Arts Councils, as well as regional or local agencies will provide speakers to your group whenever possible. Contact the offices nearest you to see what they have to offer.

☆☆☆

Cheap Seats ... Discounts on Theater Tickets

Take advantage of some special deals for those that hit the magic age of seniority. Many ballets, orchestras, museums, and art galleries offer discounted admission to senior citizens.

Here's a sample of nonprofit cultural organizations across the country that have received funding from either state arts councils and/or the National Endowment for the Arts and provide programs geared specifically toward older adults.

ARKANSAS
The Arkansas Symphony
Orchestra (ASO)
P.O. Box 7328
Little Rock, AK 72717
501-666-1761
The ASO provides discounted tickets to senior citizens. The Quapaw String Quartet performs in retirement communities and community centers.

CALIFORNIA
National Institute of Art and
Disabilities
551 23rd St.
Richmond, CA 94804
510-620-0290
Director: Carol Weinstein
National Institute of Art and Disabilities provides an on-going, 40-hour week art program for adults with developmental disabilities, many of whom are older and are developing careers as visual artists. Participants' work is facilitated by Master artist teachers.

GEORGIA
The Woodruff Arts Center
1280 Peachtree St., NE
Atlanta, GA 30309
404-733-4200
The Woodruff Arts Center provides discounted theater and museum tickets for senior citizens over age 65.

KENTUCKY
Appalshop
306 Madison St.
Whitesburg, KY 41858
606-633-0108
Appalshop provides programs that seek to break down cultural stereotypes of the Appalachian people. They have several programs that target older citizens. Roadside Theater program draws together diverse groups to examine local heritage. The community radio program features programs such as "Deep in Tradition," an old-time mountain music show.

211

ElderSprites
1816 Frankfort Ave.
Louisville, KY 40205
502-451-7302
Attn: Mary Ann Maier

Elder Dance Express
1442 Rufer Ave.
Louisville, KY 40204
502-581-1976
Attn: Chris Doerflinger

ElderSprites, a theater troupe of older adults; and Elder Dance Express, an ensemble of older dancers perform in schools, senior centers, and community centers, as well as in theaters throughout Kentucky.

MASSACHUSETTS
Boston-Fenway, Inc.
Elder Arts Project
590 Huntington Ave.
Boston, MA 02115
617-445-0047
Attn: Juanda Drumgold

This initiative involves older adults in the activities of the Boston Symphony Orchestra, New England Conservatory of Music, Huntington Theater, Stewart Garden and Museum, and Boston Museum of Fine Arts. The program provides complimentary tickets and transportation to selected events and performances. The more than 500 older adults participating in the program live in elder care centers or low-income housing complexes in Boston's Roxbury and Back Bay neighborhoods.

MINNESOTA
St. Paul's Chamber Orchestra
Hamm Building

408 St. Peters St.
Suite 300
St. Paul, MN 55102
612-292-3248

The Saint Paul Chamber Orchestra provides "The Morning Coffee Series," which is geared toward older people, and is comprised of eight morning Baroque concerts opening with informative concert previews.

NEW MEXICO
Very Special Arts New Mexico
P.O. Box 7784
Albuquerque, NM
505-768-5188

Very Special Arts New Mexico features the Buen Viaje Dancers, a modern dance troupe of all ages with multiple disabilities. They received a grant to produce, market, and distribute a video on working with individuals with disabilities in dance.

NEW YORK
Performance Space 122
150 1st Ave.
New York, NY
212-477-5288

Performance Space 122 provides dance tickets for events at a cost of $8 for eligible seniors.

Theater Development Fund
1501 Broadway Ave.
New York, NY 10036
212-221-0013 (recorded message)
212-221-0885 (staff)

The Theater Development Fund provides discounted theater and dance tickets to individuals and nonprofit community and senior citizen centers.

Elders Share the Arts (ESTA)
57 Willoughby St.
Brooklyn, NY 11201
718-488-8565
Attn: Susan Pearlstein
    Elders Share the Arts produces living history theater workshops and performances throughout New York's five boroughs. They tour and perform at city wide festivals, schools, museums, and community and senior centers.

Bronx Arts Ensemble
c/o Gulf House
Van Courtland Park
Bronx, NY 10471
718-601-7399
    The Bronx Arts Ensemble provides occasional free concerts and a series of concerts at reduced rates that are available to senior adults.

NORTH CAROLINA

Greensboro Symphony Society
P.O. Box 20303
Greensboro, NC 27420
910-333-7490
    The Greensboro Symphony Orchestra provides discounted tickets to senior citizens.

VERMONT

Grass Roots Art and Community Effort (GRACE)
P.O. Box 324
Saint Johnsbury, VT 05819
802-472-6857
    GRACE discovers, develops, and promotes visual art produced primarily by older self-taught artists in rural Vermont. GRACE has involved older adults in arts programs, many of whom are in nursing homes and other residential centers.

WASHINGTON, DC

Washington DC International Film Festival
P.O. Box 21396
Washington, DC 20009
202-274-6810
    The Washington DC International Film Festival provides two free matinee screenings for senior citizens at the Kennedy Center for Performing Arts during their May film festival each year.

Attend the Symphony for Free

    Many music groups offer special programs to older adults in the form of discounted tickets, free concerts, transportation, afternoon teas, and/or daytime events. Contact your State Arts Group (see page 215) or your state Department of Aging (listed in the Directory of State Information at the end of this book) to investigate the possibilities in your area. Some of the groups include:

Bronx Arts Ensemble in
Bronx, NY

Caramoor Center for Music
and the Arts in Katonah, NY

Chicago Symphony Chorus in Chicago, IL

Columbus Symphony Orchestra in Columbus, OH

Eastern Connecticut Symphony in New London, CT

Evansville Philharmonic Orchestra in Evansville, PA

Fort Wayne Philharmonic Orchestra in Fort Wayne, IN

Frederic R. Mann Music Center in Philadelphia, PA

Grand Rapids Symphony Society in Grand Rapids, MI

Lexington Philharmonic Society in Lexington, KY

Los Angeles Chamber Orchestra Society in Los Angeles, CA

Louisville Orchestra in Louisville, KY

Meet the Composer in New York City, NY

Memphis Orchestral Society in Memphis, TN

Missouri Symphony Society in Columbia, MO

Mississippi Symphony Orchestra Association in Jackson, MS

Nevada Symphony Orchestra in Las Vegas, NV

New York Chamber Ensemble in New York, NY

Northeastern Pennsylvania Philharmonic in Avoca, PA

Philharmonic Symphony

Society in New York City, NY

Philomel Concerts in Philadelphia, PA

Pro Musicis Foundation in New York City, NY

Queens Symphony Orchestra in Long Island, NY

Robert W. Woodruff Arts Center in Atlanta, GA

Rochester Philharmonic Orchestra in Rochester, NY

Rockford Symphony Orchestra in Rockford, IL

Rosewood Chamber Ensemble in Sunnyside, NY

Saint Paul Chamber Orchestra Society in St. Paul, MN

Santa Barbara Symphony Orchestra Association in Santa Barbara, CA

Seattle Children's Home in Seattle, WA

Shreveport Symphony Society in Shreveport, LA

South Carolina Orchestra Association in Columbia, SC

Stamford Symphony Orchestra in Stamford, CT

Theatre Development Fund in New York City, NY

Trustees of Columbia University in New York City, NY

Tucson Symphony Society in Tucson, AZ

Westwind Brass in San Diego, CA

State Arts Groups

The following is a state-by-state listing of State Arts Groups. Each listing contains a list of programs, a description of general requirements, and an estimate of the total money available.

ALABAMA
Alabama Arts Council
201 Monroe St.
Montgomery, AL 36130-5810
334-242-4076
Fax: 334-240-3269
http://www.bham.com/asca/
Money Available: $1.5 million
Eligibility Requirements:
For individual artist programs state residency is required, unless otherwise specified. Grants to organizations must be matched by at least an equal amount from other sources located by the applicant.
Programs Available:
$5,000 To Art Administrators (Fellowship in Arts Administration)
$10,000 For Artists (Artists Fellowships)
$1,000 To Develop Administrative Skills (Technical Assistance)
Money To Be An Artist-In Residence (Artist Residences)
$5,000 For Master Folk Artists (Folk Art Apprenticeships)
Grants To Large Arts Organizations (Advanced Institutional Assistance)
Money For Schools To Hire Artists (Arts in Education Projects)
Money For Designers (Design Arts Projects)
Money For Folk Artists (Folklife Program)
Money For Local Arts Councils (Local Arts Councils)
Money To Put On A Show Or Exhibition (Presenter Program)
Money For Community Arts Projects (Project Assistance Programs)
Money to bring arts to communities deprived of art (Community Arts Development Grants)

ALASKA
Alaska State Council on the Arts
411 W. 4th Ave., Suite E
Anchorage, AK 99501-2343
907-269-6610
Fax: 907-269-6601
http://www.educ.state.ak.us/asca/home.html
Money Available: $450,000
Eligibility Requirements:
State residency is required for individual grants to artists. The Council awards funds only to Alaskan non-profit organizations, schools or government agencies.
Programs Available:
$1,000 For Artists To Travel To Art Conferences (Career Opportunity Grant Program)
$2,000 To Study With A Master Craftsperson, Musician, Dancer, Or Storyteller (Master Arts and Apprentice Grants in Traditional Native Arts)
Money For Local Art Agencies (Grants to Local Arts Agencies)
Grants To Help Pay For Art Administration Costs (Season Support)

Money To Support a Local Art
Project (Project Grants)

Money To Pay Artists To Speak At
Workshops (Workshop Grants)

Money For Schools To Have An
Artist-In-Residence Program
(Artist Residency Grants)

ARIZONA
Arizona Arts Commission
417 W. Roosevelt St.
Phoenix, AZ 85003
602-255-5882
Fax: 602-256-0282
http://www.azarts.asu.edu/
artscomm

Money Available: $3,600,000
Eligibility Requirements:
Individual Artist Fellowships
require state residency. Priority for
organizational funding is given to
projects in rural areas of the state
and projects coordinated by ethnic-
run organizations or those that primarily serve ethnic communities.

Programs Available:
$7,500 For Artists and Writers
(Fellowships)

$5,000 For Artists To Use For
Research And Travel (Artist
Projects)

Money To Support Special Art
Projects (Project Support)

Grants To Help Run Art
Organizations (Administrative/
General Operating Support)

Money For Schools To Have
Artists-In-Residence Programs
(Artists-in-Residence)

Money For Schools With New Ideas
In Art (Education Initiatives)

Help For Sponsors Who Wish To
Contract With Artists (Project
Support)

ARKANSAS
Arkansas Arts Council
1500 Tower Bldg.
323 Center St.
Little Rock, AR 72201
501-324-9766
Fax: 501-324-9154
http://www.state.ar.us:80/html/
ark_her_aac.html

Money Available: year to year
average of about $1.2 million
Eligibility Requirements:
Individual Artist Fellowship program: state resident; not a previous
fellowship winner

Technical Assistance to Individual
Artists: state resident; approval as
an Arts in Education or touring
artist or previous fellowship winner

Grants to Organizations: non-profit, 501(c)(3) status; existence as an
entity for at least one year; proven
history for presenting or producing
art programs. Funds awarded must
be matched at least equally by the
applicant organization with cash
from sources other than the
Arkansas Arts Council, Mid-
America Arts Alliance, or National
Endowment for the Arts.

Programs Available:
Individual Artist Fellowship: $5,000
based on previous work

General Operating Support (to
organizations): for administrative,
non-programming operations of
the organization. Match must be
from programming expenses.

Project Support (to organizations): for
specific arts projects or programs

Arts In Education (to organizations
or schools): for artist in residence
programs

216

Arts On Tour (to organizations or schools): subsidy of 40% for costs of presenting approved artists, with maximum of $2,000 Assistance Fund: up to $1,000 to organizations for professional or board development or for unforeseen expenses and opportunities; up to $1,000 to individual artists for technical assistance

Public Art: grants related to public art in communities, Save Outdoor Sculpture projects, and Two-Percent for Art

CALIFORNIA
California Arts Council
1300 I St., Suite 930
Sacramento, CA 95814
916-322-6555
Fax: 916-322-6575
http://www.cac.ca.gov
Money Available: $14,720,000
Eligibility Requirements:
State residency is required for individual artists programs.
Programs Available:
$5,000 Award To Artists, Choreographers, and Writers (Artists Fellowship Program)

Be An Artist-In-Residence And Get $1,300 For 80 Hours (Artists-in-Residence Program)

Money For Organizations Interested In Art-Related Activities (Organizational Support Program)

$6,000 For Multi-Cultural Arts Activities (Multi-Cultural Entry Grant Program)

$40,000 For Multi-Cultural Grant Activities (Multi-Cultural Advancement Program)

Money For Organizations To Hire

Performing Artists (Performing Arts Touring and Presenting Program) In-state groups only

Matching Grants For Arts Organizations (California Challenge Program)

COLORADO
Colorado Council on the Arts (CCAH)
750 Pennsylvania
Denver, CO 80203
303-894-2617
800-291-ARTS
Fax: 303-894-2615
http://www.aclin.org/cca/index.htm
Money Available: $1,144,000
Eligibility Requirements:
For individual artist programs, state residency is required, unless otherwise specified.
Programs Available:
Grants To Individual Artists (Colorado Visions Project Grants; up to $4,000 awarded per fellowship)

Free Help With Managing An Arts Organization (Organizational Assistance Program)

Grants To Local Arts Councils (Community Arts Development Grants)

Money For Schools To Have An Artist-In-Residence (Artists-in-Residence Program)

Money for Teacher Training Art in Public Places Program

Colorado Artist Register

CONNECTICUT
Connecticut Commission on the Arts
755 Main St.
1 Financial Plaza
Hartford, CT 06103

860-566-4770
Fax: 860-566-6462
http://www.cslnet.ctstateu.edu/cca/
Money Available: $918,400
Eligibility Requirements:
State residency is required.
Programs Available:
Artists Fellowships: funding for
Connecticut resident artists. (Artistic categories alternate every year)
Arts Partnerships for Stronger
Communities: to provide funding
to CT arts organizations to form
collaborative projects with local
organizations.
Arts Presentation Grants: to provide
support to CT nonprofit organizations which present events featuring members of the CCA's
Directory of Performing Artists
and Master Teaching Artists.
Organization Challenge Grants: to
provide funding to CT's nonprofit
organizations and units of state or
local government to conduct public programs which support artistic development, arts in education
and participation in the arts.
Arts in Education Development
Grants: to provide funding to
schools for arts-related curriculum and/or pedagogy development projects.

DELAWARE
Delaware Division of the Arts
Carvell State Office Building
820 North French St.
Wilmington, DE 19801
302-577-8278
Fax: 302-577-6561
http://www.dca.net/artsdel/
Money Available: $1,180,000
Eligibility Requirements:

Individual artist programs
require state residency, unless otherwise specified.
Programs Available:
Money For New Or Established
Artists (Individual Artist
Fellowships)
Matching Grants For Arts Groups
(Project Support Grants)
Money For Operating Expenses
(General Operating Support Grants)
Money For New Arts Groups To
Help With Management (Grants
to Emerging Organizations)
Money For Schools To Have An
Artist-In-Residence (Arts in
Education Residencies)
$10,000 for Playwrights Fellowships
$5,000 for Composers Competition

DISTRICT OF COLUMBIA
District of Columbia Council of Arts
410 Eighth St., NW, 5th Floor
Stables Art Center
Washington, DC 20004
202-724-5613
Fax: 202-727-4135
http://www.capaccess.org/dccah
Money Available: $1.4 million
Eligibility Requirements:
Individual artist programs
require residency in the District of
Columbia for at least one year
prior to application deadline and
the applicant must maintain residency during the grant period.
Individuals and arts organizations
may apply in one of the following
disciplines: crafts, dance, interdisciplinary/performance art (individuals only), literature, media, multidisciplinary, music, theater, and
the visual arts.

Organizations must have their principal place of business in the District of Columbia, and have both Federal and DC Tax Exemption for at least one year prior to application.

Programs Available:
$2,5000 - $4,500 For Theater, Visual, And Literary Artists
Up To $15,000 For Art Groups (Organizational Funding)

FLORIDA

Florida Arts Council
Division of Cultural Affairs
Department of State
Tallahassee, FL 32399
850-487-2980
Fax: 850-922-5259
http://www.dos.state.fl.us/dca/
Money Available: $22,000,000
Eligibility Requirements:
Funding is offered to organizations providing cultural activities and programming. Organizations must be either not-for-profit, tax-exempt Florida corporations or governmental entities. Florida Individual Artist Fellowships ($5,000) are offered only to state residents; recipients may not be degree seeking students. Some programs for individual artists are open to out of state residents.

Programs Available:
Art in State Buildings Program (% for art) (open to out of state artists)
Arts in Education Program (up to $15,000)
Capitol Complex Exhibition Program
Challenge Grant Program (up to $75,000)
Cultural Facilities Program (up to $500,000)
Cultural Institutions Program (up to $350,000)
Discipline-based Arts Grants (up to $50,000)
Florida Cultural Endowment Program
Florida Individual Artist Fellowship Program ($5,000 each, up to 40 awarded each year)
Florida's Artist Residency Directory
International Cultural Exchange Program (up to $25,000)
Local Arts Agency and State Service Organization Program (up to $60,000)
Quarterly Grant Assistance (up to $1,500)
Science, Youth and Children's Museum Program (up to $50,000)
State Touring Program
Underserved Arts Communities Assistance Program (up to $10,000)

GEORGIA

Georgia Council for Arts
530 Means St., NW, Suite 115
Atlanta, GA 30318
404-651-7920
Fax: 404-651-7922
Money Available: $2,600,000
Eligibility Requirements:
The majority of grants available are organizational grants in the following disciplines: dance, music, literature, presenters, theater visual arts and community arts programs. Additional grants are available for individual Georgia schools and school systems.

Programs Available:
Grants To Local Governments And Nonprofits (Civic/Education/Government/Other Grants)

$500 To Hire An Arts Consultant (Technical Assistance Grants)

Georgia Folklife Program (Georgia Folklife Program)

Money For Schools To Have An Artist-In-Residence (Arts Education Partnership Program)

Up to $50,000 for School Systems to Implement Curriculum-based Arts Education Programs (Georgia Challenge Program)

HAWAII
Hawaii State Foundation on Culture and Arts (SFCA)
44 Merchant St.
Honolulu, HI 96813
808-586-0300
Fax: 808-586-0308
http://www.state.hi.us/sfca/
Money Available: $1,400,000
Eligibility Requirements:
State residency required.
Programs Available:
Grants For Concerts, Performances, Workshops, and Lectures (Organizational Funding)

$2,700 For Artists To Study As An Apprentice (The Folk Arts Program)

$5,000 For Artists (Fellowship Awards)

Arts in Education Program

Art in Public Places Program

IDAHO
Idaho Commission on Arts
304 West State St.
Boise, ID 83720
208-334-2119
800-278-3863 (ID only)
Fax: 208-334-2488
http://www.state.id.us/arts/
Money Available: $509,810

Eligibility Requirements:
Individual artist programs require state residency, unless otherwise specified. Organizations must be registered as nonprofit organizations.
Programs Available:
$3,500 For Artists, Dancers, Designers, and Craftspersons (Fellowship Awards)

$3,500 For Artists To Work With A Master (Worksites Awards)

$1,000 Plus Travel To Study With A Master Craftsperson (Traditional Native Arts Apprenticeship Program)

$8,000 To Be A Writer-In Residence (Writer-in-Residence)

Up to $7,500 For Special Art Projects (Project Support)

Up to $5,000 For Touring Arts Groups (Performing Arts Touring)

Grants To Bring Art To Small Towns (Arts in Rural Towns)

Money For Running A Local Arts Council (Local Arts Council Salary Assistance)

$3,700 For An Arts Council In A Small Town (Arts in Rural Towns (ARTs))

Money For Schools Or Nursing Homes To Have An Artist-In-Residence (Artists-in-Residence)

Money For New Ideas In Arts Education (Education Innovations)

$1,000 Quick Project (organizations and artists)

$400 for Professional Development

$2,000 for Traditional Arts Apprenticeships

ILLINOIS
Illinois Arts Council
State Of Illinois Center
100 West Randolph, Suite 10-500
Chicago, IL 60601
312-814-6750, 800-237-6994 (IL only)
Fax: 312-814-1471
http://www.state.il.us/agency/iac/
Money Available: $86,007,000
Eligibility Requirements:
   Individual artist programs
require state residency, unless otherwise specified.
   In addition to the programs
detailed, grants are funded for
choral music and opera, dance,
ethnic and folk arts, symphonies
and ensemble, theater, and visual
arts programs.
Programs Available:
$5,000 and $10,000 for Artists,
   Photographers, Writers, and
   Poets (Fellowships)
Grants To Artists To Study As
   Apprentices (Apprenticeship
   Program)
$1,000 For Writers And Non-Profit
   Magazines (Literary Awards)
Money To Provide Art To
   Communities Normally
Deprived Of Art (Access Program)
Grants To Groups That Support
   Creative Writers (Literature
   Programs)
Money For Film and Video
   Production (Media Arts Program)
Funding For Interdiscipline Art
   Programs (Multi-Disciplinary
   Programs)
Grants For Performing Arts
(Presenters Development Programs)
Money For Touring Art Groups
   (Artstour)

Special Money For Arts Programs
   and Projects (Special Assistance
   Grants)
Money For Schools Or Other
   Organizations To Have An
   Artist-In-Residence (Artists-in-
   Residence and Short Term
   Artist Residencies)
Grants For Schools To Develop
   Arts Curriculum (Arts
   Resource)
Grants to Groups That Support
   Arts Education (Arts in
   Education Program)
Grants to Groups That Support
   Dance Companies (Dance
   Programs)
Grants to Groups That Support
   Ethnic and Folk Artists (Ethnic
   and Folk Arts Programs)
Grants to Groups That Support
   Musicians (Music Programs)
Grants to Groups That Support
   Actors (Theater Programs)
Grants to Groups That Support
   Visual Artists (Visual Arts
   Programs)
Grants to Local Art Agencies for
   Support of Local Arts
   Programming (Local Arts
   Agencies Programs)
Grants to Local Arts Agencies for
   Development of Local Arts
   Programming (Arts
   Development Program)

INDIANA
Indiana Arts Commission
402 W. Washington St., Room 072
Indianapolis, IN 46204
317-232-1268
Fax: 317-232-5595
http://www.ai.org/iac/
Money Available: $2,700,000

Eligibility Requirements:
Contact the Arts Commission for guidelines.
Programs Available:
Grants To Arts Organizations (General Operating Support)
Grants To Run Special Art Projects (Arts Projects and Series)
Money For Artists-In Residence Programs (Arts in Education Grants)
Money For Multi-Cultural Or Rural Art Activities (Arts: Rural and Multi-Cultural (ARM) Program)
Money For Art Administrators To Attend Workshops (Technical Assistance)

KANSAS
Kansas Arts Commission
Jayhawk Tower
700 Jackson, Suite 1004
Topeka, KS 66603-3714
785-296-3335
Fax: 785-296-4989
Money Available: $1,000,000
Eligibility Requirements:
Matching grants from the Commission are available to Kansas not-for-profit organizations and public agencies to support arts programs and services that provide public access to the arts. Non-matching fellowships are available to Kansas artists.
Programs Available:
Fellowships for Kansas Artists (For artists creating original work)
Grants to Arts Organizations (General operating and program support)
Grants for Arts In Education Programs (For programs in schools and non-school settings)
Grants for Arts Projects and Kansas Touring Program Events (To support presenters of arts programs)
Grassroots Program Grants (For arts programs in multicultural and rural communities)
Technical Assistance (Grants and services to assist developing arts organizations)
Statewide Arts Service Organization Support (To provide services for artists and organizations)

KENTUCKY
Kentucky Arts Council
31 Fountain Place
Frankfort, KY 40601
502-564-3757
Fax: 502-564-2839
Money Available: $2,700,000
Eligibility Requirements:
Matching grants from the Council are available to Kentucky non-profit organizations committed to providing arts programs and services to the public. Grant amounts vary from year to year and depend upon the availability of funds. Non-matching fellowships are available to Kentucky artists.
Programs Available:
Organizational Support Grant Programs
Challenge Grants
Arts Development Grants
Project Grant Program
Organizational Technical Assistance Grant Program
Individual Artist Recognition and Support Program
Brown-Forman and Al Smith Artist Fellowships
1997 Writers, Composers,

Choreographers
1998 Visual and Media Arts
Governor's Awards in the Arts
Kentucky Poet Laureate
Community Arts Development
Grant Programs
Community Arts Grants
Community Artist in Residence
Grants
Folk and Traditional Arts Grants
Project Grant Program
Organizational Technical
Assistance Grant Program
Arts in Education Grant Programs
Artist in Residence Sponsor Grants
Artist in Residence Artist Application
Teacher Incentive Program Grants
Project Grant Program
Organizational Technical
Assistance Grant Program
Folklife Program
Craft Marketing Program

LOUISIANA
Louisiana State Division of the Arts
P.O. Box 44247
Baton Rouge, LA 70804
504-342-8180
Fax: 504-342-8173
http://www.crt.state.la.us/crt/ocd /doapage/doapage.htm
Money Available: $1,680,000
Eligibility Requirements:
Individual artist programs require state residency.
Programs Available:
$5,000 For Artists, Craftspersons, Designers, and Musicians (Artist Fellowships)
$5,000 For Artists To Work With A Master (Folklife Apprenticeships)
$25,000 For Art Organizations (Project Assistance Program)

$500 for Artist Mini-gate
Up To $250,000 For Local Arts Agencies (Local Arts Agency Program)
Money For Art Groups (General Operating Support)
Money For Schools To Develop Art Programs (Educational Funding)

MAINE
Maine Arts Commission
55 Capitol St.
25 State House Station
Augusta, ME 04333
207-287-2724
Fax: 207-287-2335
http://www.mainearts.com
Money Available: $750,000
Eligibility Requirements:
Individual artist programs require state residency.
Programs Available:
$3,000 To Artists (Fellowships)
$1,200 For Master Artists To Teach Others (Traditional Arts Apprenticeships)
Leadership Initiatives and Technical Assistance
Cultural Tourism
Community Arts Development
Arts in the Capitol
Maine Artist Roster
Maine Artist Registry
Arts in Education
Percent for Art

MARYLAND
Maryland State Arts Council
601 N. Howard St.
Baltimore, MD 21201
410-333-8232
Fax: 410-333-1062
http://www.msac.org

Money Available: $6,870,000
Eligibility Requirements:
The Council provides direct grants to individual artists based on artistic merit, and offers professional opportunities for Maryland artists. State residency is required for participation. The Grants To Organizations Program provides operating, program and project grants to Maryland organizations that produce or present the arts to the public. The Community Arts Development Program supports county arts councils in each of the 23 counties of Maryland and in Baltimore City. Funds are used in each county to regrant to local organizations, support arts programs and support the operations of the county arts councils. The Artists in Education program provides opportunities for visual and performing artists to hold residencies or performances in schools.
Programs Available:
Awards of $1,000, $3,000 and $6,000 for Creative and Performing Artists (Individual Artist Awards)
Money For Large Arts Organizations (Grants to Major Institutions)
Grants To Arts Organizations who Produce or Present the Arts to the Public (General Operating Grants)
Money To Support Innovative Art Projects that Reach Out to the Underserved (New Initiative Grants)
Grants To Non-Arts Organizations who Produce or Present the Arts to the Public (Arts Program and Arts Project Grants)
Help For Those Interested In

Maryland Folklife (Maryland Folklife Program)
Money For Poets, Artists, and Performers To Work At Schools (Artists in Education Program)

MASSACHUSETTS
Massachusetts Cultural Council
120 Boylston St., 2nd Floor
Boston, MA 02116-4600
617-727-3668
Fax: 617-727-0044
Money Available: $12,600,000
Eligibility Requirements:
Eligibility varies from program to program.
Programs Available:
Event and Residency Program
Education Partnership Initiative
Organizational Support Program
Professional Development Program
ADA Mini-Grants Program
Massachusetts Cultural Facilities Project
YouthReach Program
Local Cultural Council Grant Program
Local Cultural Council Matching Incentive Program
Artist Grants
Visual Arts Fellowships
Media Fellowships
Massachusetts Touring Program
Science in the Community Program
Cultural Economic Development Program
Elder Initiative

MICHIGAN
Michigan Council for the Arts
1200 Sixth St., Executive Plaza
Detroit, MI 48226-2461
313-256-3731
Fax: 313-256-3781

http://www.cis.state.mi.us/arts/
Money Available: $22,000,000
Programs Available:
Arts and Learning Program
Artists in Schools Program
Anchor Organization Program
Arts Organization Development
Program (AOD)
Arts and Cultural Projects for
Cities, Townships and Villages
Program (CTV)
Discretionary Grants Program
Local, Regional or Statewide Arts
Agencies Services Program
Mini-Grant Regional Regranting
Program
Arts Projects Program
Partnership Program

MINNESOTA
Minnesota State Arts Board
400 Sibley St., Suite 200
St. Paul, MN 55102
612-215-1600
800-8MN-ARTS
Fax: 612-215-1602
Money Available: $4,492,155
Eligibility Requirements:
Individual artist programs
require state residency, unless oth-
erwise specified.
Programs Available:
$6,000 For Visual, Literary, Or
Performing Artists (Fellowships)
$1,000 For Artists To Improve
Their Careers (Career
Opportunity Grants)
Money For Art Studio In Sausalito,
California (Headlands Residency
Project)
$4,000 To Be An Apprentice
Craftsperson (Folk Arts
Apprenticeship Grants)
$4,000 For Folk Art Research And

Festivals (Folk Arts Sponsorship
Grants)
$3,000 For Artists To Travel More
Than 60 Miles From Home
(Minnesota Touring Arts)
$50,000 To Organizations Who
Help Artists (Operating Support
Program)
$5,000 To Organizations That Help
More Than 5 Artists (Series
Presenters Programs)
Money For Schools To Improve
Their Arts Program
(Organizational Support Grants)
Money For Schools To Have An
Artist-In-Residence (School
Support Grants)

MISSISSIPPI
Mississippi Arts Commission
239 North Lamar St., Suite 207
Jackson, MS 39201
601-359-6030
Fax: 601-359-6008
http://www.arts.state.ms.us/
Money Available: $1,200,000
Eligibility Requirements:
Individual artist programs
require state residency.
Programs Available:
$5,000 For Writers, Composers,
Video Producers (Artist
Fellowships)
$30,000 For Arts And Cultural
Organizations (General
Operating Support)
$25,000 For Local Arts Agencies
(Local Arts Agencies)
$5,000 For New Arts Organizations
(Management Assistance)
$7,500 For Special Art Projects
(Project Support)
$2,000 To Help Touring Artists
(Mississippi Touring Arts)

$7,000 For Local Schools To
Improve Their Art Programs
(Arts in Education)

MISSOURI
Missouri State Council on the Arts
Wainwright Office Complex
111 N. 7th St., Suite 105
St. Louis, MO 63101
314-340-6845
Fax: 314-340-7215
http://www.ecodev.state.mo.us/
moartscouncil/
Money Available: $5,100,000
Eligibility Requirements:
The Council offers financial assistance through seven art areas: dance, literature, media, multi-discipline, music, theater, and visual arts. A program administrator supervises applications in each area.
Programs Available:
Money For Smaller Arts
Organizations (Community Arts
Program (CAP))
Money For Arts Groups Serving
The Entire State (Statewide Arts
Service Organizations)
$2,000 To Help Art Organizations
With Management Development
(Technical Assistance)
Special partners to the Missouri
State Council on the Arts are:
Missouri Alliance for Art Education
African American Cultural Initiative
Missouri Folk Art Program

MONTANA
Montana Arts Council
316 N. Park Ave., Room 252
Helena, MT 59620-2201
406-444-6430
Fax: 406-444-6548
Money Available: $1,550,000

Eligibility Requirements:
Individual artist programs
require state residency.
Programs Available:
$2,000 To Individual Artists
(Individual Artist Fellowships)
$6,000 For Arts Organizations
(Organizational Funding)
Grants For Arts Preservation,
Media Arts, Archaeology, and
Folklore (Cultural and Aesthetic
Project Grants)
Money For Schools To Have An
Artist-In-Residence (Artists in
Schools/Communities)

NEBRASKA
Nebraska Arts Council
Joslyn Castle Carriage House
3838 Davenport St.
Omaha, NE 68131
402-595-2122
Fax: 402-595-2334
http://www.gps.kl2.ne.us/
nac_web_site/nac.htm
Money Available: $1,110,000
Eligibility Requirements:
Individual artist programs
require state residency.
Programs Available:
Money For Writers, Artists, and
Performers (Individual Artist
Fellowships)
Grants To Arts Organizations
(Basic Support Grant)
$1,000 For High Risk Art Projects
(Special Opportunity Support)
Up to $5,000 For Art Festivals,
Exhibitions, and Poetry
Readings (Impact)
Money For Touring Exhibits and
Programs (Nebraska Touring
Program/Exhibits Nebraska)

Money For Educational Organizations To Use Art (Arts as Basic in the Curriculum/Community)

$500 For Artists and Groups To Tour (Nebraska Touring Program/Exhibits Nebraska (NTP) Technical Assistance Program)

Money For Art Projects At Schools (Artists in Schools/Communities)

NEVADA
Nevada State Council on the Arts
Capitol Complex
602 N. Curry St.
Carson City, NV 89701
702-687-6680
Fax: 702-687-6688
http://www.clan.lib.nv.us/docs/arts/arts-con.html
Money Available: $552,000
Eligibility Requirements:
Individual artist programs require state residency.
Programs Available:
$200 - $30,000 For Artists To Create New Works (Artists Fellowships)
$2,500 For Master Folk Artists To Teach Apprentices (Folk Arts Apprenticeships)
$22,500 For Arts Organizations (Grants to Organizations)
$15,000 To Bring Art To Small Towns (Rural Arts Development)
$30,000 To Help Art Organizations (Challenge Grant Program)
Money For Schools To Have An Artist-In-Residence (Artist-in-Residence Program)

NEW HAMPSHIRE
New Hampshire Division of Arts
Council on the Arts
40 North Main St.

Concord, NH 03301
603-271-2789
Fax: 603-271-3584
http://www.state.nh.us/nharts
Money Available: $500,000
Eligibility Requirements:
Individual artist programs require state residency, unless otherwise specified.
Programs Available:
Percent for Art
Arts in Communities
Arts C.O.R.E.
Individual Artists Grants

NEW JERSEY
New Jersey State Council on the Arts
P.O. Box 306
Trenton, NJ 08625-0306
609-292-6130
Fax: 609-989-1440
http://www.artswire.org/artswire/njsca/
Money Available: $13.1 million
Eligibility Requirements:
Individual artist programs require state residency.
Organizations must be nonprofit.
Programs Available:
Matching Organizational Grants (for operations, programs, and projects)
Fellowships for Individual Artists
Folk Arts Apprenticeships
Artist in Education Residencies
Special Initiatives

NEW MEXICO
New Mexico Arts
228 East Palace Ave.
Santa Fe, NM 87501
505-827-6490
800-879-4278 (NM only)

Fax: 505-827-6043
http://www.nmmnh_abg.mus.nm.
us/arts/arts.html
Money Available: $692,800
Eligibility Requirements:
New Mexico Arts is unable to
fund fellowships to individuals. It
strongly encourages applicant
organizations to involve resident
New Mexico artists. However, the
Division does support local sponsorship of out-of-state artists or
organizations to enrich a resident
group or when the services fill a
need that is not being met locally.
Organizational Funding:
New Mexico administers awards
to non-profit organizations. Generally,
award applicants must provide at
least a one-to-one cash match.
Programs Available:
$80,000 For Arts Organizations
    (Established Arts Organizations)
$15,000 For Local Art Groups
    (Civic and Community Arts
    Organizations)
$20,000 For Ethnic Arts Projects
    (Culturally Diverse
    Organizations)
$5,000 For Folk Art Programs
    (Arts Projects)
Money For An Artist-In-Residence
    For Schools And Community
    Homes (Artists Residencies)

NEW YORK
New York State Council on the Arts
915 Broadway
New York, NY 10010
212-387-7000
Fax: 212-387-7164
http://www.artswire.org/~nysca/
Money Available: $36,000,000

Eligibility Requirements:
Individual artist programs
require state residency and must
be sponsored by nonprofit organizations. Nonprofit organizations
can obtain support in 17 areas
including: architecture, planning
and design, arts in education, capital funding, dance, electronic media
and film, folk arts, individual
artists, literature, museum, music,
musical instrument revolving loan
fund, presenting operations, special
arts services, state local partnership, theater, and the visual arts.
Programs Available:
Please call and ask for application guideline book.

NORTH CAROLINA
North Carolina Arts Council
Department of Cultural Resources
Raleigh, NC 27611
919-733-2821
Fax: 919-733-4834
http://www.ncarts.org
Money Available: $4,200,000
Eligibility Requirements:
Individual artist programs
require state residency. Money for
arts organizations is in eight categories: community development,
dance, folklife, literature, music,
theater, touring/presenting, and
the visual arts. Support includes
funding for program support, inter-
disciplinary/ special projects, and
organizational development grants.
Programs Available:
$8,000 For Artists, Dancers,
    Musicians, and Writers Bi-annu-
    ally (Fellowships)
Money For Artists To Work With
    Schools And Community

228

Colleges (Residencies)

$3,000 For Local Folk Artists Bi-annually (Folk Heritage Awards)

Up to $10,000 To Make A Documentary Of State Folk Artists (Folklife Documentary Project Grants)

Help For Local Artists To Tour The State (Touring Artists Roster)

Money To Train As An Art Administrator (Internships)

Money For Theater And Literary Organizations (General Support)

Money For Local Governments To Support Art Groups (Local Government Challenge)

Money For Statewide Arts Groups (Management Service Organization)

Grants To Schools For Art Projects (Arts in Education)

NORTH DAKOTA
North Dakota Council On Arts
418 E. Broadway, Suite 70
Bismark, ND 58501-4086
701-328-3954
Fax: 701-328-3963
http://www.state.nd.us/arts/
Money Available: $550,000
Eligibility Requirements:
Individual artist programs require state residency, unless otherwise specified. Organizations must be 501(c)(3).
Programs Available:
Money For Artists, Dancers, Opera Singers, Photographers, and Writers (Artists Fellowships Program)

Money To Hire Consultants Or Arts Advisors (Professional Development Program)

Grants To Small Arts Organizations (ACCESS Grant Program)

$500 For Special Art Projects

Money For Schools To Have An Artist-In-Residence (Artists-in-Residence)

Money For Schools To Develop Art Programs (Local Education in the Arts Planning: LEAP)

OHIO
Ohio Council on Arts
727 East Main St.
Columbus, OH 43205
614-466-2613
Fax: 614-466-4494
http://www.oac.ohio.gov/
Money Available: $6,442,000
Eligibility Requirements:
State residency is required, unless otherwise specified. Programs/ projects must be nonprofit in intent. Proof of tax-exempt status is required. Programs/projects must be of high aesthetic quality and artistic merit. Must provide a one to one match for grant funds and demonstrate financial responsibility.
Programs Available:
Individual Artists Program
Traditional and Ethnic Arts Apprenticeship Program
Artists Projects Program
Support for Organizations (Operating support and project support)
Major Institution Support
Arts in Education Programs
Minority Arts Program
Performing Arts on Tour
Technical Assistance/Resource Center
Building Diverse Audiences

OKLAHOMA
Oklahoma Arts Council
P.O. Box 52001-2001
State Capitol Complex

Jim Thorpe Bldg.
Oklahoma City, OK 73152
405-521-2931
Fax: 405-521-6418
http://www.state.ok.us/~arts/
Money Available: $2,850,000
Eligibility Requirements:
The Council is unable to fund
individuals. Applications are
accepted from non-religious, nonprofit, tax exempt organizations.
Colleges, schools, and universities
which receive funding through the
State Regents for Higher
Education or substantial private
sources, are a lower funding priority, except in areas where the university or college is the sole source
of arts events in a community.

All funding for the Annual Project
Support, Sudden Opportunity
Support, and Festivals categories
must be matched dollar for dollar by
the applicant. Fifty percent of the
matching funds must be cash. The
Council will fund personnel or
administrative costs associated with
a project. The Council does not fund
general administrative expenses or
general organizational support.
Programs Available:
Matching funds for arts organization's projects for the year
(Annual Project Support)
Matching funds for unexpected
projects that the organization was
unable to include in the APS cate-
gory (Sudden Opportunity
Support)
Matching funds for multi-arts festivals, pow-wows, and other cultural celebrations which have activities designed to bring arts to the

public (Festivals)
Non-matching funds to organiza-
tions to contract with knowl-
edgeable consultants to address
specific management or artistic
problems, to strengthen manage-
ment and programs (Technical
Assistance)
Matching funds for Artist in
Residence in Schools or
Community Groups (Artist in
Residence Program)
Matching funds for schools and
communities to bring in
Oklahoma Roster Artists
(Oklahoma Touring Program)
Matching funds for organizations
to present performing artists
from outside Oklahoma
(Presenting Program)

OREGON
Oregon Arts Commission
775 Summer St., NE
Salem, OR 97310
503-986-0082
Fax: 503-986-0260
http://www.das.state.or.us/oac/
index.html
Money Available: $1,720,000
Eligibility Requirements:
Individual artist programs
require state residency, unless oth-
erwise specified.
Programs Available:
$3,000 To Artists, Photographers,
And Performers (Artist
Fellowships)
Up to $5,000 For Artists Living In
13 Western States (Western
States Regional Media Arts
Fellowships)
Money For Authors and Publishers
In 13 Western States (Western

States Book Awards)
Grants For Arts Organizations
(Economic Development Grants)
Grants For Artists and Small Art
Groups (Regional Regranting)
Money To Be An Artist-In-Residence
(Artist Residencies)
Up to $3,000 For Arts Programs In
Schools (Arts Education Project
Grants)

PENNSYLVANIA
Pennsylvania Council on the Arts
Room 216, Finance Bldg.
Harrisburg, PA 17120
717-787-6883
Fax: 717-783-2538
http://artsnet.heinz.cmu.edu/pca/
Money Available: $9,658,000
Eligibility Requirements:
For individual artist programs,
applicants must have lived in
Pennsylvania for two years prior to
applying for funding and should
have had a minimum of three
years professional experience in
their field. Organizational funding
programs require that organizations must be non-profit, tax
exempt corporations that provide
arts programming and/or services
to Pennsylvania. Categories
include: broadcast of the arts,
crafts, inter-disciplinary arts,
dance, literature, local arts services, local government, media arts,
museums, music, presenting
organizations, theater, and visual
arts. Non-profit organizations may
apply on behalf of an unincorporat-
ed arts group. In this capacity, the
organization becomes a "conduit"
for grant funds and is financially,
administratively, and programmati-

cally responsible for a grant.
Programs Available:
Grants To Dancers, Jazz
Composers, Writers, And Artists
(Fellowships)
Grants To Arts Organizations
(General Support)
$1,000 To Hire A Consultant For Your
Art Group (Technical Assistance)
$250 To Bus Artists To A
Performance (Busing Program)

RHODE ISLAND
**Rhode Island State Council on
The Arts**
95 Cedar St., Suite 103
Providence, RI 02903
401-277-3880
Fax: 401-521-1351
http://www.modcult.brown.edu/
risca/
Money Available: $912,400
Eligibility Requirements:
Applicants for the individual artist
programs must be eighteen years of
age or older and have lived in the
state for at least one year prior to
application. Grant applications are
received from arts organizations,
schools, community centers, social
service organizations, local governments, and nonprofit organizations,
as well as from individual artists.
Grants are awarded to organizations
for general operating support, as
well as for specific projects that
serve communities throughout the
state. Individual artists apply for our
highly competitive fellowship
grants — awarded in different arts
disciplines, such as painting, music,
and sculpture — and for individual
artist project grants. A dollar for
dollar cash match is required.

Programs Available:

$5,000 For Artists To Create New Works (Artist Projects)

$3,000 For Artists, Choreographers, Designers, and Printmakers (Fellowships)

$2,000 For Folk Art Apprenticeships (Folk Arts Apprenticeships)

Grants To Groups Providing Art To Underserved Groups (Access Initiatives)

Grants For Special Art Projects (Arts Programming)

Grants To Help Manage Art Organizations (Organizational Development)

Money For Operating Expenses (General Operating Support)

Up to $12,000 To Have An Artist-In-Residence At A School (Artist Residency Grants)

$2,500 To Develop Art For Schools (Arts as Basic in Curriculum (ABC) Grants)

Up to $2,000 For A Public School To Plan An Art Program (Rhode Island Comprehensive Arts Planning Grants)

SOUTH CAROLINA
South Carolina Arts Commission
1800 Gervais St.
Columbia, SC 29201
803-734-8696, 803-734-8526
http://www.midnet.sc.edu/scac/artweb.htm
Money Available: $1,918,895
Eligibility Requirements:

Individual artist programs require South Carolina residency for six months prior to date of application and through grant period and applicant cannot be a degree seeking full time under-

graduate student. Fellowship applicants require South Carolina residency for two years prior to date of application. Organ-izations must be chartered in South Carolina as nonprofit and must hold a federal tax exempt status or apply through a tax exempt agent.

Programs Available:

$7,500 For Artists, Performers, Writers, And Craftsmen (Fellowships)

$5,000 For Artists Projects (Project Support Grants)

$10,000 for Organization's Arts Projects (Project Support Grants)

$1,000 for Artists for Professional Development (Quarterly Grants)

$1,000 for Organizations (Quarterly Grants)

Up To $40,000 To Arts Organizations (General Support Grants)

Funding for Artists Residencies, Strategic Projects, Comprehensive Arts Education Planning and Arts in Basic Curriculum Advancement in South Carolina Schools (Arts Education Initiatives)

Funding for Multicultural Artists and Organizations (Multicultural Initiatives)

Funding to Communities and Organizations to Develop Design Excellence (limited to non-capital expenditures) (Design Arts)

Other programs and/or funding are available for South Carolina artists and South Carolina organizations. Call the Arts Commission at 803-734-8696 for details.

SOUTH DAKOTA
South Dakota Arts Council
800 Governors Dr.

Pierre, SD 57501-2294
605-773-3131
800-423-6665 (SD only)
Fax: 605-773-6962
http://www.state.sd.us/state/
executive/decal/sdarts/sdarts.htm
Money Available: $500,000
Eligibility Requirements:
Individual artist programs require
state residency. All artist project
grants (except Emerging Artist
Grants and Fellowships) are intended as seed money. Applicant organizations and individuals are funded up
to 50% of projected costs. Funding is
available in the following arts disciplines: dance, music, opera/music
theater, theater, visual arts, design
arts, crafts, photography, media arts,
literature, and folk arts.
Programs Available:
Arts Challenge Grants
Rural Arts Presenting Program
Solo Artists in Libraries
Artist Project Grants
Artists in Schools
Touring Arts
Music Residency Programs for
Native Americans

TENNESSEE
Tennessee Arts Commission
401 Charlotte Ave.
Nashville, TN 37243
615-741-1701
Fax: 615-741-8559
http://www.arts.state.tn.us/
Money Available: $2,500,000
Eligibility Requirements:
Individual artist programs
require state residency.
Programs Available:
$2,000 For Artists, Musicians,
Writers, And Dancers

(Individual Artists Fellowships)
Grants For Arts Organizations
(Arts Build Communities)
Grants To Operate An Arts Organi-
zation (General Operating
Support)
$7,500 For A Nonprofit Agency To
Have An Artist-In-Residence
$5,000 for Arts Project Support

TEXAS
Texas Commission on the Arts
920 Colorado
P.O. Box 13406
Capitol Station
Austin, TX 78711
512-463-5535
Fax: 512-475-2699
http://www.arts.state.tx.us/
Money Available: $2,910,000
Eligibility Requirements:
Texas does not offer direct fund-
ing to individuals. Individual artists
are funded indirectly through the
Arts in Education and the Touring
Programs. In addition, individual
artists may apply to the Commission
under the umbrella of a non-profit
organization or government entity.
Programs Available:
Money To Support Art Projects
(Project Assistance)
Grants For Artists To Go On Tour
(Touring Assistance)
Money For Schools To Have An
Artist-In-Residence (Arts in
Education)

UTAH
Utah Arts Council
617 E. South Temple
Salt Lake City, UT 84102
801-236-7555
Fax: 801-236-7556

http://www.ce.ex.state.ut.us/arts/
Money Available: $1,106,200
Eligibility Requirements:
Individual artist programs
require state residency, unless otherwise specified.
Programs Available:
$5,000 For Artists, Printmakers,
Photographers, and Video Artists
(Visual Artist Fellowships)
$2,000 For An Artist To Learn
From A Master (Folk Arts
Apprenticeship Program)
$5,000 For Creative Writers
(Publication Award)
$110,000 To Art Groups (Grants
Program)
Money For Community Art
Councils (Community/State
Partnership Program)
Money For Performing Artists To
Tour The State (Utah
Performing Arts Tour)
$27 An Hour For Artists To Work At
Local Schools (Arts Education)

VERMONT
Vermont Council on Arts
133 State St.
Montpelier, VT 05633-6001
802-828-3291
Fax: 802-828-3363
http://www.state.vt.us/vermont-arts
Money Available: $729,000
Eligibility Requirements:
Individual artist programs
require state residency.
Programs Available:
$250 - $400 for Professional
Development of Artists
$250 - $1,000 for Technical
Assistance for Arts Organizations
$500 - $3,000 for Project and
Program Collaboration

(Organization/Artist/School)

VIRGINIA
Virginia Commission for the Arts
Lewis House
223 Governor St.
Richmond, VA 23219
804-225-3132
Fax: 804-225-4327
http://www.artswire.org/~vacomm/
Money Available: $3,200,000
Eligibility Requirements:
Individual artist programs require
state residency. Support grant recipients must match award amount.
Programs Available:
Up to $5,000 For Professional Artists To Advance Their Careers
(Individual Artist Fellowships)
Up to $250 For Readings and
Workshops Conducted By
Writers (Writers in Virginia)
$500 To $150,000 To Run An Arts
Organization (General Operating
Support)
$1,500 To Hire Management
Consultants (Technical
Assistance Grants)
Up to $5,000 To Help Local Governments Support The Arts (Local
Government Challenge Grants)
Money For Artists To Tour The State
(Touring Assistance Programs)
Money For Schools To Have An
Artist-In-Residence (Artist in
Education Residencies)
Grants For Community Colleges
To Have An Artist-In-Residence
(Community College Artist
Residencies)
Funding For Workshops and Consultants In Arts Education (Arts
in Education Development Grants)
Up to $300 For Teachers To

Develop Innovative Art Programs
(Teacher Incentive Grant Program)
Money To Hire Consultants Or
Attend Conferences In Arts
Education (Arts In Education
Technical Assistance)

WASHINGTON
Washington State Arts Commission
P.O. Box 42675
Olympia, WA 98504
360-753-3860
Fax: 360-586-5351
http://www.wa.gov/art/
Money Available: $1,639,231
Eligibility Requirements:
501(c)(3) arts organizations and resident artists.
Programs Available:
Up to $2,000 For Short-Term Art Projects (Project Support)
Up to $9,000 For Arts Organizations (Organizational Support)
Money To Bring Performances To Schools (Touring Arts Program)
Matching Grants For Schools To Have An Artist-In-Residence (Artists-in-Residence Program, AIR)
Professional Development Assistance Grants
Folk Arts Residencies
Folk Arts/Apprenticeship Awards
Folk Arts Fellowships
Grants for Arts Curriculum
Grants for Arts Organizations/School Projects
Rural Residency Grants
Note: Fellowship awards and artist project awards are administered by another organization under contract with the Arts Commission. Contact the Arts

Commission for more information.

WEST VIRGINIA
Arts and Humanities Division
Division of Culture and History
Cultural Center
1900 Kanawha Blvd. East
Charleston, WV 25305
304-558-0240
Fax: 304-558-2779
http://www.wvlc.wvnet.edu/culture/arts.html
Money Available: $1,100,000
Programs Available:
Money For Individual Artists (Individual Artist Programs)
Money For The Professional Development Of Artists (Support for Artists Program)
Artists Lists and Register (West Virginia Artists List and Register)
Money For Craftsman and Artists (West Virginia Juried Exhibition)
Money For Special Art Exhibits (Showcase of Visual Arts Program)
Up to $5,000 For Art Organizations (Professional Development)
Grants To Bring Art To Local Schools And Communities (Mini-Grants)
Money To Fund Art Programs (Touring Program)
Money To Support New Works Of Composers, Playwrights, Writers, and Choreographers (Performing Arts)
Money To Artists and Art Administrators To Attend Conferences (Travel Fund)
Money to Develop Special Art Programs For Schools (Arts in Education)

$3,500 To Artists (Artist Fellowship)

WISCONSIN
Wisconsin Arts Board
101 E. Wilson St., 1st Floor
Madison, WI 53702
608-266-0190
Fax: 608-267-0380
Money Available: $2,500,000
Eligibility Requirements:
Individual artist programs require
state residency. For most programs,
recipients must match state awards
with cash or donated services.
Programs Available:
$8,000 For Artists, Writers, and
Folk Artists (Fellowships)
Money For Artists To Work With A
Master (Folk Art Apprenticeships)
Grants To Larger Arts Organizations
(Artistic Program Support I)
Grants To Smaller Arts Organizations
(Artistic Program Support II)
Support For The Performing Arts
Network (Performing Arts
Network (PAN)-Wisconsin)
Community Development Project
Grants
- Arts in Education
- Local Arts Agencies
- Folk Arts

WYOMING
Wyoming Arts Council
2320 Capitol Ave.
Cheyenne, WY 82002
307-777-7742
Fax: 307-777-5499
http://commerce.state.wy.us/cr/
arts/
Money Available: $506,000

Eligibility Requirements:
Individual artist programs
require state residency. For educa-
tional funding, grants require a
one-to-one cash match.
Programs Available:
$2,500 For Artists, Mimes, And
Costume Designers (Performing
Arts)
Up to $2,500 To Exhibit Wyoming
Artists (Visual Arts)
$2,500 To Writers (Literature)
Grants For Arts Organizations
(Organizational Funding)
Grants For Operating An Arts
Organization (General Operating
Support Grant)
Grants For One-Time Arts Events
(Project Grants)
Grants For Art Productions
(Presenting and Producing
Grants)
Grants To Strengthen An Arts
Organization (Technical Assistance)
Grants To Schools And
Organizations To Plan Arts
Programs (Art is Essential
Grant)
Grants For Schools To Have An
Artist-In-Residence (Artist-In-
Residence Grants)
Money To Develop Art Courses In
Schools (Project Grants)
Money To Bring Scholars and
Experts To School Art Programs
(Technical Assistance/In-Service
Grants)
Money For Trailblazer Art
Programs (Trailblazer Projects)

Choosing A Nursing Home ... If You Want To

We all know that a nursing home is not really a home, but for some folks the services that nursing homes provide are a necessary part of life.

Maybe you need some rehab after breaking your hip or having a stroke. Maybe your loved one is a little confused, and needs someone to keep a close eye on her. On any given day, approximately 5% of the elderly population is in a nursing home, but for most, the stay is only for a short time.

People want to stay at home, so new programs are springing up each day to fill the need for home care. But for those who do need a nursing home, who picks up the check for the $30,000 a year to stay in a nursing home is always an interesting discussion.

There are government resources to help you choose a good nursing home, look at your finances, and make this difficult step a little easier.

☆☆☆

Your Very Own Strong Arm

You don't need to put up with cold food or rough care. Just make a call to your state's Nursing Home Ombudsman, and there will be another person on your side.

Ombudsmen are there to help people who are denied admission to nursing homes, improve the quality of the food, and even help report stolen property.

The Ombudsman Program is designed to investigate and resolve complaints made by or on behalf of residents of long-term care facilities. They also make sure these places are running properly and up to code.

Ombudsmen act as mediators, but they are not enforcement agencies. They cannot force a nursing home to change or correct their practices. But it is in the best interest of the nursing home to work with you, before you refer your complaint elsewhere (which the Ombudsman can assist you with).

To locate the Nursing Home Ombudsman in your state, look in the Directory of State Information at the end of this book.

☆☆☆

Nursing Home Shopping List

It's not like shopping for groceries. You can't really walk into a nursing home's cafeteria and squeeze the fruit or check the expiration date on cereal boxes. But even if you could, it probably wouldn't tell you what you really need to know. So what are the ways you can make sure you are getting your money's worth?

You might first ask these simple questions. Do residents seem well cared for and generally content? Is there an activity room? Is the home certified for Medicare and Medicaid programs? Does the home have a security system to prevent confused residents from wandering away?

These are just some of the questions you will find from the nursing home checklist provided in the free publication, *When You Need A Nursing Home*. To receive your copy, contact National Institute on Aging, Information Center, P.O. Box 8057, Gaithersburg, MD 20898; 800-222-2225; or online at <http://www.nih.gov/nia/>.

The Medicare Hotline also distributes a free publication titled, *A Guide to Choosing a Nursing Home*, which provides you with information and questions you should ask when looking at facilities. Contact the Medicare Hotline at 800-638-6833; or online at <http://www.hcfa.gov/medicare/medicare.htm>.

☆☆☆

Free Workshops to Help You Decide

The decision to enter a nursing home is never an easy one, but with some preparation, the move can go smoothly.

Many County Cooperative Extension offices offer pamphlets or workshops on choosing a nursing home, or planning for it financially. Some local offices have information on estate planning and the pros and cons of nursing home insurance.

To learn more about what your local County Cooperative Extension office has for seniors, look in the blue pages of your phone book for the office nearest you, or you can find the main state office in the state-by-state directory at the end of the book.

For more information, contact Cooperative State Research Education and Extension Service, U.S. Department of Agriculture, Room 3328, Washington, DC 20250; 202-720-3029; or online at <http://www. reeusda.gov>.

☆☆☆

Get Married And Move To Arizona

Who would have ever thought that this is what you could do to lower your chances of ever having to spend some time in a nursing home? Believe it or not, nursing home use is different for each state, with Arizona being the lowest and Minnesota the highest. Must be all that dry desert air.

Research also shows that if you've been married you're less likely to use a nursing home than if you haven't. So, you might want to reconsider the marriage proposal from that guy with the plaid jacket from Tucson.

Actually, the Agency for Health Care Policy and Research (AHCPR) looks into who pays for this care, and even if it is the right facility for certain people. Some of the free publications include:

- *Characteristics of Nursing Homes that Affect Resident Outcomes*
- *Case Management Agency Systems of Administering Long-Term Care: Evidence from the Channeling Demonstration*
- *Cognitive Impairment and Disruptive Behaviors Among Community-Based Elderly Persons: Implications for Targeting Long-Term Care*
- *A Lifetime Perspective on Proposals For Financing Nursing Home Care*
- *Long-Term Care Arrangements for Elderly Persons with Disabilities: Private and Public Roles*
- *Long-Term Case Studies*
- *Measuring Cognitive Impairment with Large Data Sets*
- *Nursing Home Reform and the Mentally Ill*
- *Nursing Home Use After 65 in the United States*
- *Nursing Home Use and Costs*
- *Public and Private Responsibility for Financing Nursing Home Care*
- *Quality of Board Care Homes Serving Low-Income Elderly*
- *Lifetime Use of Nursing Home Care*
- *The Risk of Nursing Home Use in Later Life*
- *Standardizing Nursing Home Admission Dates for Short-Term Hospital Stays*

- *Use of Formal and Informal Home Care by the Disabled Elderly*
- *Use of Psychoactive Drugs in Nursing Homes*

For your free copies or more information, contact Agency for Health Care Policy and Research, P.O. Box 88547, Silver Spring, MD 20907; 800-358-9295; or online at <http://www.ahcpr.gov>.

☆☆☆

Who is Really Picking Up The Check?

A recent government study has discovered that a disturbingly large number of seniors who buy long-term care insurance will actually stop paying their premiums long before they get to the point where they need the insurance coverage the most. This trend is especially alarming given the fact that the price of nursing home care is expected to double in the next 25 years.

To find out more about this study and others on long-term care issues, contact the General Accounting Office (GAO). The GAO has a series of reports that deal with long-term care issues including:

- *Long-Term Care Insurance: High Percentage of Policyholders Drop Policies* (GAO/HRD 93-129)
- *Long-Term Care: The Need for Geriatric Assessment in Publicly Funded Home and Community-Based Programs* (T-PEMD 94-20)
- *Long-Term Care: Demography, Dollars, and Dissatisfaction Drive Reform* (T-HEHS 94-140)
- *Long-Term Care Insurance: Tax Preferences Reduce Costs More for Those in Higher Tax Brackets* (GAO/GGD 93-110)

All reports are free and can be requested by contacting the U.S. General Accounting Office, P.O. Box 6015, Gaithersburg, MD 20884; 202-512-6000; or online at <http://www.gao.gov>.

Neat Things To Do With Your Free Time

Shuffleboard, dominoes, bridge, and golf ... Excited yet? Wouldn't you rather improve your neighborhood, lead nature walks, or teach Lech Walesa's kids to become little capitalists? Being retired doesn't have to mean spending your afternoons chasing a little white ball around a glorified cow patch. And just because now you might find yourself on a fixed income, it doesn't mean that you can't take that trip to Africa you've always dreamed about. The government has hundreds of ways to help you get excited about your new-found free time.

★★★

Keep a Fellow Senior Out of a Nursing Home

Nursing homes have got to be one of the last places people want to spend the remaining years of their lives. Through a special program, you can be matched up with someone who needs just a little help to stay in the comfortable surroundings of their own home, and you can gain a friend in the bargain.

Through the Senior Companion program, Oscar Jones was matched up with a 93-year-old man named Joe, who was afflicted by everything from blindness, heart disease, lung and kidney problems, to a stroke. Before long, Oscar had Joe up, walking, and talking. Joe's family was amazed at the beautiful friendship that developed between Joe and Oscar.

As a participant in the Senior Companion Program, you will give individual care to other seniors who need help with transportation and shopping, or just sharing their reminiscences. Volunteers receive a small paycheck and other benefits.

There are fact sheets and brochures available outlining the program. For more information, contact National Senior Service Corps, 1201 New York Ave., NW, Washington, DC 20525; 800-424-8867; or online at <http://www.cns.gov>.

$3,000 to Help the Kids

After being retired for only a month, Lucy DePeppo just couldn't stand it anymore, and decided to become one of over 14,300 seniors who take part in the Foster Grandparent Program. Instead of watching soap operas, Ms. DePeppo spends her day caring for AIDS babies and babies born addicted to drugs — and she is even being paid for her work. Lucy's supervisor says she is a terrific role model for young parents.

The Foster Grandparent Program matches low-income seniors with young people who need various kinds of special help. Volunteers serve as mentors, tutors, and caregivers for children and young kids with special needs, and can also work in schools, hospitals, and recreation centers in their communities. Volunteers work twenty hours per week, and receive a small paycheck and other benefits such as transportation costs or uniforms.

If you think you are up to a challenge like this, call the toll-free hotline listed below and have some free fact sheets and brochures sent to you.

For more information, contact National Senior Service Corps, 1201 New York Ave., NW, Washington, DC 20525; 800-424-8867; or online at <http://www. cns.gov>.

☆☆☆

Share Your Know-How For Some Expense Money

You've got forty years of business experience out there with you on the golf course during your retirement. There are hundreds of businesses and even nonprofit groups starting up each day run by people who have the energy, but not the experience that you possess. You can lend your expertise to those who need your help the most.

Take John Moore, for example. He is a retired pastor who now uses his years of experience to serve as a mediator for a community program which gets criminals and victims to sit down to air their feelings, and reach an agreement on restitution.

This is only one example of how the Retired Senior Volunteer Program (RSVP) gives retired people a chance to continue using their professional experience by working with local service organizations doing such things as conducting employment workshops and acting as consultants to nonprofit organizations. You can even work in schools, libraries, hospitals, and other community service centers.

There are fact sheets and brochures available describing the program. For more information, contact National Senior Service Corps, 1201 New York Ave., NW, Washington, DC 20525; 800-424-8867; or online at <http://www.cns.gov>.

☆☆☆

Give Of Your Time And Your Heart

Over 9 million seniors a year could use your help. Over half a million seniors volunteer each year to: deliver meals to shut-ins, help others get to doctor's appointments — whatever is needed to keep them functioning in their homes and communities.

If you have the time and want to get involved, contact your State Department on Aging which is listed in the Directory of State Information at the end of this book, and they will direct you to local organizations who would love to get you started.

If you have trouble locating an appropriate organization, the Eldercare Locator can refer you to various services that aid and assist the elderly. Contact Eldercare Locator, Administration on Aging, 330 Independence Ave., SW, Washington, DC 20201; 202-629-0641, 800-677-1116; or online at <http://www.ageinfo.org/elderloc/elderloc.html>.

☆☆☆

Have Some Fun in the Woods

If you prefer saving spotted owls and counting woodchucks to playing bridge with the girls, then how about volunteering at one of our national forests? Since the government seems to be more interested in investing in obsolete bombers, volunteers are essential in managing the nation's natural resources.

That is where you can come in if you would like to help. Volunteer positions vary depending on the needs of your local forest, but can include everything from typing and filing, leading nature hikes, to conducting fascinating research.

For a list of national forests nearest you, contact U.S. Forest Service, U.S. Department of Agriculture, Human Resource Programs, P.O. Box 96090, Washington, DC 20090; 703-235-8855; or online at <http://www.fs.fed.us>.

15,000 Seniors Are Doing It in the Parks

Do you ever wonder why the National Parks seem so crowded in the summer? It might be because there are 80,000 people volunteering each year, 15,000 of whom are in the over 50 crowd! Whether it is timing Old Faithful with a stop watch, directing moose traffic, or luring grizzly bears away from stray children, the National Park Service will find something for you to do.

While some money is available for out-of-pocket expenses, and there are even limited housing opportunities at a few parks reserved for volunteers with special skills, this is strictly a volunteer program designed for those who love the great outdoors.

Contact your nearest park to discover an interesting way to spend your free time or to receive a free brochure, contact Office of Public Inquiries, National Park Service, U.S. Department of the Interior, P.O. Box 37127, Washington, DC 20013; 202-208-4747; or online at <http://www. nps.gov>.

☆☆☆

Fishing and Hunting Was Never Like This

When you hear a statistic like there are 10,318 salmon running upstream in Washington State, we hope you don't think that number was made up by some guy at a desk. In fact, statistics such as this often come from volunteers who are needed to stand out in the middle of rivers and count those fish, one-by-one.

If you like fishing or hiking, you can serve as a volunteer where you can do this kind of work all the time. The U.S. Fish and Wildlife Service counts all kinds of things — fish, owls, cranes, herons. But if you're just not very good at math, they will find something else for you to do. Whatever it is that you do, it will look great on your resume.

To find out about volunteer opportunities at your local Fish and Wildlife Office, look in the blue pages of your phone book, or contact U.S. Fish and Wildlife Service, U.S. Department of the Interior, 4401 N. Fairfax Dr., Arlington, VA 22203; or online at <http://www.fws.gov>.

Be a Big Shot Executive

Your wife wants you to slow down now that you're retired, but every time you walk into a store, you embarrass your wife by demanding to see the manager. Then you proceed to tell the guy what's wrong with the way he's running his business. Your wife hides in the frozen food section.

Instead of getting kicked out of every place you shop, try volunteering with SCORE, Service Corps of Retired Executives. SCORE volunteers are usually retired business professionals who want to share their expertise with the next generation of business owners.

You won't get paid as a volunteer, although you may get reimbursed for certain out-of-pocket expenses. SCORE even conducts seminars and workshops covering major considerations for running a business.

If you are interested in becoming one of over 13,000 SCORE members nationwide, contact them at SCORE, 409 Third St., SW, Fourth Floor, Washington, DC 20024; 202-205-6762; 800-634-0245; or online at <http://www.score.org>.

✩✩✩

Travel The World at Government Expense

The average roundtrip ticket to Nepal will cost you $2,800, Poland is $1,800, and Sudan is $2,100. Who can afford those prices on a fixed income? Bob and June Lindstrom managed to get to Poland for free by volunteering to teach those former communists how to become capitalists. Harriet Locke is teaching school in Nepal.

These are just a few of the 508 seniors who recently volunteered for the Peace Corps (out of a total of 6500). Even Jimmy Carter's mother once volunteered. Who else but Uncle Sam is going to pay all your expenses and give you a salary to boot?

As a volunteer you will serve for two years, living among the native people, and becoming part of the community. The Peace Corps sends volunteers throughout Latin America, Africa, the Near East, Asia, the Pacific, and Eastern Europe to share their expertise in education, agriculture, health, economic development, urban development, and the environment.

To learn more about serving the world, contact Peace Corps, 1990 K St., NW, Washington, DC 20526; 800-424-8580; or online at <http://www.peacecorps.gov>.

Free Help With Your Investments

You can't eliminate all the risks, but you sure can rest easier at night if you learn how to make use of government sources before you make your next big deal. Check out your broker and the information he provides by using resources available courtesy of your tax dollars.

Hello — Gimme Your Money

Shady telemarketers and investment brokers have duped more than one unsuspecting consumer out of their life savings. At last count, the number of victims climbed into the millions.

You don't want to be among the big losers; all it takes is a little self-control and a call to the Federal Trade Commission. Several of their free publications can help you become a more informed investor, including *Multilevel Marketing Plans*, *Costly Coupon Scams*, *Wealth Building Scams*, and more.

For more information, contact Federal Trade Commission, Public Reference Branch, 6th and Pennsylvania Aves., NW, Washington, DC 20580; 202-326-2222; or online at <http://www.ftc.gov>.

Foreign Investment Advice
Straight From the Experts

Your broker tells you that the hottest investment in town is selling computers in Bangladesh. Your first thought is that poor people can't afford computers.

What about your friend who wants you to go in on a company that's importing nylons from Poland? Since when are Polish women known for their beautiful legs? You can find out a great deal of information about these countries simply by making a phone call.

State Department Country Officers can provide current political, economic, and background information on marketing and business practices for every country in the world. Although they can't tell you whether your computer deal is going to fly, they can give you enough information to help you better weigh your options.

Write to the SR Coordinator for Business Affairs, E-CBA, Room 2318, U.S. Dept. of State, Washington, DC 22204; or online at <http://www.state.gov/index.html>.

Check Out Your Broker

Before making a securities investment, you must decide which brokerage firm or stockbroker to use. Talk with several firms, preferably in person (which is an especially important step to take to avoid telecommunication fraud).

Remember that they want to invest your money to earn their commission, so do not rush. Do the necessary background investigation on both the firm and the sales representative.

You can find out about the disciplinary history of any brokerage firm and sales representative by calling 800-289-9999, a toll-free hotline operated by NASD Regulation, the regulatory arm of the National Association of Securities Dealers, Inc. (NASD). The NASD Regulation will provide information on disciplinary actions, civil judgments, arbitration, indictments, criminal judgments, and other actions taken by securities regulators and criminal authorities.

Contact NASD Regulation, 1735 K St., NW, Washington, DC 20006, 800-289-9999; or online at <http://www.nasdr.com>.

Buyer Beware of Mutual Funds

Before you sink your money into that hot new biotechnology company, wouldn't you like to know if it's being sued for patent or copyright infringement? And what about the CEO of that new software enterprise — didn't you see him avoiding news cameras a couple of years ago outside the courthouse?

You can do a full background check on any company that's offering public stock simply by making a call to the Securities and Exchange Commission. They can tell you if a broker or brokerage firm has been found guilty of wrong-doing, and can provide general information about the federal securities laws, as well as information on investor inquiries and complaints. They have many free publications available including, *Invest*

248

Wisely: An Introduction To Mutual Funds, The Work of the SEC, and *What Every Investor Should Know.*

Contact Securities and Exchange Commission, Office of Consumer Affairs, 450 5th St., NW, Mail Stop 11-2, Washington, DC 20549; 202-942-7040, 800-SEC-0330 (publications only); or online at <http://www.sec.gov>.

Silver and Gold

Pennies are twelve cents a dozen, but you passed first grade math so you already know that. Since then, your investment concerns have become a little more sophisticated than that, and you now might find yourself looking into American Eagle Gold and Silver Bullion Coins produced by the U.S. Mint.

These gold coins are available in a variety of weights, while silver coins are minted only in a one ounce size. Check listings in your daily newspaper to find out current market value.

Coins may be purchased from brokerage companies, participating banks, coin dealers, and precious metal dealers. For a listing of sales locations in your area, write Customer Service, U.S. Mint, U.S. Department of the Treasury, 10003 Derekwood Lane, Lanham, MD 20706; 202-283-COIN; or online at <http://www. usmint.gov>.

Know the Difference Between
Junk Bonds and Junk Food?

Do people really invest in pork bellies? And if so, why don't you ever see people lined up in the supermarket waiting to buy them?

While the Commodities Futures Trading Commission (CFTC) may not be able to answer these sophisticated investment questions, they do offer several free booklets explaining how the commodities market operates. Some of the titles they have include *Futures and Options: What You Should Know Before You Trade, The CFTC,* and *Economic Purposes of Futures Trading.*

You can find out that commodity prices are tied to the weather, strikes, foreign exchange rates, and even storage factors. A small amount of money (the initial margin) controls a commodity futures contract worth a large amount of money.

The risk is high because a small change in the price of the commodity can either bring a large return on your money, or it can wipe out your initial margin and require that you immediately make additional margin payments. Follow that? Better get the publication yourself.

The CFTC will also send you a free copy of their annual report which includes a handy glossary of trading terms. For your copy, contact Commodities Futures Trading Commission, Office of Public Affairs, 3 Lafayette Center, 1155 21st St., NW, 9th Floor, Washington, DC 20581; 202-418-5080; or online at <http://www. cftc.gov>.

Free Lesson on How To Buy a T-Bill

On the golf course, your investment adviser tells you that with interest rates what they are, maybe it's time to consider T-Bills, and he's not talking golf tees. Treasury bills, notes, and bonds are a way to invest in this country's future, he claims.

The T-Bill hotline provides general information on buying treasury bills, notes, and bonds, and can tell you how they can be purchased and when they will be auctioned. Contact Bureau of the Public Debt, U.S. Department of the Treasury, 13th and C Sts., SW, Washington, DC 20239-0001; 202-874-4000, ext. 231 and 232; or online at <http://www.publicdebt. treas.gov>.

☆☆☆

When Your Banker Takes You To The Cleaners

Even though you have good credit and a good job, your bank won't give you a car loan because you're divorced. What if your bank makes unusual deductions from your bank account each month for maintenance charges you don't understand? What if you are having trouble with your bank issued credit card or mortgage?

Your State Banking Commissioner handles complaints about state-chartered banks doing business in their state. If you cannot resolve your problem with your bank, contact the Banking Commissioner and they will investigate for you. To locate your State Banking Commissioner, look in the Directory of State Information at the end of this book.

Money Lessons

If your bank tells you that they need to hold the amount of your Social Security check until the check clears, they are wrong. Certain checks, such as cashier's certified, or teller's checks, money orders, and electronic payments must be available on the next banking day from when they were deposited.

Teaching the grandkids about the value of money? Want to learn more about how bonds work? What about international economics? Or even consumer protection issues? The Federal Reserve has a free list of public information materials available from their various district offices. You can even learn about inflation, public debt, and macroeconomic data.

For your copy, contact Board of Governors of the Federal Reserve System, Publications Service, MS-127, Federal Reserve Board, Washington, DC 20551; 202-452-3244; or online at <http://www. bog.frb.fed.us>.

☆☆☆

Free Financial Planning

Trying to live on a limited budget is never easy. Congress can't do it, but they somehow expect you to. With so many financial options available, it's not surprising that so many seniors are confused while trying to sort out the best financial plan.

Your County Cooperative Extension Offices frequently have pamphlets or classes which can help you look at your bank book and savings, and make a plan you can live with. For example, free publications in Ohio include *Estate Planning Considerations for Ohio Families; Evaluating Nursing Home Insurance; Financial Planning For Retirement; and Personal Property Inventory.*

To learn what your local office has to offer, look in the blue pages of your phone book for the office nearest you, or you can find the main state office in the Directory of State Information at the end of this book.

For more information, contact Cooperative State Research Education and Extension Service, U.S. Department of Agriculture, Room 3328, Washington, DC 20250; 202-720-3029; or online at <http://www. reeusda.gov>.

Free Legal Help With a Franchise

Tipsy McSwiggers Restaurants claim to be the hottest franchise to come down the pike since McDonalds, and they are letting you in on the ground floor.

Before you get too flattered and lose your shirt, you should find out everything you can about this new business from the Federal Trade Commission. They can tell you all the ins and outs of the franchise world and what you need to know to ask when you actually visit a couple of the franchises and talk to the owners.

You can learn about the Franchise and Business Opportunity Rule, state disclosure requirements, and more. For your packet of franchise information, contact Federal Trade Commission, Pennsylvania Ave. at 6th St., NW, Washington, DC 20580, 202-326-3128; or online at <http://www.ftc.gov>.

Funeral Home Funny Business

When you're planning a loved one's funeral, the last thing you want to worry about is whether or not you're being taken advantage of during this emotional time. But that's exactly what happens to hundreds of people each year.

You don't have to let that overly polite funeral director play upon your grief, and get you to spend more than you want. The Federal Trade Commission has a publication entitled *Caskets and Burial Vaults*, which helps you ask the right questions of the funeral home and points out issues which need to be addressed.

To receive your free copy, contact Public Reference, Room 130, Federal Trade Commission, Washington, DC 20580; 202-326-2222; or online at <http://www. ftc.gov>.

✩✩✩

Is Your Bank Messing With Your Money?

Is Charles Keating or one of his friends sitting on your bank's Board of Directors? Before you and your friends make a run on the bank, you should check out how secure your savings are.

For example, many people have set up separate accounts to safeguard their money against bank failure, but unless they are under different types of ownership categories, such as single or joint ownership, the maximum limit per institution is $100,000. And you might not know that Treasury bonds or notes purchased through a particular institution are not covered by insurance.

The Federal Deposit Insurance Corporation's Division of Compliance and Consumer Affairs answers questions and addresses complaints regarding FDIC regulated institutions and your FDIC insured deposit. A computerized system helps to track complaints from their initial filing to their resolution.

You can request information on financial reports and compliance of different institutions, as well as free brochures such as Deposit Insurance and Consumer Protection. The FDIC even publishes a quarterly newsletter which answers common questions, and informs you about what to do in the event of a problem.

Banking questions may be directed to your nearest regional FDIC office, or Division of Compliance and Consumer Affairs, Federal Deposit Insurance Corporation, 550 17th St., NW, Washington, DC 20429; 800-934-FDIC; or online at <http://www.fdic.gov>.

☆☆☆

Make Sure You Have Credit Credibility

Securing credit is as important for older adults as it is for anyone else. Yet, older consumers, and particularly older women, may find they have special problems establishing credit.

For example, if you've paid for everything with cash all of your life, you may find it difficult to open a credit account, because you have "no credit history." If you now are living on a lower salary or pension, you may find it harder to obtain a loan because you have "insufficient income." Or, if your spouse dies, you may find that creditors try to close credit accounts that you and your spouse once shared.

To learn what legal rights and recourses you have, request the publication *Credit And Older Americans*, which explains the credit process, gives tips on establishing credit, and tells you what to do if you are denied credit.

To receive your free copy, contact Public Reference, Room 130, Federal Trade Commission, Washington, DC 20580; 202-326-2222; or online at <http://www. ftc.gov>.

☆☆☆

Check Out Phony Charities

Starving children in Bolivia who won't live another day unless you give them the help they need today. It seems like every day someone calls or sends letters asking for donations for charity.

Don't fall for appeals, especially the ones over the phone that insist you send money right away. But it may be hard to decide who is most deserving.

There are several different organizations like the National Charities Information Bureau or the Philanthropic Advisory Service at the Council of the Better Business Bureau, where you can learn more about a particular charity's activities, finances, and fundraising practices.

The free publication *Charitable Giving* outlines steps you can take to check out any organization and make sure your money is put into good hands. For your copy, contact Public Reference, Room 130, Federal Trade Commission, Washington, DC 20580; 202-326-2222; or online at <http://www.ftc.gov>.

☆☆☆

Take The Deduction

When you finally do find a good organization you'd like to donate money or gifts to, don't forget that you can take a tax deduction for that contribution. If you spend $50 to attend a special dinner for a cause, is the entire amount deductible? No, but part may be allowed.

What about if you pay $100 for a Golf for Gallstones benefit? Anything over and above the usual charge for golfing may be deductible.

Request the publication, *Charitable Contributions* (Publication 526), that explains which contributions you may deduct and what qualifies as a contribution. For your copy, contact the Internal Revenue Forms Line at 800-829-3676; or online at <http://www.irs.gov>.

Free College Tuition For Seniors

You're never too old to be the Big Man — or Big Woman — on Campus again, or get a degree in Renaissance art, or even carouse at a frat party. Don't waste any more time feeling nostalgic about how great it was to be a carefree student all those years ago. Or, if you never went to college in the first place, you can stop regretting it.

Believe it or not, more than 350 colleges and universities all across the country have special programs for seniors who are interested in going back to school. This often means free or low-cost tuition, discounts on fees and books, and even special deals on housing, if you feel like living in a dorm and blasting your Benny Goodman records to all hours of the night.

So why not go to college with your grandchildren? Sure, it will probably embarrass them to death, but you'll have loads of fun doing it, and at the same time...earn a diploma...graduate magna cum laude ... or start a new business.

Maybe you never went to college because you couldn't stand doing homework. Even if that's still the case, you could still take an art appreciation class that requires only that you show up to a couple of times a week ... or learn to swim ... or draw nude women ... or cook like a gourmet chef.

Tuition and basic fees for seniors are based on the lowest charged to all students (in-state, in-district, in-county, non-degree seeking, undergraduate etc.). Special fees may apply to some classes. Generally, lab, books and materials are additional, and vary depending upon the class. Some other additional fees include parking, health insurance, and a fee for degree seeking and graduate students.

Anyone interested should contact the school they wish to attend to find out how to apply for a discount or waiver. Some limitations and restrictions apply such as an income limit, residency, and space availability.

ALABAMA
Gadsden State Community College
Admissions
P.O. Box 227
Gadsden, AL 35902-0227
205-549-8260
Minimum Age: 60

Tuition: free
Basic Fees: none
Credit: yes

Jefferson State Community College
Admissions
2601 Carson Rd.

255

Birmingham, AL 35215-3098
205-853-1200
Minimum Age: 60
Tuition: free
Basic Fees: $4 per credit hour
Credit: yes

Livingston University
Station 2
Livingston, AL 35470
205-652-3400
Minimum Age: 55
Tuition: free
Basic Fees: $15 one time application fee
Credit: no

University of Montevallo
Station 6065
Montevallo, AL 35115
205-665-6065
800-292-4349
Minimum Age: 65
Tuition: free
Basic Fees: $15 per class
Credit: no

ALASKA

Prince William Sound Community College
P.O. Box 97
Valdez, AK 99686
907-835-2678
Minimum Age: 60
Tuition: free
Basic Fees: $2.50 for 1-3 credit hours; $5 for 4-5 credit hours; $25 for 7+ credit hours
Credit: yes

University of Alaska Anchorage
Enrollment Services
3211 Providence Dr.
Anchorage, AK 99508
907-786-1525

Minimum Age: 60
Tuition: free
Basic Fees: $45 for 3 credit hours; $57 for 6 credit hours
Credit: yes

University of Alaska Fairbanks
Admissions and Records
P.O. Box 757640
Fairbanks, AK 99775-0060
907-474-7821
Minimum Age: 60
Tuition: free
Basic Fees: $25 for 3 credit hours; $155 for 12 credit hours; parking and health insurance can be waived if not needed
Credit: yes

University of Alaska Southeast
11120 Glacier Hwy.
Juneau, AK 99801
907-465-6457
Minimum Age: 60
Tuition: free
Basic Fees: $5 for 1 credit hour; $8 for 2 credit hours; $17 for 3+ credit hours
Credit: yes

ARIZONA

Arizona Western College
P.O. Box 929
Yuma, AZ 85366-0929
520-726-1050
Minimum Age: 60
Tuition: $16 per credit hour
Basic Fees: none
Credit: yes

Central Arizona College
Student Records
8470 North Overfield Rd.
Coolidge, AZ 85228
602-426-4444

256

Minimum Age: 60
Tuition: $18 per credit hour with the 6th, 16th, 17th and 18th free
Basic Fees: none
Credit: yes

ARKANSAS

Arkansas State University
Admissions
P.O. Box 1630
State University
Jonesboro, AR 72467-1630
800-382-3030
Minimum Age: 60
Tuition: free
Basic Fees: $4 per credit hour
Credit: yes

Arkansas State University: Beebe Branch
P.O. Drawer H
Beebe, AR 72012
501-882-6452
Minimum Age: 60
Tuition: free
Basic Fees: none (auto sticker $5)
Credit: yes

Arkansas Tech University
Admissions
Russelville, AR 72801-2222
501-968-0343
Minimum Age: 60
Tuition: free
Basic Fees: none
Credit: yes

East Arkansas Community College
1700 Newcastle Rd.
Forest City, AR 72335-9598
501-633-4480
Minimum Age: 62
Tuition: free
Basic Fees: $3 per credit hour
Credit: yes

Garland County Community College
101 College Dr.
Hot Springs, AR 71913
501-767-9371
Minimum Age: 60
Tuition: free
Basic Fees: $10 per session
Credit: yes

Henderson State University
Registrar
P.O. Box 7534
Arkadelphia, AR 71999-7534
501-203-5000
Minimum Age: 60
Tuition: free
Basic Fees: $36 for 3 credit hours
Credit: yes

Northern Arkansas Community College
Pioneer Ridge
Harrison, AR 72601
501-743-3000
Minimum Age: 60
Tuition: free
Basic Fees: none
Credit: yes

Phillips County Community College
Campus Dr.
P.O. Box 785
Helena, AR 72342
501-338-6474
Minimum Age: 60
Tuition: free
Basic Fees: none
Credit: yes

CALIFORNIA

California State University —
Sacramento
Re-Entry Services
6000 J St.
Sacramento, CA 95819-6048

916-278-6750
Minimum Age: 60
Tuition: $3 per session
Basic Fees: none (students receive
free public transportation in the
Sacramento area)
Credit: yes

COLORADO

Adams State College
Alamosa, CO 81102
719-589-7712
Minimum Age: 65
Tuition: free
Basic Fees: none
Credit: no

Colorado Mountain College: Alpine
Campus
1330 Bob Adams Dr.
Steamboat Springs, CO 80487
970-870-4444
Minimum Age: 62
Tuition: 50% off (regular tuition
$32 per credit hour)
Basic Fees: $50 for 0-9 credit
hours; $65 for 12+ credit hours
Credit: yes

Colorado State University
Admissions and Records
Administrative Annex Bldg.
Ft. Collins, CO 80523
970-491-6909
Minimum Age: 62
Tuition: free
Basic Fees: none
Credit: no

Metropolitan State College of Denver
Adult Learning Services
P.O. Box 173362
Denver, CO 80217
303-556-8342
Minimum Age: 62
Tuition: free

Basic Fees: none
Credit: no

University of Colorado, Boulder
Regent Administrative Center 125
Office of Admissions
Campus Box 6
Boulder, CO 80309
303-492-6301
Minimum Age: 55
Tuition: member of alumni $5 per
session; non-alumni member $15
per session
Basic Fees: none
Credit: no

University of Colorado at Denver
P.O. Box 173364
Campus Box 146
Denver, CO 80217-3364
303-556-2400
Minimum Age: 60
Tuition: free
Basic Fees: none
Credit: no

University of Northern Colorado
Admissions
Greeley, CO 80639
970-351-2881
Minimum Age: 60
Tuition: free
Basic Fees: none
Credit: no

CONNECTICUT

Asnuntuck Community College
Admissions
170 Elm St.
Enfield, CT 06082
203-253-3043
Minimum Age: 62
Tuition: free
Basic Fees: none (lab fee also
waived)
Credit: yes

Central Connecticut State University
Admissions Office
1615 Stanley St.
New Britain, CT 06050
860-832-3200
Minimum Age: 62
Tuition: free
Basic Fees: $37 per semester
Credit: yes

Eastern Connecticut State University
Registrar
83 Windham St.
Willimantic, CT 06226
203-465-5389
Minimum Age: 62
Tuition: free
Basic Fees: $12 per credit hour for
    part-time
Credit: yes

University of Connecticut, Storrs
2131 Hillside Rd.
Storrs, CT 06269-3088
203-486-3137
Minimum Age: 62
Tuition: free
Basic Fees: $222 full-time per
    semester
Credit: yes

University of Hartford
Adult Services
200 Bloomfield Ave.
West Hartford, CT 06117-0395
203-768-4457
Minimum Age: 70
Tuition: free
Basic Fees: $30 per semester (1
    class limit)
Credit: no

Western Connecticut State
    University
Office of Continuing Education

181 White St.
Danbury, CT 006810
203-837-8230
Minimum Age: 62
Tuition: $10 per semester (non-
    credit $10 per class)
Basic Fees: Part-time none (full-
    time varies)
Credit: yes

DELAWARE

Delaware State College
Admissions
1200 N. Dupont Hwy.
Dover, DE 19901
302-739-4917
Minimum Age: 62
Tuition: free
Basic Fees: $25 per semester
Credit: yes

Delaware Technical and
    Community College:
Jack F. Owens Campus
P.O. Box 610
Georgetown, DE 19947
302-856-5400
Minimum Age: 60
Tuition: free
Basic Fees: none
Credit: yes

Delaware Technical and
    Community College:
    Stanton/Wilmington Campus
333 Shipley St.
Wilmington, DE 19801
302-571-5343
Minimum Age: 60
Tuition: free
Basic Fees: none
Credit: yes

Delaware Technical and
    Community College:

Terry Campus
1832 N. Dupont Pkwy.
Dover, DE 19901
302-741-2700
Minimum Age: 60
Tuition: free
Basic Fees: none
Credit: yes

DISTRICT OF COLUMBIA

University of the District of
  Columbia
1100 Harvard St., Room 114
Washington, DC 20008
202-274-5010
Minimum Age: 65
Tuition: free (50% off if going for a
  degree)
Basic Fees: $20 per semester
Credit: yes

FLORIDA

Broward Community College, Ft.
  Lauderdale
Registration
225 E. Lasolas Blvd.
Ft. Lauderdale, FL 33301
305-761-7465
Minimum Age: 65
Tuition: free
Basic Fees: the school will cover
  up to $181.50 of basic fees
Credit: yes

Florida Atlantic University
500 Northwest 20th St.
Boca Raton, FL 33431-0991
407-367-3294
Minimum Age: 60
Tuition: free
Basic Fees: none
Credit: no

Florida International University
University Park

Miami, FL 33199
305-348-2363
Minimum Age: 60
Tuition: free
Basic Fees: none
Credit: no

Florida State University
2249 University Ct.
Tallahassee, FL 32306-1009
904-644-6200
Minimum Age: 62
Tuition: free
Basic Fees: none
Credit: no

Santa Fe Community College
P.O. Box 1530
3000 NW 83rd St.
Gainesville, FL 32602
352-395-5443
Minimum Age: 60
Tuition: free
Basic Fees: none
Credit: yes

University of Central Florida
P.O. Box 160111
Orlando, FL 32816-0111
407-823-3000
Minimum Age: 60
Tuition: free
Basic Fees: none
Credit: no

GEORGIA

Albany State College
504 College Dr.
Albany, GA 31705
912-430-4650
Minimum Age: 62
Tuition: free
Basic Fees: $10 per session
Credit: yes

Armstrong State College
11935 Abercorn St.
Savannah, GA 31419
800-633-2349
Minimum Age: 62
Tuition: free
Basic Fees: $10 per session
Credit: yes

Athens Area Technical Institute
US Highway 29 North
Athens, GA 30610-3099
706-542-8050
Minimum Age: 62
Tuition: free
Basic Fees: $12.50 per quarter
Credit: yes

Bainbridge College
2500 E. Shotwell St.
Bainbridge, GA 31717
912-248-2500
Minimum Age: 62
Tuition: free
Basic Fees: none
Credit: yes

Brunswick College
Admissions
3700 Altama Ave.
Brunswick, GA 31520-3644
912-264-7253
Minimum Age: 62
Tuition: free
Basic Fees: none
Credit: yes

Clayton State College
Admissions/Registrar
P.O. Box 285
Morrow, GA 30260
770-961-3400
Minimum Age: 62
Tuition: free
Basic Fees: none
Credit: yes

Columbus College
4225 University Ave.
Columbus, GA 31907-5645
706-568-2035
Minimum Age: 62
Tuition: free
Basic Fees: none
Credit: yes

Georgia College
Admissions and Records
Campus Box 023
Milledgeville, GA 31061
912-453-5004
Minimum Age: 62
Tuition: free
Basic Fees: none
Credit: yes

Georgia Southern University
Admissions
Landrum Box 8024
Statesboro, GA 30460-8024
912-681-5531
Minimum Age: 62
Tuition: free
Basic Fees: none
Credit: yes

Georgia Southwestern College
800 Wheatly St.
Americus, GA 31709-4693
912-928-1273
Minimum Age: 62
Tuition: free
Basic Fees: none
Credit: yes

Georgia State University
P.O. Box 4009
Atlanta, GA 30302-4009
404-651-2365
Minimum Age: 62
Tuition: free
Basic Fees: $82 per quarter

Credit: yes

HAWAII

University of Hawaii: Hawaii
   Community College
200 West Kawili St.
Hilo, HI 96720
808-933-3611
Minimum Age: 60
Tuition: free (no summer classes)
Basic Fees: none
Credit: yes

University of Hawaii: Honolulu
   Community College
874 Dillingham Blvd.
Honolulu, HI 96817
808-845-9129
Minimum Age: 60
Tuition: free
Basic Fees: $10 per semester
Credit: yes

University of Hawaii: Kapiolani
   Community College
4303 Diamond Head Rd.
Honolulu, HI 96816
808-734-9559
Minimum Age: 60
Tuition: free
Basic Fees: $10 per semester
Credit: yes

University of Hawaii: Kauai
   Community College
3-1901 Kaomualii Hwy.
Lihue, HI 96766
808-245-8212
Minimum Age: 60
Tuition: free
Basic Fees: none
Credit: yes

University of Hawaii: Leeward
   Community College
96-045 Ala Ike

Pearl City, HI 96782
808-455-0217
Minimum Age: 60
Tuition: free
Basic Fees: none
Credit: yes

University of Hawaii at Manoa
2600 Campus
Honolulu, HI 96822
808-956-8975
Minimum Age: 60
Tuition: free
Basic Fees: none
Credit: yes

University of Hawaii: Maui
   Community College
310 Kaahumanu Ave.
Kahului, HI 96732
808-244-9181
Minimum Age: 60
Tuition: free
Basic Fees: $4 per session plus 50
   cents per credit hour
Credit: yes

University of Hawaii: Windward
   Community College
45-720 Keaahala Rd.
Kaneohe, HI 96744
808-235-7432
Minimum Age: 60
Tuition: free
Basic Fees: none
Credit: yes

IDAHO

Boise State University
1910 University Dr.
Boise, ID 83725
800-824-7017
Minimum Age: 60
Tuition: $5 per credit hour
Basic Fees: $20 per semester
Credit: yes

College of Southern Idaho
Admissions
P.O. Box 1238
Twin Falls, ID 83303-1238
208-733-9554
Minimum Age: 60
Tuition: free
Basic Fees: none
Credit: yes

Idaho State University
Enrollment Planning
Campus Box 8054
Pocatello, ID 83209
208-236-2123
Minimum Age: 60
Tuition: $5 per credit hour
Basic Fees: $20 per semester
Credit: yes

Lewis Clark State College
500 Eighth Ave.
Lewiston, ID 83501
208-799-5272
Minimum Age: 60
Tuition: $5 per credit hour
Basic Fees: $20 per semester
Credit: yes

North Idaho College
Business Office
1000 West Garden Ave.
Coeur d'Alene, ID 83814
208-769-3311
Minimum Age: 60
Tuition: 50% off (regular tuition
    $50 per credit hour)
Basic Fees: $130 full-time
Credit: yes

ILLINOIS

Belleville Area College
2500 Carlyle Rd.
Belleville, IL 62221
618-235-2700

Minimum Age: 60
Tuition: $35 per credit hour
Basic Fees: $10 one time applica-
    tion fee
Credit: yes

Chicago State University
95th St. and King Dr.
Chicago, IL 60628
312-995-2513
Minimum Age: 65
Tuition: free (income limitation of
    $12,000 annually)
Basic Fees: none (lab also waived)
Credit: yes

College of Du Page
22nd St. and Lambert Rd.
Glen Ellyn, IL 60137
708-858-2800, ext. 2482
Minimum Age: 65
Tuition: $3.45 per credit hour
Basic Fees: none
Credit: yes

Illinois State University
Adult Services
Campus Box 2200
Normal, IL 61790-2200
309-438-2181
Minimum Age: 65
Tuition: free
Basic Fees: none
Credit: no

Northern Illinois University
Office of Admissions
101 Williston Hall
Dekalb, IL 60115-2857
815-753-0446
Minimum Age: 65
Tuition: free (income limitation of
    $14,000 annually)
Basic Fees: $20-$40 per session
Credit: yes

INDIANA
Ball State University
Office of Admission
Lucina Hall
Muncie, IN 47306
317-285-8300
Minimum Age: 60
Tuition: 50% off (regular tuition
  $478 for 0-3 credit hours; $638
  for 4-5 credit hours; $1008 for 6-8
  credit hours)
Basic Fees: none
Credit: yes

Indiana University at Kokomo
P.O. Box 9003
Kokomo, IN 46904-9003
317-453-2000
Minimum Age: 60
Tuition: 50% off up to 9 hours (reg-
  ular tuition $83.30-$87.05 per
  credit hour)
Basic Fees: $15 maximum activity
  fee plus $2 per credit hour
Credit: yes

Indiana University-Purdue
  University at Fort Wayne
Financial Aid
2101 Coliseum Blvd., East
Fort Wayne, IN 46805
219-481-6820
Minimum Age: 60
Tuition: 50% off (regular tuition
  $80.25 per credit hour)
Basic Fees: none
Credit: yes

Indiana University Southeast
4201 Grant Line Rd.
New Albany, IN 47150
812-941-2212 ext. 2335
Minimum Age: 60
Tuition: 50% off up to 9 hours (regular tuition $87.05 per credit hour)

Basic Fees: none
Credit: yes

University of Southern Indiana
8600 University Blvd.
Evansville, IN 47712
812-464-1765
Minimum Age: 60
Tuition: $5 per class
Basic Fees: $10 ID fee per session
Credit: yes

IOWA
Clinton Community College
Enrollment Services
1000 Lincoln Blvd.
Clinton, IA 52732-6299
319-242-6841
Minimum Age: 62
Tuition: $3.65 per semester hour
Basic Fees: $5.50 per hour
Credit: yes

Des Moines Area Community
  College
Records and Services
2006 South Ankeny Blvd.
Ankeny, IA 50021
515-964-6241
Minimum Age: 65
Tuition: free
Basic Fees: none
Credit: yes

Indian Hills Community College
Admissions
525 Grandview St.
Ottumwa, IA 52501
515-683-5111
Minimum Age: 62
Tuition: 50% off (regular tuition
  $40 per credit hour)
Basic Fees: $4.50 per credit hour
Credit: yes

Iowa Western Community College
Business
923 East Washington St.
Clarinda, IA 51632
712-542-5117
Minimum Age: 55
Tuition: $22 per credit hour (3
    credit hour limit per semester)
Basic Fees: $15 one time applica-
    tion fee plus $6 per credit hour
Credit: yes

KANSAS
Allen County Community College
1801 North Cottonwood St.
Iola, KS 66749
316-365-5116
Minimum Age: 60
Tuition: $28 per credit hour (book
    rental and fees are free)
Basic Fees: none
Credit: yes

Barton County Community
    College
Registrar
Rt. 3, Box 1362
Great Bend, KS 67530-9283
316-792-2701 ext. 215
Minimum Age: 65 (must be resi-
    dent of CO)
Tuition: free
Basic Fees: $10 per credit hour
Credit: yes

Butler County Community College
901 South Haverhill Rd.
Eldorado, KS 67042
316-321-2222
Minimum Age: 60
Tuition: free
Basic Fees: $10 per credit hour
Credit: yes

Cloud County Community College
221 Campus Dr.

P.O. Box 1002
Concordia, KS 66901-1002
913-234-1435
Minimum Age: 55
Tuition: $24 per credit hour (fee
    will increase this fall)
Basic Fees: none
Credit: yes

Coffeyville Community College
400 West 11th
Coffeyville, KS 67337
316-251-7700
Minimum Age: 60
Tuition: free
Basic Fees: $10 per credit hour
Credit: yes

Emporia State University
Admissions
1200 Commercial
Emporia, KS 66801-5087
316-341-5465
Minimum Age: 60
Tuition: free
Basic Fees: none
Credit: no

Fort Hays State University
600 Park St.
Hays, KS 67601-4099
913-628-4222
Minimum Age: 60
Tuition: free
Basic Fees: none
Credit: no

Garden City Community College
Dean of Admissions
801 Campus Dr.
Garden City, KS 67846
316-276-7611
Minimum Age: 65
Tuition: free
Basic Fees: $7 per credit hour
Credit: yes

Hutchinson Community College
1300 North Plum St.
Hutchinson, KS 67501
316-665-3535
Minimum Age: 60
Tuition: $21 per credit hour
Basic Fees: none
Credit: yes

KENTUCKY

Ashland Community College
1400 College Dr.
Ashland, KY 41101
606-329-2999
Minimum Age: 65
Tuition: free
Basic Fees: none
Credit: yes

Eastern Kentucky University
Coates Box 2A
203 Jones Building
Richmond, KY 40475-3101
606-622-2106
Minimum Age: 65
Tuition: free
Basic Fees: none
Credit: yes

Elizabethtown Community College
600 College Street Rd.
Elizabethtown, KY 42701
502-769-1632
Minimum Age: 65
Tuition: free
Basic Fees: none
Credit: yes

Lexington Community College
203 Oswald Bldg., Cooper Dr.
Lexington, KY 40506-0235
606-257-4872
Minimum Age: 65
Tuition: free
Basic Fees: none
Credit: yes

Madisonville Community College
2000 College Dr.
Madisonville, KY 42431
502-821-2250
Minimum Age: 65
Tuition: free
Basic Fees: none
Credit: yes

Maysville Community College
1755 US 68
Maysville, KY 41056
606-759-7141
Minimum Age: 65
Tuition: free
Basic Fees: none
Credit: yes

Morehead State University
306 Howell McDowell
Morehead, KY 40351
606-783-2000
Minimum Age: 65
Tuition: free
Basic Fees: none
Credit: yes

Murray State University
Bursars Office
P.O. Box 9
Murray, KY 42071-0009
502-762-3741
800-272-4678
Minimum Age: 65
Tuition: free
Basic Fees: none
Credit: yes

Northern Kentucky University
Office of Admissions
Highland Heights, KY 41099
606-572-5220
800-637-9948
Minimum Age: 65
Tuition: free

Basic Fees: none
Credit: yes

University of Kentucky
100 Funkhouser Bldg.
Lexington, KY 40506-0054
606-257-2000
Minimum Age: 65
Tuition: free
Basic Fees: none
Credit: yes

University of Louisville
Admission AO
University of Louisville
Louisville, KY 40292
502-852-6531
Minimum Age: 65
Tuition: free (10% off non-academic)
Basic Fees: none
Credit: yes

LOUISIANA

Delgado Community College
615 City Park Ave.
New Orleans, LA 70119
504-483-4114
Minimum Age: 60
Tuition: 3 credit hours free per
   semester
Basic Fees: $15 per semester
Credit: yes

Grambling State University
P.O. Box 864
Grambling, LA 71245
318-274-2435
Minimum Age: 65
Tuition: free
Basic Fees: $15 per semester
Credit: yes

Louisiana State University and Agricultural and Mechanical College
Records and Registration
112 Thomas Boyd Hall

Baton Rouge, LA 70803
504-388-1175
Minimum Age: 65
Tuition: free
Basic Fees: none
Credit: yes

Louisiana State University at
   Alexandria
Financial Aid
8100 Highway 71 South
Alexandria, LA 71302-9633
318-473-6423
Minimum Age: 65
Tuition: free
Basic Fees: none
Credit: yes

Louisiana State University —
   Baton Rouge
Office of Admissions
Room 110 Thomas Boyd Hall
Baton Rouge, LA 70803
504-388-1175
Minimum Age: 65
Tuition: free
Basic Fees: none
Credit: yes

Louisiana State University at Eunice
P.O. Box 1129
Eunice, LA 70535
318-457-7311
Minimum Age: 65
Tuition: free (must pay one time
   application fee of $5)
Basic Fees: $10 per semester
Credit: yes

Louisiana State University in
   Shreveport
Admissions and Records
One University Place
Shreveport, LA 71115
318-797-5207

Minimum Age: 65
Tuition: free
Basic Fees: $50 for part-time; $65
  for full-time
Credit: yes

Louisiana Tech University
P.O. Box 3178
Tech Station
Ruston, LA 71272
318-257-3036
Minimum Age: 65
Tuition: 1 class per quarter free
Basic Fees: $35 per quarter
Credit: yes

McNeese State University
P.O. Box 92495
Lake Charles, LA 70609
318-475-5000
Minimum Age: 60
Tuition: 3 credit hours free per
  semester
Basic Fees: $10 per semester
Credit: yes

Nicholls State University
P.O. Box 2004
College Station
Thibodaux, LA 70310
504-448-4139
Minimum Age: 62
Tuition: 3 credit hours free per
  semester
Basic Fees: $10 per semester
Credit: yes

Northeast Louisiana University
Student Affairs
Office of the Registrar
Monroe, LA 71209-1110
318-342-5252
Minimum Age: 60
Tuition: 3 credit hours free per
  semester

Basic Fees: $15 per semester
Credit: yes

Northwestern State University
Fiscal Affairs
Cashier Section
Natchitoches, LA 71497
318-357-4503
Minimum Age: 60
Tuition: 3 credit hours free per
  semester
Basic Fees: $5 one time
  application fee
Credit: yes

Southeastern Louisiana University
Enrollment Services
P.O. Drawer 752
Hammond, LA 70402-0752
504-549-2123
Minimum Age: 60
Tuition: 3 credit hours free per
  semester
Basic Fees: $10 per semester
Credit: yes

MAINE

University of Maine
Admissions
7513 W. Chadbourne Hall
Orono, ME 04469
207-581-1561
Minimum Age: 65
Tuition: free
Basic Fees: $9 for 3 credit hours;
  $246.50 for 12 credit hours
Credit: yes

University of Maine at Augusta
Admissions
46 University Dr.
Augusta, ME 04330
207-621-3000
Minimum Age: 65
Tuition: free

Basic Fees: $4.50 per credit hour
Credit: yes

University of Maine at Farmington
102 Main St.
Farmington, ME 04938
207-778-7052
Minimum Age: 65
Tuition: No reduced rate. Case-by-case basis
Basic Fees: case-by-case basis
Credit: yes

University of Maine at Fort Kent
Admissions
25 Pleasant St.
Fort Kent, ME 04743
207-834-7500
Minimum Age: 65
Tuition: free (2 course limit)
Basic Fees: $20 for 6 credit hours
Credit: yes

MARYLAND

Alleghany Community College
Continuing Education
Willow Brook Rd.
Cumberland, MD 21502
301-724-7700
Minimum Age: 60
Tuition: free (non-academic only)
Basic Fees: up to $3 per course
Credit: no

Baltimore City Community College
Registration
2901 Liberty Heights Ave.
Baltimore, MD 21215
410-462-8300
Minimum Age: 60
Tuition: free
Basic Fees: $20 per credit hour
    (non-credit $10 per course)
Credit: yes

Bowie State University

Human Resources
14000 Jericho Park Rd.
Bowie, MD 20715
301-464-6515
Minimum Age: 62
Tuition: free
Basic Fees: $83.50 for 0-11 credit
    hours; $369 for 12+ credit hours
Credit: yes

Coppin State College
Human Resources
2500 W. North Ave.
Baltimore, MD 21216
410-383-5990
Minimum Age: 60
Tuition: free
Basic Fees: part-time $47 plus $8
    per credit hour; $333 for 12 credit hours
Credit: yes

Frostburg State University
Admissions
Frostburg, MD 21532-1099
687-680-4201
Minimum Age: 60
Tuition: free (3 course limit)
Basic Fees: 9 credit hours approximately $115
Credit: yes

Salisbury State University
Human Resources
Camden and College Avenues
Salisbury, MD 21801-6862
410-543-6035
Minimum Age: 60
Tuition: free (2 course limit)
Basic Fees: 6 credit hours approximately $18
Credit: yes

St. Mary's College of Maryland
Admission
St. Mary's City, MD 20686

301-862-0292
Minimum Age: 65
Tuition: free; apply for waiver
Basic Fees: $230 for 9-11 credit
hours, space available
Credit: yes

University of Maryland — College
Park
Golden ID Program
College Park, MD 20742
301-314-8237
Minimum Age: 65 (60 if employed
less than 20 hours per week)
Tuition: $103.50 per semester (3
class limit per semester)
Basic Fees: $30 one time applica-
tion fee
Credit: yes

MASSACHUSETTS
Berkshire Community College
1350 West St.
Pittsfield, MA 01201
413-499-4660
Minimum Age: 60
Tuition: free
Basic Fees: $25 per credit hour
Credit: yes

Boston University
881 Commonwealth Ave.
6th Floor
Boston, MA 02215
617-353-2300
Minimum Age: 60
Tuition: $20 per course
Basic Fees: none
Credit: no

Bridgewater State College
Gates House
Bridgewater, MA 02325
508-697-1237
Minimum Age: 60

Tuition: 50% off regular fee
Basic Fees: $201.42 for 3 credit
hours; $491.25 for 12 credit hours
Credit: yes

Briston Community College
777 Elsbree St.
Fall River, MA 02720
508-678-2811
Minimum Age: 60
Tuition: $42 for 3 credit hours, $55
for 4 credit hours
Basic Fees: none
Credit: yes

Bunker Hill Community College
250 New Rutherford Ave.
Boston, MA 02129-2991
617-228-2000
Minimum Age: 60
Tuition: free
Basic Fees: $35/credit hour
Credit: yes

Cape Cod Community College
Rt. 132
West Barnstable, MA 02668-1599
508-362-2131
Minimum Age: 60
Tuition: 50% off fees, apply for
waiver
Basic Fees: $138 for 3 credit hours
Credit: yes

Salem State College
352 Lafayette St.
Salem, MA 01970
508-741-6200
Minimum Age: 60
Tuition: $41.50 per credit
Basic Fees: $61 per credit hour;
full-time $743.50
Credit: yes

North Adams State College
Admissions

270

Church St.
North Adams, MA 01247
413-662-5000
Minimum Age: 65
Tuition: free
Basic Fees: none
Credit: yes

MICHIGAN

Alpena Community College
666 Johnson St.
Alpena, MI 49707
517-356-9021
Minimum Age: 60
Basic Fees: $10 per session plus $6
    per credit hour
Tuition: free
Credit: yes

Central Michigan University
Admissions
105 Warriner Hall
Mount Pleasant, MI 48859
517-774-3076
Minimum Age: 60
Tuition: free
Basic Fees: none
Credit: no

Charles Stewart Mott Community
    College
4503 East Court St.
Flint, MI 48503
810-762-0200
Minimum Age: 60
Tuition: free (50% off non-academic)
Basic Fees: none
Credit: yes

Delta College
Admissions
University Center, MI 48710
517-686-9092
Minimum Age: 60
Tuition: 50% off (regular tuition
    $65 per credit hour)

Basic Fees: $25 per session
Credit: yes

Glen Oaks Community College
62249 Shimmel Rd.
Centreville, MI 49032
616-467-9945
Minimum Age: 60
Tuition: based on context hours
Basic Fees: none
Credit: yes

Macomb Community College
2800 College Dr., SW
Sidney, MI 48885-0300
517-328-2111 ext. 215
Minimum Age: 60
Tuition: in-district 50% off tuition;
    out-of-district $22 per credit hour
Basic Fees: $1.50 per credit hour
Credit: yes

Oakland Community College
District Office
George AB
Administration Center
2480 Opdyke Rd.
Bloomfield Hills, MI 48304-2266
810-540-1567
Minimum Age: 60
Tuition: 20% off (regular tuition
    $47 per credit hour)
Basic Fees: $35 per session
Credit: yes

Wayne State University
Office of Undergraduate
    Admission
Detroit, MI 48202
313-577-3577
Minimum Age: 60
Tuition: 50% off (regular tuition
    $98 per credit hour)
Basic Fees: $70 per semester
Credit: yes

Western Michigan University
Office of Admission and
  Orientation
Kalamazoo, MI 49008-5120
616-387-2000
Minimum Age: 62
Tuition: free
Basic Fees: none
Credit: no

University of Michigan — Ann Arbor
515 East Jefferson
1220 Student Activities
Ann Arbor, MI 48109-1316
313-764-7433
Minimum Age: 65
Tuition: 50% off (regular tuition
  full-time $2,500)
Basic Fees: $87 per term
Credit: yes

MINNESOTA

Anoka-Ramsey Community College
11200 Mississippi Blvd., NW
Coon Rapids, MN 55433
612-427-2600
Minimum Age: 62
Tuition: $10 per credit hour
Basic Fees: $15 per session plus $1
  per credit hour
Credit: yes

Austin Community College
1600 Eighth Ave., NW
Austin, MN 55912
507-433-0535
Minimum Age: 62
Tuition: $6 per credit hour
Basic Fees: 0-7 credit hours free;
  8+ credit hours $15 plus $2 per
  credit hour
Credit: yes

Bemidji State University
1500 Birchmont Dr., NE

Bemidji, MN 56601
218-755-2040
Minimum Age: 62
Tuition: $6 per credit hour
Basic Fees: $15 per session
Credit: yes

Brainerd Community College
501 West College Dr.
Brainerd, MN 56401
218-828-2508
Minimum Age: 62
Tuition: $10 per credit hour
Basic Fees: $15 per session plus $2
  per credit hour
Credit: yes

Fergus Falls Community College
1414 College Way
Fergus Falls, MN 56537
218-739-7501
Minimum Age: 62
Tuition: $6 per credit hour
Basic Fees: 0-7 credit hours free;
  8+ credit hours $15 plus $3 per
  credit hour
Credit: yes

Hibbing Community College
1515 East 25th St.
Hibbing, MN 55746
218-262-6700
Minimum Age: 62
Tuition: $6 per credit hour
Basic Fees: 0-7 credit hours free;
  8+ credit hours $15 plus $2 per
  credit hour
Credit: yes

Minnesota Universities — Twin
  Cities
Room 240, Pillsbury Dr., SE
Minneapolis, MN 55455
800-752-1000
Minimum Age: 62

Tuition: $6 per credit hour
Basic Fees: none
Credit: yes

MISSISSIPPI

Copiah-Lincoln Community College
Financial Aid Office
P.O. Box 649
Wesson, MS 39191
601-643-8307
Minimum Age: 65
Tuition: free
Basic Fees: none
Credit: yes

Delta State University
Registrar
Cleveland, MS 38733
601-846-4656
Minimum Age: 60
Tuition: $10 for 1 course up to 3
    credit hours
Basic Fees: none
Credit: yes

East Central Community College
Admissions
Decatur, MS 39327
601-635-2111
Minimum Age: 65
Tuition: free
Basic Fees: none
Credit: yes

Holmes Community College
P.O. Box 369
Goodman, MS 39079
601-472-2312
Minimum Age: 65
Tuition: free
Basic Fees: none
Credit: yes

Itawamba Community College
Admissions
602 W. Hill St.

Fulton, MS 38843
601-862-3101
Minimum Age: 65
Tuition: free
Basic Fees: none
Credit: yes

Jones County Junior College
Guidance Office
900 South Court St.
Ellisville, MS 39437
601-477-4025
Minimum Age: 65
Tuition: free
Basic Fees: none
Credit: yes

Meridian Community College
910 Highway 19 North
Meridian, MS 39307
601-483-8241
Minimum Age: 65
Tuition: $2.50 per class
Basic Fees: none
Credit: yes

Mississippi Gulf Coast Community
    College: Jackson County
    Campus
Business Services
P.O. Box 100
Gautier, MS 39553
601-497-9602
Minimum Age: 65 (62-64 also quali-
    fy if retired)
Tuition: free
Basic Fees: none
Credit: yes

MISSOURI

Crowder College
601 LaClede Ave.
Neosho, MO 64850
417-451-3223
Minimum Age: 60

Tuition: free
Basic Fees: $12 per credit hour
Credit: yes

East Central College
Registration
P.O. Box 529
Union, MO 63048
314-583-5193
Minimum Age: 60
Tuition: free
Basic Fees: none
Credit: yes

Jefferson College
Continuing Education
1000 Viking Dr.
Hillsboro, MO 63050
314-789-3951
Minimum Age: 60
Tuition: 50% off (regular tuition
    $38 per credit hour)
Basic Fees: $1 for a Lifetime Card
Credit: no

Lincoln University
820 Chestnut St.
Jefferson City, MO 65102
314-681-5000
Minimum Age: 60
Tuition: $12 per course
Basic Fees: $17 per session
Credit: no

Longview Community College
500 Longview Rd. SW
Lee's Summit, MO 64081
816-672-2000
Minimum Age: 65
Tuition: free
Basic Fees: none
Credit: yes

Maple Woods Community College
Development Center
2601 Northeast Barry Rd.

Kansas City, MO 64156
816-437-3050
Minimum Age: 65
Tuition: free
Basic Fees: none
Credit: yes

Missouri Southern State College
Business Office
3950 East Newman Rd.
Joplin, MO 64801-1595
417-625-9300
Minimum Age: 60
Tuition: free
Basic Fees: none
Credit: yes

Missouri Western State College
4525 Downs Dr.
St. Joseph, MO 64507
816-271-4200
Minimum Age: 60
Tuition: free
Basic Fees: none
Credit: yes

Moberly Area Community College
Financial Aid Office
College Ave. and Rollins St.
Moberly, MO 65270
816-263-4110
Minimum Age: 60
Tuition: free
Basic Fees: none
Credit: yes

St. Louis Community College
Office of Admission
11333 Big Bend Blvd.
Kirkwood, MO 63122
314-984-7601
Minimum Age: 62
Tuition: 50% off (regular tuition
    $40 per credit hour)
Basic Fees: none
Credit: yes

MONTANA
Dawson Community College
Business Office
300 College Dr.
Glendive, MT 59330
406-365-3396
Minimum Age: 60
Tuition: free
Basic Fees: none (most books can be borrowed)
Credit: yes

Flathead Valley Community College
777 Grandview Dr.
Kalispell, MT 59901
406-756-3846
Minimum Age: 62
Tuition: $30.25 per credit hour
Basic Fees: none
Credit: yes

Fort Belknap College
P.O. Box 159
Harlem, MT 59526
406-353-2607
Minimum Age: 55 (must be a member of a federally recognized tribe)
Tuition: free
Basic Fees: none
Credit: yes

Fort Peck Community College
P.O. Box 398
Poplar, MT 59255
406-768-5551
Minimum Age: 60
Tuition: free
Basic Fees: $12 per credit hour
Credit: yes

Miles Community College
2715 Dickinson St.
Miles City, MT 59301
406-232-3031
Minimum Age: 62

Tuition: free
Basic Fees: none
Credit: yes

Montana College of Mineral Science and Technology
1300 West Park St.
Butte, MT 59701
406-496-4178
800-445-8324
Minimum Age: 62
Tuition: apply for waiver
Basic Fees: $26.25 for 3 credit hours; $171 for 12 credit hours
Credit: yes

Northern Montana College
P.O. Box 7751
Havre, MT 59501
406-265-3700
Minimum Age: 62
Tuition: free
Basic Fees: $80.25 for 3 credit hours
Credit: yes

Western Montana College at the University of Montana
Continuing Education
710 South Atlantic
Dillon, MT 59725
406-683-7537
Minimum Age: 62
Tuition: 1 credit hour $20; $3 for each additional credit hour
Basic Fees: $30
Credit: yes

University of Montana
Missoula, MT 59812
406-243-0211
Minimum Age: 62
Tuition: all state supported costs waived, no discount on tuition
Basic Fees: $30 one time fee
Credit: yes

NEBRASKA

Chadron State College
Admissions
1000 Main St.
Chadron, NE 69337
308-432-6263
Minimum Age: 62
Tuition: no discount on tuition
Basic Fees: $35 for 3 credit hours
Credit: yes

McNook Community College
Registrar
1205 East Third St.
McNook, NE 69001
308-345-6303
800-348-5343
Minimum Age: 62
Tuition: free
Basic Fees: none
Credit: no

Metropolita Community College
Student Accounts
P.O. Box 3777
Omaha, NE 68103
402-449-8418
Minimum Age: 62
Tuition: 50% off (regular tuition
$23 per credit hour)
Basic Fees: none
Credit: yes

Mid-Plains Community College
Accounting
1101 Halligan Dr.
North Platte, NE 69101
308-532-8740
Minimum Age: 60
Tuition: free
Basic Fees: $1.50 per credit hour
Credit: yes

Nebraska Indian Community
College

Financial Aid Office
Mayce, NE 42837
402-878-2414
Minimum Age: 55
Tuition: free
Basic Fees: $10 one time applica-
tion fee
Credit: yes

Southeast Community College:
Beatrice Campus
Adult Education
Rt. 2, Box 35A
Beatrice, NE 68310
402-228-3468
Minimum Age: 62
Tuition: no discount on tuition
(regular tuition $35.25 per credit
hour)
Basic Fees: none
Credit: no

Southeast Community College:
Lincoln Campus
Cashier
8800 O St.
Lincoln, NE 68520
402-437-2600
Minimum Age: 62
Tuition: no discount on tuition
Cashier: 402-437-2558
Basic Fees: varies by class
Credit: no

Southeast Community College:
Milford Campus
Student Accounts
Rt. 2, Box D
Milford, NE 68405
402-761-2131
800-999-7223
Minimum Age: 65
Tuition: no discount on tuition
Basic Fees: varies by class
Credit: no

NEVADA

Community College of Southern
  Nevada
3200 East Cheyenne Ave.
North Las Vegas, NV 89030
702-651-4060
Minimum Age: 62
Tuition: free
Basic Fees: none
Credit: yes

Northern Nevada Community
  College
1500 College Pkwy.
Elko, NV 89801
702-738-8493
Minimum Age: 62
Tuition: free
Basic Fees: none
Credit: yes

Truckee Meadows Community
  College
7000 Dandini Blvd.
Reno, NV 89512
702-673-7000
Minimum Age: 62
Tuition: free
Basic Fees: none
Credit: yes

University of Nevada: Las Vegas
4505 Maryland Pkwy.
Las Vegas, NV 89154-1021
702-895-3011
Minimum Age: 62
Tuition: free
Basic Fees: none
Credit: yes

University of Nevada: Reno
Records and Enrollment Services
Reno, NV 89557
702-784-6865
Minimum Age: 62

Tuition: tuition waiver fall-spring,
  50% off during summer
Basic Fees: none
Credit: yes

Western Nevada Community College
2201 West College Pkwy.
Carson City, NV 89703
702-887-3138
Minimum Age: 62
Tuition: free
Basic Fees: none
Credit: yes

NEW HAMPSHIRE

New Hampshire Technical
  College: Berlin
2020 Riverside Dr.
Berlin, NH 03570
603-752-1113
800-445-4525
Minimum Age: 65
Tuition: free
Basic Fees: $16 for 3 credit hours
Credit: yes

New Hampshire Technical
  College: Claremont
One College Dr.
Claremont, NH 03743
603-542-7744
Minimum Age: 65
Tuition: free
Basic Fees: $10 per course
Credit: yes

New Hampshire Technical
  College: Manchester
1066 Front St.
Manchester, NH 03102
603-668-6706
Minimum Age: 65
Tuition: free
Basic Fees: none
Credit: yes

New Hampshire Technical
   College: Nashua
505 Amherst St.
Nashua, NH 03063
603-882-6923
Minimum Age: 65
Tuition: free
Basic Fees: none
Credit: no

New Hampshire Technical
   College: Stratham
Tech Dr. and Rt. 101
277 Portsmouth Ave.
Stratham, NH 03885
603-772-1194
Minimum Age: 65
Tuition: free
Basic Fees: none
Credit: yes

New Hampshire Technical Institute
Institute Dr.
Concord, NH 03301-7412
603-225-1800
Minimum Age: 65
Tuition: free
Basic Fees: none
Credit: yes

Notre Dame College
2321 Elm St.
Manchester, NH 03104
603-669-4298
Minimum Age: 65
Tuition: free (2 course per semes-
   ter limit - 6 courses per year)
Basic Fees: $60 per semester
Credit: yes

Plymouth State College of the
   University System of New
   Hampshire
Bursars
17 High St.
Plymouth, NH 03264-1600

603-535-2237
Minimum Age: 65
Tuition: free
Basic Fees: $35/credit hour
Credit: yes

School for Lifelong Learning
Learner Services
NSNH
125 N. State St.
Concord, NH 03301
603-228-8300
Minimum Age: 65
Tuition: free
Basic Fees: $15 per session
Credit: yes

University of New Hampshire at
   Manchester
220 Hackett Hill Rd.
Manchester, NH 03102
603-668-0700
Minimum Age: 65
Tuition: free up to 8 credit hours, 8
   credit hours or 2 non-credit courses; no discount if courses are
   being taken for economic gain;
   space available basis
Basic Fees: none
Credit: yes

NEW JERSEY

Atlantic Community College
5100 Black Horse Pike
Mays Landing, NJ 08330
609-343-4922
Minimum Age: 62
Tuition: free
Basic Fees: $20 per session
Credit: yes

Bergen Community College
Admissions and Registration
400 Paramus Rd.
Paramus, NJ 07652
201-447-7857

Minimum Age: 65
Tuition: $9.50/credit hour
Basic Fees: $8.60/credit hour
Credit: yes

Brookdale Community College
765 Newman Springs Rd.
Lincroft, NJ 07738
908-842-1900
Minimum Age: 65
Tuition: free
Basic Fees: $28 for 3 credit hours
Credit: yes

Burlington County College
Admission
County Rt. 530
Pemberton, NJ 08068
609-894-9311
Minimum Age: 62
Tuition: $65 for 3 credit hours
Basic Fees: none
Credit: yes

Camden County College
P.O. Box 200
Blackwood, NJ 08012
609-227-7200
Minimum Age: 62 (55 if unem-
    ployed)
Tuition: free
Basic Fees: none
Credit: yes

County College of Morris
214 Center Grove Rd.
Randolf, NJ 07869
201-328-5000
Minimum Age: 65
Tuition: $5 per credit hour
Basic Fees: none
Credit: yes

Essex County College
303 University Ave.
Newark, NJ 07102

201-877-3100
Minimum Age: 60
Tuition: free
Basic Fees: none
Credit: yes

Rowan State College
Oak Hall
Glassboro, NJ 08028
609-256-4200
Minimum Age: 55
Tuition: no fee; space available
Basic Fees: none
Credit: no

Gloucester County College
Business Office
Tanyard Rd.
Deptford Township
RR #4, Box 203
Sewell Post Office, NJ 08080
609-468-5000
Minimum Age: 60
Tuition: $5/credit hour
Basic Fees: $10/credit hour
Credit: yes

Jersey City State College
2039 Kennedy Blvd.
Bursars Office
Jersey City, NJ 07305
201-200-3234
Minimum Age: 62
Tuition: free
Basic Fees: $73.50 for 3 credit
    hours
Credit: yes

Kean College of New Jersey
1000 Morris Ave.
Union, NJ 07083
908-527-2195
Minimum Age: 62
Tuition: free, space available
Basic Fees: $60 for 3 credit hours

Credit: yes

Mercer County Community College
1200 Old Trenton Rd.
Trenton, NJ 08690-1099
609-586-0505
Minimum Age: 65
Tuition: free, residents of Mercer Co.
Basic Fees: none
Credit: yes

Middlesex County College
155 Mill Rd.
P.O. Box 3050
Edison, NJ 08818
808-906-2510
Minimum Age: 65
Tuition: apply for waiver
Basic Fees: $20 per semester plus
$6 per credit hour
Credit: yes

Montclair State College
Normal Ave. and Valley Rd.
Upper Montclair, NJ 07043
201-655-4136
Minimum Age: 65
Tuition: free
Basic Fees: $25 per session
Credit: yes

Ocean County College
College Dr.
P.O. Box 2001
Toms River, NJ 08754
908-255-0304
Minimum Age: 65
Tuition: $24 per credit hour
Basic Fees: $15 per semester
Credit: yes

Ramapo College of New Jersey
505 Ramapo Valley Rd.
Mahwah, NJ 07430
201-529-7700
Minimum Age: 65

Tuition: free
Basic Fees: none
Credit: no

State University of New Jersey —
Rutgers
Office of University Undergraduate
Admissions
Administrative Services Bldg.
P.O. Box 2101
New Brunswick, NJ 08903-2101
908-445-3770
Minimum Age: 62
Tuition: free
Basic Fees: none
Credit: no

NEW MEXICO
Clovis Community College
417 Schepps Blvd.
Clovis, NM 88101
505-769-4025
Minimum Age: 65
Tuition: $13 first credit hour, $5 for
each additional credit hour
Basic Fees: none
Credit: yes

New Mexico State College at
Carlsbad
1500 University Dr.
Carlsbad, NM 88220
505-885-8831
Minimum Age: 65
Tuition: $6 per credit hour
Basic Fees: $10 one time admis-
sion fee
Credit: yes

New Mexico State University
Registrars Office
Las Cruces, NM 88003
505-646-3121
Minimum Age: 65
Tuition: $25 per hour (6 credit

hour limit in the fall) NM residents only
Basic Fees: $15 per semester for part-time (full-time free)
Credit: yes

New Mexico State University at Alamogordo
Admissions
P.O. Box 477
Alamogordo, NM 88311
505-439-3600
Minimum Age: 65
Tuition: $8 per credit hour for in-district, $13 per credit hour out-of-district
Basic Fees: $10 one time admission fee (6 credit hour limit)
Credit: yes

New Mexico State University at Grants
1500 North Third St.
Grants, NM 87020
505-287-7981
Minimum Age: 65
Tuition: $8 per credit hour
Basic Fees: $10 one time application fee
Credit: yes

University of New Mexico
Cashier
Student Services Center
Room 140
Albuquerque, NM 87131
505-277-5363
800-225-5866
Minimum Age: 65
Tuition: $5 per credit hour (6 credit hour limit)
Basic Fees: none
Credit: yes

NEW YORK
Adirondack Community College
Registrar
Bay Rd.
Queensbury, NY 12804
518-743-2264
Minimum Age: 60
Tuition: free
Basic Fees: none
Credit: no

Broome Community College
Student Accounts
P.O. Box 1017
Binghamton, NY 13902
607-778-5000
Minimum Age: 60
Tuition: free
Basic Fees: none
Credit: no

Cayuga County Community College
Records Office
197 Franklin St.
Auburn, NY 13021
315-255-1743
Minimum Age: 60
Tuition: free, space available
Basic Fees: none
Credit: no

City University of New York: Baruch College
P.O. Box 279
17 Lexington Ave.
New York, NY 10010
212-802-2222
Minimum Age: 62
Tuition: free
Basic Fees: $52 per session
Credit: yes

City University of New York: Bronx Community College
Bursars Office

W. 181st and University Ave.
New York, NY 10453
718-289-5100
Minimum Age: 65
Tuition: free
Basic Fees: $52 per session
Credit: yes

City University of New York:
    Brooklyn College
2900 Bedford Ave.
1602 William James Hall
Brooklyn, NY 11210
718-951-5000
Minimum Age: 65
Tuition: $50 per session
Basic Fees: $50 per session
Credit: yes

City University of New York: City
    College
Convent Ave. at 138th St.
New York, NY 10031
212-650-6977
Minimum Age: 65
Tuition: free
Basic Fees: $52 per session
Credit: yes

City University of New York:
    College of Staten Island
Registrar
2800 Victory Blvd.
Bldg. 2A-110
Staten Island, NY 10314
718-982-2000
Minimum Age: 65
Tuition: free
Basic Fees: $52 per session
Credit: yes

City University of New York:
    Hostos Community College
Admissions
500 Grand Concourse
Bronx, NY 10451

718-518-4444
Minimum Age: 65
Tuition: $75 per semester
Basic Fees: $52 per session
Credit: yes

City University of New York:
    Hunter College
Admissions
695 Park Ave.
Room 203, North Bldg.
New York, NY 10021
212-772-4490
Minimum Age: 65
Tuition: free
Basic Fees: $52 per session
Credit: yes

City University of New York:
    Kingsborough Community College
2001 Oriental Blvd.
Brooklyn, NY 11235
718-368-5079
Minimum Age: 65
Tuition: free
Basic Fees: $70 registration fee
Credit: yes

NORTH CAROLINA

Alamance Community College
Student Services
P.O. Box 8000
Graham, NC 27253
910-578-2002
Minimum Age: 65
Tuition: free
Basic Fees: none
Credit: yes

Anson Community College
P.O. Box 126
Polkton, NC 28135
704-272-7635

Minimum Age: 65
Tuition: free
Basic Fees: $2 per quarter plus $5
  per credit hour
Credit: yes

Appalachian State University
Cashier's Office
Administration Bldg.
Boon, NC 28608
704-262-2120
Minimum Age: 65
Tuition: free plus fees (lab etc.)
Basic Fees: $117.50 for 3 credit
  hours; $235 for 6 credit hours
Credit: yes

Beaufort County Community College
P.O. Box 1069
Washington, NC 27889
919-946-6194
Minimum Age: 65
Tuition: free
Basic Fees: maximum $6 activity
  fee per semester
Credit: yes

Bladen Community College
P.O. Box 266
Dublin, NC 28332
910-862-2164
Minimum Age: 65
Tuition: free
Basic Fees: none
Credit: yes

Blue Ridge Community College
Rt. 2, Box 133A
Flat Rock, NC 28731-9624
704-692-3572
Minimum Age: 65
Tuition: free
Basic Fees: $1.25 per quarter
Credit: yes

Brunswick Community College

P.O. Box 30
Supply, NC 28462
910-754-6900
Minimum Age: 65
Tuition: free
Basic Fees: $1.05 per quarter
Credit: yes

Cape Fear Community College
411 North Front St.
Wilmington, NC 28401-3993
910-343-0481
Minimum Age: 65
Tuition: free
Basic Fees: $1 ID fee per semester,
  maximum $6 activity fee per
  semester
Credit: yes

Carteret Community College
3505 Arendell St.
Morehead City, NC 28557
919-247-4142
Minimum Age: 65
Tuition: free
Basic Fees: $3.25 for 3 credit hours
Credit: yes

Catawba Valley Community College
2550 Highway 70, SE
Hickory, NC 28602
704-327-7009
Minimum Age: 65
Tuition: free
Basic Fees: $1.75 per quarter
Credit: yes

North Carolina University —
  Raleigh
Adult Credit Program
Box 7401
Raleigh, NC 27695-7401
919-515-2434
Minimum Age: 65
Tuition: free
Basic Fees: none

Credit: yes

University of North Carolina —
Chapel Hill
CB# 2200, Jackson Hall
Chapel Hill, NC 27599
919-966-3621
Minimum Age: 65
Tuition: free
Basic Fees: $10 per semester
Credit: yes

NORTH DAKOTA
North Dakota State University
P.O. Box 5454
Admissions
Fargo, ND 58105
701-231-8643
Minimum Age: 65
Tuition: free
Basic Fees: $20 per session
Credit: no

North Dakota State University:
Bottineau and Institute of Forestry
First and Simrall Blvd.
Bottineau, ND 58318
Minimum Age: 65
701-228-2277
Minimum Age: 55
Tuition: free
Basic Fees: none
Credit: no

Standing Rock College
HCI Box 4
Fort Yates, ND 58538
701-854-3861
Tuition: free (tuition, books and
fees all waived if you don't quali-
fy for Pell Grant)
Basic Fees: none (see above)
Credit: yes

University of North Dakota:
Lake Region

1801 College Dr., North
Devils Lake, ND 58301-1598
701-662-1600
Minimum Age: 65
Tuition: free
Basic Fees: none
Credit: no

University of North Dakota:
Williston
1410 University Ave.
Williston, ND 58801
701-774-4210
Minimum Age: 65
Tuition: free
Basic Fees: $10/credit hour
Credit: no

Valley City State University
101 College St., SE
Valley City, ND 58072
701-845-7990
Minimum Age: 65
Tuition: free
Basic Fees: none
Credit: no

OHIO
Belmont Technical College
120 Fox Shannon Pl.
St. Clarisville, OH 43950
614-695-9500
Minimum Age: 60
Tuition: free
Basic Fees: none
Credit: yes

Bowling Green State University
Department of Continuing
Education
McFall Center
40 College Park
Bowling Green, OH 43403
419-372-2086
Minimum Age: 60
Tuition: free, space available

Basic Fees: none
Credit: no

Bowling Green State University —
  Firelands College
901 Rye Beach Rd.
Huron, OH 44839
419-433-5560
Minimum Age: 60
Tuition: free $10 registry fee
Basic Fees: $5 per semester
Credit: no

Central Ohio Technical College
1179 University Dr.
Newark, OH 43055
614-366-9222
Minimum Age: 60
Tuition: free
Basic Fees: $5 per credit hour
Credit: no

Central State University
Registrar
1400 Brush Row Rd.
Wilberforce, OH 45384
513-376-6231
Minimum Age: 60
Tuition: free
Basic Fees: none
Credit: no

Cuyahoga Community College
  District
Downtown Campus
Office of Admissions
2900 Community College Ave.
Cleveland, OH 44115
216-987-4200
Minimum Age: 60
Tuition: free
Basic Fees: none
Credit: yes

Kent State University
P.O. Box 5190

Kent, OH 44242-0001
216-672-2444
Minimum Age: 50 and retired or 60
Tuition: free
Basic Fees: none
Credit: no

Ohio State University
Continuing Education
152 Mount Hall
Columbus, OH 43210
614-292-8860
Minimum Age: 60
Tuition: free
Basic Fees: none
Credit: no

University of Akron
381 Buchtel Common
Akron, OH 44325-2001
216-972-7100
Minimum Age: 60
Tuition: free (3 course limit)
Basic Fees: none
Credit: no

University of Cincinnati
Office of Admission
P.O. Box 210091
Cincinnati, OH 45221-0091
513-556-1100
Minimum Age: 60
Tuition: free
Basic Fees: none
Credit: no

University of Toledo
Evening Session
University of Toledo
Toledo, OH 43606-3398
419-530-4137
Minimum Age: 60
Tuition: free (income limitation of
  $50,000 annually)
Basic Fees: none

Credit: yes

OKLAHOMA

Cameron University
Business Office
2800 West Fore Blvd.
Lawton, OK 73505
405-581-2230
Minimum Age: 65
Tuition: free
Basic Fees: none
Credit: no

Carl Albert State College
P.O. Box 1507
South McLenna
Poteau, OK 74953-5208
918-647-1200
Minimum Age: 65
Tuition: free
Basic Fees: none
Credit: no

Connors State College
Business Office
Rt. 1, Box 1000
Warner, OK 74469
918-463-6250
Minimum Age: 65
Tuition: free
Basic Fees: none
Credit: no

Oklahoma Panhandle State
    University
P.O. Box 430
Goodwell, OK 73939
405-349-2611
Minimum Age: 65
Tuition: free, space available only
Basic Fees: none
Credit: no

Oklahoma State University
104 Whitehurse
Stillwater, OK 74078

405-744-6858
Minimum Age: 65
Tuition: free
Basic Fees: none
Credit: no

University of Oklahoma
Office of Admissions
1000 Asp Ave., Room 127
Norman, OK 73019
405-325-2251
Minimum Age: 65
Tuition: free
Basic Fees: none
Credit: no

OREGON

Blue Mountain Community
    College
Continuing Education
P.O. Box 100
Pendleton, OR 97801
503-276-1260
Minimum Age: 60
Tuition: $10 per credit hour
Basic Fees: none
Credit: yes

Central Oregon Community
    College
Admissions
2600 Northwest College Way
Bend, OR 97701
541-382-6112
Minimum Age: 62
Tuition: 25% off (regular tuition
    $32 per credit hour)
Basic Fees: $1.50 per credit hour
Credit: yes

Chemeketa Community College
Business Office
P.O. Box 14007
4000 Lancaster Dr., NE
Salem, OR 97305
503-399-5006

Minimum Age: 62
Tuition: 35% off (regular tuition
$32 per credit hour)
Basic Fees: none
Credit: yes

Clackamas Community College
19600 South Molalla Ave.
Oregon City, OR 97045
503-657-6958
Minimum Age: 62
Tuition: free
Basic Fees: none
Credit: yes

Clatsop Community College
Extended Learning
1653 Jerome Ave.
Astoria, OR 97103
503-325-0910
Minimum Age: 62
Tuition: 50% off (another 10% for
early payment-regular tuition $30
per credit hour
Basic Fees: none
Credit: yes

Lane Community College
Admissions
4000 East 30th Ave.
Eugene, OR 97405
541-726-2207
Minimum Age: 62
Tuition: 50% off (regular tuition
$30 per credit hour)
Basic Fees: none
Credit: yes

Linn-Benton Community College
Registration
6500 Pacific Blvd., SW
Albany, OR 97321-3779
541-917-4999
Minimum Age: 62
Tuition: 50% off (regular tuition
$32 per credit hour)

Basic Fees: none
Credit: yes

Mount Hood Community College
Business Office
26000 Southeast Stark St.
Gresham, OR 97030
503-667-6422
Minimum Age: 62
Tuition: free
Basic Fees: none (self-enrichment
classes are usually $5 each plus
materials)
Credit: yes

Oregon Institute of Technology
Registrar
3201 Campus Dr.
Klamath Falls, OR 97601-8801
541-885-1150
800-343-6653
Minimum Age: 65
Tuition: free
Basic Fees: none to audit
Credit: no

Oregon State University
Corvallis, OR 97331
503-737-4411
Minimum Age: 65
Tuition: free to audit
Basic Fees: none
Credit: no

Portland Community College
Admissions
P.O. Box 19000
Portland, OR 97280-0990
503-244-6111 ext. 4724
Minimum Age: 62
Tuition: 50% off (regular tuition
$30 per credit hour)
Basic Fees: $7 per quarter full-
time; $2 per quarter part-time
Credit: yes

Portland State University
Senior Adult Learning Center
P.O. Box 751
Portland, OR 97207-0751
503-725-3511
800-547-8887
Minimum Age: 65
Tuition: free to audit
Basic Fees: none
Credit: no

PENNSYLVANIA

Bloomsburg University of
    Pennsylvania
Extended Learning
700 West Main St.
Bloomsburg, PA 17815
717-389-4420
Minimum Age: 60
Tuition: free, space available
Basic Fees: $42.50 for 3 credit
    hours; $304 for 12 credit hours
Credit: yes

Bucks County Community College
Swamp Rd.
Newtown, PA 18940
215-968-8100
Minimum Age: 65
Tuition: free
Basic Fees: $48-$57 per semester
Credit: yes

Butler County Community College
Registrar
P.O. Box 1203
Butler, PA 16003-1203
412-287-8711
Minimum Age: 60
Tuition: free
Basic Fees: none
Credit: no

California University of Pennsylvania
COPE Program
250 University Ave.

California, PA 15419
412-938-5930
Minimum Age: 60
Tuition: free
Basic Fees: $135 for 3 credit hours;
    $408 for 12 credit hours
Credit: yes

Clarion University of Pennsylvania
Admissions
B-16 Carrier Hall
Clarion, PA 16214
814-226-2306
Minimum Age: 65
Tuition: free
Basic Fees: none
Credit: no

Community College of Beaver
    County
One Campus Dr.
Monaca, PA 15061
412-775-8561
Minimum Age: 65
Tuition: free
Basic Fees: $20 per session
Credit: yes

Pennsylvania State University
201 Shields
University Park, PA 16802
814-865-6528
Minimum Age: 60
Tuition: free
Basic Fees: none
Credit: yes (evening classes)

University of Pennsylvania
3440 Market St.
Suite 100
Philadelphia, PA 19104
215-898-7326
Minimum Age: 65
Tuition: $50 donation for 1 class;
    $75 donation for 2 classes
Basic Fees: none

Credit: no

University of Pittsburgh
407 CL
Pittsburgh, PA 15260
412-624-7308
Minimum Age: 60
Tuition: $15 per class
Basic Fees: none
Credit: no

RHODE ISLAND
Community College of Rhode
   Island
Admissions
400 East Ave.
Warwick, RI 02886
401-825-2285
Minimum Age: 62
Tuition: free, waiver
Basic Fees: $15 per session
Credit: yes

Rhode Island College
Records Office
600 Mt. Pleasant Ave.
Providence, RI 02908
401-456-8234
Minimum Age: 65
Tuition: free plus registration fee
Basic Fees: $135 full-time per
   semester
Credit: yes

University of Rhode Island
Financial Aid
Kingston, RI 02881-0806
401-792-2314
Minimum Age: 60, waiver, space
   available
Tuition: free (income limitation)
Basic Fees: $96 for 3 credit hours;
   $619 for 12 credit hours plus $480
   for insurance, which can be waived
   if they have comparable coverage
Credit: yes

SOUTH CAROLINA
Aiken Technical College
P.O. Drawer 696
Aiken, SC 29802-0696
803-593-9231
Minimum Age: 60
Tuition: free
Basic Fees: none
Credit: yes

Chesterfield-Marlboro Technical
   College
Student Development
P.O. Drawer 1007
Cheraw, SC 29520
803-921-6900
Minimum Age: 60
Tuition: free
Basic Fees: $14.50 per semester
Credit: yes

The Citadel
171 Moultri St.
Charleston, SC 29409
803-953-5000
Minimum Age: 60
Tuition: free, $15 registration fee
Basic Fees: $40 per semester
Credit: yes

Clemson University
Business Affairs
G-08 Sikes Hall
P.O. Box 345307
Clemson, SC 29634-5307
864-656-2287
Minimum Age: 65
Tuition: free
Basic Fees: none
Credit: yes

College of Charleston
Treasurers Office
Charleston, SC 29424
803-953-5592
Minimum Age: 60

Tuition: $25 per semester
Basic Fees: none
Credit: yes

Denmark Technical College
Business Office
P.O. Box 327
Solomon Blatt Blvd.
Denmark, SC 29042
803-793-3301
Minimum Age: 62
Tuition: free
Basic Fees: none
Credit: yes

Florence-Darlington Technical
College
Admissions
P.O. Box 100548
Florence, SC 29501-0548
803-661-8151
Minimum Age: 60
Tuition: free
Basic Fees: none
Credit: yes

Francis Marion College
Financial Aid
P.O. Box 100547
Florence, SC 29501-0547
803-661-1231
Minimum Age: 65
Tuition: free
Basic Fees: none
Credit: yes

Greenville Technical College
Admissions
P.O. Box 5616, Station B
Greenville, SC 29606-5616
803-250-8109
Minimum Age: 60
Tuition: free
Basic Fees: $23 per semester
Credit: yes

Horry-Georgetown Technical
College
Financial Aid
P.O. Box 1966
Conway, SC 29526
803-347-3186
Minimum Age: 60
Tuition: $10 per class; $45 for
computer classes
Basic Fees: $15 per session
Credit: yes

Lander College
Admissions
P.O. Box 6007
320 Stanley Ave.
Greenwood, SC 29649
864-229-8307
800-768-3600
Minimum Age: 60
Tuition: free
Basic Fees: none
Credit: yes

Midlands Technical College
Admissions
P.O. Box 2408
Columbia, SC 29202
803-738-7764
Minimum Age: 60
Tuition: free
Basic Fees: none
Credit: yes

SOUTH DAKOTA

Black Hills State University
Records and Admissions
USB 9502
Spearfish, SD 57799-9502
605-642-6343
800-255-2478
Minimum Age: 65
Tuition: $12.86 per credit hour
Basic Fees: none
Credit: yes

Dakota State University
Cashier
Heston Hall
Madison, SD 57042
605-256-5139
Minimum Age: 65
Tuition: $12.86 per credit hour
Basic Fees: $147.33 for 3 credit
　hours
Credit: yes

Northern State University
Finance Office
1200 South Jay St.
Aberdeen, SD 57401
605-626-2544
Minimum Age: 65
Tuition: 75% off (regular tuition
　$45.78 per credit hour)
Basic Fees: $29.05 per credit hour
Credit: yes

South Dakota School of Mines and
　Technology
Registrars Office
501 East St. Joseph St.
Rapid City, SD 57701-3995
605-394-2400
Minimum Age: 65
Tuition: $13.25 per credit hour
Basic Fees: $15 per session
Credit: yes

University of South Dakota
Admissions
414 East Clark
Vermillion, SD 57069-2390
605-677-5434
Minimum Age: 65
Tuition: 75% off (regular tuition
　$47.18 per credit hour)
Basic Fees: $15 per session
Credit: yes

TENNESSEE
Austin Peay State University
Admissions
P.O. Box 4548
Clarksville, TN 37044
615-648-7661
800-426-2604
Minimum Age: 65
Tuition: $33 per credit hour not to
　exceed $75 per session
Basic Fees: none
Credit: yes

Chattanooga State Technical
　Community College
Records Office
4501 Amnicola Hwy.
Chattanooga, TN 37406
423-634-7702
Minimum Age: 65 (60 to audit free)
Tuition: 50% of not to exceed $45
　per session
Basic Fees: $12 per session
Credit: yes

Cleveland State Community
　College
P.O. Box 3570
Cleveland, TN 37320
423-472-7141
Minimum Age: 65 (60 for audit)
Tuition: $16 per credit hour not to
　exceed $45 per session; audit free
Basic Fees: $5 per semester
Credit: yes

Columbia State Community College
Admissions
P.O. Box 1315
Columbia, TN 38402-1315
615-540-2722
Minimum Age: 65 (60 for audit)
Tuition: $20 per session
Basic Fees: $5 one time application
　fee and $5 per session

291

Credit: yes

Dyersburg State Community
  College
P.O. Box 648
Dyersburg, TN 38025-0648
901-286-3200
Minimum Age: 60
Tuition: 50% off not to exceed $50
  per session
Basic Fees: $10-$28/session
Credit: yes

East Tennessee State University
Admissions
P.O. Box 70731
Johnson City, TN 37614
423-929-4213
Minimum Age: 65 (60 for audit)
Tuition: free
Basic Fees: $75 per semester
Credit: yes

Jackson State Community College
Business Office
2046 North Pkwy.
Jackson, TN 38301
901-424-3520
Minimum Age: 65
Tuition: 50% off (regular tuition
  $43 per credit hour)
Basic Fees: $5 per session
Credit: yes

Memphis State University
Admissions Office, Room 167
Memphis, TN 38152
901-678-2101
800-669-9678
Minimum Age: 65 (60 audit)
Tuition: $75 per semester; audit
  free
Basic Fees: none
Credit: yes

Middle Tennessee State University

Accounting and Records
Murfreesboro, TN 37132
615-898-2111
Minimum Age: 65
Tuition: 50% off regular tuition
  Basic Fees: $20 per session
Credit: yes

Motlow State Community College
P.O. Box 88100
Tullahoma, TN 37388-8100
615-393-1500
Minimum Age: 65 (60 to audit)
Tuition: $20 per credit hour not to
  exceed $45 per session
Basic Fees: $5 per session
Credit: yes

University of Tennessee
451 Communication Bldg.
Knoxville, TN 37996-0341
423-974-5361
Minimum Age: 65 (60 can audit free)
Tuition: $7 per credit hour not to
  exceed $75 per session
Basic Fees: $15 one time applica-
  tion fee
Credit: yes

TEXAS
Alvin Community College
Records
3110 Mustang Rd.
Alvin, TX 77511-4898
713-388-4636
Minimum Age: 65
Tuition: no discount
Basic Fees: none
Credit: no

Amarillo College
Business Office
P.O. Box 447
Amarillo, TX 79176
806-371-5000
Minimum Age: 65 or belong to

senior citizen association
Tuition: free (some courses excluded)
Basic Fees: $3 per semester
Credit: yes

Angelina College
P.O. Box 1768
Lufkin, TX 75902
409-639-1301
Minimum Age: 65
Tuition: free
Basic Fees: none
Credit: no

Bee County College
Business Office
3800 Charco Rd.
Beeville, TX 78102
512-358-3130
Minimum Age: 65
Tuition: free
Basic Fees: none
Credit: yes

Southwest Texas State University
SWT General Accounting
601 University Dr.
San Marcos, TX 78666-4603
512-245-2541
Minimum Age: 65
Tuition: free, space available
Basic Fees: none
Credit: no

University of Houston — Central Campus
Bursars Office
Houston, TX 77204-2160
713-743-1096
Minimum Age: 65
Tuition: free
Basic Fees: none
Credit: no

University of North Texas

P.O. Box 13797
Denton, TX 76203
817-565-2681
Minimum Age: senior citizen
Tuition: free
Basic Fees: none
Credit: no

University of Texas — Austin
Office of the Registrar
Main Bldg., Room 1
Austin, TX 78712-1157
512-471-7701
Minimum Age: 65
Tuition: free
Basic Fees: none
Credit: no

UTAH
Brigham Young University
BYU Evening Classes
120 Harman Bldg.
Provo, UT 84602
801-378-2872
Minimum Age: 55
Tuition: $10 per class
Basic Fees: none
Credit: no

College of Eastern Utah
451 East 400 North
Price, UT 84501
801-637-2120
Minimum Age: 65
Tuition: $10 per class
Basic Fees: none
Credit: no

Dixie College
The Office of the Registrar
225 South 700 East
St. George, UT 84770
801-673-4811 ext. 348
Minimum Age: 62
Tuition: $10 quarter (some classes

are excluded)
Basic Fees: none
Credit: no

Salt Lake Community College
Admissions
4600 South Redwood Rd.
Salt Lake City, UT 84130
801-957-4297
Minimum Age: 63
Tuition: $10 per class
Basic Fees: none
Credit: yes

Snow College
150 East College Ave.
Ephraim, UT 84627
801-283-4021
Minimum Age: 62
Tuition: $10 per quarter
Basic Fees: none
Credit: no

Southern Utah University
Cashiers Office
351 West Center
Cedar City, UT 84720
801-586-7740
Minimum Age: 62
Tuition: $10 per quarter
Basic Fees: none
Credit: yes

University of Utah
DCE
1185 Annex
Salt Lake City, UT 84112
801-581-8113
Minimum Age: 60
Tuition: $10 per quarter
Basic Fees: none
Credit: no

Utah State University
Registrar
Logan, UT 84322-1600

801-797-1107
800-662-3950
Minimum Age: 62
Tuition: $10 per class to audit
Basic Fees: none
Credit: no

Utah Valley State College
Registrar
800 West 1200 South
Orem, UT 84058
801-222-8000
Minimum Age: 65
Tuition: $20 per class
Basic Fees: $20 one time admission fee
Credit: no

Weber State University
3750 Harrison
Ogden, UT 84408-1015
801-626-6050
Minimum Age: 62
Tuition: $10 per quarter
Basic Fees: none
Credit: no

VERMONT
Castleton State College
Admissions
Castleton, VT 05735
802-468-5611
Minimum Age: 62
Tuition: free
Basic Fees: $19/credit hour
Credit: yes

Community College of Vermont
Registrar
P.O. Box 120
Waterbury, VT 05676
802-241-3535
Minimum Age: 62
Tuition: 50% off (regular tuition
    $88 per credit hour)
Basic Fees: $42 per semester

Credit: yes

Johnson State College
Student Accounts
Stowe Rd.
Johnson, VT 05656
802-635-2356
800-635-2356
Minimum Age: 62
Tuition: 50% off (regular tuition
  $138 per credit hour)
Basic Fees: $292 per semester plus
  $125 in one time fees
Credit: yes

Lyndon State College
Business Office
Lyndonville, VT 05851
802-626-9371, ext. 163
800-225-1998
Minimum Age: 60
Tuition: 50% off (regular tuition
  $138 per credit hour)
Basic Fees: $58.50 for 3 credit
  hours ($19.50 per credit hour)
Credit: yes

University of Vermont
194 South Prospect
Burlington, VT 05401
802-656-3170
Minimum Age: 62
Tuition: free
Basic Fees: none
Credit: yes

VIRGINIA

In the State of Virginia the following rule applies: If annual federal
  taxable income is less than
  $10,000 tuition and application
  fees are waived (audit only).

Blue Ridge Community College
P.O. Box 80
Weyers Cave, VA 24486-9989

540-234-9261
Minimum Age: 60
Tuition: free
Basic Fees: none
Credit: yes

Central Virginia Community College
Student Services
3506 Wards Rd.
Lynchburg, VA 24502
804-386-4500
Minimum Age: 60
Tuition: free
Basic Fees: none
Credit: yes

Clinch Valley College of the
  University of Virginia
Admissions
College Ave.
Wise, VA 24293
540-328-0116
Minimum Age: 60
Tuition: free
Basic Fees: none
Credit: yes

College of William and Mary
Bursars Office
P.O. Box 8795
Williamsburg, VA 23187-8795
804-221-4000
Minimum Age: 60
Tuition: free
Basic Fees: none
Credit: yes

Dabney S. Lancaster Community
  College
Continuing Education
P.O. Box 1000
Clifton Forge, VA 24422
540-862-4246
Minimum Age: 60
Tuition: free

Basic Fees: none
Credit: yes

Danville Community College
1008 S. Main St.
Danville, VA 24541
804-797-3553
Minimum Age: 60
Tuition: free
Basic Fees: none
Credit: yes

Eastern Shore Community College
Student Services
Rt. 1, Box 6
Melfa, VA 23410-9755
804-787-5912
Minimum Age: 60
Tuition: free
Basic Fees: none
Credit: no

George Mason University
Office of Admissions
GMU
4400 University Dr.
Fairfax, VA 22030
703-993-2400
Minimum Age: 60
Tuition: free
Basic Fees: none
Credit: no

Germanna Community College
Admissions
P.O. Box 339
Locust Grove, VA 22508
540-423-1333
Minimum Age: 60
Tuition: free
Basic Fees: none
Credit: yes

James Madison University
Student Accounts
Harrisonburg, VA 22807

540-568-6147
Minimum Age: 60
Tuition: free
Basic Fees: none
Credit: yes

Northern Virginia Community
   College
Admissions Office
8333 Little River Turnpike
Annandale, VA 22003
703-323-3400
Minimum Age: 60
Tuition: free
Basic Fees: none
Credit: no

University of Virginia
Charlottesville Regional Programs
Div. of Continuing Education
P.O. Box 3697
Charlottesville, VA 22903
804-982-3200
Minimum Age: 60
Tuition: free
Basic Fees: none
Credit: no

WASHINGTON

Bellevue Community College
3000 Landerholm Circle, SE
Bellevue, WA 98007
206-641-2222
Minimum Age: 60
Tuition: free (2 class limit)
Basic Fees: $2.50 per class
Credit: yes

Big Bend Community College
7662 Chanute St.
Moses Lake, WA 98837
509-762-6226
Minimum Age: 60
Tuition: $10 per course (2 course
   limit)

Basic Fees: none
Credit: yes

Central Washington University
400 E. 8th Ave.
Ellensburg, WA 98926
509-963-1211
Minimum Age: 60
Tuition: $5 per credit hour up to 6
    credit hours
Basic Fees: $25 per session
Credit: no

Centralia College
600 West Locust
Centralia, WA 98531
360-736-9391
Minimum Age: 60
Tuition: $20 (2 class limit)
Basic Fees: none
Credit: no

Clark College
1800 East McLaughlin Blvd.
Vancouver, WA 98663
360-992-2000
Minimum Age: 60
Tuition: $5 per class (2 class limit)
Basic Fees: none
Credit: no

University of Washington
Access Program
Undergraduate Extension Office
5001 25th Ave., NE
Seattle, WA 98195
206-543-2320
Minimum Age: 60
Tuition: free plus $5 registration
    fee per quarter
Basic Fees: $5 per session
Credit: no

WEST VIRGINIA
Apparently, legislation has been
    proposed several times to no

avail. We were unable to find any
schools who offered a discount
to senior citizens.

WISCONSIN
Chippewa Valley Technical College
620 West Clairmont Ave.
Eau Claire, WI 54701
715-833-6244
Minimum Age: 62
Tuition: free
Basic Fees: none
Credit: no

Madison Area Technical College
3350 Anderson St.
Madison, WI 53704-2599
608-246-6205
Minimum Age: 62
Tuition: varies ($3.50 and up non-
    credit only) inquire on course #
Basic Fees: varies
Credit: no

Mid-State Technical College
500 - 32nd St., North
Wisconsin Rapids, WI 54494
715-422-5500
Minimum Age: 62
Tuition: free
Basic Fees: none
Credit: no

Milwaukee Area Technical College
Downtown Campus
700 West State St.
Milwaukee, WI 53233
414 297-6600
Minimum Age: 62
Tuition: free
Basic Fees: none
Credit: no

Northcentral Technical College
Registrar
1000 W. Campus Dr.

Wausau, WI 54401
715-675-3331
Minimum Age: 62
Tuition: varies, reduced rate
Basic Fees: none
Credit: no

Northeast Wisconsin Technical
   College
Registrar's Office
P.O. Box 19043
Green Bay, WI 54307-9042
414-498-5703
800-272-2740
Minimum Age: 62
Tuition: up to 50% off (non-credit
   only)
Basic Fees: none
Credit: no

WYOMING

Casper College
125 College Dr.
Casper, WY 82601
307-268-2110 ext. 2491
Minimum Age: 60
Tuition: free, resident of county
Basic Fees: none
Credit: yes, with Golden Age card

Central Wyoming College
Continuing Education
2660 Peck Ave.
Riverton, WY 82501
307-856-9291 ext. 181
Minimum Age: 60
Tuition: free
Basic Fees: $11.50 per credit hour
Credit: yes

Eastern Wyoming College
Records

3200 West C St.
Torrington, WY 82240
307-532-8334
800-658-3195
Minimum Age: 60
Tuition: free
Basic Fees: $9 per credit hour
Credit: yes

Laramie County Community
   College
Admissions
1400 East College Dr.
Cheyenne, WY 82007
307-778-1212
Minimum Age: 65
Tuition: $5 per credit hour
Basic Fees: $10 one time applica-
   tion fee
Credit: yes

University of Wyoming
Admissions
P.O. Box 3435
Laramie, WY 82071
307-766-5160
Minimum Age: 65
Tuition: free
Basic Fees: none
Credit: yes

Western Wyoming Community
   College
P.O. Box 428
Rock Springs, WY 82901
307-382-1600
Minimum Age: 60
Tuition: free
Basic Fees: none
Credit: yes

☆☆☆

Other Free Stuff

No need to wonder where to turn for help, or even if help is out there. Uncle Sam realizes that the over 50 crowd is growing by leaps and bounds, and he's taking action to provide needed services for you.

You can find out about meal programs, home health assistance, insurance, and more with just a phone call. You can even learn what your own state is doing to help out those in your age group. Read on to find some good starting places you can try.

Your Private Concierge

Need help finding out about local Meals on Wheels programs? Want to know about home health aides?

The Eldercare Locator provides access to an extensive network of organizations serving older people at state and local community levels. This service can connect you to information sources for a variety of services including: home delivered meals, transportation, legal assistance, housing options, recreation and social activities, adult daycare, senior center programs, home health services, elder abuse prevention, and nursing home ombudsman.

Contact Eldercare Locator, National Association of Area Agencies on Aging, 1112 16th St., NW, Suite 100, Washington, DC 20036; 800-677-1116 between 9 a.m. and 8 p.m. EST; or online at <http://www.aoa.dhhs.gov/elderpage/locator.html>.

Keep Current on Free Stuff

Ever wonder who is behind most of the programs serving the elderly? Probably not, but in case you did — it's the Administration on Aging (AoA). They're the ones who develop the government's aging programs and coordinate community services for older people.

Seniors can participate in AoA sponsored homemaker, nutrition, housing, employment, counseling, legal aid, transportation, and consumer affairs programs. You can also get your blood pressure checked and work out like Jane Fonda.

Most of these programs are handled through a national network of State Agencies on Aging (see the Directory of State Information at the end of this book for your state office). You can locate services near you through the ElderCare Locator Hotline, National Association of Area Agencies on Aging, 112 16th St., NW, Suite 100, Washington, DC 20036; 800-677-1116.

AoA also publishes a quarterly subscription magazine titled *Aging*, covering a variety of topics of interest to seniors, and the free *Aging America: Trends and Projections*, a statistical compendium covering every aging issue.

For more information about AoA, contact Administration on Aging, 330 Independence Ave., SW, Washington, DC 20201; 202-619-0641; or online at <http://www.aoa.dhhs.gov>.

★★★

Stop Getting Taken

Starving kids in Bolivia? You've just won a bizillion dollars? Precious gem stones available only to you? These are just some of the common telephone scams con artists are using these days.

Tip-offs that you are dealing with less than honest people include using lines such as: "You have to act now or the offer won't be good"; or "You can't afford to miss this high profit, no risk offer"; or "Give me your credit card number and I'll send you all the information."

If you hear these or similar lines, just hang up the phone. You're not being rude; you're just being smart.

The Federal Trade Commission protects consumers from unfair or deceptive business practices. Programs focus on truth in advertising, fair packaging and labeling of products, warranty performance, fair credit reporting, direct mail advertising, door-to-door sales, and business practices of nursing homes. They have a listing of free publications which provide tips and information to help you with all your consumer issues.

To learn more, contact the State Attorney General's office listed in the Directory of State Information at the back of this book, or contact the Federal Trade Commission, Public Reference, Room 130, Washington, DC 20580; 202-326-2222; or online at <http://www.ftc.gov>.

Your Check Is (Ripped Off) In The Mail

For many elderly people living alone and on fixed incomes, shopping by mail is convenient. At the same time, older people are attractive targets for mail-order swindles. Another mail-related crime that hits the elderly is the theft of benefit checks.

Seniors who find themselves victims of mail schemes or theft should contact their local Postmaster for an investigation. Remember also that many communities offer a Carrier Alert Program, where mail carriers watch post boxes for any unusual accumulation of mail that might indicate a need for help. They will also bring your mail to your door if your mail box is located some distance from your home.

The U.S. Postal Services have put together a booklet, *A Consumer's Guide to Postal Crime Prevention*, which offers tips on how to avoid being victimized by mail fraud and theft.

Contact your local post office for more information, or contact Public Affairs Branch, U.S. Postal Service, 475 L'Enfant Plaza, SW, Room 3018, Washington, DC 20260; 202-268-4293; or online at <http://www.usps.gov>.

☆☆☆

Bennies For Vets

You have done your duty, and now it's time to take advantage of some of the great benefits available to you and your family. The Department of Veterans Affairs can answer all your questions about benefits for veterans and their families.

They can provide information and help you apply for programs such as education assistance, vocational rehabilitation, home loan programs, life insurance, comprehensive dental and medical care in outpatient clinics, medical centers, and nursing homes around the country.

They also provide burial services, including cemeteries, markers, and flags, to veterans and others who are eligible.

For more information on benefits and eligibility requirements, contact Department of Veterans Affairs, Office of Public Affairs, 810 Vermont Ave., NW, Washington, DC 20420; 800-827-1000; or online at <http://www.va.gov>.

When You Don't Get No Respect

Some people missed the lesson about treating seniors with respect, and now prey on their elderly relatives (and maybe even their own spouses). Abuse of the elderly can be both physical and psychological, such as demanding their checks or not giving them their medications.

If you suspect someone is being abused, you should report it immediately to the proper authorities. The Clearinghouse on Abuse and Neglect of the Elderly maintains the largest collection of elder abuse and neglect information, and will conduct searches of their database for you.

Contact the Clearinghouse on Abuse and Neglect of the Elderly, College of Human Resources, Education and Public University of Delaware, Newark, DE 19716; 302-831-3525.

☆☆☆

Seniors Are Less Crime Prone ... But

According to a special report published by the Bureau of Justice Statistics (BJS), people age 65 and older are the least likely of all age groups to be the victims of crime. For those seniors who are victims, they are more likely to be victimized at or near their home, and less likely to use measures of self-protection.

BJS can answer all your crime questions, and they publish statistics on crime, victims of crime, and criminal offenders. They have a free series of reports that describe some of the research they have available. Some of the titles include:

- *Violent Crime by Strangers and Nonstrangers*
- *The Crime of Rape*
- *The Risk of Violent Crime*
- *Crime Victims: Learning how to help them*
- *Lifetime Likelihood of Victimization*
- *Robbery Victims*
- *Elderly Victims*

Contact Justice Statistics Clearinghouse, Box 6000, Rockville, MD 20850; 800-732-3277, 8:30 to 7:00 pm; or online at <http://www.ojp.usdoj.gov/bjs>.

Send It Directly To Your Account

Rather than worry each month whether or not your check will arrive in time, many programs will directly deposit your check into a bank account. You can even have this done with your tax return in some places! It allows you to access your funds on the same day each month without the fear of your check being stolen or misplaced.

For those interested in having their Social Security checks directly deposited, contact your local Social Security office or call their hotline at 800-772-1213; or online at <http://www.ssa.gov>.

☆☆☆

Elvis Presley Personally Delivered To You

Well, actually Elvis' face on a postage stamp. You do realize, of course, that the real Elvis stopped doing house calls in 1977. Anyone, especially homebound elderly, can order stamps and other postal items that will be delivered right to their door. Request an order form from your mail carrier or local post office. Orders normally take 2 to 3 business days, with no extra charge.

Postal products can also be ordered by phone by calling the Postal Service's 24-hour toll-free number: 800-STAMP-24. To order over the phone a VISA or Master Card is needed, and there is a $3 service fee per order. Orders are normally delivered within 3 to 5 business days.

Where To Find People Like You

Did you know that during colonial times half the population was under age 16? Now less than 25% are under age 16. The number of people who are 100 or older numbered 35,808 in 1990, mostly females.

If you want to hang around with people your own age, head to California or Florida. California has the largest number of persons 65 and older (3.1 million), but Florida has the largest proportion of elderly at 18%. You can learn more interesting facts, such as the diversity of the elderly, the general health of the group, living arrangements and more.

These facts are all included in a series of reports published by the

Bureau of the Census. You know, the guys who come knocking on your door every ten years, asking how many people live in your house, how many rooms do you have, etc.

They have published a series titled, *Profiles of America's Elderly*, which looks at growth of America's elderly, the racial and ethnic diversity, and living arrangements of this group.

For your copies or more information, contact Bureau of the Census, U.S. Department of Commerce, Washington, DC 20233; 301-457-4100; or online at <http://www.census.gov>.

☆☆☆

Discounts on Your Phone Bill

A house, a car, 2.3 kids, and a phone is the average American family. If you don't have a telephone because of the cost, and you're eligible for social service assistance programs, your local telephone company may offer you reduced connection and installation fees.

Under the Federal Communication Commission's Link-Up America program, low-income households seeking telephone service are given a 50% discount for connection charges, and may be able to pay installment payments on the remaining charge.

All states, the District of Columbia and Puerto Rico have federally approved connection assistance programs. If you are interested in signing up for this service, contact the consumer service representative at your local telephone company.

If you have trouble locating this service, contact Common Carrier, Federal Communications Commission, 1919 M St., NW, Washington, DC 20554; 202-418-1500.

☆☆☆

$7 Off Your Bill

Now that you've got the phone, here is some help with the monthly bill. The Federal Communication Commission's Federal Lifeline program helps low-income subscribers reduce their monthly telephone bill by waiving or reducing the line charge, up to approximately $7 per month.

To date, over 40 states and the District of Columbia have federally approved Lifeline programs. Eligibility varies from state to state, with some having income and/or age requirements. See the list below for more specifics.

For more information on Lifeline assistance, contact your local telephone company, or you can contact Common Carrier, Federal Communications Commission, 1919 M St., NW, Washington, DC 20554; 202-418-0940.

The following is a list of organizations which handle this program on the state level, along with a description of eligibility requirements for that state. The organizations listed for the state can be found by contacting the state government operator located in the state capital. If your state is not listed, contact the office of the Federal Communications Commission listed above.

Lifeline and Link-up State Eligibility Qualifications

ALABAMA
Entity: Public Service Commission
Eligibility Criteria: Recipient of: SSI, AFDC, or Food Stamps
Income Verification: Medicaid or Food Stamp Card

ALASKA
Entity: Anchorage Telephone
Eligibility Criteria: Recipient of: SSI, AFDC, or Food Stamps
Income Verification: Alaska Department of Health and Human Services

ARIZONA
Entity: Corporation Commission
Eligibility Criteria: Lifeline: Income below 150% poverty Link Up: Income at or below poverty and participant in Senior Telephone Discount Program
Income Verification: Arizona Department of Economic Security

ARKANSAS
Entity: Public Service Commission
Eligibility Criteria: Recipient of: SSI, AFDC, HEAP, Food Stamps, Medicaid, or Subsidized housing

Income Verification: Dept. of Human Services

CALIFORNIA
Entity: Public Utilities Commission
Eligibility Criteria: Income at or below 150% poverty
Income Verification: Self certified

COLORADO
Entity: Public Utilities Commission
Eligibility Criteria: Recipient of: SSI, Old Age Pension, Aid to the Blind, or Aid to the Needy and Disabled
Income Verification: Department of Social Services

CONNECTICUT
Entity: Department of Public Utility Control
Eligibility Criteria: Eligible for any low-income assistance or energy assistance program administered by the Connecticut Department of Human Resources or Connecticut Department of Income Maintenance or SSI
Income Verification: Applicable

agency of those listed

DISTRICT OF COLUMBIA
Entity: Public Service Commission
Eligibility Criteria: LIHEAP Eligible
Over age 65 (Flat rate $1.00);
Head of Household ($3.00 meas-
ured + 6.5 cents over 120 calls)
Income Verification: DC Energy
Office

FLORIDA
Entity: Public Service Commission
Eligibility Criteria: Recipient of:
Food Stamps or Medicaid
Income Verification: Department of
Health and Rehabilitative Services

GEORGIA
Entity: Public Service Commission
Eligibility Criteria: Recipient of SSI,
AFDC, and/or Food Stamps
Income Verification: Department of
Human Resources

HAWAII
Entity: Public Utilities Commission
Eligibility Criteria: Age 60 or older
or handicapped with annual
household income $10,000 or less
Income Verification: Hawaiian
Telephone Co.

IDAHO
Entity: Public Utilities Commission
Eligibility Criteria: Recipient of:
AFDC, Food Stamps, Aid to the
Aged, Blind and Disabled, or
Medical Assistance
Income Verification: Medical
Assistance or Food Stamp ID card

ILLINOIS
Entity: Illinois Commerce
Commission

Eligibility Criteria: Recipient of
public assistance in programs
administered by the Illinois
Department of Public Aid
Income Verification: Department of
Public Aid

INDIANA
Entity: Utility Regulatory
Commission
Eligibility Criteria: Recipient of:
SSI, AFDC, HEAP, Medicaid, or
Food Stamps
Income Verification: Local
Exchange Companies

IOWA
Entity: State Utilities Board
Eligibility Criteria: Recipient of: SSI,
AFDC, LIHEAP, or Food Stamps
Income Verification: Local
Exchange Companies

KANSAS
Entity: Corporation Commission
Eligibility Criteria: Recipient of:
SSI, AFDC, Food Stamps,
Medicaid, or General Assistance
Income Verification: Local
Exchange Companies

KENTUCKY
Entity: Public Service Commission
Eligibility Criteria: Recipient of:
SSI, AFDC, Food Stamps, or
Medical Assistance
Income Verification: Cabinet for
Human Resources

LOUISIANA
Entity: Public Service Commission
Eligibility Criteria: Recipient of:
SSI, AFDC, or Food Stamps
Income Verification: Medicaid or
Food Stamp card

MAINE
Entity: Public Utilities Commission
Eligibility Criteria: Recipient of:
SSI, AFDC, HEAP, Medicaid, or
Food Stamps
Income Verification: Department of
Human Services

MARYLAND
Entity: Public Service Commission
Eligibility Criteria: Recipient of:
General Assistance
Income Verification: Dept. of
Human Resources

MASSACHUSETTS
Entity: Dept. of Public Utilities
Eligibility Criteria: Recipient of:
SSI, AFDC, General Public
Welfare, Food Stamps, Medicaid,
and Fuel Assistance
Income Verification: Dept. of
Public Welfare and/or Office of
Fuel Assistance

MICHIGAN
Entity: Public Service Commission
Eligibility Criteria: Income at or
below 130% poverty
Income Verification: Department of
Social Services or Office of
Services to the Aging

MINNESOTA
Entity: Public Utilities Commission
Eligibility Criteria: Age 65 or older
or income level which meets
state poverty levels
Income Verification: Department of
Human Services

MISSISSIPPI
Entity: Public Service Commission
Eligibility Criteria: Recipient of:
SSI, AFDC, or Food Stamps
Income Verification: Medicaid or

Food Stamp card

MISSOURI
Entity: Public Service Commission
Eligibility Criteria: Recipient of:
Medicaid
Income Verification: Dept. of Social
Services

MONTANA
Entity: Public Service Commission
Eligibility Criteria: Recipient of:
SSI, AFDC, or Medicaid
Income Verification: Medicaid card
and Social and Rehabilitation
Services

NEBRASKA
Entity: Public Service Commission
Eligibility Criteria: Recipient of:
SSI, AFDC, Energy Assistance,
Food Stamps, Medicaid, or Aid
to the Aged, Blind or Disabled
Income Verification: Medicaid
Agency or Department of Social
Service or Food Stamp program

NEVADA
Entity: Public Service Commission
Eligibility Criteria: Recipient of:
SSI, AFDC, Energy Assistance,
Food Stamps, Indian General
Assist., Commodity Foods, or VA
Improved Pension
Income Verification: Proof of
enrollment in listed programs

NEW HAMPSHIRE
Entity: Public Utilities Commission
Eligibility Criteria: Recipient of:
SSI, AFDC, Food Stamps, Fuel
Assistance, Old Age Assistance,
Weatherization Assist., Aid to
Permanently/ Totally Disabled,
Women, Infants and Children
Feeding Program, Welfare, Title

XX, or Subsidized Housing
Income Verification: Respective
donor agency

NEW JERSEY
Entity: Public Service Commission
Eligibility Criteria: Recipient of:
SSI, AFDC, HEAP, Pharma-
ceutical Assist. to the Aged,
Welfare, or Lifeline Credit
Income Verification: Local
Exchange Companies

NEW MEXICO
Entity: Mountain Bell Telephone
Eligibility Criteria: Recipient of:
SSI, AFDC, or LITAP
Income Verification: Human
Services Department

Entity: Western NM Tel. Co.
Eligibility Criteria: Recipient of:
SSI, AFDC, or CCIC
Income Verification: Human
Services Department

NEW YORK
Entity: Public Service Commission
Eligibility Criteria: Recipient of:
SSI, AFDC, Food Stamps,
Medicaid, or Home Relief
Income Verification: Administering
Agency

NORTH CAROLINA
Entity: Utilities Commission
Eligibility Criteria: Recipient of: SSI
or AFDC
Income Verification: Dept. of
Human Resources

NORTH DAKOTA
Entity: Public Service Commission
Eligibility Criteria: Eligible for:
Food Stamps, Fuel Assist.,
AFDC, Medical Assist.

Income Verification: County Social
Service Board

OHIO
Entity: Public Utilities Commission
Eligibility Criteria: Recipient of:
HEAP, E-Heap, Ohio Energy
Credits Program, SSI, AFDC and
Medicaid
Income Verification: Local
Exchange Companies

OKLAHOMA
Entity: Corporate Commission
Eligibility Criteria: Recipient of aid
from state low income programs
Income Verification: Dept. of
Human Services

OREGON
Entity: Public Utilities Commission
Eligibility Criteria: Eligible for:
Food Stamps and assistance pro-
grams 135% of poverty
Income Verification: Dept. of
Human Resources

PENNSYLVANIA
Entity: Public Utilities Commission
Eligibility Criteria: Recipient of:
SSI, AFDC, Food Stamps, General
Assistance, or Blue Card Medical
Assist. Medically Needy Only
Income Verification: Department of
Public Welfare

PUERTO RICO
Entity: PR Tel. Co.
Eligibility Criteria: Recipient of:
Nutritional Assistance Program
Income Verification: Dept. of Social
Services

RHODE ISLAND
Entity: Public Utilities Commission
Eligibility Criteria: Recipient of:

SSI, AFDC, General Assistance,
or Medical Assistance
Income Verification: Dept. of
Human Services

SOUTH CAROLINA
Entity: Public Utilities Commission
Eligibility Criteria: Recipient of:
AFDC, Food Stamps, Medicaid,
or Temporary Emergency Food
Assistance
Income Verification: Local
Exchange Companies

SOUTH DAKOTA
Entity: Northwestern Bell
Eligibility Criteria: Recipient of:
HEAP or Food Stamps
Income Verification: Dept. of Social
Services

TENNESSEE
Entity: Public Service Commission
Eligibility Criteria: Recipient of: SSI,
AFDC, Medicaid, or Food Stamps
Income Verification: Medicaid card or
Food Stamp Notice of Disposition

TEXAS
Entity: Public Utilities Commission
Eligibility Criteria: Eligible for: SSI,
AFDC, LIHEAP, Food Stamps,
Medicaid, Medical Assistance, or
Maternal Health Program
Income Verification: Local
Exchange Companies

UTAH
Entity: Public Service Commission
Eligibility Criteria: Eligible for: SSI,
AFDC, Food Stamps, General
Assistance, Home Energy
Assistance, Medical Assistance,
Refugee Assistance, or Energy
Work Programs

Income Verification: Local
Exchange Companies

VERMONT
Entity: Public Service Board
Eligibility Criteria: Recipient of:
SSI, AFDC, Food Stamps,
Medicaid, or Fuel Assistance
Income Verification: Department of
Social Welfare

VIRGINIA
Entity: Corporation Commission
Eligibility Criteria: Recipient of:
Virginia Universal Service Plan
Income Verification: Department of
Medical Assistance Services

WASHINGTON
Entity: Utilities and Transportation
Commission
Eligibility Criteria: Recipient of:
SSI, AFDC, Food Stamps,
Refugee Assistance, Chore
Services, or Community Options
Program Entry System
Income Verification: Department of
Social and Health Services

WEST VIRGINIA
Entity: Public Service Commission
Eligibility Criteria: Disabled or age
60 or older and receives SSI,
AFDC, or Food Stamps or is eli-
gible for SSI
Income Verification: Department of
Human Services

WISCONSIN
Entity: Wisconsin Bell, GTE
Eligibility Criteria: Recipient of:
AFDC, SSI, Food Stamps, Title
19 Medical and Energy Programs
Income Verification: Department of
Health and Social Services

WYOMING
Entity: Public Services
 Commission United US West
Eligibility Criteria: Recipient of:

SSI, AFDC, LIHEAP, or Food
Stamps
Income Verification: Dept. of
 Health and Social Services

They Have The President's Ear

Mental health and aging, health care reform and long-term care, income security, housing and living arrangements, and even the problems faced by minority elders are just some of the topics that have been investigated by the Federal Council on Aging.

The Council is a special advisory group of a cross-section of rural and urban older Americans, national organizations with an interest in aging, business, labor, and the general public. The Council reviews and evaluates federal policies, programs, and activities that affect the lives of older Americans. The Council collects and distributes information on aging, as well as publishes an annual report to the President.

For more information on how to keep up to date on these issues, contact Federal Council on the Aging, Room 4280 HHS-N, 330 Independence Ave., SW, Washington, DC 20201; 202-619-2451.

✩✩✩

Find Out What the Government is Doing for You

You have your own special lobbying group to keep you up-to-date on what Congress is doing and you don't even have to take them golfing in Tahiti.

The U.S. Senate puts out a free report that outlines what each government agency is doing for seniors, from special arts programs at the National Endowment for the Arts to clinical trials on treatments for Alzheimer's at the National Institutes of Health. Or you can get free copies of special reports on a variety of topics like prescription drug price increases or women's health issues.

For a current listing of all publications, or to obtain one of the free publications listed below, contact Special Committee on Aging, United States Senate, SD-G31, Washington, DC 20510; 202-224-5364; or online at <http://www.senate.gov/~aging>.

Below is a partial listing of free publications:

- *Retiring Baby Boomers: Meeting the Challenge*
- *Shortchanged: Pension Miscalculations*
- *Society's Secret Shame: Elder Abuse and Family Violence*
- *Telescams Exposed: How Telemarketers Target the Elderly*
- *Nutrition and the Elderly: Savings for Medicare*
- *Hearing on Adverse Drug Reactions in the Elderly*
- *Grandparents as Parents: Raising a Second Generation*, July 29, 1992, Serial No. 102-24
- *Consumer Fraud and the Elderly: Easy Prey?* September, 24, 1992, Washington, DC, Serial No. 102-25
- *Roundtable Discussion on Intergenerational Mentoring*, November 12, 1992, Washington, DC, Serial No. 102-26*
- *The Federal Government's Investment in New Drug Research and Development: Are We Getting Our Money's Worth?* February 24, 1993, Washington, DC, Serial No. 103-1
- *Prescription Drug Prices: Out-Pricing Older Americans*, April 14, 1993, Bangor, ME, Serial No. 103-2
- *Workshop on Innovative Approaches to Guardianship*, April 16, 1993, Washington, DC, Serial No. 103-3
- *Controlling Health Care Costs: The Long-Term Care Factor*, April 20, 1993, Washington, DC, Serial No. 103-4
- *Workshop on Cataract Surgery: Guidelines and Outcomes*, April 21, 1993, Washington, DC, Serial No. 103-5
- *Workshop on Rural Health and Health Reform*, May 3, 1993, Washington, DC, Serial No. 103-6*
- *Preventive Health: An Ounce of Prevention Saves a Pound of Cure*, May 6, 1993, Washington, DC, Serial No. 103-7
- *How Secure Is Your Retirement: Investments, Planning, and Fraud*, May 25, 1993, Washington, DC, Serial No. 103-8
- *The Aging Network: Linking Older Americans to Home and Community-Based Care*, June 8, 1993, Washington, DC, Serial No. 103-9
- *Mental Health and the Aging*, July 15, 1993, Washington, DC, Serial No. 103-10*
- *Health Care Fraud as It Affects the Aging*, August 13, 1993, Racine, WI, Serial No. 103-11
- *The Hearing Aid Marketplace: Is the Consumer Adequately Protected?* Washington, DC, September 15, 1993, Serial No. 103-12
- *Improving Income Security for Older Women in Retirement: Current Issues and Legislative Reform Proposals*, September 23, 1993, Washington, DC, Serial No. 103-13

- *Long-Term Care Provisions in the President's Health Care Reform Plan,* November 12, 1993, Madison, WI, Serial No. 103-14
- *Pharmaceutical Marketplace Reform: Is Competition the Right Prescription?* November 16, 1993, Washington, DC, Serial No. 103-15
- *Home Care and Community-Based Services: Overcoming Barriers to Access,* March 30, 1994, Kalispell, MT, Serial No. 103-16
- *Medicare Fraud: An Abuse,* April 11, 1994, Miami, FL, Serial No. 103-17
- *Health Care Reform: The Long-Term Care Factor,* Washington, DC, April 12, 1994, Serial No. 103-18
- *Elder Abuse and Violence Against Midlife and Older Women,* May 4, 1994, Washington, DC, Serial No. 103-19
- *Long-Term Care,* May 9, 1994, Milwaukee, WI, Serial No. 103-20
- *Health Care Reform: Implications for Seniors,* May 18, Lansing, MI, Serial No. 103-21
- *Fighting Family Violence: Response of the Health Care System,* June 20, 1994, Bangor, ME, Serial No. 103-22
- *Uninsured Bank Products: Risky Business for Seniors,* September 29, 1994, Washington, DC, Serial No. 103-23

☆☆☆

We The American ... Elderly

Did you know that in 1900, 1 in 25 Americans were elderly, and in 1990, 1 in 8 were? Just in sheer numbers, you will be a force to be reckoned with. But what is in store for you, and what is Washington thinking about the elderly?

To learn more, the Congressional Research Service (CRS) has written several easy to understand reports on the topic. The reports are free, but you must request them through your members of Congress. Some titles relating to the elderly include:

- *Economic Status Of the Elderly Population* (87-101E)
- *The Aged: A Profile* (IP3A)
- *Older Americans Act Amendments of 1992* (93-329EPW)
- *The Aged: Bibliography In Brief* (89-258L)
- *Selected Legislation Affecting The Elderly* (91-624EPW)

These and other reports dealing with the elderly are available by contacting Your Representative or Senator, The Capitol, Washington, DC 20510; 202-224-3121.

Making Sure You Get
Your Thirty-Two Cents Worth

Before you buy a long-term care insurance policy, you should look at what the government has learned about the policies in general. Even before you go under the laser for cataract surgery, you can discover data on the appropriateness and outcomes to that surgery and other procedures.

Pension plan violators, rental housing problems for seniors, and cataract surgery complications are just a few of the issues covered in the General Accounting Office (GAO) report titled *Aging Issues.* It lists all the subjects the GAO investigated, like long-term care insurance and lump sum retirements. Each listing also includes an abstract of the report or testimony.

All reports are free (except for the cost of a phone call or stamp) and can be requested by contacting the U.S. General Accounting Office, P.O. Box 6015, Gaithersburg, MD 20884; 202-512-6000; or online at <http://www.gao.gov>.

☆☆☆

"Help! I've Fallen And I Can't Get Up"

No need to spend a fortune on an emergency call button if you take some basic precautions.

The number one cause of accidents for the over 65 age group involves bathtubs, carpets, ladders, and other home furnishings and fixtures. The Consumer Product Safety Commission (CPSC) distributes the publication, *Home Safety Checklist for Older Consumers,* which can help you make your home a safer place.

CPSC also answers questions and accepts complaints about consumer products, and can inform you of product recalls. They even maintain a clearinghouse which collects information about consumer product-related injuries.

For publications, a publications list, or other services, contact the Consumer Product Safety Commission, Office of Information and Public Affairs, 4330 East-West Hwy., Bethesda, MD 20207; 800-638-2772; or online at <http://www. cpsc.gov>.

Consumer Power

Nine Ways To Lower Your Auto Insurance Costs. Medicare Pays For Flu Shots. Understanding Social Security. Food Facts For Older Adults. Estrogens — How To Take Your Medicine. These are just a few of over 200 publications available for free or not much money from the Consumer Information Center.

Four times a year, the Center publishes the Consumer Information Catalog, which lists selected federal government publications of interest to consumers. Topics covered include automobiles, health, food, money management, nutrition, housing, employment, and education. Prices range from free to one dollar.

For your free catalog, write Consumer Information Center, P.O. Box 100, Pueblo, CO 81009.

Your Own Television Station

Tired of those shoot and kill shows on T.V. every night? Now is your chance to turn the channel and find something that's just right for you. Arizona's Office of Aging produces a weekly cable television show which airs on its public access station, as does one in Ohio.

Interview topics have included employment and volunteer opportunities, as well as legislation of interest to senior adults. Some cable stations even offer a discount rate to seniors who meet income and residency requirements.

To learn if your state provides similar programming, contact your local cable television company or your State Department on Aging listed in the Directory of State Information at the end of this book.

No Car, No License, No Problem

Getting around town without a set of wheels is a big problem for many seniors. Fortunately, many transit systems offer free or reduced fares to those over 65. They even offer special pick-up services for those who have trouble making it to the nearest bus stop or who are in wheelchairs.

New Jersey offers the Senior Citizen and Disabled Resident Transportation Assistance Program which provides door-to-door service, fixed route service, local fare subsidies, and more to those over 60.

Contact your local transit authority to see what it offers, or your state Department on Aging from the Directory of State Information at the end of this book.

Free Deadbolt Locks

You can make breaking into your home a little harder by using a deadbolt lock. The Senior Lock Program provides locks and installation for Wilmington, Delaware homeowners, age 65 and over, whose income is under $14,000. You must live within the city limits of Wilmington.

For more information, call the Wilmington Police Department Crime Prevention Unit, 300 N. Walnut St., Wilmington, DE 19801; 302-571-4470. For those outside of Wilmington, Delaware, contact your local police or fire department to learn what similar services they offer to seniors.

Free Phone Friends

Do what the telephone commercials tell you to do, and pick up the phone and call someone. Many seniors benefit from these telephone reassurance calls. They know people are calling to check on them on a regular basis, and it provides them needed contact with others. These phone calls don't require much of your time, but can offer a great deal in return.

To find out how you can become a volunteer phone friend, or to have a phone friend check on you, contact your state Department on Aging listed in the Directory of State Information at the end of this book.

Free Fans

Fan Care is a great program sponsored by Virginia Power. If you are a resident of Virginia and 60 or older, you may be eligible for a free fan to help you make it safely through the hot summer.

To learn about eligibility requirements, contact Fan Care, Department for the Aging, 1600 Forest Ave., Suite 102, Richmond, VA 23229; 804-662-9333; or online at <http://www.aging.state.va.us/>.

For those outside of Virginia, contact your state Department on Aging or your state utility commission, both listed in the Directory of State Information at the end of this book, to see what they have to offer.

Turn 65, And Get A Discount

I bet you didn't realize that just by turning that magic number, you would actually be saving money left and right.

Golf courses, parks, beaches, fishing and hunting licenses, and even automobile tags are often provided to those over 65 at a great discount. All you need to do is ask.

You can:

- Save 1% on sales tax in South Carolina
- Save $100 on hearing aids in New Jersey
- Get free admission to state parks in many states
- Get free hunting and fishing licenses in most states
- Get a discount on cable television in New Jersey
- Save 15% on groceries in some stores in Ohio
- Get cheap tickets to the movies
- Go to the ballpark for half-price at many ballfields
- Get books of airplane tickets at cheap rates from most airlines
- Choose from lower-priced menus at many restaurants

Your state Department on Aging (see the Directory of State Information at the end of this book) can tell you about many of the state programs that provide these services to seniors, as well as many private enterprises.

Now the big question is, what are you going to do with all the money you save?

$\star\star\star$

Help Close To Home

Did you know that Rhode Island will help pay for your hearing aid? Illinois will give you a reduced rate for your license tags. Ohio will give you a $50 tax credit against the amount of Ohio tax that you owe. Ohio also will provide you with a computerized printout of the special programs for which you qualify.

To learn more about programs which are specific to your state, contact your state Department on Aging. They can put you in contact with the right people to learn how you can save money on your utilities, medical bills, food, and even property taxes. Look in the Directory of State Information at the end of this book to locate your state Department on Aging.

☆☆☆

Trouble With Utility Bills?

Can't afford to heat your house in the winter? Are you having trouble paying your electric or water bill because your income is so low? Many utility offices offer special programs for seniors. Contact your local utility office to see if they have a program of discounts or reduced fees for seniors.

If the utility company is threatening to turn off your service because of unpaid bills, make sure to let them know you are a senior citizen and need this service. In many cases, they will not cut off your service.

For more information, contact your local utility office. If you have trouble locating the office or need further assistance, contact your state Public Utilities Commission which is located in the Directory of State Information at the end of this book.

☆☆☆

Sky High Bills?

Feel like your utility bill is high enough to heat your entire street? Think the meter reader needs his glasses checked?

If you are having trouble with your utility bills and have not gotten satisfaction from your local utility office, contact your State Public Utilities Commission office. This office regulates consumer services and rates for gas, electric, water, and telephone. They will help negotiate with your local office on your behalf.

To locate your state Public Utilities Commission office, look in the Directory of State Information at the end of this book.

Directory Of State Information

ALABAMA

Federal Information Center
All locations; 800-688-9889

State Information Office
334-242-8000
http://www.state.al.us

Cooperative Extension Offices
Dr. W. Gaines Smith Interim
Director
Alabama Cooperative
Extension Service
109 A Duncan Hall
Auburn University
Auburn, AL 36849-5612
334-844-4444
http://www.acesag.auburn.edu

Chinelle Henderson,
Administrator
Alabama A&M University
Cooperative Extension Service
P.O. Box 222
Normal, AL 35762
205-851-5710
http://www.saes.aamu.
edu/exten.htm

Dr. Moore, Director
Cooperative Extension Program
U.S. Dept. of Agriculture
Tuskegee University
207 N. Main St., Suite 400
Tuskegee, AL 36083-1731
334-727-8806
http://www.tusk.edu

Attorney Grievances
Alabama State Bar
Center for Professional
Responsibility
P.O. Box 671
Montgomery, AL 36101
334-269-1515
http://www.alabar.org/

Client Security Trust Fund & Fee Arbitration
Alabama State Bar
P.O. Box 671
Montgomery, AL 36101
334-269-1515
http://www.alabar.org/

State Consumer Protection Office
Consumer Protection Division
Office of Attorney General
11 S. Union St.
Montgomery, AL 36130
334-242-7334
800-392-5658 - in AL only
http://e-pages.com/aag/
cuspro.html

HUD Field Office
600 Beacon Pkwy, West
Suite 300
Birmingham, AL 35209
205-290-7617
http://www.hud.gov

State Insurance Commissioner
Insurance Commissioner
201 Monroe St., Suite 1700

Montgomery, AL 36104
334-269-3550

Nursing Home Ombudsmen
Commission on Aging
770 Washington Ave.
R.F.A. Plaza, #470
Montgomery, AL 36130
334-242-5743
800-243-5463 - (AL only)

State Government Banking Commissioner
Superintendent of Banks
401 Adams Ave., Suite 680
Montgomery, AL 36130
334-242-3452

State Office on Aging
Aging Commission
770 Washington Ave.
Suite 470
Montgomery, AL 36130
334-242-5743

State Utility Commission
Public Service Commission
P.O. Box 991
Montgomery, AL 36101
334-242-5207
800-392-8050 (AL only)

ALASKA

Federal Information Center
All locations; 800-688-9889

State Information Office
907-465-2111
http://www.state.ak.us

Cooperative Extension Office
Hollis D. Hall, Director
Alaska Cooperative Extension
University of Alaska Fairbanks
P.O. Box 756180

Fairbanks, AK 99775-6180
907-474-7246
http://zorba.uafadm.alaska.edu
/coop-ext/index.html

Attorney Grievances, Client Security Trust Fund, & Fee Arbitration
Alaska Bar Association
P.O. Box 100279
510 L. St., Suite 602
Anchorage, AK 99501
907-272-7469
http://www.alaskabar.org

State Consumer Protection Office
Attorney General
1031 W. Fourth Ave.
Suite 200
Anchorage, AK 99501
907-269-5100

HUD Field Office
Federal Bldg.
222 W. 8th Ave., #64
Anchorage, AK 99513
907-271-4170
http://www.hud.gov

State Insurance Director
Director of Insurance
P.O. Box 110805
Juneau, AK 99811-0805
907-465-2515
http://www.state.ak.us/
local/akpages/commerce/
ins.htm

Nursing Home Ombudsmen
State of Alaska Long Term
Care Ombudsman
3601 C St., Suite 260
Anchorage, AK 99503-5209
907-563-6393
800-730-6393

State Government Banking Commissioner
Director of Banking
Securities and Corporations
P.O. Box 110807
Juneau, AK 99811-0807
907-465-2521
http://www.commerce.
state.ak.us/bsc/bsc.htm

State Office on Aging
Division of Senior Services
Commission on Aging
P.O. Box 110209
Juneau, AK 99811-0209
907-465-3250
http://www.state.ak.us/
local/akpages/ADMIN/dss/
homess.htm

State Utility Commission
Public Utilities Commission
1016 W. 6th Ave., Suite 400
Anchorage, AK 99501
907-276-6222
http://www.state.ak.us/
local/akpages/COMMERCE/
apuc.htm

ARIZONA

Federal Information Center
All Locations; 800-688-9889

State Information Office
602-542-4900
http://www.state.az.us

Cooperative Extension Office
Jim Christenson, Director
Cooperative Extension Office
University of Arizona
Forbes 301
Tucson, AZ 85721
520-621-7205

http://ag.arizona.edu/ext/
coopext.html

Attorney Grievances, Client Security Trust Fund, & Fee Arbitration
Chief Bar Counsel
State Bar of Arizona
111 West Monroe
Suite 1800
Phoenix, AZ 85003-1742
602-252-4804
http://www.azbar.org

State Consumer Protection Office
Consumer Protection Division
Office of Attorney General
1275 W. Washington St.
Room 259
Phoenix, AZ 85007
602-542-3702
800-352-8431 (AZ only)

HUD Field Office
400 N. 5th St.
Suite 1600
2 Arizona Center
Phoenix, AZ 85004
602-379-4434
http://www.hud.gov

State Insurance Commissioner
Director of Insurance
2910 N. 44th St., Suite 210
Phoenix, AZ 85018
602-912-8400
http://www.state.az.us/id

Nursing Home Ombudsmen
Aging and Adult
Administration
1789 W. Jefferson
Phoenix, AZ 85007
602-542-4446

State Government Banking Commissioner
Superintendent of Banks
2910 N. 44th St., Suite 310
Phoenix, AZ 85018
602-255-4421
800-544-0708
http://www.azbanking.com

State Office on Aging
Aging and Adult Administration
Economic Security Department
1789 W. Jefferson
Phoenix, AZ 85007
602-542-4446

State Utility Commission
Corporation Commission
1200 W. Washington St.
Phoenix, AZ 85007
602-542-3935
800-222-7000 (AZ only)
http://www.cc.state.az.us

ARKANSAS

Federal Information Center
All Locations; 800-688-9889

State Information Office
501-682-3000
http://www.state.ar.us

Cooperative Extension Offices
David Foster, Director
Cooperative Extension Service
P.O. Box 391
Little Rock, AR 72203
501-671-2000
http://www.uaex.edu

Attorney Grievances
Committee on Professional
Conduct
Justice Bldg., Room 205

625 Marshall St.
Little Rock, AR 72201
501-376-0313

Client Security Trust Fund
Clerk
Clerk Office
625 Marshall St.,
Justice Bldg.
Little Rock, AR 72201
501-682-6849

State Consumer Protection Office
Consumer Protection Division
Office of Attorney General
200 Catlitt-Prien Bldg.
323 Center St.
Little Rock, AR 72201
501-682-2341
800-482-8982 (AR only)
http://www.ag.state.ar.us

HUD Field Office
425 W. Capitol, Suite 900
Little Rock, AR 72201
501-324-5931
http://www.hud.gov

State Insurance Commissioner
Insurance Commissioner
1200 W. 3rd St.
Little Rock, AR 72201
501-371-2600

Nursing Home Ombudsmen
Division of Aging and Adult
Services
1417 Donaghey Plaza South
P.O. Box 1437, Slot 1412
Little Rock, AR 72203-1437
501-682-2441

State Government Banking Commissioner
Bank Commissioner

Tower Bldg.
323 Center St., Suite 500
Little Rock, AR 72201
501-324-9019
http://www.state.ar.us/
bank/banking.html

State Office on Aging
Aging and Adult Services
Division
Box 1437
Slot 1412
Little Rock, AR 72203
501-682-2441
http://www.state.ar.us/
dhs.index2.html

State Utility Commission
Public Service Commission
1000 Center St.
P.O. Box 400
Little Rock, AR 72203-0400
501-682-1453
800-482-1164 (AR only)

CALIFORNIA

Federal Information Center
All Locations; 800-688-9889

State Information Office
916-322-9900
http://www.state.ca.us

Cooperative Extension Office
Kenneth Farrell, VP
University of California
Division of Agriculture and
Natural Resources
300 Lakeside Dr., 6th Floor
Oakland, CA 94612-3560
510-987-0060 (programs are at
county level)

Attorney Grievances
Southern California

Chief Trial Counsel
State Bar of California
1149 S. Hill St., 4th Floor
Los Angeles, CA 90015
213-765-1000
800-843-9053 (CA only)
http://www.calbar.org

Northern California
Chief Trial Counsel
State Bar of California
100 Van Ness Ave.
28th Floor
San Francisco, CA 94102
415-561-8200
800-843-9053 (CA only)
http://www.calbar.org

Client Security Trust Fund
Southern California Grievance
Committee
State Bar of California
1149 S. Hill St., 9th Floor
Los Angeles, CA 90017
213-765-1140
http://www.calbar.org

Fee Arbitration
Chief Trial Counsel
State Bar of California
100 Van Ness Ave.
28th Floor
San Francisco, CA 94102
415-241-2020
800-843-9053 (CA only)
http://www.calbar.org

State Consumer Protection Offices
Public Inquiry Unit
Office of Attorney General
1515 K St., Suite 511
P.O. Box 944255
Sacramento, CA 94244
916-322-3360

800-952-5225 (CA only)
http://caag.state.ca.us/piu/

California Department of Consumer Affairs
400 R St.
Sacramento, CA 95814
916-445-0660
800-344-4410 (CA only)

Bureau of Automotive Repair
California Department of
Consumer Affairs
400 R St.
Sacramento, CA 95814
916-366-5100
800-952-5210 (CA only-auto repair only)
http://caag.state.ca.us/piu/bar.htm

HUD Field Offices
611 W. 6th St., Suite 800
Los Angeles, CA 90017
213-894-8007
http://www.hud.gov

450 Golden Gate Ave.
P.O. Box 36003
San Francisco, CA 94102-3448
415-436-6550
http://www.hud.gov

777 12th St., Suite 200
Sacramento, CA 95814
916-498-5220
http://www.hud.gov

State Insurance Commissioner
Commissioner of Insurance
300 S. Spring St.
Los Angeles, CA 90013
916-322-3555 (Santa Monica)
213-897-8921 (Los Angeles)
800-927-HELP (complaints)

http://www.insurance.ca.gov

Nursing Home Ombudsmen
Department of Aging
1600 K St.
Sacramento, CA 95814
916-323-6681
800-231-4024 (CA only)

State Government Banking Commissioner
Superintendent of Banks
111 Pine St., Suite 1100
San Francisco, CA 94111
415-557-3535
800-622-0620
http://www.dfi.ca.gov

State Office on Aging
California Department of
Aging
1600 K St.
Sacramento, CA 95814
916-322-5290
http://www.aging.state.ca.us

State Utility Commission
Public Utilities Commission
505 Van Ness Ave.
San Francisco, CA 94102
415-703-2782
http://www.cpuc.ca.gov

COLORADO

Federal Information Center
All Locations; 800-688-9889

State Information Office
303-866-5000
http://www.state.co.us

Cooperative Extension Office
Milan Rewets, Director
Colorado State University
Cooperative Extension

1 Administrative Building
Fort Collins, CO 80523
970-491-6281
http://www.colostate.edu

Attorney Grievances
S.C.D.C
Disciplinary Counsel
Supreme Court of Colorado
Dominion Plaza Bldg.
600 17th St.
Suite 510 S.
Denver, CO 80202
303-893-8121

Client Security Trust Fund
Colorado Bar Association
1900 Grant St., Suite 950
Denver, CO 80203-4309
303-860-1115
800-332-6736 (CO only)
http://www.cobar.org

Fee Arbitration
Legal Fee Arbitration
Committee
Colorado Bar Association
1900 Grant St., Suite 950
Denver, CO 80203-4309
303-860-1112
800-332-6736 (CO only)
http://www.cobar.org

State Consumer Protection
Office
Consumer Protection Unit
Office of Attorney General
1525 Sherman St.
5th Floor
Denver, CO 80203
303-866-5189
800-332-2071 (CO only)
http://www.state.co.us/
gov_dir/dol/consprot.htm

HUD Field Office

633 17th St.
Denver, CO 80202
303-672-5258
http://www.hud.gov

State Insurance
Commissioner
Commissioner of Insurance
1560 Broadway, Suite 850
Denver, CO 80202
303-894-7490
http://www.dora.state.
co.us/insurance

Nursing Home Ombudsmen
The Legal Center
455 Sherman St.
Suite 130
Denver, CO 80203
303-722-0300
800-288-1376 (CO only)

State Government Banking
Commissioner
State Bank Commissioner
Division of Banking
1560 Broadway
Suite 1175
Denver, CO 80202
303-894-7575
http://www.aclin.org/other/
government/dora/aclin

State Office on Aging
Commission For Aging and
Adult Services
Social Services Dept.
110 16th St., Suite 200
Denver, CO 80202
303-620-4147
http://www.aclin.org/
~sherlock/colodaas.htm

State Utility Commission
Public Utilities Commission
1580 Logan St.

Logan Tower
Office Level 2
Denver, CO 80203
303-894-2000
800-888-0170 (CO only)
http://www.puc.state.co.us

CONNECTICUT

Federal Information Center
All Locations; 800-688-9889

State Information Office
860-240-0222
http://www.state.ct.us

Cooperative Extension Office
Associate Director
Cooperative Extension System
University of Connecticut
1376 Storrs Rd.
Storrs, CT 06269-4036
860-486-6271

Attorney Grievances
Statewide Grievance
Committee
P.O. Box 260888
287 Main St.
2nd Floor, Suite 3
East Hartford, CT 06118
860-568-5157

Client Security Trust Fund
George Buckley, Jr.
State Bar Association
101 Corporate Place
Rocky Hill, CT 06067-1894
860-721-0025
http://www.ctbar.org

Committee on Arbitration of Fee Disputes
State Bar Association
101 Corporate Place

Rocky Hill, CT 06067-1894
860-721-0025
http://www.ctbar.org

State Consumer Protection Office
Department of Consumer
Protection
State Office Building
165 Capitol Ave.
Hartford, CT 06106
860-566-4999
800-538-CARS (2277)
800-842-2649 (complaints line)
government information (CT
only)
http://www.state.ct.us/dcp/

HUD Field Office
330 Main St., 1st Floor
Hartford, CT 06106
860-240-4800
http://www.hud.gov/local/
har/harhome.html

State Insurance Commissioner
Insurance Commissioner
P.O. Box 816
Hartford, CT 06142-0816
860-297-3800
http://www.state.ct.us/cid

Nursing Home Ombudsmen
Department of Social Services
Elderly Services Division
25 Sigourney St.
Hartford, CT 06106
860-424-5242

State Government Banking Commissioner
Banking Commissioner
260 Constitution Ave.
Hartford, CT 06103
860-240-8299
http://www.state.ct.us/dob/

State Office on Aging
Elderly Services
Division of Social Services
25 Sigourney St.
Hartford, CT 06106
860-424-5277
http://www.dss.state.ct.us/

State Utility Commission
Department of Public Utility
Control
10 Franklin Square
New Britain, CT 06051
860-827-1553
800-382-4586 (CT only)
http://www.state.ct.us/dpuc/

DELAWARE

Federal Information Center
All Locations; 800-688-9889

State Information Office
302-739-4000
http://www.state.de.us

Cooperative Extension Offices
Dr. Richard E. Fowler, Director
Cooperative Extension
131 Townsend Hall
University of Delaware
Newark, DE 19717-1303
302-831-2504
http://www.bluehen.ags.
udel.edu/

Dr. Starlene Taylor
Assistant Administrator
Delaware State College
Cooperative Extension Service
1200 N. DuPont Hwy.
Dover, DE 19901
302-739-5157
http://www.dsc.edu

Attorney Grievances
Office of Disciplinary Counsel
P.O. Box 472
Wilmington, DE 19899
302-577-7042

Lawyer's Fund for Client Protection
200 W. 9th St., Suite 300B
Wilmington, DE 19899
302-577-7034

State Consumer Protection Office
Justice Dept.
Attorney General
Consumer Protection Unit
820 N. French St.
4th Floor
Wilmington, DE 19801
302-577-8600

HUD Field Office
Liberty Square Bldg.
105 S. 7th St.
Philadelphia, PA 19106-3392
215-597-2560
http://www.hud.gov

State Insurance Commissioner
Insurance Commissioner
P.O. Box 7007
841 Silver Lake Blvd.
Dover, DE 19903-1507
302-739-4251
800-282-8611

Nursing Home Ombudsmen
Division of Aging and
Disabilities
Milford State Service Ctr.
18 N. Walnut St.
Milford, DE 19963
302-422-1386
800-292-1515 (DE only)

State Government Banking Commissioner
State Bank Commissioner
555 E. Lockerman St.
Suite 210
Dover, DE 19901
302-739-4235
http://www.state.de.us/ bank

State Office on Aging
Aging Division
Health and Social Services
Department
1901 N. Dupont Hwy.
New Castle, DE 19720
302-577-4791
http://kidshealth.org/
nhc/divage/index.html

State Utility Commission
Public Service Commission
861 Silver Lake Blvd.
Suite 100, Cannon Bldg.
Dover, DE 19904
302-739-4247
800-282-8574 (DE only)
http://www.state.de.us

DISTRICT OF COLUMBIA

Federal Information Center
All Locations; 800-688-9889

District of Columbia Information Office
202-727-6161
http://www.ci.washington.dc.us

Cooperative Extension Office
Reginald Taylor, Acting
Director
Cooperative Extension Service
University of the District of
Columbia
901 Newton St., NE

Washington, DC 20017
202-274-6900

Attorney Grievances
Office of Bar Counsel
515 5th St., NW
Building A, Room 127
Washington, DC 20001
202-638-1501

Client Security Trust Fund
District of Columbia Bar
1250 H St., NW, 6th Floor
Washington, DC 20005
202-737-4700 x237
http://www.dcbar.org

Fee Arbitration
Attorney-Client Arbitration
Board
District of Columbia Bar
1250 H St., NW, 6th Floor
Washington, DC 20005
202-737-4700 x238
http://www.dcbar.org

State Consumer Protection Office
Department of Consumer and
Regulatory Affairs
614 H St., NW
Washington, DC 20001
202-727-7080
http://www.ci.washington.
dc.us/dcra

HUD Field Office
820 First St., NE
Washington, DC 20002
202-275-9200
http://www.hud.gov

State Insurance Commissioner
Commissioner of Insurance
441 4th St., NW
8th Floor N

Washington, DC 20001
202-727-7424

Nursing Home Ombudsmen
Legal Counsel for the Elderly
601 E. St., NW
Building A, 4th Floor
Washington, DC 20049
202-662-4933

State Government Banking Commissioner
Superintendent of Banking and Financial Institutions
717 14th St., NW
11th Floor
Washington, DC 20006
202-727-1563
http://www.ci.washington.dc.us

State Office on Aging
Aging Office
441 4th St., NW, Suite 900
Washington, DC 20001
202-724-5622
http://www.ci.washington.dc.us/aging/aghome.htm

State Utility Commission
Public Service Commission
717 14th St., NW
Suite 200
Washington, DC 20005
202-626-5110

FLORIDA

Federal Information Center
All Locations; 800-688-9889

State Information Office
850-488-1234
http://www.state.fl.us

Cooperative Extension Offices
Christine Taylor-Stephens, Dean

Florida Cooperative Extension Service
P.O. Box 110220
University of Florida
Gainesville, FL 32611-0210
352-392-1761
http://www.ifas.ufl.edu

Lawrence Carter, Director
Cooperative Extension Service
215 Perry Paige Building S.
Florida A&M University
Tallahassee, FL 32307
850-599-3546
http://www.famu.edu

Attorney Grievances, Client Security Trust Fund, & Fee Arbitration
Staff Counsel
Florida Bar
650 Apalachee Parkway
Tallahassee, FL 32399-2300
850-561-5839
800-342-8060 (FL only)
http://www.flabar.org

State Consumer Protection Office
Division of Consumer Services
Mayo Building
Tallahassee, FL 32399-0800
850-488-2221
800-HELP-FLA (FL only)

HUD Field Office
301 W. Bay St.
Suite 2200
Jacksonville, FL 32202
904-232-2626
http://www.hud.gov/local/jkv/jkv_home.html

State Insurance Commissioner
Insurance Commissioner
200 E. Gaines St.

Tallahassee, FL 32399-0300
850-922-3100, 800-342-2762
http://www.doi.state.fl.us

State Government Banking Commissioner
State Comptroller
Department of Banking and Finance
State Capitol Bldg.
Tallahassee, FL 32399
850-488-0286
http://www.dbf.state.fl.us

Nursing Home Ombudsmen
State Long-Term Care Ombudsman
501 S. Calhoun St.
Tallahassee, FL 32399
850-488-6190

State Office on Aging
Department of Elder Affairs
4040 Esplanade Way
Tallahassee, FL 32399-0700
850-414-2108
Elder Helpline:
  800-96-ELDER (in FL)
http://www.state.fl.
us/doea/doea.html

State Utility Commission
Public Service Commission
2540 Shumard-Oak Blvd.
Tallahassee, FL 32399-0850
850-413-6344
800-342-3552 (FL only)
http://www.scri.net/psc

GEORGIA

Federal Information Center
All Locations; 800-688-9889

State Information Office
404-656-2000

http://www.state.ga.us

Cooperative Extension Offices
Bob Isaac, Interim Director
Cooperative Extension Service
University of Georgia
1111 Conner Hall
Athens, GA 30602
706-542-3824
http://www.ces.uga.edu

Dr. Fred Harrison, Jr., Dir.
Cooperative Extension Service
P.O. Box 4061
Fort Valley State College
Fort Valley, GA 31030
912-825-6269
http://agschool.fvsc.
peachnet.edu

Attorney Grievances & Committee on Arbitration of Fee Disputes
State Bar of Georgia
Office of General Counsel
800 Hurt Bldg.
50 Hurt Plaza
Atlanta, GA 30303
404-527-8720
404-527-8752 for fee arbitration
404-527-8771 for client security trust fund
http://www.gabar.org

State Consumer Protection Office
Office of Consumer Affairs
2 Martin Luther King, Jr. Dr.
Suite 356, Plaza Level
East Tower
Atlanta, GA 30334
404-656-3790
800-869-1123 (GA only)

HUD Field Office
Richard B. Russell Federal Bldg.

75 Spring St., SW
Atlanta, GA 30303
404-331-5136
http://members.aol.com/
hudfiles/georgia.html

State Insurance Commissioner
Insurance Commissioner
2 Martin Luther King, Jr. Dr.
Atlanta, GA 30334
404-656-2070
800-656-2298
http://www.state.ga.us/
ga.ins.commission/

Nursing Home Ombudsmen
Office of Aging
Dept. of Human Resources
2 Peachtree St., NW
18th Floor
Atlanta, GA 30303
404-657-5319

State Government Banking Commissioner
Commissioner of Banking and
Finance
2990 Brandywine Rd.
Suite 200
Atlanta, GA 30341
770-986-1633
http://www.georgianet.org/
services/dbf/

State Office on Aging
Aging Services Office
2 Peachtree St., NW
Atlanta, GA 30303
404-657-5258
http://www.state.ga.us/
departments/dhr/aging/html

State Utility Commission
Public Service Commission
47 Trinity Ave.

Atlanta, GA 30334
404-656-4501
800-282-5813 (GA only)
http://www.psc.state.ga.us

HAWAII

Federal Information Center
All Locations; 800-688-9889

State Information Office
808-548-6222
http://www.state.hi.us

Cooperative Extension Office
Dr. Po'Yung Lai, Assistant
Director
Cooperative Extension Service
3050 Maile Way
Honolulu, HI 96822
808-956-8397
http://www.hawaii.edu

Attorney Grievances
Office of Disciplinary Counsel
Supreme Court of the State of
Hawaii
1164 Bishop St.
Suite 600
Honolulu, HI 96813
808-521-4591

Lawyers Fund for Client Protection of the Bar of Hawaii
1164 Bishop St.
Suite 600
Honolulu, HI 96813
808-599-2483

Fee Arbitration
Attorney-Client Coordination
Committee
Hawaii State Bar Assoc.
1136 Union Hall Pew House L

Honolulu, HI 96813
808-537-1868
http://hsba.org

State Consumer Protection Office
Office of Consumer Protection
Department of Commerce and
Consumer Affairs
235 S. Beretania, 9th Floor
P.O. Box 3767
Honolulu, HI 96813-3767
808-587-1234
http://www.state.hi.us/
dcca/ocp

HUD Field Office
7 Waterfront Plaza
Suite 500
500 Ala Moana Blvd.
Honolulu, HI 96813-4918
808-522-8187
http://www.hud.gov

State Insurance Commissioner
Insurance Commissioner
P.O. Box 3614
Honolulu, HI 96811
808-586-2790
http://www.state.hi.us/
insurance

Nursing Home Ombudsmen
Executive Office on Aging
250 S. Hotel St., Suite 107
Honolulu, HI 96813-2831
808-586-0100

State Government Banking Commissioner
Commissioner
Financial Institutions
P.O. Box 2054
Honolulu, HI 96805
808-586-2820

State Office on Aging
Aging Office
205 S. Hotel St., Suite 107
Honolulu, HI 96813-2831
808-586-0100

State Utility Commission
Public Utilities Commission
465 S. King St.
Room 103
Honolulu, HI 96813
808-586-2020

IDAHO

Federal Information Center
All Locations; 800-688-9889

State Information Office
208-334-2411
http://www.state.id.us

Cooperative Extension Office
Dr. LeRoy D. Luft,
Director
Cooperative Extension System
College of Agriculture
University of Idaho
Moscow, ID 83844-2338
208-885-6639
http://www.uidaho.edu/ag/
extension/

Attorney Grievances, Client Security Trust Fund, & Fee Arbitration
Bar Counsel
Idaho State Bar
P.O. Box 895
Boise, ID 83701
208-334-4500
http://www.state.id.us/isb

HUD Field Office
400 SW 6th Ave., Suite 700

Portland, OR 97204-1632
503-326-2561
http://www.hud.gov

State Insurance Commissioner
Director of Insurance
P.O. Box 83720
Boise, ID 83720-0043
208-334-4250
800-721-3272
http://www.doi.state.id.us/
homepage.htm

Nursing Home Ombudsmen
Office on Aging
State House, Room 108
700 W. Jefferson
P.O. Box 83720
Boise, ID 83720-0007
208-334-3822

State Government Banking Commissioner
Department of Finance
P.O. Box 83720
Boise, ID 83720-0031
208-332-8000
http://www.state.id.us/
finance/dof.htm

State Office on Aging
Aging Office
P.O. Box 83720
Boise, ID 83720-0007
208-334-3833
http://www.state.id.us/icoa/

State Utility Commission
Public Utilities Commission
P.O. Box 83720
Boise, ID 83720-0074
208-334-0300
http://www.puc.state.id.us

Illinois

Federal Information Center
All Locations; 800-688-9889

State Information Office
217-782-2000
http://www.state.il.us

Cooperative Extension Office
Dennis Campion, Director
University of Illinois
Cooperative Extension Svc.
122 Mumford Hall
1301 W. Gregory Dr.
Urbana, IL 61801
217-333-2660
http://www.ag.uiuc.edu

Attorney Grievances
Attorney Registration and
Disciplinary Commission of
the Supreme Court of Illinois
700 E. Adams St.
Suite 201
Springfield, IL 62701-1507
217-522-6838
800-252-8048 (IL only)

Client Protection Program
1 Prudential Plaza
130 E. Randolph Dr.
Suite 1500
Chicago, IL 60601
312-565-2600

Illinois State Bar Association
424 S. Second St.
Springfield, IL 62701
217-525-1760
http://www.illinoisbar.org

State Consumer Protection Office
Consumer Division

Attorney General's Office
500 S. Second St.
Springfield, IL 62706
217-782-9011
217-782-9012
800-252-2518 (IL only)
http://www.ag.state.il.us

HUD Field Office
77 W. Jackson Blvd.
26th Floor
Chicago, IL 60604-3507
312-353-5680
http://www.towercom.
com/chhud/

**State Insurance
Commissioner**
Director of Insurance
320 W. Washington St.
Springfield, IL 62767
217-782-4515
http://www.state.il.us/ins/

Nursing Home Ombudsmen
Department on Aging
421 East Capitol Ave
Springfield, IL 62701
217-785-3140
800-252-8966

**State Government Banking
Commissioner**
Commissioner of Banks and
Trust Companies
500 E. Monroe St.
Springfield, IL 62701
217-782-7966
800-634-5452
http://www.state.il.us/obr/

State Office on Aging
Aging Department
421 E. Capitol Ave. #100
Springfield, IL 62701-1789
217-785-2870

http://www.state.il.us/aging/

State Utility Commission
Commerce Commission
527 E. Capitol Ave.
P.O. Box 19280
Springfield, IL 62794-9280
217-782-7295
http://www.state.il.us/icc

INDIANA

Federal Information Center
All Locations; 800-688-9889

State Information Office
317-232-1000
http://www.state.in.us

**Cooperative Extension
Office**
Dr. Wadsworth, Director
1140 AGAD
CES Administration
Purdue University
West Lafayette, IN 47907-1140
317-494-8489
http://www.agcom.purdue.
edu/agcom/extension/
ces.htm

Attorney Grievances
Disciplinary Commission of
the Supreme Court of Indiana
115 W. Washington St.
South Tower, Suite 1060
Indianapolis, IN 46204
317-232-1807
http://www.state.in.us/
judiciary/welcome.html

**Clients' Financial
Assistance Fund**
Attn: Tom Pyrz
Indiana State Bar Assoc.
230 E. Ohio St., 4th Floor

Indianapolis, IN 46204
317-639-5465
800-266-2581
http://www.inbar.org

Fee Arbitration
Contact Clients' Financial
Assistance Fund for referral to
local programs.

**State Consumer Protection
Office**
Consumer Protection Division
Office of Attorney General
219 State House
402 W. Washington
5th Floor
Indianapolis, IN 46204
317-232-6330
800-382-5516 (IN only)
http://www.state.in.us/
hoosieradvocate/html/
speaker.html

HUD Field Office
151 N. Delaware St.
Indianapolis, IN 46204
317-226-6303
http://www.hud.gov

State Insurance Commissioner
Commissioner of Insurance
311 W. Washington St.
Suite 300
Indianapolis, IN 46204
317-232-2385
800-622-4461
http://www.state.in.us/idoi/
index.html

Nursing Home Ombudsmen
Aging Division
Department of Human
Services
P.O. Box 7083
Indianapolis, IN 46207-7083

317-232-7134
800-622-4484 (IN only)

**State Government Banking
Commissioner**
Department of Financial
Institutions
402 W. Washington St.
Room W066
Indianapolis, IN 46204-2759
317-232-3955
800-382-4880
http://www.dfi.state.in.us

State Office on Aging
Aging and Rehabilitative
Services Division
Family and Social Services
Administration
402 W. Washington St.
Room W454
Indianapolis, IN 46207
317-232-7020

State Utility Commission
Utility Regulatory Commission
302 W. Washington St.
Suite E306
Indianapolis, IN 46204
317-232-2701
http://www.state.in.us/iurc/
index.html

IOWA

Federal Information Center
All Locations; 800-688-9889

State Information Office
515-281-5011
http://www.state.ia.us

Cooperative Extension Office
Nolan R. Hartwig, Interim
Director
Cooperative Extension Service

315 Beardshear Hall
Iowa State University
Ames, IA 50011
515-294-9434
http://www.exnet.iastate.edu

Attorney Grievances and Fee Arbitration
Iowa State Bar Association
521 E. Locust, Suite 300
Des Moines, IA 50309-1939
515-243-3179
http://www.iowabar.org

Client Security Trust Fund
Client Security Trust Fund Commission
Iowa Supreme Court
Iowa State House
State Capitol
Des Moines, IA 50319
515-246-8076

State Consumer Protection Office
Iowa Citizens' Aide Ombudsman
215 E. 7th St.
Capitol Complex
Des Moines, IA 50319
515-281-3592
800-358-5510 (IA only)

HUD Field Office
Federal Bldg.
210 Walnut St., Room 239
Des Moines, IA 50309
515-284-4512
http://www.hud.gov

State Insurance Commissioner
Insurance Commissioner
Lucas State Office Bldg.
6th Floor
Des Moines, IA 50319

515-281-5705
http://www.state.ia.us/government/com/ins/ins.htm

Nursing Home Ombudsmen
Department of Elder Affairs
200 W. 10th St.
Clemens Bldg., 3rd Floor
Des Moines, IA 50309
515-281-4656
800-532-3213 (IA only)

State Government Banking Commissioner
Superintendent of Banking
200 E. Grand, Suite 300
Des Moines, IA 50309
515-281-4014
http://www.state.ia.us/government/com/bank

State Office on Aging
Elder Affairs Department
Clemens Bldg., 3rd Floor
200 W. 10th St.
Des Moines, IA 50309
515-281-5188
http://www.sos.state.ia.us/register/r4/r4eldaf.htm

State Utility Commission
Iowa Utilities Board
Lucas State Office Building
5th Floor
Des Moines, IA 50319
515-281-5979
http://www.state.ia.us/government/com/util/util.htm

KANSAS

Federal Information Center
All Locations; 800-688-9889

State Information Office
913-296-0111

http://www.state.ks.us

Cooperative Extension Office
Mark Johnson, Interim Director
Cooperative Extension Service
Kansas State University
123 Umberger Hall
Manhattan, KS 66506
913-532-5820
http://www.oznet.ksu.edu

Attorney Grievances, Client Security Trust Fund & Fee Arbitration
Disciplinary Administrator,
Supreme Court of Kansas
3706 S. Topeka Ave.
Suite 100
Topeka, KS 66609
913-296-2486

State Consumer Protection Office
Consumer Protection Division
Office of Attorney General
Kansas Judicial Center
301 West 10th St.
Topeka, KS 66612
913-296-3751
800-432-2310 (KS only)

HUD Field Office
Gateway Towers 2
400 State Ave.
Kansas City, KS 66101-2406
913-551-6812
http://www.hud.gov

State Insurance Commissioner
Commissioner of Insurance
420 SW 9th St.
Topeka, KS 66612
913-296-7801

800-432-2484
http://www.state.ks.us/public/kid

Nursing Home Ombudsmen
Department on Aging
Docking State Office Building
150 South
915 Southwest Harrison St.
Topeka, KS 66612-4986
913-296-6539
800-432-3535 (KS only)

State Government Banking Commissioner
State Bank Commissioner
700 SW Jackson St.
Suite 300
Topeka, KS 66603
913-296-2266
http://www.state.ks.us/public/bank_dept

State Office on Aging
Aging Department
915 SW Harrison St., Docking State Office Bldg.
Room 150
Topeka, KS 66612-1500
913-296-4986
http://www.k4s.org/kdoa/default.htm

State Utility Commission
State Corporation Commission
1500 SW Arrowhead Rd.
Topeka, KS 66604-4027
913-271-3100
800-662-0027 (KS only)
http://www.kcc.state.ks.us

KENTUCKY

Federal Information Center
All Locations; 800-688-9889

337

State Information Office
502-564-3130
http://www.state.ky.us

Cooperative Extension Offices
Dr. Absher, Director
Cooperative Extension Service
310 W.P. Garrigus Building
University of Kentucky
Lexington, KY 40546
606-257-1846
http://www.ca.uky.edu

Dr. Harold Benson
Director
Kentucky State University
Cooperative Extension
Program
Frankfort, KY 40601
502-227-5905
http://www.kysu.edu

Attorney Grievances, Client Security Trust Fund, Fee Arbitration
Kentucky Bar Association
514 W. Main
Frankfort, KY 40601-1883
502-564-3795
http://www.kybar.org

State Consumer Protection Office
Consumer Protection Division
Office of Attorney General
P.O. Box 2000
Frankfort, KY 40602-2000
502-432-9257
888-432-9257 (KY only)
http://www.law.state.ky.us/
cp/default.htm

HUD Field Office
P.O. Box 1044
601 W. Broadway
Louisville, KY 40201
502-582-5251
http://www.hud.gov

State Insurance Commissioner
Insurance Commissioner
215 W. Main St.
P.O. Box 517
Frankfort, KY 40602
502-564-3630
800-595-6053
http://www.state.ky.us/
agencies/insur/default.htm

Nursing Home Ombudsmen
Division for Aging Services
Department for Social Services
275 East Main St.
5th Floor West
Frankfort, KY 40621
502-564-6930
800-372-2991 (KY only)

State Government Banking Commissioner
Commissioner
Department of Financial
Institutions
477 Versailles Rd.
Frankfort, KY 40601
502-573-3390
800-223-2579
http://www.dfi.state.ky.us

State Office on Aging
Aging Services Division
Cabinet for Families and
Children
275 E. Main St., 5th Floor
Frankfort, KY 40621
502-564-6930

State Utility Commission
Public Service Commission
730 Schenkel Lane
P.O. Box 615

Frankfort, KY 40602
502-564-3940
800-772-4636
http://www.state.ky.us/
agencies/psc/pschome.htm

LOUISIANA

Federal Information Center
All Locations; 800-688-9889

State Information Office
504-342-6600
http://www.state.la.us

Cooperative Extension Offices
Dr. Jack Bagent, Director
Cooperative Extension Svc.
Louisiana State University
P.O. Box 25100
Baton Rouge, LA 70894-5100
504-388-4141
http://130.39.57.11/wwwac/
kes.html

Dr. Leadrey Williams
Administrator
Cooperative Extension
Program
Southern University and A&M
College
P.O. Box 10010
Baton Rouge, LA 70813
504-771-2242

Grievances Fund
Office of Disciplinary Counsel
2800 Veterans
New Orleans, LA 70002
504-828-1414

Client Security Trust Fund
Executive Counsel
Louisiana State Bar Association
601 St. Charles Ave.
New Orleans, LA 70130

504-566-1600
800-421-5722
http://www.lsba.org

State Consumer Protection Office
Consumer Protection Section
Office of Attorney General
State Capitol Building
P.O. Box 94005
Baton Rouge, LA 70804
504-342-9638
800-351-4889
http://www.laag.com

HUD Field Office
Fisk Federal Bldg.
501 Magazine St.
9th Floor
New Orleans, LA 70130
504-589-7200
http://www.hud.gov

State Insurance Commissioner
Commissioner of Insurance
P.O. Box 94214
Baton Rouge, LA 70804-9214
504-342-5900
800-259-5300
http://wwwldi.ldi.state.la.us

Nursing Home Ombudsmen
Governors Office of Elderly
Affairs
412 N. 4th St.
Baton Rouge, LA 70802
504-342-7100
800-259-4990

State Government Banking Commissioner
Commissioner
Financial Institutions
P.O. Box 94095
Baton Rouge, LA 70804-9095

504-925-4660
http://www.premier. netl~la_ofi

State Office on Aging
Elderly Affairs
412 N. 4th St.
Baton Rouge, LA 70802
504-342-1700

State Utility Commission
Public Service Commission
One American Place, Suite 1630
P.O. Box 9115H
Baton Rouge, LA 70825
504-342-4404
800-228-9368 (LA only)

MAINE

Federal Information Center
All Locations; 800-688-9889

State Information Office
207-582-9500
http://www.state.maine.us

Cooperative Extension Office
Vaughn Holyoke, Director
Cooperative Extension Service
University of Maine
5741 Libby Hall, Room 102
Orono, ME 04469-5741
207-581-3188
http://www.umext. maine.edu

**Attorney Grievances and
Fee Arbitration**
Maine Board of Overseers of
the Bar
P.O. Box 1820
Augusta, ME 04332-1820
207-623-1121

**State Consumer Protection
Office**
Consumer Assistance Svcs.
Office of Attorney General

6 State House Station
Augusta, ME 04333-0006
207-626-8849
http://www.state.me.us/
ag/homepage.htm

HUD Field Office
Norris Cotton Federal Bldg
275 Chestnut St.
Manchester, NH 03101
603-666-7681
http://www.hud.gov

**State Insurance
Commissioner**
Superintendent of Insurance
34 State House Station
Augusta, ME 04333-0034
207-624-8475
http://www.state.me.us/
pfr/ins/inshome2.htm

State Nursing Home
State Long-Term Ombudsman
21 Bangor St.
P.O. Box 126
Augusta, ME 04332
800-499-0229
207-621-1079

**State Government Banking
Commissioner**
Superintendent of Banking
36 State House Station
Augusta, ME 04333-0036
207-624-8570
http://www.state.me.us/
pfr/bkg/bkghome2.htm

State Office on Aging
Elder and Adult Services
Human Services Department
11 State House Station
35 Anthony Ave.
Augusta, ME 04333-0011
207-624-5335

http://www.state.me.us/
beas/dhs_beas.htm

State Utility Commission
Public Utilities Commission
18 State House Station
Augusta, ME 04333-0018
207-287-3831
800-452-4699 (ME only)
http://www.state.me. us/mpuc

MARYLAND

Federal Information Center
All Locations; 800-688-9889

State Information Office
800-449-4347
http://www.state.md.us

Cooperative Extension Offices
Dr. Thomas Fretz
Regional Directors Office
Cooperative Extension Svc.
Room 1104, Simons Hall
University of Maryland
College Park, MD 20742
301-405-2907
http://www.agnr.umd.
edu/ces/

Dr. Henry Brookes, Administrator
Cooperative Extension Service,
UMES
Princess Anne, MD 21853
410-651-6206
http://www.umes.umd.
edu/dept/rudept.html

**Attorney Grievance Commission
and the Committee on
Resolution of Fee Disputes**
100 Community Place
Suite 3301
Crownsville, MD 21032
410-514-7051
800-492-1660 (MD only)

Client Security Trust Fund
100 Community Place
Suite 3301
Crownsville, MD 21032
410-514-7051

**State Consumer Protection
Office**
Consumer Protection Div.
Office of Attorney General
200 St. Paul Pl.
Baltimore, MD 21202
410-528-8662
http://www.oag.state.md.us

HUD Field Office
Equitable Bldg., 3rd Floor
10 N. Calvert St.
Baltimore, MD 21202
410-962-2520
http://www.hud.gov

**State Insurance
Commissioner**
Insurance Commissioner
501 St. Paul Place
7th Floor S.
Baltimore, MD 21202
410-468-2090
800-492-6116

Nursing Home Ombudsmen
Office on Aging
301 W. Preston St., 10th Floor
Baltimore, MD 21201
410-767-1100
http://www.inform.umd.
edu:8080/umststate/
md_resources/ooa

**State Government Banking
Commissioner**
Bank Commissioner
501 St. Paul Place, 13th Floor
Baltimore, MD 21202-2272
410-333-6808

http://www.dllr.state.md.us/dllr

State Office on Aging
Aging Office
301 W. Preston St.
Room 1004
Baltimore, MD 21201-2374
410-767-1100
http://www.inform.umd.
edu:8080/umststate/
md_resources/ooa

State Utility Commission
Public Service Commission
6 St. Paul St.
Baltimore, MD 21202
410-767-8000
800-492-0474 (MD only)
http://www.psc.state.md.
us/psc/

MASSACHUSETTS

Federal Information Center
All Locations; 800-688-9889

State Information Office
617-722-2000
http://www.state.ma.us

Cooperative Extension Office
Dr. John Gerber
Associate Director
212C Stockbridge Hall
University of Massachusetts
Amherst, MA 01003
413-545-4800
http://www.umass.edu/umext/

Attorney Grievances and Client Security Trust Fund
Massachusetts Board of Bar
Overseers
75 Federal St.
Boston, MA 02110
617-728-8700

http://www.state.ma.us/
obcbbo/obcbbo.htm

Fee Arbitration
Massachusetts Bar Association
Fee Arbitration Board
Attn: Stacy Shunk
20 West St.
Boston, MA 02111-1218
617-542-3602
http://www.massbar.org

State Consumer Protection Office
Consumer Protection Division
Department of Attorney
General
131 Tremont St.
Boston, MA 02111
617-727-8400
http://www.state.ma.us/
ag/ago8.htm

HUD Field Office
Thomas P. O'Neill Jr., Federal
Bldg.
10 Cassoway St.
Room 375
Boston, MA 02222
617-565-5234
http://www.hud.gov

State Insurance Commissioner
Commissioner of Insurance
470 Atlantic Ave.
6th Floor
Boston, MA 02210
617-521-7777
http://www.state.ma.us/doi/

Nursing Home Ombudsmen
Executive Office of Elder Affairs
1 Ashburton Pl., Room 506
Boston, MA 02101
617-727-7750
800-882-2003 (MA only)

State Government Banking Commissioner
Commissioner of Banks
100 Cambridge St.
Boston, MA 02202
617-727-3145
800-495-2265
http://www.state.ma.us/dob/

State Office on Aging
Elder Affairs Department
1 Ashburton Place
5th Floor, Room 506
Boston, MA 02108
617-727-7750

State Utility Commission
Department of
Telecommunications and Energy
100 Cambridge St.
12th Floor
Boston, MA 02202
617-305-3500
http://www.magnet.state.ma.us/dpu

MICHIGAN

Federal Information Center
All Locations; 800-688-9889

State Information Office
517-373-1837
http://www.state.mi.us

Cooperative Extension Office
Arlen Leholm, Director
Michigan State University
Extension
Room 108, Agriculture Hall
Michigan State University
East Lansing, MI 48824
517-355-2308
http://www.msue.msu.edu/msue

Attorney Grievances
Michigan Attorney Grievance
Commission
243 W. Congress
Marquette Bldg., Suite 256
Detroit, MI 48226
313-961-6585

Client Protection Fund and Fee Arbitration
State Bar of Michigan
306 Townsend St.
Lansing, MI 48933-2083
517-372-9030
http://www.michbar.org

State Consumer Protection Office
Consumer Protection Division
Office of Attorney General
P.O. Box 30213
Lansing, MI 48909
517-373-1140

HUD Field Offices
Patrick V. McNamara Federal
Bldg.
477 Michigan Ave
Detroit, MI 48226
313-226-7900
http://www.hud.gov

2922 Fuller Ave., NE
Grand Rapids, MI 49505
616-456-2100
http://www.hud.gov

State Insurance Commissioner
Commissioner of Insurance
Insurance Bureau
P.O. Box 30220
Lansing, MI 48909-7720
517-373-9273
http://www.cis.state.mi.us/ins

Nursing Home Ombudsmen
Citizens for Better Care
416 N. Homer, Suite 101
Lansing, MI 48912-4700
517-336-6753
800-292-7852 (MI only)

State Government Banking Commissioner
Commissioner
Financial Institutions Bureau
P.O. Box 48909
Lansing, MI 48933
517-373-3460
http://www.cis.state.mi.
us/fib/

State Office on Aging
Aging Office
P.O. Box 30026
Lansing, MI 48909
517-373-8230
http://mass.iog.wayne.edu/
masshome.html

State Utility Commission
Public Service Commission
6545 Mercantile Way
P.O. Box 30221
Lansing, MI 48909
517-334-6445
800-292-9555 (MI only)
http://ermisweb.cis.state.
mi.us

MINNESOTA

Federal Information Center
All Locations; 800-688-9889

State Information Office
612-296-6013
http://www.state.mn.us

Cooperative Extension Office

Catherine Fennely, Director
Minnesota Extension Service
University of Minnesota
240 Coffey Hall
1420 Eckles Ave.
St. Paul, MN 55108
612-625-1915
http://www.mes.umn.edu

Attorney Grievances and Client Security Trust Fund
Office of Lawyers' Professional
Responsibility
25 Constitution Ave.
Suite 105
St. Paul, MN 55155-1500
612-296-3952
800-657-3601 (MN only)

Fee Arbitration
Minnesota Bar Association
514 Nicollet Mall
Suite 300
Minneapolis, MN 55402
612-333-1183
800-882-MSBA (MN only)
http://www.mnbar.org

State Consumer Protection Office
Office of Consumer Services
Office of Attorney General
1400 N.C.L. Tower
445 Minnesota St.
St. Paul, MN 55101
612-296-3353
800-657-3787
http://www.ag.state.mn.
us/consumer

HUD Field Office
220 2nd St., South
Minneapolis, MN 55401
612-370-3000
http://www.hud.gov

State Insurance Commissioner
Minnesota Department of
Commerce
Insurance Division
133 E. 7th St.
St. Paul, MN 55101
612-297-7161
http://www.commerce.
state.mn.us

Nursing Home Ombudsmen
Board on Aging
Office of Ombudsman for
Older Minnesotans
444 Lafayette Rd.
St. Paul, MN 55155-3843
612-296-0382
800-657-3591

**State Government Banking
Commissioner**
Minnesota Department of
Commerce
Division of Financial
Examinations
133 E. 7th St.
St. Paul, MN 55101
612-296-2135
http://www.commerce.state.m
n.us

State Office on Aging
Aging Program Division
Social Services Department
444 LaFayette Rd.
St. Paul, MN 55155-3843
612-296-2770

State Utility Commission
Public Utilities Commission
121 7th Place East
St. Paul, MN 55501-2147
612-296-7124
800-657-3782 (MN only)
http://www.puc.state.mn.us

MISSISSIPPI

Federal Information Center
All Locations; 800-688-9889

State Information Office
601-359-1000
http://www.state.ms.us

**Cooperative Extension
Offices**
Ronald A. Brown
Director
Cooperative Extension Service
Mississippi State University
P.O. Box 9601
Mississippi State, MS 39762
601-325-3034
http://www.ces.msstate.
edu/ces.html

LeRoy Davis
Dean
Co-operative Ext. Service
1000 ASU Dr. #479
Lorman, MS 39096
601-877-6128
http://www.alcorn.edu

**Attorney Grievances, Client
Security Trust Fund, & Fee
Arbitration**
Mississippi State Bar
P.O. Box 2168
Jackson, MS 39225-2168
601-948-4471
800-682-6423 (MS only)
http://www.msbar.org

**State Consumer Protection
Office**
Consumer Protection Division
Office of Attorney General
P.O. Box 22947
Jackson, MS 39225
601-359-4230

800-281-4418
http://www.ago.state.ms.
us/consprot.htm

HUD Field Office
Dr. A.H. McCoy Federal Bldg.
100 W. Capitol St.
Room 910
Jackson, MS 39269
601-965-5308
http://www.hud.gov

State Insurance Commissioner
Commissioner of Insurance
1804 Walter Sillers Bldg.
P.O. Box 79
Jackson, MS 39201-0079
601-359-3569
800-562-2957
http://www.doi.state.ms.us

Nursing Home Ombudsmen
Division of Aging and Adult
Services
750 N. State St.
Jackson, MS 39202
601-359-4927
800-948-3090 (MS only)

**State Government Banking
Commissioner**
Commissioner
Department of Banking and
Consumer Finance
P.O. Box 23729
Jackson, MS 39225-3729
601-359-1031
800-844-2499
http://www.dbcf.state.ms.us

State Office on Aging
Aging and Adult Services
Division
Human Services Department
P.O. Box 352
Jackson, MS 39205-0352

601-359-4925
http://www.mdhs.state.
ms.us/aas.html

State Utility Commission
Public Service Commission
P.O. Box 1174
Jackson, MS 39215
601-961-5400
http://www.mslawyer.com

MISSOURI

Federal Information Center
All Locations; 800-688-9889

State Information Office
573-751-2000
http://www.state.mo.us

**Cooperative Extension
Offices**
Ronald J. Turner
Interim Director
Cooperative Extension Service
University of Missouri
309 University Hall
Columbia, MO 65211
573-882-7754
http://outreach.missouri.edu

Dyremple Marsh
Director
Cooperative Extension Service
Lincoln University
110A Allen Hall
P.O. Box 29
Jefferson City, MO 65102-0029
573-681-5550

Attorney Grievances
Office of Chief Disciplinary
Council
3335 American Ave.
Jefferson City, MO 65109
573-635-7400

**Client Security Trust Fund
& Fee Arbitration**
Missouri Bar Association
P.O. Box 119
Jefferson City, MO 65102
573-635-4128
http://www.mobar.org

**State Consumer Protection
Office**
Public Protection Division
Office of Attorney General
P.O. Box 899
Jefferson City, MO 65102
314-751-3321
800-392-8222 (MO only)
http://services.state.mo.
us/ago/homepg.htm

HUD Field Offices
(Eastern)
1222 Spruce St.
St. Louis, MO 63103
314-539-6560
http://www.hud.gov

(Western)
Gateway Towers 2
400 State Ave.
Kansas City, KS 66101-2406
913-551-6812
http://www.hud.gov

**State Insurance
Commissioner**
Director of Insurance
301 W. High St., Room 630
P.O. Box 690
Jefferson City, MO 65102
573-751-4126
http://www.state.mo.us/
insurance/

Nursing Home Ombudsmen
Division of Aging
P.O. Box 1337

Jefferson City, MO 65102
573-526-0727

**State Government Banking
Commissioner**
Commissioner of Finance
P.O. Box 716
Jefferson City, MO 65102
573-751-3242
http://www.ecodev.state.
mo.us/finance

State Office on Aging
Aging Division
P.O. Box 1337
Jefferson City, MO 65102
573-751-3082
http://www.state.mo.us/
dss/da/da.htm

State Utility Commission
Public Service Commission
P.O. Box 360
Jefferson City, MO 65102
573-751-3234
800-392-4211 (MO only)
http://www.ecodev.state.
mo.us/psc

MONTANA

Federal Information Center
All Locations; 800-688-9889

State Information Office
406-444-2511
http://www.state.mt.us

**Cooperative Extension
Office**
Vice Provost for Outreach and
Director of Extension
212 Montana Hall
Montana State University
Bozeman, MT 59717
406-994-4371

http://extn.msu. montana.edu

Attorney Grievances
Commission on Practice of the
Supreme Court of Montana
Justice Bldg.
Room 315
215 N. Sanders
Helena, MT 59620-3002
406-444-2634

**Client Security Trust Fund
& Fee Arbitration**
State Bar of Montana
P.O. Box 577
Helena, MT 59624
406-442-7660
http://www.montanabar.org

**State Consumer Protection
Office**
Office of Consumer Affairs
Department of Commerce
1424 9th Ave.
Helena, MT 59620
406-444-4312

HUD Field Office
301 South Park
Drawer 10095
Helena, MT 59626
406-441-1300
http://www.hud.gov

**State Insurance
Commissioner**
Commissioner of Insurance
P.O. Box 4009
Helena, MT 59604-4009
406-444-2040
800-332-6148 (MT only)
http://www.mt.gov/sao

Nursing Home Ombudsmen
Senior and Long Term Care
Division
P.O. Box 8005

Helena, MT 59604-4210
406-444-5900

**State Government Banking
Commissioner**
Commissioner
Division of Banking and
Financial Institutions
846 Front St.
Helena, MT 59620-0546
406-444-2091
http://commerce.mt.gov/
finance.index.htm

State Office on Aging
Senior and Long Term Care
Division
Department of Public Health
and Human Services
Box 4210
Helena, MT 59604
406-444-5900
http://www.dphhs.mt.gov/
whowhat/sltc.htm

State Utility Commission
Public Service Commission
1701 Prospect Ave.
P.O. Box 202601
Helena, MT 59620-2601
406-444-6199
http://www.psc.mt.gov

NEBRASKA

Federal Information Center
All Locations; 800-688-9889

State Information Office
402-471-2311
http://www.state.ne.us

**Cooperative Extension
Office**
Randy Cantrell, Director
University of Nebraska

S.E. Research and Extension
Center
Room 211, Mussehl Hall
East Campus
Lincoln, NE 68583-0714
402-472-2966
http://ianrwww.unl.edu/
ianr/coopext/coopext.htm

**Attorney Grievances &
Client Security Fund**
Counsel for Discipline
Nebraska State Bar Association
635 S. 14th St.
Lincoln, NE 68508
402-475-7091
http://www.nebar.com

**State Consumer Protection
Office**
Consumer Protection Division
Office of Attorney General
2115 State Capitol
Room 2115
Lincoln, NE 68509
402-471-2682
800-727-6432

HUD Field Office
Executive Tower Centre
10909 Mill Valley Rd.
Omaha, NE 68154-3955
402-492-3100
http://www.hud.gov

State Insurance Commissioner
Director of Insurance
941 O St., Suite 400
Lincoln, NE 68508
402-471-2201
800-833-0920
http://www.nol.org/
home/ndoi/

Nursing Home Ombudsmen
Department on Aging

State Office Building
P.O. Box 95044
Lincoln, NE 68509
402-471-2306
402-471-2307
800-942-7830 (NE only)
http://www.hhs.state.ne.us/
ags/agsindex.htm

**State Government Banking
Commissioner**
Director of Banking and
Finance
P.O. Box 95006
Lincoln, NE 68509
402-471-2171
http://www.ndbf/org/

State Office on Aging
Aging Department
P.O. Box 95044
Lincoln, NE 68509-5044
402-471-2308
http://www.hhs.state.ne.
us/ags/agsindex.htm

State Utility Commission
Public Service Commission
1200 N St.
P.O. Box 94927
Lincoln, NE 68509-4925
402-471-3101
800-526-0017
http://www.nol.org/home/npsc/

NEVADA

Federal Information Center
All Locations; 800-688-9889

State Information Office
702-687-5000
http://www.state.nv.us

Cooperative Extension Office
Janet Usinger, Director

Nevada Cooperative Extension
2345 Redrock
Las Vegas, NV 89102
702-222-3130

**Attorney Grievances, Client
Security Trust Fund, & Fee
Arbitration**
State Bar of Nevada
600 E. Charleston
Las Vegas, NV 89104
702-382-0502

**State Consumer Protection
Office**
Consumer Affairs Division
Department of Business and
Industry
4600 Kietezke Lane
Building B, Suite 113
Reno, NV 89502
702-688-1800
800-326-5202 (NV only)
http://www.state.nv.us/
busi_industry/cad/index.htm

HUD Field Office
333 North Rancho Dr., Suite 700
Las Vegas, NV 89106-3714
702-388-6500
http://www.hud.gov

**State Insurance
Commissioner**
Commissioner of Insurance
1665 Hot Springs Rd.
Capitol Complex 152
Carson City, NV 89710
702-687-4270
800-992-0900 (NV only)
http://www.state.nv.us/
busi_industry/id/index.htm

Nursing Home Ombudsmen
Division for Aging Services
Department of Human

Resources
340 N. 11th St., Suite 203
Las Vegas, NV 89101
702-486-3545

**State Government Banking
Commissioner**
Commissioner
Financial Institutions
406 E. Second St.
Carson City, NV 89710
702-687-4259
http://www.state.nv.us/b&i/fi/

State Office on Aging
Aging Services Division
Human Resources Dept.
340 N. 11th St.
Howard Cannon Center
Las Vegas, NV 89101
702-486-3545
http://www.state.nv.us/
hr/aging/

State Utility Commission
Public Service Commission
727 Fairview Dr.
Carson City, NV 89710
702-687-6007
http://www.state.nv.us/puc/

NEW HAMPSHIRE

Federal Information Center
All Locations; 800-688-9889

State Information Office
603-271-1110
http://www.state.nh.us

**Cooperative Extension
Office**
Peter J. Horne
Dean and Director
UNH Cooperative Ext.
59 College Rd., Taylor Hall
Durham, NH 03824

603-862-1520
http://www.ceinfo.unh.edu/

Attorney Grievances
New Hampshire Supreme Court
Professional Conduct Committee
4 Park St., Suite 304
Concord, NH 03301
603-224-5828

**Clients' Indemnity Fund &
Fee Resolution Committee**
New Hampshire Bar
Association
112 Pleasant St.
Concord, NH 03301
603-224-6942

**State Consumer Protection
Office**
Consumer Protection and Anti-
trust Bureau
Office of Attorney General
33 Capitol St.
Concord, NH 03301-0397
603-271-3641
http://www.state.nh.us/
oag/cpb.html

HUD Field Office
Norris Cotton Federal Building
275 Chestnut St.
Manchester, NH 03101-2487
603-666-7681
http://www.hud.gov

**State Insurance
Commissioner**
Insurance Commissioner
169 Manchester St.
Concord, NH 03301
603-271-2261
800-852-3416 (NH complaints
only)
http://www.state.nh.us/
insurance

Nursing Home Ombudsmen
Division of Elderly and Adult
Services
New Hampshire Long-Term
Care Ombudsman Program
6 Hazen Dr.
Concord, NH 03301-3843
603-271-4375
or toll free in-state:
800-443-5640 (Calls for long
term care ombudsman only)

**State Government Banking
Commissioner**
Bank Commissioner
169 Manchester St.
Concord, NH 03301
603-271-3561
http://www.state.nh. us/banking

State Office on Aging
Elderly and Adult Services
Division
State Office Park South
115 Pleasant St.
Annex Bldg. 1
Concord, NH 03301-3843
603-271-4680
http://www.state.nh.us/
dhhs/ofs/ofscstlc.htm

State Utility Commission
Public Utilities Commission
8 Old Suncook Rd.
Bldg. #1
Concord, NH 03301
603-271-2431
800-852-3793 (NH only)
http://www.state.nh.us/
puc/puc.html

NEW JERSEY

Federal Information Center
All Locations; 800-688-9889

State Information Office
609-292-2121
http://www.state.nj.us

Cooperative Extension Office
Zane Helsel, Director
Rutgers Cooperative Extension
P.O. Box 231
New Brunswick, NJ 08903
732-932-9306
http://www.rce.rutgers.edu

Attorney Grievances & Fee Arbitration
Supreme Court of New Jersey
Justice Complex
CN-963
Trenton, NJ 08625
609-530-4008

Client Protection Trust Fund
Supreme Court of New Jersey
Justice Complex
CN-961
Trenton, NJ 08625
609-984-7179

State Consumer Protection Office
Division of Consumer Affairs
124 Halsey St.
Newark, NJ 071021
973-504-6200
http://www.state.nj.us/
lps/ca/home.htm

HUD Field Office
One Newark Center
13th Floor
Newark, NJ 07102
973-622-7900
http://www.hud.gov

State Insurance Commissioner
Commissioner
Department of Insurance

20 W. State St.
CN-329
Trenton, NJ 08625
609-292-5316
http://www.naic.org.nj/
div_ins.htm

Nursing Home Ombudsman
Ombudsman Office for
Institutionalized Elderly
101 S. Broad St., 6th Floor
Trenton, NJ 08625
609-984-7831

State Government Banking Commissioner
Commissioner of Banking
20 W. State St., CN-040
Trenton, NJ 08625
609-984-2777
http://www.naic.org.nj/
consumer.htm

State Office on Aging
Aging Division
Community Affairs Dept.
101 S. Broad St., CN807
Trenton, NJ 08625
609-292-3766
800-792-8820
http://www.state.nj.us/
health/senior/sraffair.htm

State Utility Commission
Board of Public Utilities
Two Gateway Center
Newark, NJ 07102
973-648-2027
800-624-0241 (NJ only)
http://www.njin.net/njbpu/

NEW MEXICO

Federal Information Center
All Locations; 800-688-9889

352

State Information Office
505-827-4011
http://www.state.nm.us

Cooperative Extension Office
Dr. Jerry Schickenanz
New Mexico State University
Box 3AE
Las Cruces, NM 88003
505-646-3016
http://www.cahe.nmsu.
edu/cahe/ces

Attorney Grievances
Disciplinary Board of the
Supreme Court of New Mexico
400 Gold SW, Suite 800
Albuquerque, NM 87102
505-842-5781

Fee Arbitration
State Bar of New Mexico
Fee Arbitration Committee
P.O. Box 25883
Albuquerque, NM 87125
505-797-6000
800-876-6227 (NM only)
http://www.nmbar.org

State Consumer Protection Office
Consumer Protection Division
Office of Attorney General
P.O. Drawer 1508
Santa Fe, NM 87504-1508
505-827-6060
800-678-1508 (NM only)

HUD Field Office
625 Truman St., NE
Albuquerque, NM 87110
505-262-6463
http://www.hud.gov

State Insurance Commissioner
Superintendent of Insurance

P.O. Drawer 1269
Santa Fe, NM 87504-1269
505-827-4500
800-947-4722

Nursing Home Ombudsmen
Agency on Aging
228 East Palace Ave.
Ground Floor
Santa Fe, NM 87501
505-827-7663
800-432-2080 (NM only)

State Government Banking Commissioner
Director, Financial Institutions
Division
P.O. Box 25101
Santa Fe, NM 87504
505-827-7100
http://www.state.nm.us/
rld/rld_fid.html

State Office on Aging
State Agency on Aging
224 E. Palance Ave.
Santa Fe, NM 87501
505-827-7640

State Utility Commission
Public Utility Commission
224 E. Palace Ave.
Santa Fe, NM 87501-2013
505-827-6940
800-663-9782
http://www.puc.state.nm.us/

NEW YORK

Federal Information Center
All Locations; 800-688-9889

State Information Office
518-474-2121
http://www.state.ny.us

Cooperative Extension Office

William Lacy, Director
Cornell Cooperative Ext.
276 Roberts Hall
Ithaca, NY 14853
607-255-2237
http://www.cce.cornell.edu/

Attorney Grievances
Departmental Disciplinary
Committee for the First
Judicial Department
41 Madison Ave.
39th Floor
New York, NY 10010
212-685-1000

New York State Grievance
Committee for the 2nd and
11th Judicial Districts
210 Joralemon St.
Municipal Bldg., 12th Floor
Brooklyn, NY 11201
718-624-7851

Grievance Committee for the
9th Judicial District
Crosswest Office Center
399 Knollwood Rd., #200
White Plains, NY 10603
914-949-4540

New York State Grievance
Committee for the 10th Judicial
District
6900 Jericho Turnpike
LL 102
Syosset, NY 11719
516-364-7344

3rd Department Committee on
Professional Standards
Alfred E. Smith Bldg.
22nd Floor
P.O. Box 7013
Capitol Station Annex
Albany, NY 12225-0013

518-474-8816

Appellate Division
Supreme Court
4th Judicial Department
Office of Grievance Committee
295 Main St.
1036 Ellicott Square Bldg.
Buffalo, NY 14203
716-858-1190

**Lawyers' Fund for Client
Protection**
119 Washington Ave.
Albany, NY 12210
518-474-8438
800-442-3863 (NY only)

**State Consumer Protection
Office**
Bureau of Consumer Frauds
and Protection
Office of Attorney General
120 Broadway
New York, NY 10271
212-416-8000
800-771-7755
http://www.oag.state.ny.us

HUD Field Offices
(Upstate)
Lafayette Ct., 465 Main St.
Buffalo, NY 14203
716-551-5755
http://www.hud.gov

(Downstate)
26 Federal Plaza
New York, NY 10278
212-264-6500
http://www.hud.gov

**State Insurance
Commissioner**
Superintendent of Insurance
Consumer Services Bureau
25 Beaver St.

New York, NY 10004
212-480-6400
800-342-3736 (NY only)
http://www.ins.state.ny.
us/nyins.htm#top

Nursing Home Ombudsmen
Office for the Aging
Agency Building 2
Empire State Plaza
Albany, NY 12223
518-474-0108
800-342-9871 (NY only)

State Government Banking Commissioner
Superintendent of Banks
Two Rector St.
New York, NY 10006
212-618-6642
800-522-3330 (NY only)
http://www.banking.state.
ny.us

State Office on Aging
Aging Office
Bldg. 2
Empire State Plaza
Albany, NY 12223-001
518-474-5731
800-342-9871 (NY only)
http://aging.state.ny. us/nysofa/

State Utility Commission
Public Service Commission
3 Empire State Plaza
Albany, NY 12223
518-474-7080
800-342-3377 (NY only)
http://www.dps.state.ny.us

NORTH CAROLINA

Federal Information Center
All Locations; 800-688-9889

State Information Office
919-733-1110
http://www.state.nc.us

Cooperative Extension Offices
Dr. Jon F. Ort, Director
Cooperative Extension Svc.
North Carolina State
University, Box 7602
Raleigh, NC 27695-7602
919-515-2811
http://www.ces.ncsu.edu/

Dr. Dalton McAfee, Director
Cooperative Extension
Program
North Carolina A&T State
University
P.O. Box 21928
Greensboro, NC 27420-1928
910-334-7956
http://www.ncat.edu/~soa

Attorney Grievances, Client Security Trust Fund, & Fee Arbitration
North Carolina Bar Association
P.O. Box 3688
Cary, NC 27519
919-677-0561
800-662-7407
http://www.ncbar.org

State Consumer Protection Office
Consumer Protection Div.
Office of Attorney General
P.O. Box 629
Raleigh, NC 27602
919-716-6000
http://www.jus.state.nc.us/
justice/cpsmain/

HUD Field Office
2306 W. Meadowview Rd.

Greensboro, NC 27407
910-547-4000
http://www.hud.gov

State Insurance Commissioner
Commissioner of Insurance
Dobbs Bldg.
P.O. Box 26387
Raleigh, NC 27611
919-733-7343
800-662-7777 (NC only)
http://www.sips.state.nc.us/doi/

Nursing Home Ombudsmen
Division of Aging
Dept. of Human Resources
693 Palmer Dr.
Raleigh, NC 27626-0531
919-733-3983
800-662-7030 (NC only)
http://www.csc.state.nc.
us/dhr/doa/home.htm

State Government Banking Commissioner
Commissioner of Banks
P.O. Box 10709
702 Oberlin Rd.
Raleigh, NC 27605
919-733-3016
http://www.banking.
state.nc.us

State Office on Aging
Aging Division
Human Resources Dept.
693 Palmer Dr.
Raleigh, NC 27603
919-733-3983
http://www.state.nc.us/
dhr/doa/home.htm

State Utility Commission
Utilities Commission
P.O. Box 29510

Raleigh, NC 27626-0510
919-733-4249
http://www.ncuc.commerce.
state.nc.us

NORTH DAKOTA

Federal Information Center
All Locations; 800-688-9889

State Information Office
701-224-2000
http://www.state.nd.us

Cooperative Extension Office
Dr. Sharon Anderson, Director
Cooperative Extension Service
North Dakota State University
Morrill Hall, Room 311
Box 5437
Fargo, ND 58105
701-231-8944
http://www.ext.nodak.edu/

Attorney Grievances
Disciplinary Board of the
Supreme Court
P.O. Box 2297
Bismarck, ND 58502
701-328-3925

Client Security Trust Fund & Fee Arbitration
State Bar Association of North
Dakota
P.O. Box 2136
Bismarck, ND 58502
701-255-1404
800-472-2685 (ND only)

State Consumer Protection Office
Consumer Fraud Division
Office of Attorney General
600 E. Blvd.

Bismarck, ND 58505
701-328-3404
800-472-2600 (ND only)
http://www.state.nd.us/ndag

HUD Field Office
653 2nd Ave. North
P.O. Box 2483
Fargo, ND 58108-2483
701-239-5136
http://www.hud.gov

State Insurance Commissioner
Commissioner of Insurance
Capitol Bldg., 5th Floor
600 E. Boulevard Ave.
Bismarck, ND 58505
701-328-2440
800-247-0560

Nursing Home Ombudsmen
Aging Services
Department of Human Services
600 S. 2nd St.
Bismarck, ND 58505
701-328-7577
800-472-2622 (ND only)

State Government Banking Commissioner
Commissioner of Banking and Financial Institutions
2000 Schafer St., Suite G
Bismarck, ND 58501
701-328-9933
http://www.state.nd.us/
bank/banking.htm

State Office on Aging
Aging Services Division
Human Services Dept.
600 South 2nd St., Suite 1-C
Bismarck, ND 58504-5729
701-328-8910

State Utility Commission
Public Service Commission
State Capitol Bldg., 12th Fl.
Bismarck, ND 58505-0480
701-328-2400
http://www.psc.state.nd.us/

OHIO

Federal Information Center
All Locations; 800-688-9889

State Information Office
614-466-2000
http://www.state.oh.us

Cooperative Extension Office
Keith Smith, Director
OSU Extension
2120 Fiffe Rd.
Agriculture Administration Building
Columbus, OH 43210
614-292-6181
http://www.ag.ohio-state.edu/

Attorney Grievances
Office of Disciplinary Counsel of the Supreme Court of Ohio
175 S. 3rd St., Suite 280
Columbus, OH 43215-5196
614-461-0256

Clients' Security Fund
175 S. 3rd St., Suite 285
Columbus, OH 43215
614-221-0562
800-231-1680 (OH only)

Fee Arbitration
Ohio State Bar Association
1700 Lake Shore Dr.
P.O. Box 16562
Columbus, OH 43216-6562
614-487-2050

800-282-6556 (OH only)
http://www.ohiobar.org

State Consumer Protection Office
Consumer Protection Division
Office of Attorney General
30 E. Broad St.
State Office Tower, 25th Floor
Columbus, OH 43215-3428
614-466-4986
800-282-0515 (OH only)
http://www.ag.ohio.gov/

HUD Field Offices
525 Vine St., 7th Floor
Cincinnati, OH 45202
513-684-2884
http://www.hud.gov

One Playhouse Sq.
1350 Euclid Ave., 5th Floor
Cleveland, OH 44114
216-522-4065
http://www.hud.gov

200 N. High St.
Columbus, OH 43215
614-469-5737
http://www.hud.gov

State Insurance Commissioner
Director of Insurance
2100 Stella Court
Columbus, OH 43215-1067
614-644-2651
800-686-1526
800-686-1527 (fraud)
http://www.state.oh.us/ins/

Nursing Home Ombudsmen
Department of Aging
50 West Broad St.
9th Floor
Columbus, OH 43215-5928
614-466-7922

toll free in-state:
800-282-1206 (long term complaint line only)

State Government Superintendent of Financial Institutions
Ohio Dept. of Commerce
Division of Financial Institutions
77 S. High St., 21st Floor
Columbus, OH 43266-0121
614-728-8400
http://www.state.oh.us/
com/fin/index.htm

State Office on Aging
Aging Department
50 W. Broad St., 9th Floor
Columbus, OH 43215-5928
614-466-5500

State Utility Commission
Public Utilities Commission
180 E. Broad St.
Columbus, OH 43215-3793
614-466-3016
800-686-7826 (OH only)
http://www.puc.state.oh.us/

OKLAHOMA

Federal Information Center
All Locations; 800-688-9889

State Information Office
405-521-2011
http://www.state.ok.us

Cooperative Extension Offices
Dr. C.B. Browning, Director
Oklahoma Cooperative
Extension Service
Oklahoma State University
139 Agriculture Hall

Stillwater, OK 74078
405-744-5398
http://www.okstate.edu/
osu_ag/oces

Dr. Ocleris Simpston, Director
Cooperative Research and
Extension
P.O. Box 730
Langston University
Langston, OK 73050
405-466-3836
http://www.lunet.edu/

**Attorney Grievances, Client
Security Trust Fund, & Fee
Arbitration**
General Counsel
Oklahoma Bar Center
1901 N. Lincoln Blvd.
P.O. Box 53036
Oklahoma City, OK 73152
405-524-2365

**State Consumer Protection
Office**
Consumer Protection Unit
Office of Attorney General
4545 N. Lincoln, Room 260
Oklahoma City, OK 73105-4894
405-521-4274

HUD Field Office
500 W. Main St., Suite 400
Oklahoma City, OK 73102
405-553-7401
http://www.hud.gov

**State Insurance
Commissioner**
Insurance Commissioner
P.O. Box 53408
Oklahoma City, OK 73152
405-521-2828
800-522-0071 (OK only)
http://www.oid.state.ok.us

Nursing Home Ombudsmen
Special Unit on Aging
312 NE 28th St.
Oklahoma City, OK 73105
405-521-6734

**State Government Banking
Commissioner**
Bank Commissioner
4545 N. Lincoln Blvd.
Suite 164
Oklahoma City, OK 73105
405-521-2782
http://www.oklaosf.state.
ok.us/~sbd/

State Office on Aging
Aging Services Division
Human Services Dept.
P.O. Box 25352
Oklahoma City, OK 73125
405-521-2327

State Utility Commission
Corporation Commission
Jim Thorpe Office Building
P.O. Box 52000-2000
Oklahoma City, OK 73152-2000
405-521-2211
http://www.occ.state.ok.us

OREGON

Federal Information Center
All Locations; 800-688-9889

State Information Office
503-378-3111
http://www.state.or.us

Cooperative Extension Office
Dr. Lila Houghlum, Director
Oregon State Extension
Service Administration
Oregon State University
Ballard Extension Hall #101

Corvallis, OR 97331-3606
541-737-2711
http://wwwagcomm.ads.
orst.edu/agcomwebfile/
extser/index.html

**Attorney Grievances &
Client Security Trust Fund**
Oregon State Bar
P.O. Box 1689
Lake Oswego, OR 97035
503-620-0222
http://www.osbar.org

**State Consumer Protection
Office**
Financial Fraud Section
Consumer Complaints
1162 Court St., NE
Department of Justice
Justice Building
Salem, OR 97310
503-378-4320
http://www.doj.state.or.us/
FinFraud/welcome3.htm

HUD Field Office
400 SW 6th Ave.
Suite 700
Portland, OR 97201
503-326-2561
http://www.hud.gov

**State Insurance
Commissioner**
Insurance Commissioner
Labor and Industries Building
350 Winter St. NE
Room 440-2
Salem, OR 97310
503-378-4271
http://www.cbs.state.or.
us/external/ins/index.html

Nursing Home Ombudsmen
Office of LTC Ombudsman

2475 Lancaster Dr., Bldg. B, #9
Salem, OR 97310
503-378-6533
800-522-2602 (OR only)

**State Government Banking
Commissioner**
Administrator
Division of Finance and
Corporate Securities
Labor and Industries Bldg.
350 Winter St. NE, Rm. 21
Salem, OR 97310
503-378-4140
http://www.cbs.state.or.
us/external/dfcs/index.html

State Office on Aging
Senior and Disabled Svcs.
500 Summer St., NE
Salem, OR 97310-1015
503-945-5811
http://www.sdsd.hr.
state.or.us/

State Utility Commission
Public Utility Commission
550 Capital St., NE, 2nd Floor
Salem, OR 97310
503-378-6611
800-522-2404 (OR only)
http://www.puc.state.or.us

PENNSYLVANIA

Federal Information Center
All Locations; 800-688-9889

State Information Office
717-787-2121
http://www.state.pa.us

Cooperative Extension Office
Dr. Ted Alter, Director
Pennsylvania State University
Room 210, A.G. Administration

University Park, PA 16802
814-863-3438
http://www.cas.psu.edu/
docs/coext/coopext.html

Attorney Grievances & Fee Arbitration
District 1:
Office of the Disciplinary
Counsel
1635 Market, 16th Floor
Philadelphia, PA 19103
215-560-6296

District 2:
Office of the Disciplinary
Counsel
One Sentry Pkwy
Bluebell, PA 19422
610-270-1896

District 3:
Office of the Disciplinary
Counsel
2 Lemoyne Dr., 1st Floor
Lemoyne, PA 17043
717-731-7073

District 4:
Office of the Disciplinary
Counsel
Suite 400
Union Trust Building
501 Grant St.
Pittsburgh, PA 15219
412-565-3173

Pennsylvania Client Security Fund
5035 Ritter Rd., Suite 900
Mechanicsburg, PA 17055
215-560-6335
800-962-4618

State Consumer Protection Office
Bureau of Consumer Protection

Office of Attorney General
Strawberry Square, 14th Floor
Harrisburg, PA 17120
717-783-5048
800-441-2555 (PA only)
http://www.oca.state.pa.us

HUD Field Offices
Wanamaker Bldg.
100 Penn Sq. East
Philadelphia, PA 19107
215-656-0600
http://www.hud.gov

State Insurance Commissioner
Insurance Commissioner
1326 Strawberry Square
Harrisburg, PA 17120
717-787-2317
http://www.state.pa.us/
pa_exec/insurance/
overview.html

Nursing Home Ombudsmen
Department of Aging
400 Market St.
State Office Bldg., 7th Floor
Harrisburg, PA 17101-2301
717-783-3126
http://www.state.pa.us/
pa_exec/aging/overview. html

State Government Banking Commissioner
Secretary of Banking
333 Market St., 16th Floor
Harrisburg, PA 17101-2290
717-787-2665
800-PA-BANKS (PA only)
http://www.state.pa.us/
pa_ exec/banking/

State Office on Aging
Aging Department
400 Market St.

State Office Bldg., 6th Floor
Harrisburg, PA 17101-2301
717-783-1550
http://164.156.7.66/
pa_exec/aging/overview. html

State Utility Commission
Public Utility Commission
P.O. Box 3265
Harrisburg, PA 17120
717-783-1740
800-782-1110 (PA only)
http://puc.paonline.com/

RHODE ISLAND

Federal Information Center
All Locations; 800-688-9889

State Information Office
401-222-2000
http://www.state.ri.us

Cooperative Extension Office
Marsha Morreira, Director
Cooperative Extension
Education Center
University of Rhode Island
East Alumni Ave.
Kingston, RI 02881-0804
401-874-2900
http://www.edc.uri.edu/

Attorney Grievances & Fee Arbitration
Disciplinary Board of the
Supreme Court of Rhode Island
David D. Curtin Judicial Annex
24 Weybuffet St., 2nd Floor
Providence, RI 02903
401-222-3270

Client Security Trust Fund
Rhode Island Bar Association
115 Cedar St.

Providence, RI 02903
401-421-5740
http://www.ribar.com

State Consumer Protection Office
Consumer Protection Division
Department of Attorney
General
150 South Main St.
Providence, RI 02903
401-274-4400
800-852-7776

HUD Field Office
10 Weybuffet St.
Providence, RI 02903
401-528-5351
http://www.hud.gov

State Insurance Commissioner
Insurance Commissioner
233 Richmond St.
Providence, RI 02903
401-222-2246

Nursing Home Ombudsmen
Department of Elderly Affairs
160 Pine St.
Providence, RI 02903-3708
401-222-2858
800-322-2880 (RI only)

State Government Banking Commissioner
Director and Superintendent of
Banking and Securities
233 Richmond St.
Suite 231
Providence, RI 02903-4231
401-222-2405

State Office on Aging
Elderly Affairs Department
160 Pine St.
Providence, RI 02903

401-222-2858
http://www.sec.state.ri.
us/stdept/sd23.htm

State Utility Commission
Public Utilities Commission
100 Orange St.
Providence, RI 02903
401-222-3500
800-341-1000 (RI only)
http://www.state.ri.us/
stdept/sd14.htm

SOUTH CAROLINA

Federal Information Center
All Locations; 800-688-9889

State Information Office
803-734-1000
http://www.state.sc.us

Cooperative Extension Offices
Carroll Culvertson, Director
Clemson University
Cooperative Extension Service
P.O. Box 995
Pickens, SC 29671
864-868-2810
http://www.clemson.
edu/extension

Director
Cooperative Extension Service
P.O. Box 8103
South Carolina State University
Orangeburg, SC 29117-8103
803-536-8928
http://192.231.63.160/
scsu/state.htm

Attorney Grievances
Grievance Commission
South Carolina Supreme Court
P.O. Box 11330

Columbia, SC 29211
803-734-2038

Client Security Trust Fund & Fee Arbitration
South Carolina Bar
P.O. Box 608
Columbia, SC 29202-0608
803-799-6653
http://www.scbar.org

State Consumer Protection Office
Dept. of Consumer Affairs
P.O. Box 5757
Columbia, SC 29250
803-734-9452
800-922-1594 (SC only)
http://www.state.sc.us/
consumer/

HUD Field Office
Strom Thurmond Federal Bldg.
1835 Assembly St.
Columbia, SC 29201
803-765-5592
http://www.hud.gov

State Insurance Commissioner
Chief Insurance Commissioner
P.O. Box 100105
Columbia, SC 29202-3105
803-737-6117
800-768-3467
http://www.state.sc.us/doi/

Nursing Home Ombudsmen
State Long Term Care Ombudsman
Division on Aging
202 Arbor Lake Dr.
Suite 301
Columbia, SC 29223
803-737-7500

State Government Banking Commissioner
Commissioner of Banking
P.O. Box 12549
Columbia, SC 20211
803-734-2001

State Office on Aging
Office on Aging
South Carolina Department of
Health and Human Services
P.O. Box 8206
Columbia, SC 29201
803-253-6177

State Utility Commission
Public Service Commission
P.O. Drawer 11649
Columbia, SC 29211
803-737-5230
800-922-1531 (SC only)
http://www.psc.state.sc.us

SOUTH DAKOTA

Federal Information Center
All Locations; 800-688-9889

State Information Office
605-773-3011
http://www.state.sd.us

Cooperative Extension Office
Mylo Hellickson, Director
SDSU
Box 2207D
AG Hall 154
Brookings, SD 57007
605-688-4792
http://www.abs.sdstate.
edu/ces

Attorney Grievances
State Bar of South Dakota
Attn: Tom Barnett
222 East Capitol

Pierre, SD 57501
605-224-7554
http://www.sdbar.org

Client Security Trust Fund
State Bar of South Dakota
222 E. Capitol
Pierre, SD 57501
605-224-7554
800-952-2333 (SD only)
http://www.sdbar.org

State Consumer Protection Office
Div. of Consumer Affairs
Office of Attorney General
500 East Capitol
Capitol Building
Pierre, SD 57501
605-773-4400
800-300-1986 (SD only)
http://www.state.sd.us/
state/executive/attorney/
consumer.htm

HUD Field Office
2400 West 49th St.
Suite 1-201
Sioux Falls, SD 67106-5558
605-330-4223
http://www.hud.gov

State Insurance Commissioner
Director of Insurance
Insurance Bldg.
118 W. Capitol
Pierre, SD 57501
605-773-3563
http://www.state.sd.us/
insurance

Nursing Home Ombudsmen
Office of Adult Services and
Aging
700 Governor Dr.

Pierre, SD 57501
605-773-3656
http://www.state.sd.us/state/
executive/social/asa/asa.htm

State Government Banking Commissioner
Director of Banking
State Capitol Bldg.
500 E. Capitol Ave.
Pierre, SD 57501-5070
605-773-3421
http://www.state.sd.us/state/
executive/dcr/bank/bank-
hom.htm

State Office on Aging
Adult Services on Aging Office
Social Services Department
700 Governors Dr.
Pierre, SD 57501
605-773-3656
http://www.state.sd.us/state/
executive/social/asa/asa.htm

State Utility Commission
Public Utilities Commission
500 E. Capitol Ave.
Pierre, SD 57501
605-773-3201
800-332-1782
http://www.state.sd.us/state/
executive/puc/puc.htm

TENNESSEE

Federal Information Center
All Locations; 800-688-9889

State Information Office
615-741-3011
http://www.state.tn.us

Cooperative Extension Offices
Dr. Billy G. Hicks, Dean
Agricultural Extension Service

University of Tennessee
P.O. Box 1071
Knoxville, TN 37901-1071
423-974-7114
http://tunnelweb.utcc.
utk.edu/~utext/

Cherry Lane Zon Schmittou,
Extension Leader
Davidson County Agricultural
Service
Tennessee State University
800 Second Ave. N., Suite 3
Nashville, TN 37201-1084
615-254-8734

Attorney Grievances & Fee Arbitration
Board of Professional Responsibility of the Supreme Court of
Tennessee
1101 Kermit Dr., Suite 730
Nashville, TN 37217
615-361-7500

State Consumer Protection Office
Division of Consumer Affairs
500 James Robertson Parkway,
5th Floor
Nashville, TN 37243-0600
615-741-4737
800-342-8385 (TN only)
http://www.state.tn.us/consumer

HUD Field Offices
710 Locust St., 3rd Floor
Knoxville, TN 37902
423-545-4384
http://www.hud.gov

251 Cumberland Bend Dr.
Suite 200
Nashville, TN 37228
615-736-5213
http://www.hud.gov

State Insurance Commissioner
Commissioner of Insurance
500 James Robertson Pkwy.
Nashville, TN 37243-0565
615-741-2176
800-342-4029
http://www.state.tn.us/
commerce

Nursing Home Ombudsmen
Commission on Aging
500 Deaderick St.
9th Floor
Nashville, TN 37243-0860
615-741-2056

State Government Banking Commissioner
Commissioner
Financial Institutions
John Sevier Bldg.
500 Charlotte Ave., 4th Fl.
Nashville, TN 37243
615-741-2236
http://www.state.tn.us/
financialinst

State Office on Aging
Aging Commission
500 Deaderick St.
9th Floor
Nashville, TN 37243-0860
615-741-2056

State Utility Commission
Tennessee Regulatory
Authority
460 James Robertson Parkway
Nashville, TN 37243
615-741-2904
800-342-8359 (TN only)
http://www.state.tn.
us/tra/tra.htm

TEXAS

Federal Information Center
All Locations; 800-688-9889

State Information Office
512-463-4630
http://www.state.tx.us

Cooperative Extension Offices
Dr. Zerle Carpenter, Director
Texas Agricultural Extension
Service
Administration Bldg. 106-A
Texas A&M University
College Station, TX 77843
409-845-7967
http://agcomwww.tamu.
edu/agcom/taex/taex.htm

Dr. Linda Willis, Director
Cooperative Extension Program
P.O. Box 3059
Prairie View, TX 77446-3059
409-857-2023
http://www.pvamu.edu/

Attorney Grievances, Client Security Trust Fund, & Fee Arbitration
State Bar of Texas
P.O. Box 12487
Capitol Station
Austin, TX 78711
512-463-1463
800-204-2222

State Consumer Protection Office
Consumer Protection Division
Office of Attorney General
Capitol Station
P.O. Box 12548
Austin, TX 78711
512-463-2070

800-621-0508 (TX only)
http://www.oag.state.tx.us

HUD Field Offices
1600 Throckmorton
P.O. Box 2905
Fort Worth, TX 76113-2905
817-978-9000
http://www.hud.gov

Norfolk Tower
2211 Norfolk, Suite 200
Houston, TX 77098
713-313-2274
http://www.hud.gov

Washington Square
800 Dolorosa
San Antonio, TX 78207
210-472-6806
http://www.hud.gov

**State Insurance
Commissioner**
Director
Claims and Compliance
Division
State Board of Insurance
P.O. Box 149091
Austin, TX 78714-9091
512-463-6169
800-252-3439
http://www.tdi.state.tx.us/

Nursing Home Ombudsmen
Department on Aging
P.O. Box 12786
Capitol Station
Austin, TX 78711
512-424-6840
800-252-2412 (TX only)

**State Government Banking
Commissioner**
Banking Commissioner
2601 N. Lamar Blvd.
Austin, TX 78705-4207

512-475-1300
http://www.banking.
state.tx.us

State Office on Aging
Aging Department
Box 12786
Austin, TX 78711
512-424-6840
http://www.texas.gov/
agency/340.html

State Utility Commission
Public Utility Commission
1701 N. Congress Ave.
Austin, TX 78701
512-936-7000
http://www.puc.state.tx.us

UTAH

Federal Information Center
All Locations; 800-688-9889

State Information Office
801-538-3000
http://www.state.ut.us

**Cooperative Extension
Office**
Dr. Robert Gilliland
Vice President for Extension
and Continuing Education
U.M.C. 4900
Utah State University
Logan, UT 84322-4900
801-797-2200
http://ext.usu.edu/

**Attorney Grievances & Fee
Arbitration**
Bar Counsel
Utah State Bar
645 S. 200 East
Salt Lake City, UT 84111-3834
801-531-9110

http://www.utahbar.org

Client Security Trust Fund
Bar Counsel
Utah State Bar
645 S. 200 East
Salt Lake City, UT 84111-3834
801-531-9077
http://www.utahbar.org

State Consumer Protection Office
Division of Consumer Protection
Department of Commerce
160 E. 300 South
P.O. Box 146704
Salt Lake City, UT 84114-6704
801-530-6601
http://www.commerce.state. ut.us/web/commerce/conpro/ consprot.htm

HUD Field Office
257 Tower
257 East, 200 South
Suite 550
Salt Lake City, UT 84111-2048
801-524-5241
http://www.hud.gov

State Insurance Commissioner
Commissioner of Insurance
Room 3110
State Office Bldg.
Salt Lake City, UT 84114
801-538-3805
800-439-3805
http://www.ins-dept.state.ut. us/welcome.htm

Nursing Home Ombudsmen
Division of Aging and Adult Services
P.O. Box 45500

Salt Lake City, UT 84145
801-538-3910

State Government Banking Commissioner
Commissioner
Financial Institutions
P.O. Box 89
Salt Lake City, UT 84110-0089
801-538-8830

State Office on Aging
Aging and Adult Services Division
Human Services Dept.
120 North, 200 West
Salt Lake City, UT 84107
801-538-3910
http://www.dhs.state.ut.us/ agency/daas/homeage.htm

State Utility Commission
Public Service Commission
160 East, 300 South
P.O. Box 45585
Salt Lake City, UT 84145
801-530-6716
http://web.state.ut.us/bbs/ psc/html/index.htm

VERMONT

Federal Information Center
All Locations; 800-688-9889

State Information Office
802-828-1110
http://www.state.vt.us

Cooperative Extension Office
Dr. Larry Forchier, Dean
Division of Agriculture
Natural Resources, and
Extension
University of Vermont

601 Main
Burlington, VT 05401-3439
802-656-2990
http://ctr.uvm.edu/ext/

Attorney Grievances
Professional Conduct Board
c/o Bar Counsel
59 Elm St.
Montpelier, VT 05602
802-828-3368

**Client Security Trust Fund
& Fee Arbitration**
Vermont Bar Association
P.O. Box 100
Montpelier, VT 05601
802-223-2020
http://www.vtbar.org

**State Consumer Protection
Office**
Consumer Assistance Program
104 Morrill Hall
University of Vermont
Burlington, VT 05405
802-656-3183
800-649-2424

HUD Field Office
Federal Bldg.
11 Elmwood Ave.
Room 244
P.O. Box 879
Burlington, VT 05402-0879
802-951-6290
http://www.hud.gov

**State Insurance
Commissioner**
Commissioner of Banking and
Insurance
89 Main St.
Drawer 20
Montpelier, VT 05620-3101
802-828-3302

http://www.state.vt.us/bis/

Nursing Home Ombudsmen
Vermont Legal Aid
264 N. Winooski
Burlington, VT 05402
802-863-5620

**State Government Banking
Commissioner**
Commissioner
Banking and Insurance
89 Main St.
Drawer 20
Montpelier, VT 05620-3101
802-828-3307
http://www.state.vt.us/bis/

State Office on Aging
Vermont Department of Aging
and Disabilities
103 S. Main St.
Waterbury, VT 05676
802-241-2400
http://www.state.vt.us/
dad/busdir.htm

State Utility Commission
Public Service Board
112 State St.
Chittenden Bank Bldg.
4th Floor, Drawer 20
Montpelier, VT 05620-2701
802-828-2358
800-622-4496 (VT only)
http://www.state.vt.us/psb

VIRGINIA

Federal Information Center
All Locations; 800-688-9889

State Information Office
804-786-0000
http://www.state.va.us

Cooperative Extension Offices
Dr. Clark Jones
Interim Director
Virginia Cooperative Extension
Virginia Tech
Blacksburg, VA 24061-0402
540-231-5299
http://www.ext.vt.edu/

Lorenza Lyons, Administrator
Cooperative Extension
Virginia State University
Rox 9081
Petersburg, VA 23806-9081
804-524-5961

Attorney Grievances
Virginia State Bar
707 E. Main St., Suite 1500
Attn: June Fletcher, Esquire
Richmond, VA 23219-2900
804-775-0500
http://www.vsb.org

Client Security Trust Fund
Virginia State Bar
707 E. Main St., Suite 1500
Attn: Susan Busch
Richmond, VA 23219-2900
804-775-0500
http://www.vsb.org

State Consumer Protection Office
Div. of Consumer Affairs
P.O. Box 1163
Richmond, VA 23218-1163
804-786-2042
800-552-9963 (VA only)
http://www.state.va.us/
~vdacs/vdacs.htm

HUD Field Office
3600 West Broad St.
P.O. Box 90331
Richmond, VA 23230
804-278-4507
http://www.hud.gov

State Insurance Commissioner
Commissioner of Insurance
P.O. Box 1157
Richmond, VA 23218
804-371-9741
800-552-7945 (VA only)

Nursing Home Ombudsmen
Virginia Association of Area
Agencies on Aging
530 E. Main St., Suite 428
Richmond, VA 23219
804-644-2804
800-552-3402 (VA only)

State Government Banking Commissioner
Commissioner
Financial Institutions
P.O. Box 640
Richmond, VA 23218-0640
804-371-9704
800-552-7945 (VA only)

State Office on Aging
Aging Department
1600 Forest Ave.
Suite 102
Richmond, VA 23229
804-662-9333
http://www.aging.state.va.us/

State Utility Commission
State Corporation Commission
P.O. Box 1197
Richmond, VA 23218-1197
804-371-9967
800-552-7945 (VA only)
http://www.state.va.us/
scc/index.html

WASHINGTON

Federal Information Center
All Locations; 800-688-9889

State Information Office
360-753-5000
http://www.state.wa.us

Cooperative Extension Office
Dr. Harry Burcalow
Director
Cooperative Extension
411 Hulbert
Washington State University
Pullman, WA 99164-6230
509-335-2811
http://www.cahe.wsu.edu/ce/html

Attorney Grievances, Client Security Program, & Fee Arbitration
Washington State Bar
Association
2101 4th Ave., 4th Floor
Seattle, WA 98121
206-727-8200
http://www.wsba.org

State Consumer Protection Office
Consumer and Business Fair
Practice Division
Office of Attorney General
900 4th Ave., Suite 2000
Seattle, WA 98164
206-464-6684
800-551-4636 (WA only)
http://www.wa.gov/ago/cpd/cphone.html

HUD Field Office
Seattle Federal Office Bldg.
909 1st Ave., Suite 200
Seattle, WA 98104
206-220-5101
http://www.hud.gov

State Insurance Commissioner
Insurance Commissioner
Insurance Bldg. AQ21
P.O. Box 40255
Olympia, WA 98504-0255
360-753-7301
800-562-6900 (WA only)
http://www.wa.gov/ins/

Nursing Home Ombudsmen
South King County Multi-
Service Center
1200 South 336 St.
P.O. Box 23699
Federal Way, WA 98903-0699
206-838-6810
800-422-1384

State Government Banking Commissioner
Supervisor of Banking
P.O. Box 41200
Olympia, WA 98504-1200
360-902-8700
http://www.wa.gov/dfi/

State Office on Aging
Aging and Adult Services
P.O. Box 45050
Olympia, WA 98504-5600
360-586-8753

State Utility Commission
Utilities and Transportation
Commission
1300 South Evergreen Park Dr.
SW
Olympia, WA 98504
360-753-6423
800-562-6150 (WA only)
http://www.wutc.wa.gov/

WEST VIRGINIA

Federal Information Center
All Locations; 800-688-9889

State Information Office
304-558-3456
http://www.state.wv.us

Cooperative Extension Office
Robert Maxwell
Interim Director
Cooperative Extension
8th Floor,
Knapt Hall
P.O. Box 6031
West Virginia University
Morgantown, WV 26506-6031
304-293-3408
http://www.wvu.edu/~exten

Attorney Grievances and Client Security Trust Fund
West Virginia State Bar
2006 Kanawha Blvd. East
Charleston, WV 25311
304-558-2456
http://www.wvbar.org

State Consumer Protection Office
Consumer Protection Division
Office of Attorney General
812 Quarrier St.
6th Floor
Charleston, WV 25301
304-558-8986
800-368-8808 (WV only)

HUD Field Office
405 Capitol St., Suite 708
Charleston, WV 25301
304-347-7000
http://www.hud.gov

State Insurance Commissioner
Insurance Commissioner
1124 Smith St.
P.O. Box 50540
Charleston, WV 25305-0540
304-558-3394
800-642-9004

Nursing Home Ombudsmen
Commission on Aging
State Capitol-Holly Grove
1900 Kanawha Blvd. East
Charleston, WV 25305
304-558-3317

State Government Banking Commissioner
Commissioner of Banking
State Capitol Complex
Bldg. 3, Room 311
Charleston, WV 25305
304-558-2294
800-642-9056

State Office on Aging
Aging Commission
1900 Kanawha Blvd.
State Capitol
Holly Grove
Charleston, WV 25305
304-558-3317
http://www.wvdhhr.org/
pages/bcs/aging.htm

State Utility Commission
Public Service Commission
201 Brooks St.
P.O. Box 812
Charleston, WV 25323-0812
304-340-0300
800-344-5113 (WV only)
http://www.state.wv.us/
psc/default.htm

WISCONSIN

Federal Information Center
All Locations; 800-688-9889

State Information Office
608-266-2211
http://www.state.wi.us

Cooperative Extension Office
Dr. Aeyse Somersan
Director
432 N. Lake St.
Room 601
Madison, WI 53706
608-262-7966
http://www.uwex.edu/ces/

Attorney Grievances
Board of Attorneys
Professional Responsibility
Tenney Bldg.
110 E. Main St.
Room 410
Madison, WI 53703
608-267-7274

Client Security Trust Fund and Fee Arbitration
State Bar of Wisconsin
P.O. Box 7158
Madison, WI 53707
608-257-3838
800-728-7788
http://www.wisbar.org

State Consumer Protection Office
Office of Consumer Protection
and Citizen Advocacy
Department of Justice
P.O. Box 7856
Madison, WI 53707-7856
608-266-1852

HUD Field Office
Henry Rouss Federal Plaza
310 W. Wisconsin Ave.
Milwaukee, WI 53203
414-297-3214
http://www.hud.gov

State Insurance Commissioner
Commissioner of Insurance
P.O. Box 7873
Madison, WI 53707-7873
608-266-3585
800-236-8517 (WI only)
http://badger.state.wi.us/
agencies/oci/oci_home.htm

Nursing Home Ombudsmen
Board on Aging and Long
Term Care
214 N. Hamilton St.
Madison, WI 53703
608-266-8944

State Government Banking Commissioner
Commissioner of Banking
345 W. Washington Ave.
4th Floor
Madison, WI 53703
608-266-1621
http://badger.state.wi.us/
agencies/dfi

State Office on Aging
Aging and Long Term Care
Board
217 S. Hamilton St.
Suite 300
Madison, WI 53703
608-266-2536

State Utility Commission
Public Service Commission
610 North Whitney Way
Madison, WI 53707

608-266-2001
800-225-7729
http://badger.state.wi.us/
agencies/psc

WYOMING

Federal Information Center
All Locations; 800-688-9889

State Information Office
307-777-7011
http://www.state.wy.us

Cooperative Extension Office
Darryl Kautzman, Director
CES
University of Wyoming
Box 3354
Laramie, WY 82071-3354
307-766-5124
http://www.uwyo.edu/ag/
ces/ceshome.htm

Attorney Grievances, Client Security Trust Fund, & Fee Arbitration
Wyoming State Bar
P.O. Box 109
Cheyenne, WY 82003-0109
307-632-9061
http://www.wyomingbar.org

State Consumer Protection Office
Consumer Affairs
Office of Attorney General
123 State Capitol Bldg.
Cheyenne, WY 82002
307-777-7841
800-438-5799 (WY only)

HUD Field Office
4225 Federal Office Bldg.
100 East 8th St.

P.O. Box 120
Casper, WY 82602-1919
307-261-6254
http://www.hud.gov

State Insurance Commissioner
Commissioner of Insurance
Herschler Bldg.
122 W. 25th St
Cheyenne, WY 82002
307-777-7401
800-438-5768 (WY only)

Nursing Home Ombudsmen
Long Term Care Ombudsman
756 Gilchrist St.
Wheatland, WY 82201
307-322-5553

State Government Banking Commissioner
Manager
Division of Banking
Herschler Bldg.
122 West 25th St.
Cheyenne, WY 82002
307-777-6600
http://audit.state.wy.us

State Office on Aging
Division on Aging
Department of Health
117 Hathaway Bldg.
Room 139
Cheyenne, WY 82002
307-777-7986
http://wdhfs.state.wy.us/
wdh/default.htm

State Utility Commission
Public Service Commission
2515 Warren Ave.
Hansen Bldg., Suite 300
Cheyenne, WY 82002
307-777-7427

Index

A

Abuse, 302
Acetaminophen, 131
Actors, 210
Addiction, 115
Administration on Aging, 299, 300
Adopt a Horse, 201
Adult day care, 299
Advertising, 300
Advisory Council on Historic
 Places, 138
Advisory Council on Historic
 Preservation, 138
African art, 194
Age discrimination, 76
Agency for Health Care Policy and
 Research, 122
Aging Magazine, 300
AIDS, 190
Airborne allergens, 114
Alabama
 arts grants, 215
Alaska
 arts grants, 215
Alcohol abuse, 115
Allergies, 113, 114
Alzheimer's disease, 111, 112, 115,
 124, 125, 133
 research centers, 125
American Battle Monuments
 Commission, 139
AMTRAK, 137
Amyotrophic lateral sclerosis, 111
Animal care, 196
Antacids, 112
Anti-inflammatory drugs, 131
Anticancer drugs, 106
Antihistamines, 131

Archaeology, 193, 195, 196
Arizona
 arts grants, 216
Arkansas
 arts grants, 216
Army Corps of Engineers, U.S.,
 137
Arthritis, 109
 quackery, 116
Asthma, 106
Attorneys, 73
 complaints, 78
Auctions
 Customs Service, U.S., 199
 Defense Department, 200
 FDIC, 201
 Marshals Service, 201
 postal, 200

B

Back disorders, 109
Baldness, 116, 188
Bands
 armed services, 144
Banking, 251
Bathtubs, 313
Battle monuments, 139
Behcet's syndrome, 109
Beta blockers, 131
Biofeedback, 108
Bird watching, 197
Blood sugar, 108
Boating, 137
Boating safety, 144
Boats, 144
Bonds, 249, 250
Botanic Gardens, U.S., 145
Broccoli, 110